A NEW PHILOSOPHY
OF HISTORY

Critical Views

In the same series

A NEW PHILOSOPHY OF HISTORY

Edited by Frank Ankersmit
and Hans Kellner

REAKTION BOOKS

Published by Reaktion Books Ltd
11 Rathbone Place
London WIP IDE, UK

First published 1995

Copyright Reaktion Books Ltd, 1995

Designed by Humphrey Stone
Jacket designed by Ron Costley
Photoset by Parker Typesetting Service, Leicester
Printed and bound in Great Britain
by The Alden Press Oxford

British Library Cataloguing in Publication Data:

New Philosophy of History. – (Critical Views Series)
I. Ankersmit, F. R. II. Kellner, Hans
III. Series
901
ISBN 0–948462–78–7

Part of Philippe Carrard's essay 'Theory of a Practice: Historical
Enunciation and the *Annales* School' first appeared in his *Poetics
of the New History: French Historical Discourse from Braudel to
Chartier,* published by the Johns Hopkins University Press in
1992.

Robert B. Berkhofer's essay includes material reprinted with
permission from Patricia Limerick's *The Legacy of Conquest,*
W. W. Norton & Co. (New York, 1988).

Contents

IMAGES

Photographic Acknowledgements

The editors and publishers wish to express their thanks to the following sources of illustrative material and/or permission to reproduce it: Musées d'Angers: p. 202; British Museum, London: dust-jacket.

Notes on the Editors and Contributors

FRANK ANKERSMIT is Professor of Intellectual History and Historical Theory at the University of Groningen, The Netherlands. He is the author of several books in Dutch, and, in English, *Narrative Logic: A Semantic Analysis of the Historian's Language* (1983) and *History and Topology* (1994). He was also the editor of the 1986 issue of *History and Theory*.

HANS KELLNER is Professor of Rhetoric in the Department of English at the University of Texas at Arlington. He is the author of *Language and Historical Representation: Getting the Story Crooked* (1989). He has published widely on history, critical theory, philosophy, the history of music and rhetoric.

STEPHEN BANN is Professor and Director of the Centre for Modern Cultural Studies at the University of Kent. His recent books have included *Frankenstein: Creation and Monstrosity* (as editor published by Reaktion Books, 1994) and *Utopias and the Millennium* (co-edited with Krishan Kumar, published by Reaktion Books, 1993). His previous books include *The Clothing of Clio* (1984) and *The True Vine* (1989).

ROBERT F. BERKHOFER, JR. is Professor of History at the University of California at Santa Cruz. He has taught previously at the universities of Michigan, Minnesota and Wisconsin. He is the author of *A Behavioural Approach to Historical Analysis* (1969), *The White Man's Indian: Images of the American Indian from Columbus to the Present* (1979) and 'The Challenge of Poetics to (Normal) Historical Practice' (in *Poetics Today*, IX, 1988), among other publications.

PHILIPPE CARRARD is Professor of French and teaches French literature and critical theory at the University of Vermont (USA). He has published in the area of 20th-century literature, literary criticism and the rhetoric of historiography. His books include *Malraux ou le récit hybride* (1976) and *Poetics of the New History: French Historical Discourse from Braudel to Chartier* (1992).

ARTHUR C. DANTO is Johnsonian Professor Emeritus of Philosophy at Columbia University, New York. His recent books include *Beyond the Brillo*

Box: *The Visual Arts in Post-Historical Perspective* (1992) and *Embodied Meanings: Critical Essays and Aesthetic Meditations* (1994).

ALLAN MEGILL is Professor of History at the University of Virginia. He is the author of *Prophets of Extremity: Nietzsche, Heidegger, Foucault, Derrida* (1985), co-edited *The Rhetoric of the Human Sciences* (1987) and edited *Rethinking Objectivity* (1994). He is currently working on a book on Marx, rationality and history.

LINDA ORR is Professor in the Department of Romance Studies at Duke University, Durham, NC; she is the author of *Headless History: Nineteenth-Century French Historiography of the Revolution* (1990) and 'Céline, Jean Zay, and the Mutations of Hate' in the *South Atlantic Quarterly* (spring 1994).

NANCY F. PARTNER is Associate Professor of History at McGill University, Montreal. She specializes both in medieval cultural history and in the development and theory of historical writing. Her publications include *Serious Entertainments: The Writing of History in Twelfth-Century England* (1977), (as editor) *Studying Mediaeval Women: Sex, Gender, Feminism* (1993), 'The New Cornificius: Mediaeval History and the Artifice of Words' in *Classical Rhetoric and Mediaeval Historiography*, ed. E. Breisach (1985), 'Making up Lost Time: Writing on the Writing of History' in *Speculum* 61 (1986), and 'History without Empiricism/Truth without Facts' in *Transformations: Languages of Culture and Personhood after Theory*, ed. Christie McDonald and Gary Wihl (1994).

ANN RIGNEY is lecturer in literary theory at the University of Utrecht. Author of *The Rhetoric of Historical Representation: Three Narrative Histories of the French Revolution* (1990), she has also published many articles on narrative theory and historiography, and co-edited *Cultural Participation* (1993).

RICHARD T. VANN is Professor of History and Letters at Wesleyan University in Middletown, CT, and Senior Editor of *History and Theory*. He is the author of *Century of Genius: European Thought in the Seventeenth Century*, *The Social Development of English Quakerism, 1655–1755* (1969), and (with David Eversley) *Friends in Life and Death: The British and Irish Quakers in the Demographic Transition* (1992).

Introduction:
Describing Redescriptions

HANS KELLNER

During the last twenty years, the nature of reflection about history has changed in ways that are both obvious and subtle. The primary philosophical emphasis upon historical explanation which had relied heavily on models that were either logical or sociological has broadened considerably to include a far wider range of literary devices. Ancient rhetoric and modern poetics have provided tools for reconceiving historical works. The older philosophical interest in specific arguments, statements or interpretations of evidence has been joined, if not supplanted, by a focus upon the historical work as a whole vision which draws its meaning from a plot and its authority from a voice. Historiography has been revitalised as historians moved beyond the political and social pigeonholing of histories – the *Napoleon: For and Against* version of historiography – to testing the role of formal conventions in creating historical credibility. Literary critics who once would have rejected historical writing as lacking the 'fictionality' and 'illusion' of great literature have shown a growing fascination with revealing precisely these aspects of history as the literature of the realist illusion. Philosophers have shown less interest in the truth-value of the historical statement and have turned to the narrative as a whole, which will have a truth more akin to the truth of a novel or a painting than to that of a syllogism.

It is an exaggeration to call this *new*. We might agree with Richard Lanham that the basic course of Western cultural history has been the fluctuation between the serious and the playful, the sense of language as something to be looked *through* and something to be looked *at*, and the varying notions of the self that accompany these visions of language.[1] The role of the Sophists in this tale is fairly clear. Their penchant for redescription made them suspect, for Plato and his heirs. Their Protagorean intuition that man is the measure of things in this world, and that language use is the key to human *being* always disturbs. It is a version of reality that poses greater demands on the concept itself. It will not, however, go away. Nor, on the other hand, will the sense of the real as what is essential, given, found. The tension between these visions of the world and its representations seems as permanent as we can imagine things to be.

This volume of essays on current historical reflection is full of the tensions and contradictions involved in our capacities to represent and find meaning in the past. Historians (from a variety of areas), literary critics and philosophers have contributed to the collection, but there is a shared vision here. It is that history can be redescribed as a discourse that is fundamentally rhetorical, and that representing the past takes place through the creation of powerful, persuasive images which can be best understood as created objects, models, metaphors or proposals about reality. The philosopher may show an interest in the implications of narratives for knowledge, the critic on the nature and limits of representation, the historian on topics and authority, but all see history as a discourse founded on its genre conventions and the expectations and beliefs of its community. And all, I think, believe that attention to the historical text both as an aesthetic object and as part of a persuasive social discourse will broaden and deepen our understanding of how and why we represent the past.

In the first section of the book Nancy Partner, Richard Vann and Arthur Danto place the current redescriptions of historical discourse within various contexts. In 'Historicity in an Age of Reality-Fictions' Nancy Partner reminds us that the shifting boundaries of fact and fiction which characterize recent thinking about historical discourse is by no means new, but has rather been the norm for representations of the past since the beginnings of formal historical writing. Greek, Roman and medieval historiography abound with not only the sort of 'Incorporated Fictions' that suggest a postmodern historical technique, but also established a host of literary devices which have changed so little or been challenged so rarely that they are invisible, as though they were part of reality itself. But the institution of the author as narrator, information replacing inspiration, lengthy prose narrative, attention to causes and motives and attention to the state are not natural things at all. They are *devices*, and the inventions of classical literature, for Western culture, at least. Partner's conclusion: despite the received faith that modern historians are the descendants of Ranke with a special sort of critical historical method, we are, in fact, more Greek than German.

Above all, Partner is concerned about the civic implications of current historicity and the sliding scale between fact and fiction that defines its place in current 'reality-fictions.' While much professional historical writing retains a serene indifference to either the traditions of discourse which are embodied in academic history or to the implications of the re-emergence of a primarily fictional vision in the popular uses of the past, Partner worries that a breakdown of faith in the sources of information available to us may weaken the connections between citizen and polity, creating a sophisticated cynicism. Just as Stephen Bann, in *The Clothing of Clio*, described how the nineteenth-century British reading public became increasingly sophisticated in spotting the fictionality in realistic works that had seemed convincing a few decades before (e.g. Scott's novels), so Partner fears that a cynicism will prevail, in which only irony serves as a realistic view of human affairs. Yet Partner is far from rejecting the narrativist awareness of the formally fictional aspects of all reality-fictions. Her essay rather calls for a scrupulous examination of the nature of historical truth.

Through his involvement with the American journal *History and Theory* since its beginning in 1960, Richard Vann is in an excellent position to survey the development of narrativist philosophy of history in the crucial period of its inception. Vann's essay, 'Turning Linguistic: History and Theory and *History and Theory*, 1960-1975' reflects the developments of historical discourse as conducted in that journal.[2] As a case study of one moment in the ongoing tension between reality and representation that Partner found in historiographical tradition, Vann's account identifies the moment when consideration of historical rhetoric changed tone. The genteel aestheticism with which the historian's language had been evaluated by historians like Trevelyan and Emery Neff gave way in the 1960s to a very ungenteel discourse on representation driven by structuralist literary theory, which had no use for the idea that the process of writing began only after the historian felt that his research had taught him all he was likely to learn about his subject. For Roland Barthes the process of research itself, and the definition of a historical problem in the first place, are not given encounters with reality, but processes deeply mediated by structures of literary and psychological complexity, as Vann demonstrates.

In America, however, it was not the French connection that brought a change in philosophy of history; it was rather the working of the Anglo-American analytic tradition itself. Arthur Danto describes how the 'World according to Hempel' gave way to a world much more attuned to the ideas of Thomas Kuhn. Indeed, Danto's essay self-consciously enacts the sort of change of paradigms which Kuhn suggests are the source of understanding at a given place and time. This undeniable shift of attention away from the verification of statements about the past was not the product of any process of proof or disproof. Rather, Hempel's questions lost their ability to compel interest, while a different rendering of the issues gained authority. The questions remain, but as ghosts. As Danto puts it, the problem with the world according to Hempel was that it could not account for its own historical moment.

The three essays in the second section of the book deal with the 'Voices' of historians. The historian's voice has traditionally been an embarrassment to those who envision an unmediated view of the past as the utopia of historical discourse. The ideal for these historical realists would be a composite history of the world in which every particular history would blend seamlessly with the rest in a vast whole consisting of many authors but one transparent *voice*.[3] The complexities of voicing and the diversity of historians' solutions concern Linda Orr, Philippe Carrard, and Ann Rigney, all literary theorists working with the tools of contemporary poetics and discourse theory.

In her essay 'Intimate Images: Subjectivity and History – Staël, Michelet and Tocqueville', Linda Orr responds to the problem of linguistic 'shifters', which Barthes had signalled as the critical lacuna of the historical text. The shifter, which in historical discourse bridges the gap between the scene of writing and the scene of representation, is a problem for all realistic discourse because it points out that any text is being composed by an individual at a desk in a particular life-world, and that none of *this* reality appears in the text itself. Not only does Orr focus on the moment of personal self-consciousness in Madame de Staël, Michelet and Tocqueville, each experiencing in one way or another the *absence* of the past from their world, and their need to conquer that absence, but she also places herself in her essay, noting its origin in her own bemusement, hunches and wagers. The shift and shifter are both her theme and her mode of writing. In *Headless History: Nineteenth-Century French Historiography of the Revolution*, (Ithaca 1990), Orr writes:

Every writer should leave space to show how undefinable and traumatic her or his objects of study are, before rushing to explain them. Every work of history needs a moment of uncertainty, a moment given over to the disarray, or rather, the still point of uncertainty (p. 160).

The brutal decisiveness necessary to write a narrative of complex events, and the inevitable hesitation and remorse felt by historians in making these decisions is Orr's terrain. She hears the voice that others have not heard. Indeed, we may ask whether the linguistic turn comes to herald a revival of the personal voice that has been repressed since the de-rhetorization of historical study.

If the first stage of the linguistic turn was largely formal, aiming at a description of how historical texts work (i.e. a poetics), it has been followed by a rhetorical phase that is keenly sensitive to genre, where the expectations of an audience may be said to guide the writing of the text. At this point, the question of voice – who is speaking, for whom, and from what standpoint – comes to the fore. On the one hand, the personal position of the historian is no longer repressed. On the other, the problem of representing diverse, contesting, historical voices becomes an issue of considerable interest.

The voice, however, that Orr displays – both her own and that of her subjects – resounds against the grain of a professional practice. Staël, Michelet and Tocqueville wrote, despite the great differences in their personal conditions, before the professionalization of history set standards analogous to those of the natural sciences in which the voice of the historian was to be anonymous. To focus on the voice, the subject who writes, the moment of writing and on writing about writing (as historians often do) is to enter a kaleidoscopic world in which past, present and future shift, blur and change places. The act of writing about the past bears upon some vision of the future, as dream or as nightmare. Tocqueville's present, for example, is Orr's past; Orr's present is Tocqueville's future; what past they share cannot mean the same thing to them.

These conundrums are not new to historical reflection. Michelet's allusion to the death of his father, in the preface of 1847 to his *Histoire de la Révolution Française*, is a remarkable evocation of the father whose presence had been the presence of the past, of that Revolution which Michelet would now make reappear in writing. In pointing this out, Orr reminds us that the trend towards a more visible writing presence, the historian who is *there* on the page, a part of the process of shifting viewpoints and voices, is recent but not new. As Philippe Carrard maintains in his essay 'Theory of a Practice: Historical Enunciation and the *Annales* School,' the rules of positivist enunciation, based upon the classical premise that the "I" is despicable, are nowhere more transgressed than among the postwar French historians of the *Annales* school, hardly a likely locus for personal appearances given the largely quantitative and social scientific bent of the group.[4]

Carrard's meticulous study of the function of enunciation (what Barthes and Orr would call the 'shifters' that move attention from the matter at hand to the speech act that presents it), suggests that the *Annales* historians envision a new epistemology, one that does not 'pretend,' although they seem to have little sense of the conceptual basis of that epistemology. When historians emphasize political beliefs and their party affiliations rather than the days spent in libraries and archives, or tinkering with computers and software, more pretence is at hand. In their desire to represent what actually happened, historians who are showing less reluctance to speak of what actually happens in their work of representation are, both Orr and Carrard agree, returning to an earlier practice of unashamed, interventionist, authorship. That earlier practice of historical writing, before professionalization had established the standards of nineteenth century science as epistemology and the realist novel as literary model, has been the centre of attention for many recent students of historical discourse, in part because the French structuralists chose historical writing as their zero-degree model of realistic representation. Roland Barthes, Hayden White, Lionel Gossman, Stephen Bann, Linda Orr, Rigney, Jörn Rüsen and numerous others, including myself, have turned their attention to the classic historians, and have discovered there a richness of expression, variety of voices, creativity in argument, sensitivity to language and flexibility of genre that has been repressed, at least to some extent, and rarely studied.[5]

Ann Rigney, in 'Relevance, Revision and the Fear of Long Books,' considers how four historians of the early nineteenth century dealt with the problem of everyday life, making the silences of history speak, as Michelet put it. Inventing 'voices' for those who have left no documentary record, Augustin Thierry, Thomas Macaulay, Amans-Alexis Monteil and Jules Michelet chose quite diverse modes of discourse, and in so doing blazed trails which have been followed, often unawares, by historians to the present. The tensions which Rigney describes – between the inchoate mass of documentation and the communicative demands of discourse, between local and global forms of argumentation, between too little and too much (the 'Fear of long books') – are the tensions felt in any discourse that wants to articulate silence. There is so much silence to which one can give voice.

The modern scientific social historian and the French Romantic historians of a century and a half ago are peculiarly tied together by habits of enunciation which mark the presence of the historian's voice in the text and by the formal discursive genres that are always in the play of trial and error when the formless message of the voiceless must meet the demands of prose. This formlessness (*flou*, in Rigney's word) calls to mind that 'moment of uncertainty' invoked by Linda Orr.

The narrative poetics of the second section give way to rhetoric in the third, where two historians debate the argumentative dimensions of historical practice. Allan Megill's '"Grand Narrative" and the Discipline of History' endorses a powerfully self-conscious historical practice, in which confronting the formal fictions of historical writing is an integral part of its effective realism. For Megill, a world that no longer believes in a single grand narrative of human life must continually theorize the shifting and divergent stories that are told. The historian should be in several places, within and outside the profession, gaining methodological perspective in the same way that he or she has traditionally sought empathetic perspective on the strangeness that is always, somehow, the subject of historical research.

Robert Berkhofer, in 'A Point of View on Viewpoints in Historical Practice,' confronts the end of the single story through examining the problem of viewpoint in recent work in multicultural history. The powerful notion of the cumulativity of history, that is, the proposition that all valid historical writing could become part of ever-larger and more inclusive histories, ultimately constituting a Great Story, would apparently rule out any history written *for* or from the point of view of one group or another. If different groups experience different stories, in the sense of different plots, how can their stories be synthesized by any historian or historical understanding ? If all the possible plots envisioned by winners and losers, slaves and masters, women and men, professors and citizens, are amalgamated into a multi-focal form conceived according to some kind of fairness doctrine, what happens to meaning? And if we take seriously the rhetorical demand that any history must take some audience as its source of meaning, won't the result inevitably be the sort of 'Babel' described by Peter Novick in *That Noble Dream* (Cambridge 1988)? Berkhofer's argument, based on a sense of 'normal' historical professionalism and its need to answer the ultimate question of 'what really happened,' confronts finally the prospect of the historian as ironist, always noting with each statement that it could be quite otherwise.

In the final section of the book the implications of irony and seeing otherwise are developed. Stephen Bann takes up and transforms Berkhofer's interest in multiple points of view in his discussion of how the new vision brought forth by the stereoscope in the early nineteenth century led to a new sort of historical representation, culminating in the 'ironic museum.' Bann's interest in all the ways in which historical artefacts are collected, ordered and displayed, whether in a 'proper' historical narrative or in a novel, parody, painting, diorama or museum, leads him to questions about the development of historical sensitivity that go far beyond the limits of traditional historiography.

The ironic or postmodern practices described by Bann reveal the fissures in style and even individual artistic personality that Berkhofer notes in modern social groups. A postmodern solution to the problem of difference, Bann suggests, is juxtaposition, which places a differing point of view on continuous display, thus calling into question any illusion that the past can be present in a more figural sense. The 'focalization of historical competence' demanded by this sort of irony is absent in the modern historical reconstruction exemplified by Old Sturbridge Village. For Bann, what is wrong with Old Sturbridge Village is its ambition to present the past in an unmediated form. The multiple viewpoints that Berkhofer ponders in his essay take quite a different form in Bann's, where the emphasis is on the competence of the 'reader' or visitor.

In the final essay 'Statements, Texts and Pictures,' F. R. Ankersmit follows Bann's use of juxtaposition as mediation in a philosophical challenge to the literary model of historical discourse. In contrast to the prevailing textualization of all aspects of representation, Ankersmit offers a 'preference for the pictural' which makes of the text, and especially the historical text, a primarily imagistic form. Following Nelson Goodman's discussions of visual codes of representation, Ankersmit maintains that histories have the 'density' and 'repleteness' characteristic of pictures as opposed to sentences. The key to Ankersmit's work is the crucial distinction between the historical statement and the whole historical text, or 'narrative substance.' The confusion of the two has created most of the problems for philosophers of history.[6] The statement is falsifiable and subject to correspondence tests with reality; the historical text is not falsifiable (although its statements are), and the evaluations of its 'truth' are more analogous to the 'true-to-lifeness' of a novel or a painting. Ankersmit draws a clear line between history and historiography because he views historical texts as primarily objects, monads which create a world from the statements they contain. In a sense, Ankersmit's response to what Megill calls the 'paradox' of historiography – why do historical classics retain their power after their scholarship is outmoded – might be to ask why Guardi's vision of Venice retains its power in an age of Kodachrome photography; indeed, why

Guardi's vision so often guides the photographer. The real is what we are accustomed to see as real, Gombrich and Goodman suggest, and historiographic reality follows from this social coding created from a string of true, documented, sentences, but not dependent upon their truth alone for its effect. It is interesting that in his desire to downgrade the literary in favour of the pictorial model of historical representation, Ankersmit relies heavily upon metaphor, which is both textual and pictorial in its basis in resemblance.[7] By juxtaposing text and picture, by the reversing of dominance in comparisons ('the picture is like a text' becomes 'the text is like a picture'), Ankersmit sets our understanding off balance with a powerful redescription.

Multiple voices, ironic juxtapositions, strangely unbalanced magnitudes of cause and effect, redescriptions – the topics of discussion in this volume cannot fail to strike some readers as excessive or irrelevant. History has been the most commonsensical of the human sciences, the most resistant to formalization, the most persistently committed to the simple task of telling what happened and telling it straight. To focus on different aspects of the historical enterprise, bringing to the foreground for discussion what had in practice been ignored – that the historical text is an object in itself, made entirely from language, and thus subject to the interrogations devised by the sciences of language use, from ancient rhetoric to modern semiotics – is often taken as a hostile act. Rorty, whom we may call the philosopher of redescription, has noted this.

Ironism, as I have defined it, results from awareness of the power of redescription. But most people do not want to be redescribed. They want to be taken on their own terms – taken seriously just as they are and just as they talk. The ironist tells them that the language they speak is up for grabs by her and her kind. There is something potentially very cruel about that claim. For the best way to cause people long-lasting pain is to humiliate them by making the things that seemed most important to them look futile, obsolete, and powerless.[8]

A lot of the antagonism towards the attempts to redescribe historical texts is based on such emotions. Some will attack it as 'bloodless scholasticism and cold formalism.'[9] Others feel that it 'trivializes' the historical endeavour and counters some of the strongest intuitions and convictions held by historians.[10] Yet others feel that it fosters political extremism by breaking the bonds of historical understanding from the presumably moderating influence of reality.[11] Certainly, a profession like modern historical research has a particular investment in the authority to offer its own self-descriptions.

It is difficult today to find any proponents of naïve realism in historical practice, if that term is taken to mean that the past can be recaptured, explained, represented in historical discourse. Ranke's undeniable greatness and originality has been compromised by his stated aspiration to present the past as it actually was. However that expression may be qualified, explained and set in a context which makes it meaningful, it seems an unfortunate choice of words today. Each new wave of historical innovation unleashes a new group or technique or jargon which redefines the field of data, or invents new fields of data. Further, these new historical practices and discourses make no sustainable claim to be integrated with other versions of the past, nor even to deny them. They jostle to displace one another in a sort of struggle of wills.

At the same time, historians just as routinely behave as though their research were into the past, as though their writings were 'about' it, and as though 'it' were as real as the text which is the object of their labours. Everyone is a naïve realist where the past is concerned, except in a theoretical sense that may sometimes foster an unfortunate naïve anti-realism. Implicitly or explicitly, the response to this dilemma is dismissal – 'so what?' Whether I am reporting my day to my wife, or describing the course of narrative philosophy of history, or imagining as I read the course of the February revolution of 1848 or the events of autumn 1989, I am reporting or describing or imaging *something*, which I can only name as the past, as it really was. My wife, my audience and I myself expect no less than naïve realism. It is a moral, perhaps a categorical, imperative.

Now naïve is what no one today wishes to be. To speak of 'naïve realism' is to designate an outgrown view, one more benefitting childhood and innocence than maturity and experience. In historical matters, where realism is taken as the hallmark of responsible judgement, and utopianism a dangerous weakness, the expression 'naïve realist' seems not only patronizing, but also self-contradictory. To be a realist is not to be naïve; to be naïve is not to be a realist. And yet, when we commit ourselves to historical labour, there it is, whether we are reporting on a holiday in Egypt or describing modern historiographic thought. We are talking about *something*, and that *something* was real. The ghost of naïve realism haunts all of us, however much we deny it. It afflicts our formal understanding of historical thinking, even while it motivates this thinking. One may go as far as to say that historical thought in general exists only through the dispensation of these presuppositions. We examine them, find their flaws and try to correct them, but to do all of that and maintain a historical consciousness that corresponds to modern professional standards is difficult indeed.

We may learn from the great theorist of the 'naïve,' Friedrich von Schiller, why this naïve reflection on things maintains its strength and moral prestige. The moral superiority which our tradition attributes to naïve historical realism is, as Schiller implies, a nostalgia for existence in accord with itself and its inner necessity.[12] This 'eternal unity' of self with self is what we were, and ought to become again. To be naïve is to 'overlook' the artificial aspect of things, heeding only their 'simple nature.'[13] This 'overlooking' of artifice, through a nostalgia for an identity of self with self, sounds quite up-to-date. Schiller may have something to tell us. His alternative to naïve reflection, you recall, is the sentimental, a darker, less joyful wisdom.

. . .with naïve accounts, regardless of their subject matter, we always rejoice in our imagination in the truth, in the living presence of the object, and seek nothing further beyond these; whereas with the sentimental we have to reconcile the representation of imagination with an idea of reason and hence always fluctuate between two different conditions.[14]

Sentimental consciousness must confront the issue of *representations*, that is to say 'historical discourse.' It cannot 'overlook' the absence of historical representation. But it is torn, however, by an intense fluctuation, as Schiller knew.

If we can easily imagine a naïve historical consciousness regarding our relation to the evidence of the past as analogous to the relation of the scientist to his or her evidence, and equally governed by laws of logical proof and inference (which we find in the positivist or 'covering-law model' debate), it is not so obvious what follows from a more sentimental historical consciousness. For example, Hayden White holds the view that the function of historical writing is to 'test the capacity of a culture's fictions to endow real events with the kinds of meaning which literature displays to consciousness through its fashioning of patterns of "imaginary" events.'[15] Here, the sentimental striving for unity of the inner understanding and the outer reality of the past is, as Schiller puts it, 'an idea still to be realized, no longer as a fact of his life .'[16] For White, it can never be realized, only reproduced in ever more forms.

White's view of progress in historical understanding derives from this insight.

And if the tropes of language are limited, if the types of figuration are finite, then it is possible to imagine how our representations of the historical world aggregate into a comprehensive total vision of that world, and how progress in our understanding of it is possible. Each new representation of the past represents a further testing and refinement of our capacities to figure the world in language, so that each new generation is heir, not only to more information about the past, but also to more adequate knowledge of our capacities to comprehend it.[17]

If, however, our modes of comprehension and representation are not finite and permanent, but rather are in some sense historical themselves, subject to changes which we cannot understand except with their help, then White's model of progress looks fragile indeed. This is a progress of formal representational modes, not of knowledge of the past. Ironically, it founders on the possibility that these representational modes may be fundamentally historical, so that the theory cannot guarantee our knowledge of them at all.

An interesting aspect of this widespread re-examination of the conceptual foundations of the learned discourses is the marked revival of passionate interest in the ancient Greek Sophists, long the scapegoats of the story of Western philosophy. Nietzsche had remarked that any advance in moral or epistemological knowledge has reinstated the Sophists, who, for him, represented the high culture of Thucydides.[18] The question of an advance, of course, is a matter of viewpoint, but the revival of the Sophists – (Gorgias, Protagoras, Isocrates and the fragmentary others) – is indisputable. I suspect that the Sophists tend to emerge from the background when things appear to be up for grabs; as opposed to the more nomothetic, scholastic, rhetorical brethren – Plato, Aristotle, Cicero, Quintilian – who tend to regulate the traffic of an orderly discursive scene, the Sophists are 'usable.' Their meaning is not quite fixed. They can help to deflect a debate, to resituate its arguments, to reframe its terms. What brands the Sophists morally is what Nietzsche admired in them, their pragmatism, their willingness to demonstrate their own immorality, their delight in overturning the self-righteousness of the diversity of interests which confront each other. It was the Sophistic example that led Thucydides to create the dialogue of conflicting moral claims when the Athenians presented their famous ultimatum to the Melians.

In this reading, the Sophists were first to 'transvalue all values,' the first cultural relativists, the first *historicists* in their way. For far from being the dazzling word-jugglers of the tradition, the Sophists offer some modern readers a powerful ethical stance – and a dreadful immoralism. On the one hand, the Sophistic stance – one hesitates to call it a movement – unfurls the ethical banner later waved by Vico and Herder, a sense of wonder at the forms of human variety. Although their profession was to sell techniques for victory and domination in power disputes, the Sophists are credited with fathering genuine diversity because of their appeals, when timely, to fundamental disagreements and essentially contested concepts.[19]

The teaching of the Sophists made possible an active citizenry precisely because they were for hire, selling their techniques openly for what they were, with no moral claims attached. The image of history as a 'field of dreams,' in which every group, even everyone, may have a past shaped by desire, may have its appeal in a democracy, although not to me, but to call for close attention to historical *discourse* rather than more research and 'new' viewpoints is not to cause the problem. If we need citizens anymore, they may benefit most of all from the rhetorical *techne* bequeathed by the great citizen-builders, the amoral Sophists, who taught how to conduct debate on all matters, including Sophism itself.

The twelve essays in this volume address a perennial question: 'How is historical thought to be conceived and described in our time?' When R. G. Collingwood wrote in his *Autobiography*, published in 1939, that the major task of twentieth century philosophy was to account for the innovations and accomplishments of twentieth-century historical discourse, just as the philosophers of the seventeenth century were confronted with the world-transforming scientific discourse of that era, he may have had a number of things in mind.[20] He almost certainly meant to suggest that the historical work of his own time was of an importance equal to the revolutions of Galileo and Newton. He also intended, it seems to me, to reverse the traditional categories which decreed that while philosophy might be properly concerned with the immediacy of historical events, it hardly need concern itself in any but a passing way with a secondary discourse like historical writing. After all, the philosophy of history had generally chosen as its task to straighten out the historian, to tidy up the muddle it took to be historical thought, and to prescribe a set of rules which might allow historians to aspire to the lofty status of a bona fide proto-science.

Now neither Collingwood, nor Louis Mink, a philosopher who often cited this passage, believed that historical discourse was secondary. Yet they could not foresee a situation in which both philosophical and historical discourse faced a challenge from a third point. The 'scientific revolution' in the seventeenth century and the 'discovery' of history in the nineteenth founded discourses of representation and explanation of the natural and human worlds; essentially, their discourses *are* their fundamental aspect. At least this is implied by the 'linguistic turn,' the tendency of late twentieth century thought to look *at* rather than *through* a telescope (figuratively speaking) and see prisms and lenses, to stand in front of a looking-glass and see the mirror. The modernist discourse of an independent subject (the investigator) peering at a discrete, definable subject (a part of the world) through a refracting tool intended to clarify the true contours of the object seems a bit less absolute.[21] The Galilean telescope which served all modernist discourses as a figure of scientific power looks to some less like a natural extension of the subject's eye, and more as it appeared to the Paduan Peripatetics, as a distorting contraption, put in place for a particular use among other possibilities. Today, of course, this 'telescope' is *language*. In a sense, it always was. The post-Kantian, Romantic sense of a reality composed of 'both what they half create and what perceive' has been pushed towards a full-blown concept that language constitutes the knowable world, limits the ways in which we can know and represent it, and offers us as natural what is in fact conventional. There is scarcely any area in which this notion has not been applied, invariably yielding copious discourse.

Collingwood's comments were clearly aimed at the 'historical culture' bequeathed to Western society by the nineteenth century.[22] If *Historismus* proper had run its course by Collingwood's time, the habits of *historicism* had not.[23] Respect for the idea of context, a tactful reluctance to judge before making an exhaustive attempt at sympathetic understanding had taken place, a general sense of the hierarchical priority of the group and its ethical institutions (especially the state) over the private sphere and its psychological whims – these and many other habits remained to be examined. Above all, the nineteenth-century flowering of historical thought bequeathed a conviction that the foundation of proper historical understanding involved a basically narrative understanding of history as the story of change in time.

The nineteenth century did not, however, come to terms with the primarily discursive nature of the historical work. It bequeathed to us essentially modernist ambitions, to know all life-forms with the certainty afforded by the historical intuition. What is not so apparent is the extent to which historicism, or more precisely its early forms, often called historism, resembled recent ideas. For in envisioning the historical world as a plenum of ideas in the mind of God, Herder, Humboldt and later Ranke, saw peoples or states as elements of a divine vocabulary, whose restriction, corruption, frustration or limitation would limit the possibilities of divine expression, a thing devoutly not to be wished. Thus, according to Herder:

If Nature has anywhere attained her end, she has attained it everywhere. The practical understanding of man was intended to blossom and bear fruit in all its varieties; and hence such a diversified earth was ordained for so diversified a species.[24]

As is well known, the question of historical progress fares poorly in this discussion, since the best we can hope for is a fullness of divine expression in the flowering of many isolated cultures, each, as it were, directly connected to the divine.[25] Progress in this view is more, diverse, forms, not better ones; to judge would clearly be to challenge the wisdom of the Divine Author and thus not recommended.

Compare these essentially eighteenth century ideas, which hinge in my opinion on the inscrutability of God's plan, with some twentieth-century expressions of the possibility of progress in historical understanding. In our day, of course, the deity is absent, but the analogous lack of a firm standard of formal judgement is not. All that is needed is the replacement of the concept of a people (or a nation, or a race, gender, any entity) with that of a historical model of presentation, a narrative image.

But, since there would be no way of arbitrating among the different modes of explanation that might be chosen by a given historian (Organicism, Contextualism, Mechanism, Formism) on the one hand or the different modes of emplotment he might use to structure his narrative (Romance, Comedy, Tragedy, Satire) on the other, the field of historiography would appear to be rich and creative precisely in the degree to which it generated many different possible accounts of the same set of events and many different ways of figuring their multiple meanings.[26]

This passage from White's *Metahistory* certainly resonates with Humboldt's classic formulation of 1821.

The goal of history can only be the actualization of the idea which is to be realised by mankind in every way and in all shapes in which the finite form may enter into a union with the idea.[27]

And of course, for Humboldt, language is a major exemplar of the ideal forms, each one a unique, incommensurable vehicle.

To read the early historists as I have is to reverse the charges levelled at postmodernist students of historical discourse; far from being historicist in any classic sense, it was the early *historists* who were the postmoderns, as Jean-François Lyotard suggested when he noted that a postmodernism *precedes* every modernism.[28] However one wishes to name, unname and rename such movements – not after all, a very postmodern thing to do – the role of rhetoric as the self-conscious attention to the forms and techniques of discourse remains intact. Some will surely see rhetoric as the poison that caused the disease, others the medicine that can cure, but the attention to rhetoric which has not been given by mainstream American historians can hardly be said to have *caused* any problems for history. It is business as usual that has led to the relativism that seems to define the present moment. That is to say, the new descriptions of historical discourse, for all their emphasis on discourse as the basis of historical reality, only point to the remarkable evaporation of any sense of the past as a story with other than a temporary, provisional, coherence. And this evaporation has been the product of the best and most scientific of professional historical work.

Perhaps the nature of the current moment in public historical understanding can be clarified by contrasting two influential and quite different books: Hayden White's *Metahistory* of 1973 and Peter Novick's *That Noble Dream* of 1988. White sought the deep structures of thought that made historical thinking possible and would account for the coexistence of many diverse and incommensurable representations of historical events. He named these structures in largely linguistic terms, and tried to show how what it is that makes historical accounts hang together hangs together.[29] Novick, by contrast, writes what purports to be an account of the American historical profession in the 20th century, following the fluctuating fortunes of 'the objectivity question.' He spends a number of pages on White's work, but makes clear that in his opinion White's influence has largely been outside the historical profession.[30]

The distance from *Metahistory* to *That Noble Dream* is not easy to calculate. A considerable cultural change had taken place in the fifteen years between 1973 and 1988. While *Metahistory* was conceived in the ferment of the late 1960s, whose tendency was to dismiss a past that could be perceived as irrelevant to the making of the desired future, *That Noble Dream*, a book of the 1980s, seems a work of 'after-ness.' The current terms postmodern, post-structuralist, appear to name positively what is gone; ethics are situated *After Virtue*, and thought *After Philosophy*, to cite the title of two influential and quite characteristic books. And the interest stirred up by Francis Fukuyama's article 'End of History' (1989) certainly continues the theme.[31] White's obsessive mapping and charting reflect the goal of high modernist structuralism to establish clearly a sense of where one stands in the world of predictably varied formations, while Novick, concluding that in the 'collapsed comity' of historical studies there is no longer 'a king in Israel,' has little idea of where we stand or how we might find out – a very postmodern, decentred attitude. White revealed the power of metanarratives to afford meaning to historical accounts, and called for a freer sensitivity to the possibilities offered by plots. On the other hand, the distrust of metanarratives trumpeted as constitutive of both the 'postmodern condition' and the 'end of history' prevails in Novick's book. Significantly, *That Noble Dream* concludes with a voice not the author's; it is that of Jean-Paul Sartre, whose influence on White's *Metahistory* seems clear.[32]

The moment comes when you just can't take the work any further. . . At this point, my friend Giacometti explains, you can throw your piece of sculpture in the rubbish bin or exhibit it in a gallery. So there it is. You never quite grasp what you set out to achieve. And then suddenly it's a statue or a book. The opposite of what you wanted. If its faults are inscribed methodically in the negative which you present to the public, they at least point to what it might have been. And the spectator becomes the real sculptor, fashioning his model in thin air, or reading the book between the lines.[33]

In this final passage, a narrative *locus* traditionally reserved for the author's own voice in its least 'objective' mode, Novick cites Sartre citing Giacometti to the effect that the object of creative labour has neither a *proper* form, the achievement of which would signal its completion, nor a *proper* meaning, which would be the fulfilment of the creator's intent. The ambiguity in the identity of the voice which ends *The Noble Dream* re-enacts the tenor of the passage. Compared with this heteroglossic flourish, White's notorious and shunned 'rhetorical relativism' looks almost like positivism. What *it* (the work, the future, the past) is, is what *someone* will make of it, *someday*. Or so Novick implies. As Nietzsche put it, ' "Being" – we have no idea of it apart from the idea of "living." – How can anything dead "be?" '[34]

Novick's most troubling and provocative chapter again appeals to a ventriloquistic allusion. 'Every Group its Own Historian,' the title of Novick's chapter 14, echoes Carl Becker's 'Everyman his Own Historian' of 1931.[35] In this chapter, Novick recounts the development of black history and women's history, and in particular, the disruptions that their flourishing caused within the historical profession in the 1970s and 1980s, especially to the notion of professional objectivity as opposed to advocacy of group interests. The question certainly arises why *Doonesbury* revisionists (after the American political cartoon strip) or white supremacists or conspiracy mongers with film studios might not produce

their own advocacy histories, asserting, when challenged, their right to
cast off the old oppressive standards which have silenced them. Why not
produce their own canon of actualities and interpretations? Every group
its own. . ., etc. This particularism, however, extends far beyond the
group identifications that have institutionalized themselves of late in
American academia. Histories of nature, of the bodily functions, of
almost anything that can be named, are beginning to appear, regularly
amazing us with the ingenuity of their authors in resituating object after
object from the realm of the ostensibly natural to the realm of the
historical, and, of course, socially constructed. The realm of the
historical, which once had fairly clear tacit definition, largely as past
politics, lacks one now as never before. The 'historical' is clearly a
rhetorical practice, a form of discourse; to look for it elsewhere is to
encounter the chaos that Novick describes superbly.

What is interesting is the way in which each group tends to behave as
though its discourse were in fact perfectly commensurable with the
others, and to show emotions ranging from disappointment to outrage
when the other discourses of history fail, in one way or another, to profit
from the 'other' discourses (or 'new perspectives,' as they are often
called).[36] The vision of a 'Universal History', or at least a bigger, better,
story, long dismissed by philosophers and certainly put out of reach by
the historical developments of the recent past, still seems to inspire
respect.

Ironically, we are back to Collingwood's statement. It is the
accomplishments of twentieth century historical practice, functioning in
earnest with no sense of relativism, that have led to the vision, if not the
actuality, of a post-historical world. This is not an 'end of history' in
terms of directional ideological process as Francis Fukuyama describes,
but a process in which histories will be recognised for what they are:
formalized aesthetic objects which make certain claims about the world
and our relation to it, and which we take as provisional guides in making
sense of experience. The notion of a congeries of incompatible historical
worlds is potentially as troubling as the idea of the universe as a chaotic
fun-house where different physical rules prevail in different places.

RUBRICS OF STYLE

I

Historicity in an Age of Reality–Fictions

NANCY F. PARTNER

For who does not know history's first law to be that an author must not dare to tell anything but the truth? And its second that he must make bold to tell the whole truth? That there must be no suggestions of partiality anywhere in his writings? Nor of malice? Cicero, *De Oratore*, 11.62–4

Ms. Malcolm went on to explain that she had 'compressed' conversations over a long period, in this case seven months, into one 'monologue,' rather like 'sketches incorporated into one painting.' From her many conversations with Mr. Masson, Ms. Malcolm testified, she 'selected the things that seemed most characteristic, most expressive.' If relocating those conversations 'doesn't change the meaning,' she added, 'it's O.K. to do it.' *New York Times*, 14 May 1993

THE ISSUE: EXACTLY WHAT IS IT OK TO DO?

For the past twenty-five years, more or less, a multi-faceted, philosophically serious and analytically acute movement throughout the *sciences humaines*, synoptically referred to as the 'linguistic turn', has relentlessly revolved about the forms of discourse which create and mediate our evolving knowledge of ourselves, our institutions and our histories.[1] History itself, regarded as both practice and product, has been one of the chief, if reluctant, beneficiaries of this intellectual trend. It therefore seems fair to ask if the 'linguistic turn' has turned professional historians around to face language as primary, active and meaningful in their work (rather than secondary, passive and transparent – the pre-turn story). Then how are we doing now since this revolution of words? Has the impact of non-referential language theory, deconstruction and the exposure of hegemonic interests embedded in what used to pass for neutral description left the ancient discipline shattered beyond recuperation?;[2] or have historians perhaps launched themselves into postmodern, post-structuralist, post-empiricist cyberspace and are even now sending back messages encrypted in unprecedentedly novel forms? From the evidence so far, judging from my own non-scientific but not atypical sampling of conference papers, journal articles and university press books, it is my impression that the 'linguistic turn' was a revolving door and that everyone went around and around and got out exactly where they got in. For all the sophistication of the theory-saturated part of the profession, scholars in all the relevant disciplines that contribute to or depend on historical information carry on in all essential ways as though nothing had changed since Ranke, or Gibbon for that matter: as though invisible guardian angels of epistemology would always spread protecting wings over facts, past reality, true accounts, and authentic versions; as though the highly defensible, if not quite the definitive, version would always be available when we really needed it.

This show of stiff-upper-lip doggedness, which enables trained historians to proceed through any number of epistemological 'crises' without any fundamental alteration of method or presentation, strikes me as quite interesting and entirely commendable, although the collective motives and institutional forces that account for it are merely self-interested and self-perpetuating. The theoretical destabilizing of history achieved by language-based modes of criticism has had no practical effect on academic practice because academics have had nothing to gain and everything to lose by dismantling their special visible code of evidence-grounded reasoning and opening themselves to the inevitable charges of fraud, dishonesty and shoddiness. Many successful careers ride the shifting waves of relevance, revisionism and the slow-motion polemics of debate in scholarly publications, but perceived violations of the basic methodological constraints which are tacitly understood to apply to everyone bring down nothing but ignominy and exclusion.[3] So all historians – Marxist, feminist, old historicist, new historicist, empiricist – still speak the same basic language of evidentiary syntax, logical grammar and referential semantics. Florid superficial differences have yet to touch the 'critical apparatus', as the acknowledgements, explanatory introduction, footnotes with elaborated conventions of bibliographical reference, lists of manuscripts, monograph and scholarly journal sources, appendices and indexes are still known; taken together, these constitute the formalized structure of good faith and integrity in modern historical practice.

This particular formal structure frames every serious work of history as a semiotic scaffolding – a readable code of extratextual reference and inductive reasoning whose category meaning is: verification. More fully decyphered, the apparatus code reads: (1) in this text, declarative sentences which are susceptible of verification *can* be verified; and (2) interpretative or inferential sentences have been constructed following generally accepted rules of reasoning. The appearance of a work supported by a conventional critical apparatus is no guarantee of quality, of course, only of intention. Individual histories may be more or less plausibly and cogently reasoned from more or less adequate amounts of evidence which itself may have been selected, assembled, translated, copied, collated and assessed with varying degrees of aptness, thoroughness, accuracy and judgement.[4] But even thin, careless, slack histories, if they are constructed under professional auspices, locate themselves as history by implicit appeal to a certain set of practices, in the text and out.

The iconoclastic weapons of the 'linguistic turn' were the exposure of 'transparent' language as a rhetorical voice like any other;[5] a destabilized theory of reference connected to semiotics: and the deconstructive analysis of historical 'facts' as constructed artefacts no different in cognitive origin than any other made thing or 'fiction'.[6] The hectic phase of that attack on positivism, much of it mischievous and antic, seems to have played itself out. It has to be emphasized that nothing whatever was settled or decided, much less defined or disproven, but purely philosophic battles are too abstract to remain heated for long among historians unless closely connected to much more immediate and politically fraught concerns. For the most part, unreconstructed or closet positivists are no longer made the butt of erudite epistemological fun; it is even safe again to say the word 'fact' in public, so long as it is done with a certain arch reserve. Tempers fray currently over feminist, gay, afro-centric, multicultural, and post-colonial claims to a central position in publishing and pedagogy. Yet each of these groups, and others just coming into full voice, claims to speak to a reality which was and is really 'there' and each claims to speak a fully adequate language of historical evidence and reasoning. So it would seem that the basic epistemological challenge has disappeared (or 'been disappeared' in the police-state sense) by silent consensus, or was somehow deflected or collapsed of itself.

But it has not. It has reappeared, dramatically strengthened and more aggressive, but in a practical form that historians are not well equipped to recognize – in popular forms of history-derived culture in television, film, journalism and verisimilar entertainments or 'reality-fictions'. Experimentation with purposeful blurring of the distinction between fiction and history in the various formats of near-news, factoid fictions or 're-enactments' are pandemic in the mass media, even in its most elite venues. In a bizarre way, it is almost as though the postmodern games which academics tired of and discarded have been discovered and put to serious use by the only people who can actually reach a mass audience.

Since I have raised this subject in an essay directed to a knowledgeable audience, I feel bound to admit that these developments caught me entirely by surprise. In one way and another, I have been working on the subject of the formal and cultural relations between history and fiction for a long time now,[7] and while I have always been certain that the subject was intrinsically interesting, I never imagined it was anything but a learned, rather philosophic pursuit – an 'academic' subject in the colloquial and slightly patronizing sense. I did notice, at some point, that medieval historical narratives held a surprising and as yet unexamined interest for the origins of the kind of fictional realism that issued eventually in the English eighteenth-century novel, and that seemed about as 'modern' as the subject could reasonably get.[8] The overlap of modern history and fiction, which received so much attention via the 'linguistic turn' inspired by semiotics and French literary criticism, turned out to be quite an abstract and rarefied business. Only the *formal fictions* – for example significant event, plot, narrative structure, closure, all the artefacts of intelligibility created by language and imposed on the formless seriatim of experience – fill the category of 'the fictions of history' in modern lit. crit. discourse, the area Hayden White brought forward so strongly in *Metahistory*. 'Fiction' in this modern critical realm is a term limited strictly to depictions which impose meaningful form on events by actions of the intellect, not passively copy from nature.[9]

The old offhand, unchallenged, unconcealed use of outright fictional *invention* inside what purported to be histories (all the invented speeches, trumped-up anecdotes, scenes interpolated from other books, hearsay miracles, verbatim renditions of secret conversations, etc, the familiar stuff of ancient and medieval histories) had been effectively banished well before history became a university subject. Powerful strictures were in place by the seventeenth century; by the time Gibbon wrote, readers were expected to regard footnotes in classical languages as a normal feature of the history page. By the twentieth century, academic history by professional historians set the genre rules for the derivative form of contemporary reportage: 'news' in print and television, documentary film, political and cultural journalism and so forth. That much seemed settled. Or at least it used to seem settled.

And yet now, I discover that all the charmingly useless erudition I acquired from the study of ancient and medieval histories about the techniques for interlacing fiction and history *applies*. Currently, if I want to find some example of literary or cinematic practice to compare directly with something characteristic and typical of a premodern history, I hardly have to look – some new 'simulation' broadcast on a purported news programme, or a controversial documentary film, or biography or other book by a journalist, presses itself on my attention. The civil suit brought by the psychoanalyst Jeffrey Masson against the *New Yorker* journalist Janet Malcolm has been the most seriously contested case so far. Malcolm, a highly respected writer, defended her practice of creating a coherent monologue set in a specific time and place (attributed to her subject by the normal typographical conventions of quotation marks, as well as interviewer–narrator's remarks), from a pastiche of interviews held over many months in different circumstances by claiming, in court, that if such practice 'doesn't change the meaning, it's OK to do it'.[10] She is certainly not alone in her certainty that custody of 'the meaning' justifies all manner of authorial 'improvements' in the presentation. A Canadian film board documentary by the McKenna brothers, *The Valor and the Horror*, contained actors playing historical persons who apparently spoke newly written words which strongly sustain the film-maker's polemical view of events during World War II; then there was the NBC *Dateline* programme on which film of a General Motors truck exploding after a side collision turned out to have been rigged with gasoline and other props;[11] and there are all the proliferating reality-shows on television (the mixed-genre docudramas, the heavily edited videos of police work, the crime reenactments), and the dinosaur simulations being exhibited in museums of natural history, recordings in which the living and the dead sing together, and on and on.

I used to keep a brief list of what I thought were oddities of this sort, what seemed to me modern instances of practices outmoded for centuries struggling strangely back to life. It is important to keep in mind that the ancient practice of blending fictions with reported information is not essentially altered by the addition of modern technologies of film, computer imaging, sound enhancement and the like. Now I hardly bother to keep track of them anymore. Since my purpose is the analysis of principles, techniques, cultural functions and formal devices, in order to isolate out some concepts and a useful critical language for under-standing history and fiction, this proliferation of new examples, always different yet increasingly the same, does not advance intellectual clarity.

But I feel that against my will, I understand what is going on. In fact, I sometimes feel I have come to possess some arcane and appalling knowledge that in a more rational and less self-destructive world would have no use.

IS THERE ANYTHING NEW HERE?
ANCIENT PROTOTYPES AND MODERN PRACTICES

In its first fully elaborated form, the yet-to-be-defined genre *historia* was offered by a clearly self-identified author, identical with the textual narrator, who pointedly did *not* do two things: he did not invoke inspiration from a muse; and he did not speak as self-sufficient source of his information.[12]

I, Herodotus of Halicarnassus, am here setting forth my history [*historia*], that time may not draw the color from what man has brought into being, nor those great and wonderful deeds, manifested by both Greeks and barbarians, fail of their report, and, together with all this, the reason why they fought one another. (1.1).[13]

Standing out in positive relief from the narrator's frank yet reticent self-introduction (*not* an inspired epic poet, *not* a lyric poet, *not* a philosopher), the word *historia*, with its loose meaning of researches or findings, opened a literary category which Herodotus filled with a complex overarching narrative built of hundreds of interlocking stories, many of them multiple variants of some single disputed event:

That is how the Persians say it happened . . . But about Io herself the Phoenicians disagree with the Persians. For they say . . . These are the stories of the Persians and the Phoenicians (1.5).[14]

And so the history proceeds: what people remember; what people say. Many of these hearsay accounts are filled out, pointed up and completed with the writer's fictions of dialogue, private actions and the exposed thoughts and feelings of his characters.[15] The narrator, presenter of his *historia*, the emerging historian is the seeker, recipient and tentative adjudicator of the versions competing for dominance,[16] and in this complicated process, he is the maker of a 'found-object' work whose coherence depends on his ability to construct a meganarrative out of hundreds of already narrated incompatible segments – the 'historia' – conflicting, overlapping record of memory.

Herodotus' use of small-scale fictions in the form of dramatized anecdotes involving details of action, invented speeches and conversations, the dreams and thoughts of long-dead persons, did not subvert or overwhelm the narrative intention's announcing 'history'; all the major signals of genre, or textual intention, announce a serious truth-claim for this complex work. But neither can the fictions be regarded as expendable decoration. Fictions were incorporated into large-scale prose narratives whose dominant textual intention plainly announced 'not fiction' because the fictions fulfilled crucial and necessary functions in the cultural project which crystallized around the term history. The censorious Thucydides, a generation younger, announcing a more rigorous, more serious discipline for his own history, discarded many of Herodotus' characteristic procedures *except* (to the dismay and confusion of generations of scholars) the use of fiction of which he made a speciality in elaborate invented speeches which lay out an entire social psychology and theory of politics.

Fiction, as deployed by Herodotus and Thucydides, raised history from a mere descriptive record of events in sequence to a level nearer philosophy, nearer to those permanently apt generalizations about human character, politics and the causes of war so prized in Greek intellectual life. To be serious, valuable, elevated in classical culture, was to move beyond the particular. The fictions allowed history to be *about something*. The interpolated fictional voice was the voice of the contemplative, analytical historian *demonstrating*, not merely asserting, from within events and in the very voices of historical actors, the underlying meaning caught in the flux and confusion of events in progress. Fiction carried the metanarrative discourse of explanation, distant causation, human nature revealed, throughout the narrative duration of the recorded events. Without the fictions, history really would have been the minimal record of constrictedly local events, the dumb sequence of formless time and accident that Aristotle grudgingly permitted it to be in the ungenerous, programmatic mood of the *Poetics*.

The distinction between historian and poet is not in the one writing prose and the other verse – you might put the work of Herodotus into verse, and it would still be a species of history; it consists really in this, that the one describes the thing that has been, and the other a kind of thing that might be. Hence poetry is something more philosophic and of graver import than history, since its statements are of the nature rather of universals, whereas those of history are singulars.[17]

To regard the early use of historical fiction as a response to the rhetorical demands of Greek literary culture for colour, drama and variety is to see something obvious, if resisted by many classicists, but also to miss much of the point.[18] In the new genre of history, fiction was the expressive instrument of interpretation, supralocal significance, psychological analysis, large-scale pattern; all the passages from raw event to intelligible additions to permanent knowledge, from the jumble of actuality to truth, were negotiated via fiction. Aristotle exaggerated the contrast between fiction and history in the *Poetics*, presumably for schematic clarity; he was certainly not describing the historical practice of his own age which incorporated fiction precisely for the sake of philosophic depth and significance.

Fiction carried and continues to carry the most persistent and serious of human impulses: *to know* beyond the opaque surfaces of other lives and the distracting chaos of quotidian event. To the extent that reality eludes quantification and extends beyond photographable surfaces, knowledge limited to what can be supported by conventional evidence will never feel satisfying. The imaginative push through the impermeable membrane of other minds and lost actions will always be a movement towards truth, not fantasy. As E. M. Forster acutely observed:

In this direction fiction is truer than history, because it goes beyond the evidence, and each of us knows from his own experience that there is something beyond the evidence.[19]

If we work from the premise that fiction was drawn into history to satisfy its most serious intellectual aims, not merely as a slack or unevolved device for entertainment, the questions we might ask about why and under what conditions fictional invention might be utterly banned from history writing are greatly altered. Seen in this light, the elimination of fictional invention is not always and self-evidently a matter of history getting serious; the move to this self-denial and self-discipline requires some manifest and overwhelming justification.

At the same time, this apologia for historical fictions can only go so far. The blameless, shameless unselfconscious freedom to use fictions within the genre envelope of history belonged only to writers who were effortlessly confident of speaking from the moral centre of a near-universal consensus about every locus of meaning from the personal use of food and sex through all gradients of social relations out to the important public world of politics and war. If, in antiquity, the historian could not speak from deep ingrained and acculturated certainties about human nature in its great social settings, then he (and the *he* is important here) could not, and would not, write history. He wrote for and about readers identical with himself; that he and they together constituted only a fraction of the social world was of no importance since they monopolized the governing power in their world, together with formal education and high culture. 'The meaning' of things, to glance back at Janet Malcolm's use of this never neutral term, was their meaning and they had no literary competitors.

This sense of certainty about the truths that define reality, not self-effacing reportage, was what Cicero meant by the historian's duty to tell the truth:

> For who does not know history's first law to be that an author must not dare to tell anything but the truth? And its second that he must make bold to tell the whole truth? That there must be no suggestion of partiality anywhere in his writings? Nor of malice? (*De Oratore*, 11.62–4).

The stern enunciation of ethical judgements pronounced regardless of the consequences to fortune, career or even life of the historian, neither fawning nor malice, was the 'truth' appealed to here. This truth was the ethical standard of a specific, limited, if dominant class of persons and it has nothing whatever to do with objectivity or restraints on any literary technique, including wholesale invention.[20] The archetypal historian spoke as ethical witness from the centre of the action. He might be Sallust, bitter moralist with no more political career to lose, perfectly free to conduct his readers to the furthest room in the house of the revolutionary, Catiline, where, 'excluding all witnesses' Catiline exhorted his debased followers to a conspiracy to burn Rome – in a speech presented word for word.[21] Or he might be Tacitus, equally contemptuous of fear or favour, writing in a temporary lull when 'we can think as we please, and speak as we think', filling his horrific scenes of mob violence with poignant and shocking detail of no known provenance, or using the same battle scene in two different books.[22]

Classical histories 'read' with such effortless conviction, with, even now, such mind-subduing authority (try, *while reading*, to disagree with Tacitus!), because in their historical moment these writers were, in all essentials, their own readers, and their histories powerfully summon up a social world with no other readers in it.[23] We have to presume that the dramatizing fictions of historical narrative which aggressively interpreted events aroused no revulsion or scepticism because, for writer and reader both, the truths thus conveyed were so self-evidently, so self-justifyingly true. The contamination of credibility introduced by the incorporated fictions must have seemed beneath serious notice.

The crude contrast between Cicero and Janet Malcolm in the epigraphs with which I opened this essay turns out to be illusory. Her calm certainty of holding the true 'meaning' which itself justifies any striking and persuasive mode of expression is perfectly classical; Cicero would have approved. Broadly defined, all historiographical practice descends from ancient models set by Herodotus and Thucydides with respect to its epistemology as a set of practices in prose; and from the late republican Roman writers with respect to moral stance, the historian becomes political and ethical observer. We are currently seeing every ancient practice of verisimilar representation 'standing for', dramatizing or extending historical truth paralleled by a modern instance from some medium; so far this has excluded academe. Instances when actuality is felt to be inadequate in filling the logical and dramatic gap between event and meaning invite gap-filling according to all the ancient rhetorical techniques.

These include all the Incorporated Fictions which in ancient and medieval histories were placed under the 'genre umbrella' created by such devices as framing, authorial voice, invocations of authority and so on, which announce textual intention and establish 'history' as the operative contract between writer and reader.[24] These fictions which, in their ancient context, carried an implicit supratextual request to the reader to be accepted as heightened expressions of truthful meaning, harmless ornaments with a degree of permitted dramatic licence are now routinely found in journalism, biography, history-based film and 'true-life' television drama. The increasingly familiar docudrama techniques of simulation, compression, gap-filling, impersonation and so on look very like contemporary equivalents of ancient rhetorical fictions; 'fact-based' serves now as the code for a representation of a highly partisan view of events and persons whose meaning is felt to require *and justify* dramatic alteration. In both cases, ancient and modern, truth is not grounded in verification but in intention – lodged in the author who grasps the essential meaning and must find a suitable verbal (or visual) equivalent for the audience. In this set of practices, intention or 'truth-telling' always overrides the claims of actuality and the irritating restrictions it places on expression.

History as a set of practices involving research, reasoning and writing did not begin in the nineteenth century. The vague persuasion current among historians that we are as much the product of advanced industrial and scientific culture as empirical medicine or physics is an unexamined and foolish illusion. As an illusion it allows us to proceed uncritically in some of the more self-deceiving notions about our 'scientific' practices and the negligible role of language in our work; it has also produced a collective amnesia about our true origins and what student historians ought to know about the deeply ambivalent impulses we express and suppress when we write as historians. Our common ancestor is not German but Greek wedded to Roman.

Insisting on the importance of the literary and discursive techniques used by the first major historians in the Western tradition is not antiquarian fussiness. Only the narcissistic shortsightedness of a rather too self-flattering professionalism prevents historians, as a discipline, from recognizing that the basic literary forms and authorial intentions established in Greek and Latin antiquity have continued, with astonishingly few alterations, into modern times. The openly identified narrator who is the known author; the substitution of collected information for inspiration by muse or authorial omniscience; the use of prose for a complex extended narrative; close attention to causal relations, motive and fortune as the determinants of events; the organized state as the defining unit of human society, and the predominance of political action and war as subject matter are all legacies from antiquity.[25] The difference between immediate local provocations and distant, long-term causes, between individual motive and collective impulse, even between such very modern forms as the author's introduction, acknowledgements and attribution of sources can be traced clearly to the conventions of ancient historical narrative. And in addition, antiquity left us, calmly and without apology, its use of *incorporated fictions* within plainly signalled history as an instrument of the historical purpose. The modern suppression of this instrument required substitutions and a degree of collective self-denial that itself needs explanation.

THE 'LINGUISTIC TURN' RETURNED

. . . but I draw courage from the remembrance that history is never, in any rich sense, the immediate crudity of what 'happens,' but the much finer complexity of what we read into it and think of it in connection with it. Henry James, *The American Scene*

Perhaps only a medievalist would find classical and medieval antecedents in the shabby practices of television near-news; to Herodotus, Thucydides and Sallust we can add late antique extracanonical gospels, Gregory of Tours and other long-departed company. But the point here is not the pedantic one, but important issues of cultural practice – the functions of 'true knowledge' or justifiable belief in an organized society and the acceptable conditions for producing knowledge and offering it to the public. It is worthy of comment when the same techniques of

representation continue essentially unchanged for centuries, and also
when these techniques are suppressed for a time only to reappear
essentially unaltered but in drastically different circumstances. The
question suggested is how and how much historical change affects the
communicative value of enduring linguistic practices.[26]

To make useful sense, this question has to anticipate an answer open to
fine discriminations and calmly aloof from alarmist postmodern
prophesies of the decline and death of fact, truth, external reality,
objectivity and other candidates for postmodern extinction. The
intellectual life of Western societies, with its deeply ingrained bias for
realism, mimesis, factuality and verification, has done very well without
attainable absolutes; the failed candidates are transparent language,
irreducible concepts, demonstrable facts, an extralinguistic check on
reality and a single satisfactory mode of comprehending reality.[27] All of
these (regularly annihilated in post-structuralist criticism) are still
regularly claimed by one system of thought or another, but none seems
to exist except as rhetorical instruments of conflicting systems. Yet even
that is an important intellectual function, because if there are no
permanent or fixed forms anchoring thought and expression, then high
degrees of pragmatic stability and continuity of use will have to serve the
purpose of anchoring one end of a spectrum whose other end is pure
sliding relativity.

The central question which haunts Western culture is some version of:
How can we depend on words to connect us to reality? This is the
philosophical expression of the deep reality-principle of the mind which
yearns to capture reality in language, and yet resists and rebels against
the punishing indifference of the world we encounter. Since Greek
philosophy first formulated this anxious ambition, we have never yet
come to terms with mimesis and its paradoxes: that a mimetic
commitment to reality (James's 'immediate crudity of what "happens"')
is necessary but fails to satisfy our demand for meaning (James's 'finer
complexity'), yet asserting a poetic licence to improve on mimesis
compromises the reality-principle. How is the reality-principle translated
into language? Only with great difficulty and a systematic exertion of
wish-denial. The reality-principle is very powerful (the loss of it is our
definition of madness) but it is the conduit of frustration and anger as our
hopes are thwarted and our wishes denied; it is countered by wishes for
pleasure, self-flattery, glorification of impulse and, most of all, for sheer
uncontested dominance. Carried into the public arena of knowledge and
belief, collective myths of group superiority justifying hatred and

contempt for others (whoever the designated 'others' are) show the dark side of importing fictional freedoms into historical mimesis.

The philosophic and social expression of these concerns is the question of exactly what we want to mean by history, admitting that the history in question is always a complex artefact of language. History, in order to be written at all, has to call on the fiction-making capacity of the mind to such an extent (to impose form on time, to locate 'event', to impose plot on the seriatim of reality) that the essential question about history is how it can separate itself out from fiction at all. All books, to be books, begin in fiction and some assert 'history' as a certain kind of announced authorial commitment and contract or understanding between writer and reader. The meaning of history depends on the meaning of fiction, not the other way around because fiction is analytically prior – the larger category. I am using fiction here in the inclusive sense of linguistic artefacts: verbal objects whose coherence and intelligibility are made, not found, by exploiting the grammatical, syntactical and rhetorical capacities of language. Fictional *invention*, the imaginative construction of events, speech and so on beyond the knowledge of the writer, is a subcategory, a specific application of the larger capacity called fiction. A great deal of unnecessary confusion results from writers and readers blurring the primary and secondary uses of fiction: (1) the creation of form in language; and (2) the invention or imaginary description of events and persons. The primary or formal fictions which create intelligible event and narrative structure are necessary to all depictions of event; without these artefacts history is not conceivable. But history dissociates itself from fiction as a special category of verisimilar prose through a system of (implicitly) announced limitations and accepted restrictions. In the past, a flexible standard allowed history to incorporate certain kinds of fictional invention for certain purposes, but history was not allowed to *be* fiction.

Expressed as a quality *literary historicity* is the characteristic of representations and assertions in prose that qualify for inclusion in justified belief, or knowledge of the world. The rules or constraints accepted by an author who writes history are most usefully called a *protocol*.[28] A protocol for literary historicity is not exceptionally difficult to define and understand (so long as we do not attempt to link it to intellectually inappropriate canons taken from the physical sciences). A formal analysis of any acceptable modern history will yield the characteristic small-scale usages (related to pronouns, verb moods, conditionals, reported speech, etc) and large-scale forms related to verification. A second-century protocol or a twelfth-century protocol will look somewhat different from a twentieth-century one, but this systematic approach towards the system of formal elements or implicit rules which differentiate history from fiction will also point to the stable and continuing aspects of historical writing. And an analogous protocol can certainly be created for historicity in the visual media (although it will always be looser and less reliable with respect to verification). The problem is in creating the cultural imperative to enforce these standards – making people willing to accept the formal constraints of historicity when creative impatience, commercial pressures and ideological sanctimoniousness combine to offer a more flexible permission under the rubric of Art or Truth, or both.

Academic historians might be supposed to be the custodians of what counts now as historicity in representations. In my experience and observation, history students are not taught anything at all about historicity as an attribute of writing (much less television, film, photography, etc).[29] It is hard to speak about a topic so uniformly suppressed, but it seems to be assumed that the appropriate modes of expression (Form) will be absorbed subliminally by students as they read articles and books for purposes of information (Content). That, after all, is how the writers of the articles and books generally learnt how to write themselves, and successive generations of historians are (reasonably enough) relied on to clone themselves into producers of recognizable, unalarming academic prose. Probing our institutional silence further, I intuit an unformulated assumption that a certain special virtue vaguely linked to honest intentions, dispassion and fairness animates modern historical writing and will accrete by moral osmosis to habitual readers (so few in any case) without any embarrassing preaching by the professoriate.

The apprenticeship route to writing history works well enough for academe. Ordinary professional practice amounts to a problem only when a genuine *problem* (not a rhetorical, publication-justifying pseudo-problem) arises[30] – such as the silence and near-total absence of comment from professional historians on the increasingly frequent disregard of the protocol of historicity by journalists, television producers, biographers, documentary makers and the like. The most egregious instances come in for moral chiding in the media,[31] and the occasional lawsuit, but these reactions do not quite get to the point: the social necessity of having certain kinds of information consistently presented within certain formal constraints, and the intellectual necessity of having some persons who know how to talk about it.

I am beginning, reluctantly, to think that even the largish number of historians who have followed the debates over epistemology and history have skimmed off the most simplified lessons as directives for personal sophistication and knowingness without really understanding the logic and limitations of the anti-empiricist argument. This would not matter except that these basic issues do touch every historical subspeciality equally, and the ranks of professional historians cannot be counted on to say anything clear and to the point about the increasing (and increasingly undetectable) blurring of genre forms in all the many varieties of purported non-fiction. Historians are hardly ready to tackle the trickier issues of visual literacy while they remain naive or patronizing about literary literacy.

'TRUTH' AND ACTUALITY: WHICH DO PEOPLE WANT WHEN?

It has become a truism of the age of global electronic communications that the flow of information cannot ultimately be contained or controlled, but there are no clichés about maintaining some control over the *form* of information. Yet the form information takes is not a secondary, superficial or merely decorative aspect; form is the decipherable intention of the author and determines how information is received – *what* it is taken to be. This is what Hayden White meant by choosing *The Content of the Form* as the title of his book of essays: that the formal properties of verbal information carry its inscribed and readable intentions with respect to the basic distinctions of fiction or history, as well as rhetorical inflections of irony, exhortation, satire and so on. The communicative valence of information is conveyed by its form.

A stable and clear distinction between fiction and non-fiction is the product of a strict protocol of literary historicity imposed by the force of a strong cultural demand. To judge by the actual products offered as history over the 2500 years available in the Western tradition, in most societies most of the time, a flexible and capacious protocol of historicity is sufficient for the cultural purposes served by history. Maintaining traditions, glorifying the past and socializing the young into widely shared values have usually taken precedence over the reality-commitment of history. Long after Thucydides had debunked the Athenian legend of Harmodius and Aristogiton into its historical components of sex, jealousy and vengeance, Greek boys, and presumably some girls, were still learning the tale of heroic and self-sacrificing tyrant-killers.[32]

The question usually addressed to ancient or more generally, premodern, historians, is some variant of why they were so naive or undiscriminating as to include so much obvious myth, unfounded legend and outright gap-filling invention in what they insisted were histories. The more sympathetic and sophisticated variant on this inquiry is to ask what purposes or functions were being fulfilled with this material. The answer built into this kind of question is some version of the relativist view that their socially constructed field of reality was different, their values were not ours, they did not have a scientific or nature-based worldview, they were spiritual, or traditional, or had a different conception of truth.[33] The scrutiny is always addressed to the fictions-in-history as the factor that has to be explained, the aberration.

But if we start again by acknowledging that the systematic exclusion of fictional invention from histories is itself the aberration, considered over the centuries, then the question interestingly changes. The question becomes one addressed to the strict protocol of literary historicity: how it works and when and why it seems important enough to accept and impose. This is a different kind of question from the quite important inquiries into what the fictions are doing in earlier histories, but it is also a question of understandings between writer and reader, of communicative intent.

One can ask simply whether readers, the appropriate, intended, contemporary readers, always understand what it is that they are reading. The evidence here is rather sparse and not altogether reassuring. It does seem clear that the course of the seventeenth century saw the beginnings of an anti-rhetorical bias against elaborated language connected with the interest in natural science, and a certain rigour with respect to the permissible contents of histories. But a period of rapid developments in science, religion, literature and politics may produce writers and readers who no longer inhabit the same communicative world of assumptions and conventions. In the early eighteenth century, Daniel Defoe produced a body of work of unparalleled verisimilar realism and equally unparalleled ambiguity of intention. Of his most successful book, *The Adventures of Robinson Crusoe*, no one, contemporary readers, modern critics, and quite possibly the author himself, seemed to know with certainty how it was intended to be read.[34] But people were angry when they discovered that the startling techniques that made them accept the veracity of the book's announced authorship, by Robinson Crusoe himself, were the artifices of a London journalist. By the time Defoe got to the Preface to the third sequel called *Serious Reflections during the Life and Surprising Adventures of Robinson*

Crusoe, with his Vision of the Angelic World, Written by Himself (1720),
he had trapped himself in an epistemological corner:

I have heard, that the envious and ill-disposed part of the world have raised some
objections against the first two volumes, on pretence, for want of a better reason;
that (as they say) the story is feigned, that the names are borrowed, and that it is
all a romance; that there never were any such man or place, or circumstances in
any man's life; I, Robinson Crusoe, being at this time in perfect and sound mind
and memory, thanks be to God therefore; do hereby declare, their objection is an
invention scandalous in design, and false in fact; and do affirm, that the story,
though allegorical, is also historical.

Defoe's panic (which is what I think is exposed here) to defend his well-
intended work from accusations of a fraud he had never intended,
resulted from what was, even in 1720, a too comfortable fit between
history and 'truthful fiction': the story, though allegorical, is also
historical. If textual intention is a complex set of signals sent and
understood, it only works when senders and receivers are using the same
code book.

The situation of popularly circulated information remained ambiguous.
In eighteenth-century England, reporters were barred from parliament but
an interested public wanted to read the MPs' speeches; naturally enough,
this market was satisfied. The editor of the *Gentleman's Magazine*
furnished a hack journalist, for instance the poor Samuel Johnson, with
whatever scraps and hints were available and the writer wrote a speech
which was attributed to a specific MP. After a few months of this work,
Johnson felt too uneasy about it to continue and declined to write any
more parliamentary speeches. But as usual, Johnson was sensitive beyond
the standards of his age. At the end of the century, Jane Austen had one of
her characters declare: 'If a speech be well drawn up, I read it with
pleasure, by whomsoever it may be made – and probably with much
greater, if the production of Mr. Hume or Mr. Robertson, than if the
genuine words of Caractacus, Agricola, or Alfred the Great' (*Northanger
Abbey*). Mr. Hume would have been fairly affronted, but the idea that all
historians wrote fictional speeches was still a commonplace; as late as
1834, the author of a heavily fictionalized autobiographical novel scored
patronizing points off the compromised reputation of history:

As I have rigidly adhered to truth, I have been compelled to state what I have to
say in a form almost entirely narrative; and have not imitated those great
historians, who put long speeches into the mouths of their kings and generals,
very much suited to the occasions undoubtedly, and deficient only in one point –
that is, accuracy. (Edward Howard, *Rattlin, The Reefer*, 1834).

The very sliding scale of what constitutes history in highly developed
societies at various times demonstrates clearly enough that fact-based
natural standards for truth are the exception, not the rule. A certain kind
of commitment to truth can easily coexist with semi-verifiable history;
true-to-actuality and true-to-meaning seem to most people most of the
time to be separable.

You instance, Sir, the liberty of the press; which you would persuade us, is in *no*
danger, though not secured, because there is no express power granted to
regulate literary publications. [Various arguments follow, to the effect that the
general power to define offences in the constitution can and most likely will come
to touch on freedom of publication in the future.] . . . The freedom of the press,
the sacred palladium of public liberty, would be pulled down; – all useful
knowledge on the conduct of government would be withheld from the people –
the press would become subservient to the purposes of bad and arbitrary rulers,
and imposition, not information, would be its object ('Cincinnatus' or Arthur
Lee, *New York Journal*, 1 November 1787).

The idea broached here, though it was not a subject of frequent
discussion in the widespread debate following the publication of the
proposed American constitution, was that some future evil authority
would want to control information for self-interested purposes, 'imposition, not information'. The extent and population of the United States in
1787, emphasized by regional differences of climate, agriculture, mode of
life and livelihood, which were felt to be great, already made the problem
of representation in governing institutions seem an acute and troublesome one. The ready diffusion of information was clearly felt to be a
crucial link between the dangerous authority of government and a
populace at risk of being made impotent through ignorance and
disconnection from the centres of power. Ready, accessible, and it has to
be assumed, reliable, information was central to all ideas of workable
democracy in societies larger than ancient Athens, a favourite comparison. In other words, written history in its short-term contemporaneous
and provisional state as 'news' was clearly understood to be indispensable to democracy.

The grim warning of Montesquieu, widely known to many Americans
and repeatedly cited in the public debate on the proposed constitution,
that democracy was possible only in very small nations where nearly all
the citizens could assemble for face-to-face debate and voting, was a
source of serious foreboding. Both sides in the constitutional debate were
acutely and anxiously aware that only the obligation of high office
holders to stand for re-election at fairly short intervals before an

electorate armed only with their knowledge of public affairs weighed against Montesquieu's predictions that large-scale democracies inevitably deteriorate into oligarchies.

The slightly bombastic epithet 'palladium of liberty', so often attached to any mention of an uncensored press, was a shorthand rhetorical reference to the crucial extra-constitutional function of information quickly and widely communicated (to produce an informed electorate), free from prior constraint (to prevent control by those in power) and accurate or subject to open correction (although this passed as assumed). Without an assured constant flow of information on public affairs, eighteenth-century Americans could hardly have dared to envision a democracy on the scale of the thirteen states.

The ancient anxiety expressed throughout Thucydides' history – democracy rests on words, and words cannot be trusted – was transposed into the more optimistic Enlightenment hope: democracy rests on words, and so words must be as prolific and unconstrained as possible. It may have been unsophisticated of the constitutional debaters to ignore the many possibilities of cunning manipulations of information, but then even the most adept fabrications could do only localized harm in the absence of true mass communications. (One can also note that Thucydides' pessimism was an essentially aristocratic fear of the emotion-driven minds of nearly everyone except the few like himself, and the American optimism was itself a democratic principle.)

The role of information, from the constant and prolific natter of the media through the increasingly deliberative stages of journalism, criticism and history, remains central to political life. And so does the prevailing code, the entire array of visual and verbal signals, usages, conventions and forms shared by writer and reader, sender and seer. These metaphorically enclose information and announce the terms of their approach: whether as candidates for inclusion in knowledge of the world, or under the privilege of fiction. We are dependent on the stability of these codes, on the willingness of professional purveyors of informa-tion and entertainment to work within their appropriate protocols, far more than we are aware. The danger inherent in capricious, opportunis-tic violations of the protocol of historicity is really not that millions of people will absolutely come to believe this or that, but that millions of people will come to be cynical, disabused and wary, to believe nothing and thus feel no connection with the polity at all.

2

Turning Linguistic: History and Theory and History and Theory, 1960–1975

RICHARD T. VANN

> It seems . . . that philosophy of history is the business of
> those who teach novels. Frank Kermode, 1968[1]

Kermode's view would have been considered bizarre indeed in 1950. In 1968 it was still avant-garde; by 1975 the problems that such a comment raises had moved to the forefront of debate in the philosophy of history in the English-speaking world. I shall try to show how, and in what institutional settings, this happened.

Until the end of World War II – and to a considerable extent even today – philosophy of history has been almost everywhere an academic orphan. While it is taught as a normal part of instruction in history in the Netherlands,[2] most American history departments confine the subject to introductory seminars in methodology, entrusted – except in rare instances where someone has an idiosyncratic interest in the subject – to a rota of professors willing to share in the burden of beginning graduate instruction.[3] In Britain, as usual, postgraduates in history are left to their liberty; some stumble onto the subject, but (like most historians) suffer no penalties if they remain immune to any formal reflection about their subject.

The situation in philosophy faculties has not been very different. Philosophy of history has traditionally been regarded as 'soft', a merely optional area of study. (Ethics and aesthetics are just as squishy, but few philosophy faculties have no ethicists or philosophers of art, whereas it is virtually unheard of for them to have a full-time philosopher of history.) Insofar as philosophy of history has been written by philosophers at all, it has often been done by historians of philosophy – sometimes Hegelians, though seldom concurring that the philosophy of history *is* the history of philosophy. Before the outbreak of World War II the only considerable works in philosophy of history in English were Michael Oakeshott's *Experience and its Modes* (Cambridge, 1933) and Maurice Mandelbaum's *The Problem of Historical Knowledge: An Answer to Relativism*

(New York, 1938). There is still no professional association of philosophers of history.

Until 1960 there was also no journal specifically devoted to philosophy of history. Occasional articles appeared in philosophical journals, especially in the *Journal of Philosophy* and *Philosophical Quarterly* and also in *Mind*. The *Journal of the History of Ideas*, however, published more in this area than any other journal, followed closely, somewhat surprisingly, by the *South Atlantic Quarterly*. Historical journals occasionally published brief reflections on history by working historians, especially when they became presidents of some organization and decided that a certain amount of pontification was appropriate to their new dignities.

This lack of institutional definition was reflected in the inchoate variety of argument and speculation, from numerology to *Moses and Monotheism*, that some people, at least, called 'philosophy of history'. When *History and Theory* was founded in 1960 one of the aims of its editor George Nadel, as articulated in many rejection letters, was to establish some boundaries around what, at least for the journal, would count as 'philosophy of history'. The great speculators, Vico and Hegel and later Marx, were (if treated analytically) in; Toynbee was taken seriously, if critically;[4] but Spengler and Voegelin were out. More recent speculative constructions, like those of Lloyd DeMause on the history of childhood or Shulamith Firestone on the history of women,[5] would not have been published, and were not even reviewed, on the grounds that no reader or reviewer could be found who could evaluate their claims. This was a polite way of saying that these were not falsifiable.

As this suggests, the main interest of the journal was in what was conventionally called analytical philosophy of history. In 1960 this was still configured by reaction to Carl Hempel's article 'The Function of General Laws in History',[6] which was written eighteen years earlier. The topics of law, causality, explanation and prediction were to the fore, whether conceived as Hempel and his followers had done, or in some variant of 'rational explanation'.[7] No matter which side of this dispute they embraced, philosophers tended to argue without much attention to the way that historians write. When they quoted from historians, they analysed extremely short and simple bits of historical prose, but more often they wrote about cars with burst radiators, or the indigestion that afflicted Jones after his ingestion of parsnips.

Although it had largely escaped the attention of these philosophers, historians were by no means obsessed with explanation; there was just as long a tradition of calling attention to, and in fact glorifying, the literary qualities of historiography as there was of claiming that history was a science. Emphasis on historical writing, however, was usually a reaction formation to the more aggressive claims of scientific history. The classic example is J. B. Bury's inaugural lecture at Cambridge in 1903, in which he declared that 'history is a science, no less and no more' and also made some derogatory remarks about Macaulay.[8] These irritated George Macaulay Trevelyan into writing *Clio, a Muse*. Trevelyan claimed that history could not be 'scientific' in the strong sense, since it was impossible for historians to discover causes; it was instead 'an imaginative guess at the most likely generalisations' and had educational, not scientific, value. As his title proclaims, Trevelyan exalted history's literary qualities, and especially the art of narrative, which is its 'bed rock'.[9] Invoking Trevelyan, a professor of literature at Columbia, Emery Neff, published *The Poetry of History* (New York, 1947). This book was largely devoted to readings of various eighteenth- and nineteenth-century historians; but though Neff endorsed Trevelyan's view that history is 'art added to scholarship', he believed the 'scientific' component should be held firmly in check. Neff argued that excessive indulgence in discovering facts, which was the fault of the German school of historians, had prevented Theodor Mommsen from writing more than one good book and kept Acton from writing one at all.[10]

Clio was the muse of epic poetry as well as of history; but writers like Trevelyan and Neff (despite the titles of their books) did not take the poetics of history entirely seriously. They relied on a professionally safe but philosophically questionable distinction between historical research (the domain of 'science' where historical facts were produced) and historians' writing (where the imagination might play upon the already discovered facts and imbue them with significance in the course of producing a text for an audience). This posture, as Hayden White was later to point out, easily allowed for a sort of bad faith, in which attacks on history for its lack of rigour could be deflected by pointing to its artistic character, while critics who pointed to the poverty of imagination and reliance on outmoded literary forms displayed by historians could be fobbed off by the claim that these arose from the constraints imposed by fidelity to fact.[11]

It is not surprising that philosophers, especially those of analytical bent, were immune to incantatory references to the poetry of history; but philosophy of history after World War II did not entirely ignore the fact that historical texts are verbal artefacts, constructed almost entirely on the basis of other verbal artefacts. Actual historical discourse presented itself as an object of philosophical reflection to ordinary-language Oxford philosophers. Rather than attempting, as Hempel had done, to establish a norm for explanation *tout court* and to cram history into that mould, these thinkers tried to start from what historians typically write, and take seriously that they have no specialized language to write in. Isaiah Berlin, for example, addressed the chronic issue of whether the historian should make moral judgements by pointing out that as long as history is written in ordinary language, it will be suffused with the moral meanings and connotations which are inextricably embedded in everyday speech. It is no more possible, he claimed, for a historian to write without any imputation of praise or blame than to write as if historical agents had no free will.[12] In a somewhat similar vein Patrick Gardiner tried to dissolve some of the issues clustered around law and explanation by invoking the way historians (like everyday people) wrote and talked.[13]

Some philosophers were also beginning to attend to narrative as the characteristic form of historical writing. In 1956 Arthur Danto argued 'that *stories* play an important cognitive role in historical inquiry' and 'that a story is an hypothetical recounting of what happened in a more or less determinate stretch of the past'.[14] The distinction between chronicles and history proper, first made by Benedetto Croce, had been naturalized in W. H. Walsh's path-breaking *Introduction to Philosophy of History* (London, 1951), and had already been contested (by Danto).[15] William H. Dray, inaugurating his effort to widen the concept of explanation and demote covering laws to only one species of the genus, noted in 1954 that 'when asked for an explanation of a certain event or state of affairs, the historian often responds by telling a story' and the 'narrative he offers sometimes explains in the "how" rather than the "why" sense'.[16] All the 'narratives' that these writers considered were extremely short (sometimes only two sentences) and were often not taken from real historical works; the only aspect treated was how, or whether, such narratives constituted explanations.

This then was the situation in 1960, when, having been rejected by all American and British publishers who were approached, the first issue of *History and Theory* was brought out by Mouton & Co. in The Hague: (1) Most debate still raged around the applicability of positivist or 'covering-law models' to historical explanation. (2) Some historians and literary critics upheld the literary nature of history, but this generally did not go far beyond exhorting historians to write well.[17] Nobody was willing to pursue the implications of a poetics of history far enough to compromise the scientific aspirations of the discipline. (3) Insofar as historical writing had become a subject for philosophical reflection, it was with few exceptions more or less at the lexical level. The word 'rhetoric' had not yet been uttered in this context, at least not in English.

The first volume of a new journal is like the first week of a baby's life – the most hazardous to its survival. For the first volume of *History and Theory* George Nadel assembled well in advance the strongest collection of articles and reviews he could find; and, mindful that considerable time might elapse before a comparably good second volume could be assembled, carefully warned subscribers that volume I might take more than a year to appear.[18] The lead article (the order of articles was always important to Nadel) was Isaiah Berlin's 'The Concept of Scientific History', about which he expressed great doubts.[19] Issues of laws, explanation and causality dominated the volume, whether applied to Toynbee (by William Dray), to Gibbon (by Gerald Gruman), to international relations (by Arthur Lee Burns) or to the American Civil War (by Lee Benson and Cushing Strout).[20]

Hayden White also made his first appearance in volume I, not as a subject, but as an object – the object of a drubbing by Bruce Mazlish for his translation and editing of Carlo Antoni's *From History to Sociology: The Transition in German Historical Thought* (Detroit, 1959).[21] Mazlish drew up a severe bill of particulars and found White guilty on all counts: a 'too frequently turgid' translation which occasionally skipped a phrase, misspelling Dilthey's name, and – worst of all – an 'annoying' and 'tendentious' editorial introduction.

What particularly aroused Mazlish's ire, it appears, was White's hostile attitude towards 'objective history'. He patronized Ranke – 'Ranke, poor soul, spent a lifetime in his study and ruined his eyesight attempting to "tell how it really happened"' – and described as 'vicious' the Enlightenment tendency 'to view individual manifestations of human creativity as mere instances of the abstract laws which govern machines'.[22] Mazlish correctly identified the powerful influence of Croce on both Antoni and White, but criticized him for treating Croce as quasi-sacred.

Yet the actual difference between Mazlish and White was much less than it appeared. Mazlish, for his part, was willing to grant an important place to what White called 'aesthetic historicism':

In part, history is a story, a narrative presented to us so that we may *experience* it. And we experience it as we do a play or a painting. Such an experience enlarges our understanding, and awakens in us aesthetic, or moral, or even philosophical reactions. It makes us more fully human.[23]

And White was not totally unsympathetic to 'scientific' history; he merely, in a Hegelian (or rather Crocean) manner criticized it for one-sidedness. For 'aesthetic historicism' was also one-sided: it

> went too far and ended by asserting that the traditional objects of historical reflection, past human thought and action, were less important than the original, imaginative creation of the individual historian. Fact must give way to the creative imagination which confronted it, and in opposing it, it found itself limited and imprisoned. The *effect* of the narrative was considered more important than its truth or falsity.[24]

Against the view 'that reason is . . . the tool of an animal will, having no regulative function whatsoever', White championed 'a balanced view of humanity which does justice to its creative and regulative elements at one and the same time'.[25]

Thus both still seemed to believe history was 'an art added to scholarship'. To get beyond this formulation required more serious investigation of the obvious bridge, narrative. But narrative had received a bad name among historians themselves, even while they were, willy-nilly, practising it. 'Narrative historians' – the phrase always seemed to be prefixed by an unuttered 'mere' – appeared to be engaged simply in chronicling events, without making any effort to explain them. For philosophers, too, narrative looked like an unpromising subject. As Morton White (in the course of devoting a chapter to narrative) observed, narratives characteristically are complex, sprawling and resistant to analysis; for this reason it was not surprising that his predecessors had devoted themselves chiefly to single sentences picked out from historical prose.[26] Typically, too, articles on philosophy of history were short (four or five pages). The challenge of analysing narrative required that contributors have space for a comprehensive treatment; so one of the editorial principles of *History and Theory* was that there be no prescribed limit for the length of either articles or reviews.[27]

The first essay in this direction still began with single sentences – narrative sentences, as Arthur Danto was to call them. In an article too rich for a simple paraphrase, Danto produced an argument to resolve the stale science–art controversy by declaring history to be neither. Examining the truth conditions of statements about the past and the future, Danto imagined an Ideal Chronicler able to give a total account of all events as they occurred, but without any knowledge of the future. Even if there were an Ideal Chronicler, Danto pointed out, historians would not be put out of business, for events in the past are characteristically described with reference to their future consequences, which the Ideal Chronicler could not have recorded. The model here is such sentences as 'The Thirty Years' War began in 1618', since in 1618, nobody could know its duration. The far-reaching consequence of Danto's argument is that 'there are no events except under some description' – a fatal objection to theories which founded history on unit-events susceptible to a definitively accurate description, but one which opened the door to uncertainty about how many truthful descriptions might be made at the same time.[28]

Though Danto had emphasized that narratives are the characteristic form of historical explanation, the move confronting historical narrative in all its rambling diversity began only a year later, with W. B. Gallie's proposal that explanations in history subserved the general purpose of narratives, rather than vice versa.[29] 'I find it astonishing', Gallie began, 'that no critical philosopher of history has as yet offered us a clear account of what it is to follow or to construct a historical narrative.'[30] This had been made possible by a persistent confusion of delineation and analysis of historical understanding with the problem of how it can be vindicated (i.e. how historical theses can be tested). Gallie proposed to analyse only historical understanding, leaving aside the problem of how the claims of historians can be verified.

Historical understanding, for Gallie, consists in following a story, since history is a species of the genus story (novels, presumably, being another species).[31] All of his examples of how to follow a story come from the experience of reading novels rather than histories; but even the experience of reading novels was elucidated by a second-order analogy, which Gallie found in watching cricket, one of those summer bat-and-ball games whose apparently inherent narrative structure always seems to fascinate literary types.[32] In following a game, the attention of the spectator is drawn onward by the anticipated outcome. Many sorts of improbable contingency can be accepted as the game unfolds, so long as they are neither acts of God (playing field broken up by an earthquake) nor violations of the spirit of the game (such as a strategy of not putting out any of the opposing batsmen). At times the game becomes difficult to follow, when the strategy of the captain seems unintelligible; and it is at these junctures that an expert can supply an explanation, based upon superior knowledge of the local conditions (and only very infrequently on better knowledge of the rules). Although a game is in a sense constituted by its rules, it can be played and enjoyed without knowledge of all of them – but not without a modicum of physical dexterity and strategic acumen.

The analogy between following games and stories, Gallie acknowledges, is far from perfect, since (among other things) stories have no rules; but it is good enough for the argument Gallie wishes to make. Following them is a similar activity in that the attention is directed towards the anticipated end; contingencies are not only acceptable, but essential to enjoyment; and explanations play a relatively subordinate role.

Despite a fleeting reference to 'constructing' narratives, Gallie focussed almost entirely on reading or following them; and although he characterized and exemplified what he called '*the* historical understanding', it cannot be said that he gave a very comprehensive philosophical account of it. In particular, by leaving the relationship between constructing a plausible narrative and presenting an acceptable explanation unexplored, Gallie did not directly challenge covering-law theory; he merely made room beside it for an 'understanding' of narrative form.[33] Furthermore, as Louis Mink was to point out, Gallie's conception of following a story or a game required the element of suspense; the interest of the reader or spectator had to be captured by uncertainty about how it would turn out. Readers of historical narratives, however, are unlikely to be surprised by the turns in the plot; almost all of them know from the beginning that Mary Stuart is going to be executed and the Armada defeated, but this does not spoil their pleasure and comprehension in reading Garrett Mattingly's *The Armada* (Boston, 1959).[34] The writer of histories is in fact a rewriter – not a commentator watching a game develop, but more like (if the sports analogy may be continued) a general manager poring over many box scores to decide whether what the team most needs is a left-handed reliever. To that extent, therefore, Gallie's treatment was defective, and Mink devoted himself for much of the rest of his career to exploring the spaces that Gallie and the others had created and then left vacant.

This required, in the first place, treating the entire question of what understanding is. For Mink, all of the effort to assimilate historical understanding to scientific explanation was misconceived. There were, he postulated, three irreducible and equally valid modes of understanding: theoretical, categoreal, configurational – characteristic of science, philosophy and history respectively.[35]

The distinctive feature of historical understanding, Mink argued, was its capacity to render comprehensible at one time a sequence of events that unfolded over a chronological span. '[I]n *some* sense we may understand a particular event by locating it correctly in a narrative sequence as well as by classifying it as an instance of a law', he claimed – but this does not imply that sequential explanation is 'the *only* explanation possible of a specific fact or sequence of facts, or that it is a satisfactory answer to a different question "Why did it happen?"'[36] Mink thus proposed to 'loosen the tie that binds the concept of *understanding* to that of *explanation*'.[37] Historical understanding resembled the way one might understand a musical composition rather than a geometrical demonstration; and the 'synoptic judgement' of the historian – the ability to represent at a single time events in a chronological stream – typically takes the form of narrative.

For some years after the seminal articles by Danto, Gallie and Mink, *History and Theory* continued to devote most of its philosophical articles to further refinements of the controversy about explanation, causation and covering laws. Finally the editors decided the subject was exhausted except as a first-year seminar exercise for graduate students; so an editorial moratorium was declared. But some voices did carry forward the discussion begun in these three articles, although Gallie and Morton White turned their attention from narrative to other things.[38]

Not all, of course, approved the new direction. Mandelbaum, a doughty foe of relativism for thirty years, declared that the 'tendency to view history as narrative is unfortunate, and stands in need of correction'.[39] Even when the historian does present an account in which the precise sequence of occurrences provides the essential framework, s/he is not telling a story, which for Mandelbaum is either recounting what is already known or making things up. But historians are forbidden to make things up, and are engaged in inquiry into what is not yet known; thus history cannot be *essentially* narrative. The teleological sense that Gallie found in stories, Mandelbaum claimed, is present in any explanation (or even in a syllogism).

Mandelbaum criticized the model of history as narrative as 'far too simplistic', and so it would have been had narrative been presented in so restricted a view as his, since he confined it to a series of causal statements arraying events in chronological order. He had some warrant to do so from the habit of giving oversimplified examples into which some of the writers he criticized had fallen. Morton White, for instance, adapted E.

M. Forster's story about a demographic catastrophe which struck the English royal family. A chronicle would simply report the deaths in order; but a history would go as follows:

> The king of England died, so the queen of England grieved. Her grief led her to death. Her death led the prince to worry, and he worried to the point of suicide. His death made the princess lonely, and she died of that loneliness.[40]

Even White's concocted 'history' included no statements about conditions or dispositions, such as one which might explain the extraordinary susceptibility to depression which accounted for three of the four royal deaths. Mandelbaum seemed to assume that such statements could not be accommodated by any narrative form. He even denied that biographies were characteristically narratives, since the biographer

> must frequently take into account not merely the situations by which his subject was confronted, but must appeal to factors of intelligence, temperament, and personality which often cannot be accounted for in terms of specific episodes which enter into his narrative.[41]

Gallie, as the boldest of the narrativists, came in for further and fuller criticism, which typically focussed on the exemplary cricket match and thus moved away from the more complex issues posed by novels and histories. C. J. Arthur asserted that he had underplayed the role of generalizations, even in following the unfolding of a game, since no event could be identified as contingent or surprising except against the background of generalizable knowledge about the normal course of play.[42] But Arthur did not challenge the basic contention that histories are species of the genus story. This step was taken by Richard G. Ely, who rejected the theories of both Danto and Morton White on one of the same grounds advanced by Mandelbaum, namely that 'conditions' cannot be admitted into narratives, and yet obviously have great influence on the course of events; therefore history cannot be *essentially* narratives. Gallie, however, was exempted from this criticism, because he specified that other aspects, such as discussions, analyses and explanations, could find a proper place in historical works.[43]

Rolf Gruner, while agreeing with Mandelbaum that histories are not essentially narrative, found his arguments unsatisfactory. He pointed out that many of Mandelbaum's points could be deflected by adopting a broader view of narrative – one that, like the classic realist novels of the nineteenth century, could incorporate extensive descriptions of background and social circumstances as well as narrate the actions taken by the various characters. Gruner's strategy was rather to name certain works – he instanced Burckhardt's *Civilization of the Renaissance in Italy* and Huizinga's *Waning of the Middle Ages* – which were obviously not narratives and yet could not be anything else but histories. A mere glance at the table of contents, Gruner claimed, would dispel the idea that these two works were narratives, since they were not organized on chronological lines, and 'chronological order is the external hallmark of a story'. Denying this would be 'violating common usage'.[44] They might, it is true, contain some 'narrative elements', just as 'non-narrative' elements (that is, description of states of affairs) can be found in largely narrative works. However, if a completely non-narrative work like Burckhardt's were ever to be found, it would still have to be classed as a work of history.

William Dray, showing less sympathy with the narrativists than he was later to manifest, agreed with Mandelbaum's conclusion and Gruner's argument to support it. It is even false, he wrote, 'that a work must *contain* narrative to be properly considered a work of history'.[45] But though it is conceivable that a totally non-narrative historical work could be written (even if this is still a null class), Dray granted that explanations 'would often properly assume narrative form'; and in a characteristically irenic move he noted that an inquiry focussing on 'what is the story?' may just as legitimately follow 'what did in fact occur?' as 'what is the explanation?'[46]

The topic of narrative excited other philosophers as well. A. R. Louch's 'History and Narrative'[47] went even further than Gallie, arguing that, as a way of filling in the gaps of our experience of a world of things that endure through change, narrative is essential to historical explanation, and can in fact allow the historian to repudiate the covering-law model altogether. Frederick A. Olafson attempted to improve upon the way that Morton White and Danto had tried to reconcile narrative with some sort of regularity theory by stressing the concept of human action as an essential one for historical explanation.[48]

It would appear that Morton White, Danto, Gallie and Mink had not changed many minds, but this can hardly be evaluated from the published record. Philosophers who are so unprofessional as to agree entirely with their colleagues have no material for writing articles. The 'narrativists', as William Dray called them, did at least push the largest units of historical discourse into the glare of philosophical analysis. It cannot be said that there was any 'school' of narrativists, and there were loose ends aplenty for more philosophers to worry. Even those sympathetic to narrative were far from united in their views. Beginning with those questions that had the strongest claims: is history narrative, or essentially narrative, as Gallie, Danto, and Louch argued? or is it just that all histories must contain some narrative elements? or, descending to the undeniable, is it simply that *some* histories are narratives?

Are narratives themselves explanatory – perhaps even self-explanatory – or is it merely that historical explanations become so just by being incorporated in narratives? If they do explain, is it entirely by offering a series of causally linked statements? Should the right model not be Danto's of causal *input* rather than of causal chains? Or Mink's, that narrative is required to delineate an entire complex of relations?

Can any significant or useful distinction be made between 'chronicle' and 'history' (Morton White), 'story' and 'plot' (E. M. Forster) or 'plain' and 'significant' narrative (W. H. Walsh)?[49] If narratives are held to be in themselves explanatory, then the notion of a set of statements that past events merely occurred would seem to be incoherent.[50] But then – to recapitulate Mandelbaum's arguments – does emphasis on narrative form *preclude* the historian from giving proper explanations, and divert our attention from inquiry, which is truly distinctive of historical scholarship? Can it be, as C. Behan McCullagh believed, that narrative is just an incidental feature of some histories, being introduced only when the historian must 'write up' what has been discovered?[51]

If there was no agreement that narrative was a necessary condition for historiography, or whether, and if so how, narratives explain, it was generally agreed that the most histories, especially histories of some central subject, typically took a narrative form. No philosopher, however, produced any convincing criteria for deciding what constituted a narrative, or how to recognize one; and opinions about whether narratives are explanations seemed polarized between cheerful pluralists like Mink or Dray and those with scientific leanings, like Mandelbaum or McCullagh.

McCullagh's dismissive remark that narrative was merely a literary device to spice up the historian's presentation of his findings was in fact quoted from a historian, H. Stuart Hughes.[52] Parallel with, but almost never intersecting, the philosophical interest in historical discourse, which since 1960 was increasingly conducted mainly in *History and Theory*, was a distinctive treatment of historians' language and narrative by a few reflective historians. A good, and early, example, of these is J. G. A. Pocock, who called for a historical criticism 'closely intermingled with the philosopher's, though necessitating different skills' which would inquire where the historian found the terms of his conceptual vocabulary; how they were normally used and how he used them, what logical, sociological, and other implications they carried; how their significance changed as, and has changed since, he used them; and how his construction of his statements was affected by the state of his language at the time when he made use of it.

Such an inquiry, he continued, would be 'less immediately concerned with logic and verifiability than with language as a social instrument and thought as social behavior'.[53] This was of course to sketch out a research programme which Pocock himself has subsequently accomplished; but the occasion for his remarks was the work of J. H. Hexter, who, he remarked, had made a plea for 'a "revolution" in historical thought which would amount to historians' assuming critical responsibility for their own professional vocabulary'. Such a revolution might enable historians to overcome the 'vagueness and apparently chronic conceptual poverty' which currently infested their language.[54]

It is not surprising that historians would pursue their own agenda in the analysis of historical discourse. Philosophers, as Louis Mink remarked,

are really discussing . . . logical theory, and historical inference interests them not because it is historical, but because it is *inference* . . . On the other hand, what the historians are really discussing is whether history is a discipline or just an aggregation of parts of a number of other disciplines, and they are not interested in the logic of arguments in general but in the *differentiae* of *historical* arguments.[55]

As Marvin Levich noted, 'history is an organized discipline of study, neither science nor poetry, and endowed with the imprimatur of academic respectability', which made it 'an ideal case-in-point for controversies about the privileged character of "scientific" models of explanation'.[56] This explains the persistence of the controversy about covering laws, even though it was of negligible interest to all but a handful of historians. On the other hand, historians' interest in philosophy of history arose from 'problems encountered in the concrete pursuit of their craft'.[57] Of these, the most pressing (in the mid-1960s, at least) was the role (if any) that generalizations of the social-science type should play in historical work.

This was not the problem which preoccupied Pocock and Hexter. Hexter made one of his most important contributions to the hoped-for 'revolution' in historical studies with 'The Rhetoric of History'.[58] Tacitly accepting a distinction between historical research and writing, Hexter sets himself to analyse what goes on between the time an historian says to himself: "Well, I guess I understand this matter about as well as I ever will, so I may as well start writing," and the time he lays down his pen ruefully beside a stack of scrawled pages and says: "Well, it's a damned bad job, but it's about as good as I can do, so that's that."[59]

This historian (who, one hopes, used better grammar in his writing than in his soliloquies) made use of three devices distinctive of historiography, but not peculiar to it: footnotes, name lists and direct quotations. None of these, Hexter was easily able to show, figures importantly in scientific writing; but the first two, at least, are almost necessary conditions for historiography.[60] Nor is this a trivial difference; to Hexter it indicated that history is 'a unique and separate domain of human knowing'.[61]

This was to administer another blow – albeit a glancing blow – to the moribund carcass of 'the unity of scientific explanation' as expounded by Hempel and his followers. But Hexter's intention went further than delivering a *coup de grâce* in this ancient philosophical quarrel. Unlike those ordinary-language philosophers who were content to explicate what historians actually wrote, Hexter was unabashedly prescriptive. There are, he claimed, Rules of historical rhetoric. The first of these is the Reality Rule: that the historian write about the past *wie es eigentlich gewesen*. Hexter did try to reformulate Ranke's 'much-derided aphorism' as follows: 'historians are concerned and committed to tell about the past the best and most likely story that can be sustained by the relevant extrinsic evidence'. This reformulation only says 'what Ranke intended in a form hopefully more satisfactory to a generation acutely conscious of linguistic niceties' – which could easily be abandoned, for brevity's sake, in propounding the Reality Rule.[62]

Next comes the Maximum Impact Rule: 'Place in footnotes evidence and information which, if inserted in the text, diminishes the impact on the reader of what you, as an historian, aim to convey to him.'[63] Closely related – indeed a corollary of that rule – is the Economy-of-Quotation Rule: 'Quote from the record of the past only when and to the extent that confrontation with that record is the best way to help the reader to an understanding of the past *wie es eigentlich gewesen*.'[64] Now it would seem that the more evidence presented to the reader in footnotes and direct quotations, the closer s/he would be brought to the past as it actually happened; so the Reality Rule apparently conflicts with the other two. Hexter puts the paradox thus: *'in the interest of conveying historical reality to the reader with maximum impact, the rules of historiography may sometimes require an historian to subordinate completeness and exactness to other considerations*.[65] But, Hexter believes, there is a way to transcend this paradox. The direct quotation is a device which confronts the reader with key pieces of evidence, challenges one to judge for oneself, and aims at inducing not only assent, but enthusiastic assent. The purpose of the confrontation would be frustrated if the reader were overwhelmed by the *entire* body of evidence. It is thus preferable at times for the historian to *withhold* information – a tactic Hexter neatly illustrates by a bare list of evocative names, which requires the reader to provide for oneself knowledge about the people named and the reasons for the construction of the list.

Hexter drew three conclusions: that history is 'a rule-bound discipline by means of which historians seek to communicate their knowledge of the past'; that rhetoric is not merely decorative, but is necessary to such communication; and that the rhetoric of history is irreducibly different from that of natural science.[66] The third conclusion is surely warranted; but the first, although it looks like a truism, is ambiguous; and the sense of it that Hexter favours contradicts the second principle.

This can be seen by looking more closely at what Hexter says about the Reality Rule; for there he tries to conflate a realist and a narrativist view of historical knowledge. What Ranke said is that, unlike more high-flown purposes of other historians, he would merely show how it actually happened. This is quite different from 'telling the most likely story that can be sustained by the relevant extrinsic evidence'. Hexter treats the difference as a mere matter of 'linguistic niceties' – itself an odd put-down for one so brilliantly successful in criticizing and clarifying historians' language – and claims (without producing any evidence) that his formulation is what Ranke intended. Nevertheless, showing is not telling, no matter how often the two are coupled in primary schools, and superior plausibility is hardly what sustained Ranke's belief in *Geschichtswissenschaft*.

Furthermore, we must examine what Hexter means by 'rules'. These, as Louis Mink has pointed out, are not anything that a logician would recognize as 'rules'. They are not rules which state principles, but are merely pragmatic reminders of principles. In fact Hexter elsewhere calls them '*maxims* generally applicable . . . leaving the identification to the *experience* of the *trained* historian'.[67] The Reality 'Rule' contains no criterion for identifying the best or most likely story, and so, unlike a real rule, neither specifies what is against the rule nor provides assurance that something can be done if the rule is followed.[68]

It is in fact that 'experience of the trained historian' to which Hexter is appealing. And why not? What prevented him from recognizing this is apparently his aversion, dating as far back as the 1930s, to the sort of historical relativism then being championed by Carl Becker.[69] Hence the talk of rules, and the desire to maintain both that narrative is a cognitive instrument and that it ideally represents the past *wie es eigentlich gewesen*. Although Hexter had read Danto's *Analytical Philosophy of History*, he did not take Danto's point that the only conceivable representation of the past as it actually was would be the Ideal Chronicle; and that falls short of history because it cannot contain narrative sentences. Furthermore – another argument of Mink's – the structure of narrative would only by accident be the same as that of historical actuality, and

even worse, no one could possibly know whether it did, since to do so would require comparing the two and thus would require knowing the structure of historical actuality in itself independently of any representation of it. But this is impossible.[70]

That Hexter got himself into these difficulties should not obscure the originality and merits of his position. At a time when most historians were assuming that narrative was antithetical to explanation,[71] and rhetoric a meretricious embellishment of the plain truth, Hexter made a pioneering and perspicacious analysis of historical prose; and his appeal to historical craftsmanship adumbrated a move to be made subsequently by philosophers as well as historians.[72] While Mandelbaum had tried to defend against relativism by discrediting narrativism, Hexter attempted to defend the cognitive status of narratives without falling into relativism. No matter how one judges the success of his effort, the goal was one which virtually every historian would approve, even if maintained by arguments many sought to improve.

Furthermore, Hexter was both informed about what philosophers were saying and did his best – not always successfully – to come to grips with it. One would have thought that similar exertions would not have been beyond the capacity of at least some of his fellow historians, and that their superior grasp of actual historical practice, and acquaintance with live examples of substantial historical discourse could have corrected the errors of the philosophers. Unfortunately, most historical writing about historical writing tended to be graceful essays, in which philosophical issues, when they were noticed at all, were alluded to rather than confronted.[73] They were useful in pointing out how various are the kinds of history, and how differently, for example, theory was used in economic history than in art history; or how the problem of selectivity presents itself to the modern than to the ancient historian, who conceivably can read all the relevant primary sources pertinent to the problem in a few days.[74] Overall, however, except for Pocock, Hexter and Sevcenko, historians left the philosophers to fight it out, almost entirely in the pages of *History and Theory*, over how they were writing.[75]

Meanwhile – and entirely *outside* the pages of *History and Theory* – the logomachies of the philosophers and the complacency of the historians were about to be disturbed by the intervention of literary critics. The more emphasis being put on style and narrative, the more pertinence such an intervention might be presumed to have; but both historians and philosophers proved as adept at ignoring literary critics as they were at ignoring each other. Even so learned a philosopher as Louis Mink, writing (informally) as late as November 1968, professed surprise that 'very little has been done by literary critics to analyze the features of narrative fiction'.[76] Although books like Wayne Booth's *The Rhetoric of Fiction* (1961), E. M. Forster's *Aspects of the Novel* (1927), Northrop Frye's *Anatomy of Criticism* (1957) and Erich Auerbach's *Mimesis* (1953) may not have produced the comprehensive theory that Mink apparently wanted, they had certainly not left narrative in a surprisingly unexamined state.

The first challenge to the way narrative and the rhetoric of history had been conceived, however, came from none of the above. It was launched by Roland Barthes in three articles published between 1966 and 1968. The most important of these was 'Le discours de l'histoire'.[77] Barthes immediately poses a question which neither philosophers nor historians had directly confronted: should a structural analysis of 'discourse' – which he defined as 'sets of words beyond the level of the sentence' – retain the difference between fictional and historical narratives? In other words, does history differ in some identifiable and important way from fictional narrative?[78]

Like Hexter, Barthes made a formal analysis of historical writing, but with rather different results. He began to answer the question he posed by considering those conditions under which 'the classic historian is enabled – or authorized himself – to designate, in his discourse, the act by which he promulgated it.' This means a study of what Roman Jakobson called 'shifters': those devices which 'assure the transition from the utterance to the act of uttering (or *vice versa*)'.[79] This formulation (had any historian at the time read it) would doubtless have been relatively opaque; but Barthes does go on to clarify the issue by listing the various levels of shifters. The first is where classic historians listen and incorporate what they heard into their own discourse. The obvious example here is Herodotus; also Barthes' beloved Michelet represented himself as 'listening' to the French Revolution. At a second level comes the 'organizing' shifter, when the historian, in his own voice, breaks into the text to say that he will now leave a topic, or declare that he has treated the same matter earlier, or will do so later. The third kind of shifter is provided in the inaugural statement or preface (like that in the *Histoire de France* which Michelet wrote only after the rest of the text was finished). The use of these shifters, Barthes claims, 'dechronologizes' the time of history; it allows for such effects as Machiavelli's treatment of two decades in one chapter and several centuries in another, and by rising above a linear unfolding of time creates instead a quasi-mythic sense of it.[80]

The argument now takes a radically relativistic turn as Barthes points out the general tendency of historians to suppress reference to themselves, thus creating a 'referential illusion' of objectivity. Furthermore, historians confine themselves to stating what has been, not what has not been, or what is uncertain. In this respect, though not otherwise, he says, they resemble – 'strangely enough, but significantly' – psychotics. So-called objective historical discourse is like that of schizophrenics, since there is a 'radical censorship of the act of uttering' so that the discourse flows back massively to the utterance with nobody to take responsibility for the utterance.[81]

Barthes then sketches a tropology of historiography: when predominantly indexical, it is metaphorical, like Michelet's; when functional units predominate, it is metonymic, like Thierry's. There is a third type, which tries to reproduce in the discourse the choices made by the agents. Barthes calls this 'strategic' and gives Machiavelli as an example; it is clearly the classical notion of 'philosophy teaching by examples' or what Hegel called 'pragmatic history'.[82] Finally he produces a contrast between a totally non-signifying history – a 'pure, unstructured series of notations' and histories that signify, either on a discrete level, like that of the lessons derived by Machiavelli in the *Discorsi* and *Il Principe* or those which organize their signified so completely as to amount to a philosophy of history as a whole. The historian's task is not so much to collect facts as to relate signifiers – write Walsh's 'significant narrative' – filling the vacuum of 'pure, meaningless series'. But the choice not to settle for meaningless series at once implicates the historian in ideology:

As we can see, simply from looking at its structure and without having to invoke the substance of its content, historical discourse is in its essence a form of ideological elaboration, or to put it more precisely, an imaginary elaboration.[83]

Barthes can now call historical 'facts' into question:

From the moment that language is involved (and when is it not involved?) the fact can only be defined in a tautological fashion: what is noted derives from the notable, but the notable is only . . . what is worthy of recollection, that is to say, worthy of being noted. We thus arrive at the paradox which governs the entire question of the distinctiveness of historical discourse (in relation to other types of discourse). The fact can only have a linguistic existence, as a term in a discourse, and yet it is exactly as if this existence were merely the 'copy', purely and simply, of another existence situated in the extra-structural domain of the 'real'. This type of discourse is doubtless the only type in which the referent is aimed for as something external to the discourse, without it ever being possible to attain it outside the discourse.[84]

Historical discourse, Barthes concludes, pretends to operate with only two terms, a referent and a signifier, concealing the signified – the historian's account – under the referent – 'what really happened'. Thus, presumably, the characteristics of historical rhetoric to which Hexter drew attention, such as footnotes and direct quotations from the sources, achieve only an *effet du réel*.[85] As an example of this, Barthes points to apparently insignificant details which often figure in historical writing. Michelet relates that someone came to paint the portrait of Charlotte Corday just before her execution, and then 'after an hour and a half, someone knocked softly at a little door behind her'.[86] Such details, Barthes says, seem 'scandalous' from a structural point of view; they appear to be a 'narrative luxury'. Their function is to serve as a weapon of the real against the intelligible, 'as if there were some indisputable law that what is truly alive could not signify – and vice versa'.[87] Histories, which became prominent at the same time as realistic novels, like them are premised on the idea that 'the *having-been-there* of things is a sufficient reason for speaking of them'.[88]

Narration, as employed by the classic historians such as Thierry, was 'the privileged signifier of the real'. And this is the final paradox: narrative structure, which had developed in myth and epic, was now 'at once the sign and the proof of reality'.[89] But Barthes foresaw the decline and perhaps the fall of narration in the work of the *Annales* school, since its interest was much more in structures than chronologies. With some satisfaction he concluded: 'Historical narration is dying because the sign of History from now on is no longer the real, but the intelligible.'[90]

We can never know what anglophone philosophers of history or historians writing at the time would have made of these remarkable articles, since there is little evidence that any of them read them.[91] Although 'Le discours de l'histoire' was translated as early as 1970, neither this translation nor any of Barthes' three articles in French appeared in the series of bibliographies of works in philosophy of history published by *History and Theory*, and for a long time their influence appears to have been confined to literary studies. Historians, for obvious reasons, would have been reluctant to admit that they were necessarily engaged in 'ideological' or 'fudged-up' (*truqué*) discourse; and almost all, no matter how much they praise literary talent and the historical imagination, are historical realists.

Philosophers, and any conceivable *History and Theory* editorial referees, would certainly have noted that the rhetorical rush of Barthes' text sweeps by without bothering to offer arguments at crucial points. He presupposes something like a chronicle; but why is the 'meaningless series', since it is also linguistically encoded, less 'ideological' than a significant narrative? If one looks not at the substance but only at the form of a historical narrative, its resemblance to fictional narratives is certainly heightened. But is an exclusively formal analysis justified?

Barthes' root-and-branch rejection of historical realism also seems a trifle cavalier. Just as he relies on a strict distinction between chronicle and history, he seems to define realism as requiring knowledge by acquaintance of the past, and the ability to make a perfect verbal icon of it. On this showing historical realism would indeed be unviable; but Barthes' is not the only other position; nor is it free from its own difficulties. Can propositions about the past be fully 'intelligible' if their references to real events are dismissed as so much ideological elaboration? Barthes says nothing about historical evidence; so how could contradictory (but both intelligible) claims be judged? Or must we accept every intelligible story about the past? And how could we appraise the truthfulness of a story at all, if it was unintelligible?

The linguistic turn, in Barthes' hands, became a U-turn. Narration was still held to be distinctive of historical practice, but only as it was carried on in bad faith. The question of explanation was bracketed, and the features of historical rhetoric that writers like Hexter had emphasized were construed as tricks of the trade of producing the most deceptive of texts, those that feign to be true.

Uninviting as these propositions might appear as assertions about philosophy of history, especially in their distinctively Gallic exposition, their appeal to literary critics, given that the departmental organization of academic life fails to preclude absolutely reading outside one's discipline, was bound eventually to bring them to the attention of philosophers and historians. While some literary critics looked to structuralism to found a science of criticism, the ideal of a 'man of letters' lingered, and it was these all-purpose intellectuals who made the first bridging efforts. Frank Kermode, for example, had read Gallie and Danto, and noted that much of what they said about explanation and followability of stories could apply to novels no less than to historical accounts. What most interested him was the claim that explanations must 'embody some plausible view of the world accepted by the historian as in accordance with known types'.[92] 'Types', for Kermode, were not mythical archetypes, but 'reduction of experience to some flexible pre-existing set, rather as an alphabet reduces words to its set, or a computer reduces information to its binary terms or analogues'. To the historian, he concluded, 'myth and ritual are no longer relevant except as material; but the radical requirement of coherence, the need for explanation, is still with him, and he cannot avoid his types'.[93]

At roughly the same time Fredric Jameson began to play with tropes as types. His specific problem was to analyse cultural history and to reconceive the clearly crude and outmoded Marxist notion that culture merely reflects what is going on in the economic 'base' of a society. The relationship between culture and base, he speculated, might not be a thought or philosophical position at all, but rather

something on the order of a rhetorical figure, a kind of metaphor, a trope, one of those new poetic forms through which the new historical consciousness, the new type of historical, synthesizing, dialectical thinking, plays and expresses itself, in sharp contrast to the old static analytical modes of thought.[94]

After this massive pile-up of appositives Jameson turns to Adorno, leaving his suggestion (like that of Kermode) more or less at the programmatic stage.

Both these articles appeared in newly begun literary journals – hardly the venues to strike sparks in the minds of most philosophers or historians. For such ideas to cross-fertilize the discourse of history, they had to appear where they might be read. *History and Theory* had, in the late 1960s, almost 2500 subscribers, even though comparatively few of these were historians.[95] It had published a number of *plaidoyers* for historians to become aware of contemporary developments in literary theory, of which the most sustained and controversial was Hayden White's 'The Burden of History', which arraigned historians for failing to match either the rigour of the natural sciences or the imaginative scope of twentieth-century literary works. But no articles developing these programmatic hints were submitted, and none were successfully solicited. The journal, in the minds of potential contributors and perhaps also of the editors, seemed to some degree stuck in the problematic of the late 1950s, when it had come into being. It also, in this respect, doubtless suffered from the defects of its sedulously nurtured *Archiv* quality. It was hardly the place to take an intellectual flier.

For these reasons there was certainly an ecological niche for a quite different sort of journal – just the sort that *Clio* turned out to be. Founded by two professors of literature in Wisconsin, its subtitle announced it to be *An Interdisciplinary Journal of Literature, History, and the Philosophy of History*. It was thus well placed to serve as the forum for literary theory to impinge on history. *Clio* was as breezy as *History and Theory* was austere; it published all sorts of ephemeral matter which an *Archiv* would never include, but which served to alert its readers to conferences and interesting articles in other journals. *New Literary History* was founded in 1969 and *Critical Inquiry* in 1974, and they, together with *Clio*, took a prominent part in exhibiting, if not philosophizing about, the literariness of history.

Once history is seen as literature, questions of genre, plotting and the fundamental organizing principles of historiography come to the fore. These had been systematically repressed in so-called analytical philosophy of history, which like all analysis tended to decompose historical discourse into its smallest intelligible units, like the two-sentence narrative. But analysis – especially analysis of language and narrative – evoked, dialectically, a recurrence of 'speculative' or substantive philosophy of history. Haskell Fain spoke of this as a 'resurrection' of speculative philosophy of history within the analytical tradition, by which he meant that analysis of the analyses brings to light certain questions that cannot be answered without some theory of human nature and the historical process. Analytical procedures, for example, cannot answer the vital question 'What are histories about?'[96] He might have added: 'How do historians decide which established facts are relevant to their accounts?' Danto's objection to the distinction between 'plain' and 'significant' narratives is that the so-called plain narrative must be constructed on some grounds which will exclude obviously irrelevant

statements: 'Naram-Sin built the Sun Temple at Sippar; then Philip III
exiled the Moriscos; then Urguiza defeated the forces of Buenos Aires at
Cepaada; then Arthur Danto awoke on the stroke of seven, 20 October
1961' is not a narrative at all.[97]

While analysts have focussed on the ways historians establish isolated
'facts', Fain argues, speculative philosophy of history is selfconsciously
concerned with problems of narrative.[98] He concludes that the very
distinction between ordinary history and speculative philosophy of
history has to be reconceived. Some 'ordinary' histories make claims
about the significance of their central subjects which imply a speculative
philosophy, and many others presuppose such philosophies. It is not that
the 'speculative philosopher of history' has a different intention from the
ordinary historian; the real difference is *the way that intention is
displayed* in the written work'. Ordinary history submerges this intent;
the historian spends a minimum amount of time saying why he is writing
and why he chooses certain themes. With the speculative philosopher of
history, 'the skull shows beneath the skin'.[99]

What sort of speculative philosophy of history, or organizing principles
of historical work, should the historian choose? Kermode thought that
contemporary types would have to be like alphabets or analogue
computers but in an early essay Hayden White, evidently unchastened
by Mazlish's rebukes, argued that the historian's language makes
mythical thinking inevitable:

The social theorist who does not realize that legendary modes of thought will
inevitably intrude themselves into his narratives is either epistemologically naïve
or is concerned only with trivial questions. The fall into legend is the price science
pays to myth for the use of language. Hence, whether a particular age may be
considered "scientific" or not depends less upon its actual contribution to
knowledge than upon the attitude with which it confronts its innate propensity
for mythic modes of thought. Historians of Auerbach's generation regarded the
use of legendary techniques as a forced concession; in our own time such
techniques are often wilfully, and respectably, embraced as a welcome liberation
from the irritating restraints of rational inquiry.[100]

In his comprehensive and radical attack on contemporary historiography
in 'The Burden of History', White invoked metaphors rather than myths.
He took an uncompromisingly presentist and constructivist view of
historiography; the only 'reason why we ought to study things under the
aspect of their past-ness rather than under the aspect of their present-ness'
is to 'transform historical studies in such a way as to allow the historian to
participate positively in the liberation of the present from *the burden of*

history'; and this requires the historian to recognize that historical 'facts' are 'not so much "found" as "constructed' by the kinds of questions which the investigator asks of the phenomena before him'.[101] But White did not at this time align himself with narrativists (perhaps because he was at pains to disparage Stuart Hughes' (guarded) endorsement of the historian's 'traditional story-telling function'). Narrative, he remarks, is only one of the possible modes of representation offered to the historian today.[102] And he sought to support a constructivism which would avoid radical relativism. An explanation, he wrote, 'need not be assigned unilaterally to the category of the literally truthful on the one hand or the purely imaginary on the other'. It should be

judged solely in terms of the richness of the metaphors which govern its sequence of articulation. Thus envisaged, the governing metaphor of an historical account could be treated as a *heuristic rule which self-consciously eliminates certain kinds of data from consideration as evidence*. The historian operating under such a conception could thus be viewed as one who, like the modern artist and scientist, seeks to exploit a certain perspective on the world that does not pretend to exhaust description or analysis of all of the data in the entire phenomenal field but rather offers itself as *one way among many* of disclosing certain aspects of the field.[103]

Historians would thus be forced to 'recognize that there is no such thing as a *single* correct view of any object under study, but there are *many* correct views, each requiring its own style of representation'. Statements about events in the past cannot be expected to 'correspond' to 'some pre-existent body of "raw facts"' because *what constitutes the facts themselves* is the problem that the historian, like the artist, has tried to solve in the choice of the metaphor by which he orders his world, past, present, and future.'[104]

We can ask of the historian only to

show some tact in his use of his governing metaphors; that he neither overburden them with data nor fail to use them to their limit; that he respect the logic implicit in the mode of discourse he has decided upon; and that, when his metaphor begins to show itself unable to accommodate certain kinds of data, he abandon that metaphor and seek another, richer, and more inclusive metaphor than that with which he began – in the same way that a scientist abandons a hypothesis when its use is exhausted.[105]

Metaphors – it is not clear whether the historian should use one master metaphor or several – thus establish relevance and justify selectivity; and would be sufficiently powerful to inform an entire historical work. But on White's argument they would always be this powerful, because the historian, like the artist, has used them '*to constitute the facts themselves*'. White does not explain where the 'data' which might cause the abandonment of a metaphor could come from. The resemblance between contemporary art and contemporary science, upon which White insists throughout the article, is most dubious in the analogy between metaphor and scientific hypothesis, since it would be hard to argue that the scientist has the same freedom to constitute facts as the artist – or, in White's view, the historian – enjoys.

'The Burden of History' is the programme fulfilled by *Metahistory*, which Louis Mink called 'the book around which all reflective historians must reorganize their thoughts on history'.[106] In a series of articles White developed parts of the complex argument of that book; but none of these was submitted to *History and Theory*.[107] In particular, the conceptual scheme of the first part of *Metahistory* is laid out, in especially accessible form, in 'Interpretation in History'.[108] Here is White's entire four-fold path: the four modes of emplotment; the four kinds of explanation; the four types of ideological implication; and, at the most basic level, the undifferentiated 'metaphors' of 'The Burden of History' are now identified – somewhat diffidently – as the four tropes of classical rhetoric. White acknowledges in a footnote

The whole question of the nature of the tropes is difficult to deal with, and I must confess my hesitancy in suggesting that they are the key to the understanding of the problem of interpretation in such proto-scientific fields as history.[109]

He raises the question, however, whether tropes are intrinsic to natural languages, and if so, whether 'they function to provide models of representation and explanation within any field not yet raised to the status of a genuine science' – which may be a field of study where one trope has succeeded in monopolizing the discourse.[110] An affirmative answer to these questions, left by White as hypotheses for future study by psychologists and linguists, would justify his claim ten years earlier that 'The fall into legend is the price science pays to myth for the use of language'; this would make science not merely analogous to art but a species of it.

It would also put the discussion of the cognitive status of narratives in a new light. White now took historical writing to be essentially narrative; but he broadened its definition. Partly on etymological grounds he claimed that a narrative is

any literary form in which the voice of the narrator rises against a background of ignorance, incomprehension or forgetfulness to direct our attention, purposefully, to a segment of experience organized in a particular way.[111]

It thus did not need its Aristotelian beginning, middle and end; to those, like Gruner, who objected that Burckhardt's *Civilization of the Renaissance in Italy* was obviously not a narrative, White replies that it is a story, but one which is all middle – that is, its plot is ironic, designed to frustrate the expectation of readers that it move towards some end. He was now able to rework the story-plot distinction. The events in the story-line are not – or, as he added, not supposed to be – made up by the historian; but historical stories are not just the procession of events that would only make up a chronicle, since any given event could be described either as a beginning or an end. The relationship of plot to story is like that of a theory to evidence; plots explain the evidence organized as a story by identifying that story as belonging to a certain class of stories. Plots thus do not explain events, as Forster thought; they explain stories. Borrowing some categories from Louis Mink, White concluded that only the story level affords configurational understanding; the historian's arguments must be understood at the theoretical level, and at the level of plot understanding is categoreal.[112]

In these two articles White's own 'ideological implication' remained tacit; but it was unmistakably present in *Metahistory*[113] and even more so in a polemical lecture which he delivered in 1969.[114] Detecting a conservative bias in Anglo-Saxon philosophy of history, White championed the continental tradition as more sympathetic to speculative philosophy of history or 'metahistory' – he treated the terms as synonyms and suggested that scholars should begin to take seriously the cries of the 1960s for 'involvement' and 'relevance' of history that militant social reformers were legitimately demanding of the academic community. Only a radical questioning of the cultural utility of history, he argued, can 'contribute to the salvation of the human *species* which it is our duty as thinkers to serve'.[115]

In contrast to those who spoke of the 'prisonhouse of language', White conceived his analysis of the tropes and plots of historiography as liberating. In particular, although the analysis itself could not escape an ironic mode, White hoped to show that the historian is free to embrace any trope, mode of emplotment, style of explanation or ideology. So-called analytical philosophy of history tended to confirm the historian in the belief that the rules of the historical guild or tribe required a mode of ironical detachment with its tacit corollary that history, in Nietzsche's formulation, had nothing to contribute to life. To White, language should be the servant of the historian, not the historian an instance of language.

We have traced the adventures of philosophy of history with historians' language from the lexical to the individual statement and, with White, to the entire historical work. And, with White, we have reached a thinker, trained as a historian, who was fully conversant not only with the pertinent philosophical literature, but also with the contributions which literary theorists were making. However, as a literary critic would, White treated the classic works he discussed as self-contained works of art. It was left for Louis Mink to pose a number of issues which troubled all historians who were not prepared to collapse any distinction between historical and fictional narratives or accept that indefinitely many true stories can be worked up from the same set of events.

How, if at all, he asked, do different narrative works of history fit together? At one time, he acknowledged, such a question perhaps would not even have been raised, because of the general acceptance of paradigmatic stories such as the progressive triumph of European civilization over the less-civilized world, or the inevitable development of the world towards freedom and reason; but now these stories have lost their credibility.

One possibility would simply be to add together the books of different historians. Suppose one wrote a diplomatic history in the more traditional way, emphasizing the actions of statesmen and the successes or failures of their manoeuvres, and someone else wrote from the standpoint that all the statesmen were basically in conspiracy to provoke wars and diplomatic crises in order to fend off the demands of their working classes for political enfranchisement and economic justice. Historians often say in such circumstances that each has part of the story; but Mink claimed that the omissions or subordinations of one could not be cured merely by juxtaposing it with the other; rather 'Each needs to be rewritten as a sub-plot, so to say, of a single story.'[116] But in view of the apparent unfeasibility of constructing credible master narratives, Mink later concluded that perhaps the relationship of discrepant historical accounts is not that one can be added to another, but rather that one displaces the other.

But this in turn raises a difficulty; although 'individual statements about the past may be true or false . . . a narrative is more than a conjunction of statements, and insofar as it is *more* it does not reduplicate a complex past but constructs one.'[117] How can whatever it is that narrative form adds to the conjunction of its (presumably true) statements be displaced? Certainly not by comparison with the past, since Mink always denied that the past – and the present, for that matter –

have any intrinsic or inherent narrative form: 'life is not a story and does not have the form of one except insofar as we give it that form, then supposing ourselves to have found it there.'[118] There would thus appear to be no empirical grounds for one story to displace another.

In the Enlightenment a regulative role had been played by the idea of universal history. The idea of writing a history of all of humanity – still vital in Ranke's day[119] – disappeared, but, Mink argued:

the idea of a determinate past, of 'history-as-lived' as a single complex field of bygone reality, survives as a presupposition . . . part of the a priori structure of our views about inquiry and knowledge.[120]

This presupposition is in tacit or explicit contradiction to other 'presuppositions' which Mink claimed to be 'widely shared': that there are 'not only different stories about different events, but even different stories about the same events'; that 'there are many central subjects or themes for these stories'; and that all stories 'are at least in principle fully *intelligible* without ensconcing them within a more comprehensive narrative whose narrative form is not entirely visible in the segment which they represent'.[121] These of course are all positions maintained by Hayden White. Yet, as Danto's Ideal Chronicler demonstrates, the idea that 'everything which has happened belongs to a realm of an unchanging actuality, and that this is a single determinate realm' is perfectly intelligible, and (as he did not add) is in fact basic to historical realism.

If there is an unchangeable totality of 'what actually happened', all historical narratives should in principle be related to one another. For Collingwood the requirement that 'the historical world is one' is one that differentiates between historical and fictional works, and Mink points out that this might be an important criterion for distinguishing the two. Yet historical narratives cannot be added together or put end to end, since the unity of a narrative depends on its having its own beginning, middle and end. There is thus a dilemma: 'narrative histories should be aggregative, insofar as they are histories, but cannot be, insofar as they are narratives.'[122]

Furthermore, the assumption of the determinate past means that although 'narrative structure claims to represent real relations in historical actuality . . . when we come to describe narrative structures we treat them as artifices, the products of different imaginations and sensibilities.'[123] If we are reduced to comparing historical narratives purely on our preference for the trope that informs them, then there seems to be no way to evaluate their truth-claims *as narratives*.

Finally, given that, as Danto has shown, we can refer to events only under some description, Mink questioned the claim that different stories can be told about the same events. It seems natural, he granted, to suppose that a number of different accurate descriptions, at different levels of generality, could be given of events – but would they be the *same* events? We could be sure they were only if we could delimit events and provide standard descriptions of them, thus making them the equivalent of atoms in classical physics. But not only have no such limits ever been agreed, or standard descriptions devised; if they were, Mink shows, the narrative form would be 'wholly superfluous for the explanation of events'. He was thus able to bring to light a contradiction between the concepts of event and of narrative:

the concept of event is primarily linked to the conceptual structure of science, where it is purged of all narrative connections; it is taken to be something which can be identified and described without any necessary reference to its location in some process of development and change which only narrative form can represent. Therefore, to speak of a "narrative of events" is virtually a contradiction in terms.[124]

The upshot of this argument is that 'we cannot without confusion regard different narratives as differently emplotting the *same* events. In fact, a narrative is not *built* up out of events or their descriptions; rather the appropriateness of a description is controlled by the narrative order from which it is abstracted.'[125] Since it was in his judgement impossible to resurrect the eighteenth-century genre of universal history, he proposed the radical alternative: 'to abandon the presupposition that there is a determinate historical actuality, the complex referent for all our narratives of "what actually happened," the *untold* story to which narrative histories approximate'.[126] Mink had thus, by a different route, reached a conclusion close to that of Barthes, though he was much less comfortable with it.

As often happens in philosophy, White and Mink had raised many new and troubling questions in the process of answering some old ones. The most awkward ones, as Mink demonstrated, beset anyone who tried to retain at least sense of the past *wie es eigentlich gewesen* while acknowledging the intrinsically rhetorical character of historical narrative. As we have seen, Hexter's 'rules' were one attempt to keep both. White also, in the writings discussed above, clung to some notions of 'data' and of events that 'really happened' as opposed to those imagined by novelists.[127] Although many true stories might be told about the same events, he did not deny that some false ones could also be told – although he said nothing about how historians could tell the difference. But those philosophers like Mandelbaum who had detected a dangerous opening towards relativism even in the earliest writings by Morton White and Danto could now see their worst fears apparently confirmed. All who took the 'linguistic turn' had at the very least to confront its antinomies.

This was now, a bit belatedly, at the top of *History and Theory*'s editorial agenda. Mink was its associate editor; but all of his later writing on historical narrative appeared in other journals. White was made one of two consultant editors in 1974; but he also did most of his writing for other journals (and it must be said he was already on the editorial boards of both *Clio* and *New Literary History*).[128] Some of *History and Theory*'s editorial committee, notably Mandelbaum and Arnaldo Momigliano, retained a deep scepticism about narrative and the rhetorical elements in historical writing (Mandelbaum recommended Johns Hopkins Press not to publish Hayden White's *Metahistory*; Momigliano reviewed the book adversely).[129] Nobody on the editorial committee ever interfered in day-to-day editorial decisions; but the presence of these names on the masthead may have had a chilling effect on some potential contributors. But, beginning with the conference which produced *Beiheft* 19 (1980), devoted entirely to *Metahistory* and to a (probably doomed) effort to force historians to come to terms with its arguments, the editors worked to stimulate discussion of the varieties of historians' writing. They, like others, had barely understood structuralism when it was overwhelmed by post-structuralism; and some rarefied arguments have been as befuddling to editors as to readers.[130] What only now becomes clear is that something like a paradigmatic shift had occurred; for the next twenty years historians' language, not explanation or causality, would be *the* topic around which most reflections on history would centre.

3

The Decline and Fall of
the Analytical Philosophy of History

ARTHUR C. DANTO

The history of the analytical philosophy of history very largely begins with the publication, early in 1942, of C. G. Hempel's classical paper 'The Function of General Laws in History'. In the mid-1950s, and for some years thereafter, there was a heated controversy over Hempel's central thesis – that historical explanation, like scientific explanation in general, involves bringing the event to be explained under ('covering it with') a general law – but the argument was but a skirmish in the wider wars of the time which concerned competing views of ordinary language and the relationship to language of analytical philosophy. So far as I know, Hempel never saw great reason either to revise or retire his account of historical explanation, or the much wider general theory of explanation which he worked out with Paul Oppenheim in 'Studies in the Logic of Explanation', published in 1948; and when he came to publish a postscript to his essays on explanation in *Aspects of Scientific Explanation* in 1964, he did not even bother to defend the paper on history (reprinted without comment), and dwelt on a few matters only of logical detail, as if the theory of explanation as entailing general laws were in all essentials sound.

I do not think this was a case of mere philosophical stone-walling: Hempel offered, over these same years, some of the most remarkable pieces of philosophical dismantling I know of, of theories he himself had advanced. In 1946, in *Mind*, his 'A Note on the Paradoxes of Confirmation', with its demonstration that examining a swan and finding it white must confirm the proposition that all ravens are black if his own analysis on confirmation were correct, pretty much blew that theory sky-high: either one had to sacrifice one's intuitions about confirmation, or surrender a basic piece of logic. His paper 'Problems and Changes in the Empiricist Criterion of Meaning' made plain to the world that no one knew how to heal the logical wounds inflicted on the dread Verifiability Principle by those who had believed it to be true until it was found hopeless, unable to resist attacks from the side of its logic. Indeed – this was 1950 – nobody any longer greatly cared to try: I recall talking about it with the logician Richard Jeffries one evening at a rooftop party in Manhattan, when he said that whenever he thought of the Verifiability Principle, he was reminded of the Sybil of Cumae as described in the epigraph to T. S. Eliot's *The Waste Land*; when asked what she really wanted, the Sybil responded that she wanted to *die*. In 1958 Hempel published 'The Theoretician's Dilemma', a brilliant discussion of why no one was any longer interested in empiricist foundationalism, even though it had been demonstrated, through an astonishing theorem of William Craig's, that in any language minimally formalized, any proposition using 'non-empirical' predicates can be trivially replaced with propositions using predicates from the favoured vocabulary. With these two papers, the props had been knocked out from under the reconstructionist programmes of logical positivism, which had envisioned erecting the 'language of science' on strictly observational bases. These were philosophical criticisms of an almost breathtaking finesse, worthy entries in the Encyclopedia of Refutations along with Russell's devastation of Frege, or Wittgenstein's devastation of Russell when he showed that the latter's theory of judgement – the keystone to his epistemology – was inconsistent with his theory of types – the keystone to his way of handling the logical paradoxes. If deconstruction as a philosophical position had a single contribution as powerful as any of these, every analytical philosopher in the world would take deconstruction seriously: by contrast with Hempel's arguments, something like the charge of the 'metaphysics of presence' levelled against Husserl is the kind of argument that belongs in the *classe terminale* of a middling *lycée*.

In these three remarkable papers, then, Hempel showed himself to be a thinker ready to reconsider his views when the arguments, many of them invented or discovered by himself, went against them. So he evidently felt nothing especially damaging in the various criticisms offered of his model of historical explanation. My own book *Analytical Philosophy of History*, published in 1965, sought to demonstrate an equivalence between explanation as construed by Hempel, and narratives, thus vindicating the so-called 'covering-law model' against the claim that narrational models were deeply alternative to it, but it was for quite other reasons that the book attracted the considerable philosophical attention that it did; and when Rex Martin, in 1977, published a very balanced and judicious account of Hempel's model, I think Martin would be the first to concede that no one much cared one way or the other. The whole analytical philosophy of history, like its cousin the Verifiability Principle, hardly had enough life left in it to want to die. Thomas Kuhn's epochal *The Structure of Scientific Revolutions* appeared in 1962 (as an instalment in volume II of the uncompleted *International Encyclopedia of Unified Science*, which was after all to have been the great monument to a philosophical vision of science which Kuhn's book did as much as anything to abort). Kuhn advanced a view of history so powerful that, rather than being an applied science, as Hempel holds history to be, history came to be the matrix for viewing *all* the sciences. It all at once became the philosophical fashion to view science historically rather than logically, as an evolving system rather than a timeless calculus, as something whose shifts over time are philosophically more central to its essence than the timeless edifice of theories, related to laws which in turn were related to observation sentences; this had been the standard way in which the philosophy of science thought about its subject *ante* Kuhn. That architectonic conception is embalmed in the article on the philosophy of science (written by me) in Paul Edwards's *Encyclopedia of Philosophy*, published in 1967. It was as though science had been swallowed whole by one of its offspring, which, under the influence of Wittgenstein, N. R. Hanson and Stephen Toulmin, not to mention Kuhn himself, had become the philosophical *history* of science. This transformation was consolidated under the immense prestige of Foucault's archeologizing politics of science. The world as idea became the world as will, and science itself seen more and more as an all-too-human endeavour, a view of it confessed in such works as James Watson's *The Double Helix*. And this overall view was nailed in place with the heavy anti-scientism of the late 1960s and the decade that followed. Except for a few desultory efforts to account for paradigm shifts, or in what Foucault designates *enoncés*, I can think of very little in the philosophy of history from the middle-1960s to the present. Somewhere someone sometime in the last decade must have written about explanation, even about historical explanation – but I cannot think of an example offhand. (It should be noted that, as editor of the *Journal of Philosophy*, I see a fair sample each year of what philosophers offer as their most advanced work: my estimate is that a contribution on any aspect of the philosophy of history occurs at a rate of one per thousand submissions.) It is not just that the topic is under extreme neglect. It is, rather, that there is hardly room in the present scene of philosophy for discussion of its issues. So to find someone actively working at them would be almost to encounter a historically displaced person, like someone doing abstract expressionist canvasses as if the whole subsequent history of art had not taken place. Or like encountering Japanese soldiers on some obscure atoll who never found out that the war had ended.

I have now written a little narrative, treating a fragment of the philosophy of history as a fragment of the history of philosophy. My aim has been to emphasize that the problem of historical explanation itself belongs to history and that it has a history of its own, and that a solution of the problem can and should be tested against itself: if a theory of historical explanation is incapable of explaining its own history, it can have little claim to philosophical assent elsewhere. Philosophers are prone to exempt themselves from their own analyses. This is harmless enough when the latter bear on subjects to which philosophy does not belong, but the position is seriously compromised when philosophy does belong by rights to the subject analysed, for example if the subject should be thought. In that case philosophy must be hostage to its own accounts, in that if, again for example, philosophers should accept an account of thought to which the thinking that went into the analysis fails to conform, then the analysis is seriously limited or flawed. A first test of a philosophical theory should be that it account for itself whenever relevant. A theory of knowledge, for example, ought to be able to explain how, in its own terms, we know it to be true, and if it is not up to this, then it is either inadequate or incomplete. A theory of meaning should be able to explain how *it* gets its meaning, and a theory of understanding how we understand it. If somebody insists that 'belief' belongs to a superannuated theory of ourselves, and that in truth there are no such things as beliefs, the question naturally arises as to the status of this very belief and what *its* status is, and whether, for example, we could express what looks like a belief about beliefs in a favoured neurophysiological vocabulary which allowed itself no psychological terms whatever. Indeed, it would be extremely interesting to see how an account could be given of the argument that there are no beliefs in an idiom that had no room for the concept of belief. Possibly the argument could be expressed in terms of some transformation of states of nervous tissue, but then we would surely want to add to the normal language of neurophysiology concepts like truth and falsity and entailment, for otherwise it would not be an *argument*. And then it would be interesting to see what would have been gained: all that would have been shown, admittedly a great deal, is what happens in nervous tissue when someone arrives at a philosophical belief. But that is a far cry from denying that there are beliefs at all. Philosophy must in general include itself in whatever account it constructs, for otherwise true philosophical closure will not have been attained, and the account is partial at best.

Hempel's model of explanation had, as its most controversial feature in the case of *historical* explanation, the proviso that the event to be explained – the *explanandum* in the logical patois of the era – must be 'covered' by a general law. And there really is one place in my narrative where something like a tacit appeal to general laws might be located, but this is crucially at the very point at which Hempel's distant opponents (in contrast with his immediate critics) might have insisted that a very different operation altogether from explanation is called for, namely a kind of understanding (or *Verstehen* in the metaphysical patois of *its* era). This is where we ask ourselves why Hempel did not change his view on explanation despite the fact that his immediate opponents argued vigorously against them. Now it is possible that there is something very like a law, modelled on Newton's First Law of Motion, that a person who has formed a view tends to maintain that view with uniform tenacity until something – some 'impinging force' as Newton would say – causes him to modify or abandon it. There are no doubt views which no impinging force will cause us to change short of damage to the brain: these would be the deep *a priori* principles that define experience for creatures with brains such as ours, though there is an interesting peripheral question regarding the degree of intervenability in regard to these. Quine, not a man likely to alter his political views, has an evidently light grip on the Principle of Excluded Middle, which he feels one can give up easily if the cost of not doing so is assessed as too high. But others have wondered whether it is psychologically possible to give up a principle which may be, just as Aristotle says, a Law of Thought, even if for computational purposes one can get along without it. Quine offers a general picture of the system of beliefs as totally subject to the doxastic will, where we can pick and choose in accordance with competing priorities. But in actual practice how possible really is it to change the beliefs that perhaps define the world and ourselves together and reciprocally? Hempel's view of explanation may in fact be pretty deep, psychologically, in that it characterizes the way we do in fact proceed when we endeavour to explain, emitting hypotheses which harden into laws when they pass the tests of further experience and which are revised when they do not. Thus, learning that a certain logical positivist did not change his views on a certain subject, despite the fact that for a dozen years or more arguments against it were found compelling by a number of clever philosophers, I might explain this by saying that as a general rule logical positivists are terribly dogmatic, and that such resistance is to be explained as a matter of course. And then *you* tell me that Hempel is an extremely liberal and open person, as evidenced by the way he cheerfully gave up his views on confirmation and verification and meaning, not to mention what Quine identified as the Second Dogma of Empiricism, namely reduction to an observational base as the mark of scientific credibility. But these are views that historically defined logical positivism and which in some cases enshrined Hempel's own contribution to philosophical knowledge. And we can go further in this discussion. It might be observed that Hempel, in each of the three retractions, made a rational decision, namely to sacrifice a piece of philosophical analysis rather than a piece of logic. Many of the difficulties with the Verifiability Principle were generated, for example, by certain features of logical adjunction, namely that if P is true, then P or Q is true, whatever Q may be. The difficulties with the theory of confirmation could have been met by sacrificing the concept of logical equivalence or of contraposition. And Craig's theorem really *was* a theorem. So there are priorities here: Hempel was going to hold onto logic 'come what may', as Quine likes to put it. On the other hand, to his mind at least, none of the objections to the covering-law model entailed a choice between it and some principle of logic, and meanwhile his own account rested on some intuition of what we do and how we behave when we explain, whether we are historians or not. Challenged to explain his resistance, Hempel would be able to give an account of it which in fact exemplified his model. And he might at the same time have been really unable to give an account which did *not* exemplify it, to be sure within its relatively loose and accommodating formulation, which only required in any actual case that an 'explanation sketch' be provided.

This, then, is a kind of historical explanation of a non-change, but in history non-changes are as important as changes. It more or less reconstructs, in admittedly rough strokes, what we might call 'the World according to Hempel'. It was very much a world of its own time, in that the imperatives and priorities of logical positivism were among its foundations, though parts of the foundation were tested against one another, and where, whenever there was a choice between logic and some other kind of proposition, logic held sway, even if, in the end, this meant sacrificing finally a great many principles, verificationism and reductionism being two, which were canonical to those who lived, philosophically, in 'the World according to Logical Positivism'. 'Sacrifice' is perhaps too strong a word: perhaps there were other reasons in the air which made verificationism and reductionism decreasingly adequate accounts of how science ideally works, so that it seemed decreasingly worth the effort to try to patch them up. And so they were allowed to languish and if – no more than the Sybil of Cumae who had struck a bargain in which she was given immortality – they were able to die, at least the distinction between death and the philosophical life grew increasingly difficult to draw.

Because mathematical logic was so firm a component in its geography, the World according to Hempel was very much a World of its own time, for logic in the form that Hempel used it had not existed before Russell or, perhaps, before Frege. It was not a world available to anyone in 1742 or 1642 or 1242, to cite some pre-anniversaries of the paper on historical explanation of 1942. A world is (at least) a stratified system of representations, and it is a matter of history that certain representations cannot be formed at certain times (and though they can be formed at other times, they perhaps cannot always be *lived* at those times). Hempel's world was overlapped by the worlds of other logical positivists, other non-positivist philosophers, other non-philosopher scientists, other refugees, and there may very well have been not one single other person whose world was congruent with the World according to Hempel in every particular. A world is something that we *grow*. To be human at all is to have grown a world. A world is what a soul construes itself as living in, so there is little sense in a soul surviving death if the world it projects for itself does not survive. In any case, to understand Hempel, to apply *Verstehen* to Hempel is to reconstruct the World according to Hempel, which in effect is to 'abduct' to its laws. But that of course is exactly what Hempel supposes we do when we explain historically!

'The World according to X' (hereafter W(x)) is, to paraphrase Wittgenstein, everything that is the case for X. It is by no means necessary that whatever is the case for X is the case, though enough of W(x) must be true in order that X survive. There is, moreover, no great need to make the kinds of fact-value distinctions when we talk about worlds – for that we had to worry about when we talked about the world *tout court*: that all unsupported bodies fall may be as much or as little part of W(x) as that it is wrong to break promises. And false beliefs may count as heavily towards X's survival as true ones, if, for example, X lives in a society the worlds of whose members has as the case a belief in fact false, and where failure of it to be the case for X may mean the end of W(x) because X gets executed for infidelity or impiety. We in general understand one another's behaviour with reference to one another's worlds, which means in effect that we identify W(x) when we endeavour to explain a piece of behaviour B of X: B happens as a matter of course for X when W(x). But this in effect is to have identified, via abduction, a world-defining law for X: W(x)→B. It does not greatly matter that there should be another individual Y such that W(y)→B, for the law to be general: it is general just because it holds that anyone whose world relevantly overlaps W(x) will do B when X does B, even if there is no such anyone.

Worlds of course are holistic and stratified: they are not simply conjunctions of whatever is the case for whoever's world it is. In the World according to Hempel, logic trumps whatever would entail revision of it if the latter were true; and his own theory of confirmation is more readily jettisoned than the Verifiability Principle, which was a long time a-dying, and which in his heart of hearts he may never have given up, just because it may continue to have struck him as close to scientific practice, in a world in which scientific practice was canonical. But to see whether this were true, we would have to examine more of Hempel's behaviour than we so far have done, and see what choices he might make where we would expect him, *ceteris paribus*, spontaneously to invoke verification-ism. But that is a task for another occasion when, so to speak, one undertakes a systematic cosmography of W(hempel). It would, beyond that, be a philosophically rewarding and even indispensable task to undertake the cosmography for the worlds of everyone, which is in effect to identify the laws of all the worlds. I take it that the Transcendental Deduction of the Categories was such an undertaking. These would be the laws for rational beings, inasmuch as to be a rational being is to behave in such a way that what one does can be understood in terms of a world. There of course may be 'cracked worlds', worlds where one or another fundamental law fails, which makes the behaviour of one whose world it is irrational. But these schematic remarks carry me far downstream from where I mean to be in an essay on the philosophy of history, and I return to my true course.

It is somewhat ironical that my effort to explain Hempel's continued advocacy of the covering-law model by actually *using* his model, should have involved me in a concept, that of a world, from within which it becomes a matter of course that he should continue advocating that model, when the very idea of 'from within a world' must be repugnant to Hempel – from within Hempel's world. It is repugnant on perhaps two grounds. In the first place, it sounds very much like the very thing he meant to escape from in offering his famous model, namely, an operation like *Verstehen* which was meant by *its* advocates to set historical off from natural scientific understanding. And second, the concept of a world is not one we would ordinarily invoke in the explanation of physical phenomena, so another philosophical notion that Hempel was especially anxious to confront and to deny seems to insinuate itself at the very heart of my analysis, namely that there after all does seem to be a natural distinction between the *Geisteswissenschaften*, which concerns the explanation among other things of the behaviour of philosophers, and the *Naturwissenschaften*, if the physical sciences should be their paradigm. And this runs counter at least to Hempel's ideas of unified science. Remember, I am talking about the World according to Hempel as indexed to 1942, when his paper on history was published. The various attacks against it did not seriously begin for perhaps another decade, since the kind of ordinary-language analysis which underlies some of the criticism of the covering-law model did not enter the mainstream of analytical philosophy until after the death of Wittgenstein and the ascendancy of Oxford philosophy in the 1950s. But worlds do not change especially rapidly: world-holders are by nature conservative. I am not certain I would know what to make of a person who changed his world every year, or every month.

In 1942 and for some while afterwards, the ideal of a psychology modelled on what the positivists supposed physics was like would have been given in works like Egon Brunswick's 'The Conceptual Framework of Psychology', (which was part of the *International Encyclopedia of Unified Science*), where the 'principle of Extensionality' was the reigning ideal in analysing psychological concepts, and where something like behaviourism would have been widely endorsed as best conforming to the verificationist criteria of respectable science, as that was construed by the positivists whose world in these respects was certainly shared by Hempel. It is in terms of such views as these in the World according to Logical Positivism, that we would have to understand – would have to *interpret* – Hempel's resistance to change. The philosophy of psychology would today of course be greatly different from that subscribed to in 1942, largely in consequence of a much deeper appreciation of the logic of propositional attitudes, which was very much over the horizon of the future when Hempel was working out his ideas on explanation. Even the sketchy way I have been developing the concept of worlds depends upon discoveries in the concept of intentionality, which were hardly in place in 1942.

I shall now comment on the two points I proposed would account for Hempel's resistance. Needless to say, I am not saying he was wrong in resisting: I am after all adapting the covering-law model to Hempel's own case, to be sure elaborated with the support of the concept of worlds.

The idea of *Verstehen* is often connected with the idea of an 'internal understanding', a taking of the agent's point of view, as if this required of the interpreter a vicarious act of sympathetic identification, a leap across the barriers of the self, into the world of the other, with the outcome that one knows what it is like to be that person. We get an echo of this in Thomas Nagel's celebrated title 'What's it like to be a Bat', where it was Nagel's overall thought that there is something it is like to be something to which consciousness can be ascribed. Now I think there are certain barriers to empathic leaps, and a sense in which no one will ever really know what it is like to live in the world of the bat the way a bat lives in it. But I do not think it especially important that we worry about these barriers. In part this is because not everything that belongs to $W(x)$ is necessarily accessible to, or forms part of the consciousness of X. Nevertheless, there is something of very deep importance in the idea of *Verstehen*, and I have touched upon it so casually, so *en passant*, that it could easily have been missed, namely, that of a *point of view*. Analytical philosophers certainly invoke the idea of point of view in a non-psychological way, as in Quine's title *From a Logical Point of View* or Kurt Baier's *The Moral Point of View*, where points of view define horizons of relevance, define what, though it may be true of a subject under investigation, is not relevant to that in the subject which is being investigated. I spoke in fact of 'the agent's point of view', and here again, I think, this defines a horizon of relevance in the sense that certain things may be true of the objects the agent has to deal with in making a decision which are not really relevant to the decision the agent has to make. I was one day looking at an exhibition of some works by the Italian *arte povere* master Mario Merz in the company of a German critic I know casually, who said she was uncertain this was art. She went on to say that Mario Merz could certainly draw, and that he painted not badly, but *this* – and here she swept her hand grandly across to indicate the main objects being displayed in the Guggenheim Museum – *this* had no *aesthetic* quality at all. And my response, not particularly deep, spontaneously referred to the point of view from which it was not art, namely, that point of view from which it belongs essentially to art that it have aesthetic quality. That was in no sense *my* point of view, but it took very little by way of empathy for me to identify it as her point of view: I did not need vicariously to share it to know that it was hers. In fact it matters very little that I cannot imagine what it is like to have that point of view, what it is like to live in a world in which aesthetics defines what art is, as long as I can identify that point of view and describe that world when explaining someone's critical exclamations. That point of view defines my companion as a critic, and truly it identifies her as a person: 'the aesthetic point of view' as criterial of art comes close, I think, to what Sartre might identify as her original project, the basic choice which defines the horizon of relevance for all the choices one is going to make in following through one's plan of life. She *was*, I all at once realized, that point of view. All the ways she surrounded herself with things and presented herself to the world and to herself radiate outwards from that point of view. To change that point of view would be to shatter her world and to shatter her.

Very few philosophers have dealt with points of view as an ontological category, and as constitutive of representational beings. In a sense, the monad, in Leibniz's system, is more or less a point of view and nothing more, and of course, perspectivism in Nietzsche's metaphysics requires point of view as centres of power, each seeking to impose itself on blank passive reality. But in general, I think, points of view are crucial in the explanation of behaviour, especially when understood as action, and indeed I am not sure what behaviour could be considered as an action which did not refer back to the horizon within which the decision of what to do arose for the agent, and with it the issues of relevance. But it is precisely with points of view that historical considerations enter explanation. Consider, for example, the point of view of the woman, which men in our culture are increasingly required to show sensitivity to, and which will be held different from the point of view of the man. The basic components of sexual bimorphism have been present immemorially in human beings, and the human genome has not changed in all that time. Is there a woman's point of view which has defined the perspective of women invariantly through, say, the past 100,000 years? The likelihood is not: we have to index the point of view of women to specific times: 1992, 1942, 1802, 1492. The point of view of a woman in the post-feminist era is certain to differ in basic respects from the point of view of a woman in the pre-feminist era; and post-feminist men are more sensitive to that point of view, whatever it is, than pre-feminist men. History, in brief, defines the world available to us. Marxism insisted upon the point of view of the proletariat, but envisioned a time when points of view definitive of class position would disappear. Points of view can be consistent with behaviourism, of course, which insists that all that is required to explain behaviour are differing schedules of reinforcement. It is on the other hand insufficiently stressed that schedules of reinforcement themselves are historically indexed, though there is little doubt that Skinner allowed for historicism merely in virtue of his utopian point of view.

In any case, the World according to Hempel is more than a stratified set of beliefs: it is a point of view which defines a horizon; and explaining Hempel's non-change refers us to the point of view with regard to which the objections raised against his model of historical explanation were perceived by him either as irrelevant or uncompelling. And this gets to be very close to what *Verstehen* itself prescribed as a method for the human sciences. Nothing could be more revealing, I think, than a comparison of the opening passages of volume II, number 2 of the *International Encyclopedia of Unified Science*, which was 'The Structure of Scientific Revolutions' – and of volume II, number 7, which was Hempel's 'Fundamentals of Concept Formation in the Empirical Sciences'. Kuhn's words virtually embody what they are about:

The essay that follows is the first full published report on a project originally conceived fifteen years ago. At that time I was a graduate student in theoretical physics within sight of the end of my dissertation. A fortunate involvement . . . my first exposure to the history of science . . . To my complete surprise . . . The result was a drastic shift in my career plans.

Hempel writes this way:

Empirical science has two major objectives: to describe particular phenomena in the world of our experience, and to establish general principles by means of which they can be explained.

The point of view expressed in these two passages is respectively historical and conceptual, or logical. What I have endeavoured to do, has been to force the latter into the former, and insist that we explain historically the position that historical explanation is itself a matter of logical analysis, to which history has no relevance whatever. In the passage cited, Hempel speaks timelessly, and states what he perceives as truths for any time and all times. And I have been asking what the *history* of that ahistorical outlook is, and have endeavoured to think of it as indexed to a specific historical moment.

So much, for now, for *Verstehen*; now for the ascription of beliefs. This is an exercise of what philosophers, since Paul Churchland's truculent and celebrated essays, have come to class as folk psychology. Folk psychology is the theory that we explain one anothers' behaviour relative to sets of beliefs (etc), a theory that our survival as humans with humans very much depends upon our capacity to master in a remarkably nuanced way. Churchland's view is that as a theory it is moribund, destined sooner or later to be replaced with another theory in which we describe one another and ourselves only in the idioms of a neuroscience which admittedly is not yet in place. I have often argued against this view as follows. The new theory must be achieved by science. But science itself is a human activity described in precisely the terms it is supposed to outlaw, namely believing, observing, performing, testing, inferring and the like – all categories of folk psychology. How is science to represent *itself* in the promised tongue of utopian neuroscience? Imagine trying to represent science when everything that belongs to science is taken way: it is in fact unimaginable, as is Churchland's proposal. Now I think it true that Hempel would have found the Churchland proposal philosophically congenial, but he could hardly suppose it possible to give an account of historical explanation in terms of it, for just the reason that the language of neuroscience (I am supposing) has no room in it for concepts like points of view, of worlds, of horizons and the like, and certainly the laws of neurophysiology would hardly have ways for the kind of historical indexing we have had to introduce – for that would make it a strictly non-predictive science. Who can predict the points of view of historical periods as yet unhappened? If one represents us in some timeless ahistorical idiom of neuroscience, there can at best be laws of a kind which depend upon no historical differences, which are the same for every stage in the long history of the human genome. Once we think of ourselves as historically situated, folk psychology re-emerges. Try to imagine what it would be like to explain Hempel's non-change in terms referring solely to synaptic discharges and neuronal impulses!

Now it is true that each science wields predicates of a kind that cannot easily be defined in terms of the predicates of other sciences, though of course, a unified science, which envisioned relationships of reduction between the predicates of the various sciences ultimately to those of physics was a dream of the philosophy of science in Hempel's era. In the 'Theoretician's Dilemma' Hempel expressed certain reservations on the possibility of reduction to a strictly observational base, but overall I imagine he thought of reduction as desirable and inevitable. I am not certain what altogether he thought of psychology, but at the very least reduction to some sort of behavioural base was doubtless compassed within the horizon of desirability generated by his point of view. But it is less and less clear today that psychological predicates can be reduced in this way, and to the degree that this is so, something in the concept of unified science must give way. To refer to the World according to Hempel as a set of beliefs given unity through a consistent point of view is to bring into our description of this philosopher a dimension of intentionality, and it would have been among the axioms of positivism at the time when he was one of its great champions that the language of science is through and through *extensional*. But that means that science, even if its language is through and through extensional, would then have no way of representing itself, would have no way of housing in the universe something through and through intensional. What one might call the World of Science, if the Positivists characterized it correctly, could not include science itself. Hence science in its nature would be incomplete or inadequate. Or better, science, construed in terms of a completely extensional language, would itself be addressable only through the resources of the *Geisteswissenschaften*, which alone allows itself the conceptual resources to represent the kinds of things science does – observes, infers, tests and the like. In brief, the very things the positivists left outside defeat its enterprise of elaborating a unified science: and when we bring them in, and do so in such a way that science itself becomes something to be represented by science, the world of the positivist is burst asunder.

I want to conclude on a programmatic note. In various places I have discussed four types of causal episode which may figure in the histories of what I term *representational* beings, beings in the explanation of whose behaviour the way they represent the world enters. Let R designate a representational state of an *ens representans*, and R̸ a non-representational state. A belief is the standard exemplar of the former; perhaps the end-state of the Krebs cycle will serve as an exemplar of the latter. Then there are four kinds of episode: (1) RR; (2) RR̸; (3) R̸R; and (4) R̸R̸. There are necessarily then four different kinds of law if indeed laws are entailed by causal explanation. These would be: (1) psycho-psychic laws; (2) psycho-physical laws; (3) physico-psychic laws; and (4) physico-physical laws, which are the laws of the physical sciences. I can do no more than mention these here, but examples of the four types of episode would be: (1) believing that someone loves me because I read a letter in which she said she loves me and I believe the letter genuine; (2) believing I see a snake, which causes me to shudder involuntarily; (3) hearing the door open, which causes me to fear that someone has broken into the house; and (4) undergoing a drop in blood sugar, which causes me to faint. In the psycho-psychic and the psycho-physical cases at least we may appeal to laws only against the background of the worlds of the individuals, which is to say: against the bodies of belief, unified under points of view, of the individuals under explanation. In physico-physical laws we do not need these background considerations: or we need only the background of the way *the* world is made: not W(x) or W(y) but W: the world to which perhaps Wittgenstein's *Tractatus* refers. Of course *the* world contains among other things the individuals X and Y each with his or her own world.

All this is perhaps ontological boiler-plate. I want to talk about a special kind of episode, one in which someone's world changes. I have illustrated in fact two kinds of case already, one in which, according at least to his testimony, Kuhn's world changed, and one in which, as judged by the constancy with which he adhered to his account of historical explanation, Hempel's world did not change. The World according to Hempel, from 1942 until at least 1964, is pretty much the same world, in that Hempel's point of view did not change in any basic way through that interval. It was very much as though there were no 'impinging force' to knock Hempel off his philosophical tracks. A number of his beliefs of course changed in that time without this entailing that his *world* changed. But the world according to Kuhn in 1962 was a very different world indeed from his World, reckoning back fifteen years, of 1947, just because of the transformation in his basic point of view about science and its history. His world was different, though of course many of his beliefs were the same. In effect, he describes what caused him to exchange one world for another by virtue of changing his fundamental point of view – or changing a point of view which turned out to be fundamental. What makes Kuhn's work *historically* important is the fact that a good many thinkers, whose worlds very largely overlapped Hempel's at crucial points, were caused by Kuhn's work to turn into thinkers whose world overlapped Kuhn's world instead. It was very painful for many of them to undergo this change, and I can remember one of them saying with a cry of anguish that he wished Kuhn had never written that damned book. My colleague, the medievalist James Walsh, quoted a sixteenth-century scholastic who said, in much the same spirit, that 'The wretched Luther had emptied the lecture halls'. For a long period there were questions with which scholastic thinkers dealt and with which everyone who shared their world regarded as of the greatest moment. And then, all at once, almost overnight, nobody cared any longer. The issues stopped being what the rebel students of 1968 were correct to call 'relevant'. I recall people saying (it may have been J. L. Austin who phrased it so): 'Relevance isn't relevant; truth is.' They were wrong. The point of bringing the apparatus of worlds, horizons and points of view into the discussion is to underscore the relevance of relevance. Hempel's theory in fact strikes me still as true. It just stopped being relevant, the way the whole philosophy of history it defined stopped being. It was replaced with a different set of questions, a world in effect, into which it no longer fit. As with the questions of scholasticism which were never answered but merely abandoned, it belongs to the history of philosophy to summon up enough of the world of 1942 philosophy to see what Hempel's theory meant.

I would think that when worlds in this way give way to other worlds through changes in shared points of view, we may mark moments which define the end and beginning of historical periods. Kuhn opened a new period in the history of thought, and definitely a new one in the philosophy of science. In the earlier period it was of some importance to show the continuity between history and science, which Hempel did; in the later period the historical nature of science was so taken for granted that the earlier question lost its urgency. Hempel, of course, lived on into the new period, but he was not *of* that period. He belonged to a fading philosophical culture, one in which those who acquired their worlds in the new period required special instruction to understand, as much so as they would with scholasticism. Kuhn's theory of paradigm shifts beautifully accounts for itself, since that is just what it itself was. A lot of course goes unaffected by the change, and there are many beliefs invariant to the two worlds – beliefs which do not change when the worlds change. It is because of this that discussion between worlds remains possible, but there remains the fact that the discussion between Hempel and his critics, who largely shared a world, differs markedly from the discussion between either of them and someone from the world generated by *The Structure of Scientific Revolutions.*

In any case, since points of view are essential to worlds *of* individuals but have no place in the natural sciences (henceforward defined by that fact), historical explanation – dealing as it must with points of view – will be different from explanations in the natural sciences, not in terms that the latter entail covering laws and the former do not, but in the kinds of law they respectively entail. But I as yet have too shallow a philosophical understanding of points of view to go further than this here. What I can say is that since points of view are historically indexed, since, that is, the worlds of historical beings are penetrated by their historical locations, the *new* philosophy of history is in effect a new understanding of ourselves as through and through historical.

VOICES

4

Intimate Images: Subjectivity and History – Staël, Michelet and Tocqueville

LINDA ORR

Three images placing the historians themselves in their nineteenth-century histories of the French Revolution continue to haunt me. Madame de Staël, worldly and cranky after her extended exiles, visits with great disdain the salons of Restoration Paris. Michelet, moody and alone, hallucinates revolutionary panoramas on the empty Champs de Mars. Tocqueville, retired from the pressures of politics, cringes in horror at his desk (under a lamp) to see the shape of history emerging before his eyes. These images inform the three nineteenth-century histories like transparencies through which we read the events of the Revolution narrated there. Michelet's self-portrait is deliberate and explicit in his preface of 1847 to the *Histoire de la Révolution française* (1847–53). The image of Staël in her *Considérations sur la Révolution française* (1818) and the presence of Tocqueville in his *L'Ancien Régime et la Révolution* (1856) are not so much implicit as embedded in the narrative situation.

These intimate images have stuck with me because they represent the charged emotional scene or convergence in which the three histories come into being. The scenes are not themselves an empirical cause or origin, not primal scenes, but they figure the place where I as a reader sense that something fundamental is at stake for the subject writing the history. That urgency is often missing in much of contemporary history. Professional historians today often leave unexplored their emotional connection with the historical material they spend so much time and energy studying. My essay on nineteenth-century historians is not a nostalgic return to the past where historians were looser about their forms and more open about their political and personal involvements. Nor is this essay a simple call for more passion in history writing. I am not reversing the old subject/object binary and privileging subjectivity or a selfconscious narrative presence for its own sake. By leaving out the historian's relationship to her or his work, we have left out whole areas of how analytical decisions are made, areas that are crucial in the process of historical thinking – as if we don't see them or they are not worth mentioning. To miss the emotional intensity of the historical operation is to miss a major part of its meaning.

Objectivity is not as effective as it used to be. Or rather, references to the codes of objectivity do not function as well as before. Literary, poetic and rhetorical studies of the historical text have described how the codes of objectivity work. Suppressing all signs of subjectivity is as important as an empirical method or logical argument in the construction of an objective historical text.[1] I mean subjectivity in the broadest sense, related to the linguistic term *énonciation*. Subjectivity refers primarily to the first-person pronoun but, as an act of enunciation or utterance (as opposed to the *énoncé* or strict content, argument or narrative in a text), subjectivity can be anything that clues the reader into a writing, arguing presence. This presence can be an autobiographical 'I' or narrative 'I' with no reference to a real life. A narrative subject, similar to the enunciation, can also refer to the situation of narration: the time and space of writing (e.g. last year), an implicit reader, any evidence of evaluation (I doubt, without a doubt) and any reflection of textual organization (in the above paragraph). In other words, scientific histories must remove all hints of something going on in the wings of the final, smoothly announced product of knowledge.

The story of the historical subject is inseparable from the historical knowledge being produced. Separating subjectivity from objectivity (thus creating the possibility of objectivity) is an arbitrary, if not violent, act. It not only obliterates the narrator in the process but determines the situation of the reader. The reader cannot enter into the process and is reduced to a passive, dependent role. Although scientific history, even the most liberated and qualified kind, appears more definitive than a history mixed with personal uncertainties, that scientific history loses the opportunity to create another kind of authority, more responsive to the complexity of historical thinking. It is worth our while to listen to Staël and Michelet, as well as to Tocqueville, no matter how outlandish the first two sometimes sound. At the very least, they give us a whiff of our own difference that helps us see our impasses and entrenched habits. These nineteenth-century or 'Romantic' historians can joggle us out of our own conformities.

It may appear that I have arranged the three historians in order of their ascending objectivity, in addition to the usual chronological order, culminating in Tocqueville. Staël is supposedly a fiction writer and Michelet writes narrative history. But Tocqueville does analytic or 'problem' history – the first of its kind in the historiography of the French Revolution, according to François Furet.[2] Once I have established this presupposed gradation among them, I will collapse it. In addition to that discredit of writing fiction, Staël is also considered unprofessional because she is supposedly too close to the events. The fact that she was a partisan participant works against her. Michelet's passionate interjections in his own text (*Chose horrible!*)[3] give the impression that he might as well have been present at the events. Tocqueville points up the fact that he is situated at the perfect distance from the events of the Revolution, 'far enough' to judge calmly yet 'close enough' to remember how agitated, grave and important the period was.[4] So Tocqueville was already observing or beginning to institute, for his own purposes, new codes of objectivity. Yet, in the end, his 'I' or subjectivity, no matter how discreet, is just as invasive as Staël's or Michelet's.

Despite their different ranks in history or literature, all three historians display a subject position and appear to assume that this presence of the subject advances, rather than detracts from, the historical argument. They even set up a similar, almost archetypal, portrait of themselves as historians. All three feel overwhelmed by the insurmountable tradition they must overturn. Each complains that she or he is completely alone in the task. No one sees history in the same way as they do – and they believe deeply that they have seen something terribly important, a matter of national and personal life or death. All their energy is put into both the subtle and desperate goal: you must believe me! Their books are not just an account of interesting research. For Staël and Tocqueville especially, these histories are among their last words at the end of their lives.

If I have collapsed the generic and professional distinctions among the three historians and brought out the singleness of their purpose, I also want to emphasize the individual emotional tone and message. Each historian is addressing a particular audience in addition to an unpredictable future readership. Staël looks around her in the Parisian salon of 1814–15 and says, can't you see what has become of yourself since the heyday of the Revolution? Like a prophet, she cries out: look before it's too late and you don't even know what you've lost. Michelet also chides his reader, who senses the uncertainty and agitation of the late bourgeois monarchy, saying, you've forgotten the real Revolution. I have preserved it (in my heart). Let me play it all back grandly for you. Then you'll be so inspired you'll rush out and do it right this time (1848?). Tocqueville sees this horrible thing, the unseen real revolution that no one else has noticed because of the big, blustery one in 1789–94 until that real revolution has become so intertwined with cultural life as to be imperceptible, natural. He can only say: look out! – for what has already happened. Or he gestures: look out! – for whatever is coming.

In her *Considérations sur la Révolution française*, a mélange of memoir, history, political philosophy and travelogue, Madame de Staël herself plays, along with her father and Napoleon, one of the major roles. She uses her first-person pronoun freely and occupies centre stage at several instances, especially during her hair-raising escape from Paris in September 1792. The chapter on the early revolutionary salon is not autobiographical like the escape scene but simply lets a private scene flash by in the midst of the overall narrative. 'It happened to me sometimes, in the spirit of enterprise, to try mixing somewhat the two parties, by having the sharpest men [*les plus spirituels*] of both benches dine together'.[5] Trained in the high cultural tradition of the Parisian salon by her mother, Madame de Staël held her own brilliant social receptions in her living-rooms during the 1791–2 season. By that time her father and mother had again taken the road to exile, and the daughter reached her own pinnacle of power in the limited months that remained to her in Paris. Later, looking back over twenty years of exile in all the corners of Europe, Staël judged these early months of the Revolution as a fragile, almost utopian, time. Liberty had moderated the aristocracy without diminishing its elegance, and the scaffold was not operating yet. On the personal side, her lover the compte de Narbonne was named Minister of War, and the Constitution of 1791 was supposedly composed in part at those extraordinary dinners or gatherings at her house. In her chapter on 'Parisian Society during the Constituent Assembly', she locates that society's brilliance in its free, high-level conversation. Here her observation takes on the (third-person) distance of judgement:

'It was the last time, and in many ways also the first, that Parisian society could give the idea of this communication of superior minds [*esprits*] among themselves, the noblest enjoyment of which human nature is capable' (p. 229).

If Staël's view of the best in French political culture centres on the elitist salon, she singles out women as the reason for the salon's success.

In this chapter on Parisian society, Staël compares the situation of French women more favourably to those of English hostesses, and the reader suspects that she is speaking of herself. 'Women in France directed in their homes almost all the conversations. . . . Discussions of public affairs were therefore softened by them, and combined often with amiable and taunting [*piquantes*] pleasantries' (p. 228). These pleasantries will have their own ambiguous and even tragic history, but at this moment they represent a culmination of individual, feminine, national and international accomplishment and skill. Yet even here, the chapter is framed by the proleptic knowledge that all this glory dies. The first sentence begins: 'Foreigners cannot know how to conceive of the much-touted charm and *éclat* of Parisian society if they have seen France only in the last twenty years' (p. 228). And the chapter ends with a hint of that bile that keeps rising up because at the time of writing Staël sees how the witty, intellectual conversation of women has been ruined (*gâtée*) by the 'sophisms' and 'baseness' (*bassesse*, p. 229) of the now fashionable post-Napoleonic fops.

Madame de Staël must pose the question that provokes a history: what happened? What made them or us end up here from the promise of there? How can I the historian deflect the history that I see towards something different, both reminding me of the lost, preferable past and taking today's conditions into account? For Staël, in the meantime there was Napoleon, her *bête noire*. Napoleon created a suffocating emptiness around his pervasive despotic power. Staël thinks through her body: 'I felt . . . difficulty in breathing which became since then, I think, the sickness of all those who lived under Bonaparte's authority' (p. 358). Here Staël separates out her two selves, the one in the past and the one in the (writing) present. Her past reaction is associated with feeling ('I felt') and her present activity with belief (*je crois*) or judgement, some form of thought. All of these modes of understanding go into the result of the final insight.

When he took power, Bonaparte banished the brilliant Parisian women, banned and seized Madame de Staël's *De l'Allemagne*, and covered over the silence, the cultural void with the noisy journalism of yes-men and hack critics. Madame de Staël had drawn a sinister portrait of silence under foreign occupation: 'As in prison where silence placates the jailers more than complaints you have to be quiet as long as locks have closed down both feeling and thought' (p. 190). But under Napoleon, founder of a modern despotism, the situation was worse: 'Because it is not a question of demanding silence of a nation that needs to be making sentences in whatever way possible. . . . Bonaparte established from then on this chattering tyranny' (p. 368). What hurt Staël the most was her inability to answer back and defend herself against the state-subsidized jibes (p. 419).[6] She was forced into silence. Ironically, Napoleon shut her up by imposing the image of her as the gossipy gadfly.

It was doubly hard, if not impossible, for her to overcome the block that had settled itself into history, as history, obscuring other possible realities.

The following hypothesis that emerges from Staël's history seems incredible: Napoleon repressed all brilliant artistic and intellectual activity around him because he could not succeed in this domain himself. But how can we know? Staël depicts the future military hero as a man yearning to have social graces, and he failed. Back when he tried hard, those champions of repartee, the Parisian women, made fun of him. Had Madame de Staël herself or someone in her salon put him down when he was a gauche, vulgar new Corsican in the big city? 'He retained his old behaviour from during the revolution, a certain Jacobin antipathy against brilliant Parisian society, where women exercised great ascendancy; he feared in them the art of banter [*plaisanterie*]' (p. 386). In Staël's *Considérations* – note this example of her own Parisian style of *plaisanterie* – Napoleon is Molière's ridiculous 'bourgeois gentilhomme'.

But when he had designs on becoming an upstart king, bourgeois gentilhomme on the throne, he exposed himself precisely to the high-toned mockery, and he could not restrain it except as he did, through spies and terror (p. 387).

Staël laughs herself at the incongruity: such overkill to get rid of a 'coalition of two women [herself and Madame Récamier] on the banks of Lake Geneva' (p. 387).

Much was at stake for Madame de Staël in her *Considérations*. Writing, although a different kind of imaginary dialogue, had become the extension of her salon.[7] It was not enough that Napoleon was now the one exiled, at Saint Helena. Staël had to change the whole perception of revolutionary history so she herself would occupy her rightful place as daughter of the Revolution (both literally as Jacques Necker's daughter and metaphorically).[8] She had to convince her public that Napoleon, if any son of the Revolution at all, was the upstart, illegitimate, regicide son who destroyed all the ideals of the true Revolution (as formulated by her father). She also had to dislodge military legend as the stuff of history and get back to or on with history as political reform. A giant ghost was blanking out the history she had to tell: 'It is time that twenty-five years, fifteen of which belong to military despotism, no longer set themselves like a ghost between history and us' (p. 604). The task was enormous, and she would not live to finish writing and assembling the different texts, dating from 1804 to 1816, that make up the *Considérations* (published in 1818).

The rhetorical and emotional intensity of Staël's history reaches a

climax in her last chapter, 'On the Love of Liberty' (or at least these are
the inspired pages which her editors, her son, son-in-law and Schlegel,
put last in the book).⁹ The images of the revolutionary utopia and the
degradation of the present come face to face. Staël can hardly believe
what she sees. Napoleon may be gone but he has left a whole breed of
descendants, what Staël calls, in disgust, *le fat* – the sons of Bonaparte,
shameful and false grandsons of the Revolution. In a seventeen-line
sentence, Staël employs anaphora (the repetition of the when-clause) to
build up to the immense disappointment of the new Parisian social scene:

> When for so many centuries all generous souls have loved liberty; when the
> greatest actions have been inspired by it; when antiquity and the history of
> modern times give us so many prodigious examples carried out by public spirit;
> . . . what is there to say about these most fatuous of little men who declare to you
> in a dull and mannered tone of voice resembling their whole being, that it is in
> very bad taste to care about freedom. . . . Good heavens! what are they thinking
> about, these young men brought up under Bonaparte's regime, for the sole
> purpose of going to war, with no other education, no interest for literature and
> the arts? (p. 602).

Staël aims her critique at the post-revolutionary generation of self-
important, detached yet opportunistic young men. The object of her
satire partly resembles the main character Adolphe in Benjamin
Constant's novel of the same name – or resembles Constant himself. The
novel, written much earlier, was published in 1816, just two years before
Staël's history.¹⁰ Staël's despicable petty characters also anticipate Victor
Hugo's *Napoléon le petit* by over thirty years. Is her vision more
nightmarish than Hugo's or Constant's? In Staël's eyes, Napoleon's fatal
combination of military hero and social *raté* full of resentment created a
proliferation of little Frankensteinian monsters, small-minded men who
were bored and just as indifferent as Napoleon was to human life and to
the important concepts of political freedom – all the values that defined
the meaning of Staël's life. Like so many J. Alfred Prufrocks, the fatuous
men go from waiting-room to drawing-room, that place of past lustre
that has fallen so low:

> 'But what do they want to substitute for politics, that they deign to condemn? A
> few hours spent in the antechamber of ministers . . . a few words in the salons,
> not even up to the level of the women of shallow wit they are talking to. . . . That
> is what is really in bad taste' (p. 602).

Even the women seem to have been contaminated by the historical and
social situation.

This backhanded jibe at the women reminds us that Staël was more

ambiguous towards women than it might appear, and her utopian salon
was, in fact, not perfect. The picture of Staël's desired history has cracks
from the beginning. She admitted that salon conversation could become
snide and petty in the eyes of outsiders, and through her father she was
male-identified enough to turn against the intelligence of women at the
very time she praised them. 'Necker', she noted, 'was too smart not to
unravel these ruses of [women's] conversation which produced no effect
on enlightened and natural intelligence' (p. 101). Besides taking a swipe
at her mother, Staël is incredibly destructive to herself in this sentence.
Marilyn Yalom also has a nuanced, intriguing view of the older Staël as
less heroic:

> In concluding her prodigious memoirs, the author was not above flattering the
> reigning monarch, Louis XVIII, in the hope that flattery would serve the cause of
> liberty and promote some of the early Revolution's lost ideals.[11]

Did Staël have some female *fat* in her?

In the end I hear another voice from Staël which I find chilling because
of its prophetic tone. Staël is passionately trying to shake up her reader
whom she addresses using the second-person pronoun. 'You whom it has
bent down, just hope that at no time, under no prince in whatever form,
[despotism] can ever reach all the way to you' (p. 603). These words have
the modern ring of a Hannah Arendt or Kundera.

Michelet's preface of 1847 to his *Histoire de la Révolution française* is
one of the richest, most suggestive self-portraits of a historian we have in
historical literature. It should be read in any class dealing with the
historian's relation to the historical text. Instead of those sporadic,
rambunctious interventions of the author in his historical narrative,
Michelet's preface lays out a quiet, intimate view of himself as a professor
of history. He takes the reader into his confidence in this reflective, almost
nostalgic moment – so how can the reader resist going along with such a
sympathetic guide and mentor?

> Every year, when I descend from my chair and see the crowd disperse, another
> generation I will not see again, my thoughts turn inward.
> Summer comes on, the city is less populated, the streets less noisy, the
> pavement echoes around my Pantheon. . . .
> I go then to the Champs de Mars and sit down on the dry grass, I breathe in the
> strong breeze wafting across the arid plain (1, p. 1).

Michelet's landscape begins poetically – like Wordsworth's *Prelude* with
a 'gentle breeze' or like Lamartine's 'L'Isolement' in which the poet

surveys the countryside. But Michelet's landscape is rife with the ghosts of history past and the figures of history future. Michelet begins in the founding, symbolic moment where history appears to be empty, where the most crucial moments are left out.

Nothing remains of the French Revolution. Michelet has to build his voluminous history on the desert terrain of this emptiness.

The Champs de Mars! This is the only monument that the Revolution has left. . . . The Empire has its column, and it still took almost for itself alone the Arc de Triomphe; the royalty its Louvre, its Invalides; the feudal church of 1200 is still enthroned at Notre-Dame; nor does it not go back to the Romans, who have Caesar's Baths. And the Revolution has for its monument . . . the void (*le vide*) . . . (Michelet's ellipses, 1, p. 1).

As it turns out, the void is an appropriate monument for the Revolution. Nothing can adequately stand for or even commemorate the Revolution but open space. As Marie-Hélène Huet puts it, Michelet reconstructs 'on the Champs de Mars, the verbal architecture of an inexpressible Revolution'.[12]

The open space, as in Staël, is never really empty or silent. A lacuna is the sign of historical and political repression we can no longer read. Background noise, all kinds of interference covers the repression up so that even the silence is hard to hear. The Champs de Mars served in 1847 as a race track. The race track represents much of what Michelet criticizes in contemporary French life, but despite the distraction, an eerie reminder remains:

Yes, although a forgetful generation dares to take this place as a theatre for its vain amusements, imitated from a foreign country, although the English horse pounds its hoofs insolently against the plain . . . a great breath crosses it that you cannot feel anywhere, a soul, an all-powerful spirit . . . (Michelet's ellipses, 1, p. 1).

The sacred space of the Revolution is occupied by frivolity, just as journalistic gossip covered up resistance in Staël's Napoleonic society. In addition, this frivolity is foreign – English. Michelet was troubled by the fact that France's bourgeois monarchy of 1830 took modern Britain as its uncritical model. Britain denied the poverty resulting from its industrial development and clung to vestiges of aristocratic culture. Under all this, the 'strong breeze' carried the old voices within it – that Michelet alone hears. That breeze is the breath or afflatus of inspiration for his book.

The light wind is not the only reminder of the Revolution on the Champs de Mars, but Michelet has to show the reader, who cannot see

them on his own, two barely perceptible hills that break the flatness of
the plain. The hills provide the barest suggestion of a shape that triggers
Michelet's massive reproduction of the desired historical moment.

Its monument, it is this sand, as flat as Arabia . . . A *tumulus* on the right and a
tumulus on the left, like the ones that Gaul raised up, obscure and dubious
witnesses of the memory of heroes . . . (Michelet's ellipses, 1, p. 1).

The hills are the sacred burial mounds of France's history that span from
the ancient days of Gaul up to the Revolution.

Michelet re-creates from the soil of these symbolic mounds and the
voices in the breeze the bodies of those people who moved the earth and
made 'mountains' in preparation for that miraculous day, the *fête de la
fédération*, 14 July 1790.

For in that soil is deeply mingled the fruitful sweat of their brows who, on a
sacred day, piled up those hills – that day when, aroused by the cannon of the
Bastille, France from the North and France from the South came forward and
embraced – the day when three million men, who rose up as one armed man,
decreed eternal peace (1, p. 2).

Seated on the empty field of the Champs de Mars under the hot sun,
Michelet replays for himself and his readers the pageant, the *son et
lumière* of the Revolution. At the boom of the cannon, the empty
landscape fills with the clamour of different crowds arriving on all sides.
The boisterous, pacific crowd of men, women and children sparkles with
the glimmer of arms, the first makeshift uniforms of the provincial
military federations. All meet in the huge circle dance of the newly unified
nation, 'the immense farandole' (I, p. 423) of all France.

Michelet derives so much pleasure from reliving, resurrecting this
scene, a gesture which marks his pleasure as a historian, that he is doubly
compensated for not having attended the event at the time it occurred. He
gets to go back and relive it, and he gets to re-create the scene as he
desires.

But Michelet discovers, like Staël, that a history of the Revolution must
deal with more than the fugitive space and time of the utopian moment.
(Michelet measured Staël's four months of triumph in his chapter title
'Madame de Staël and Narbonne in Power, December 91 – March 92'.)
Both Staël and Michelet had to stay at the historian's post far beyond
where they thought the real Revolution ended – where it had barely
begun. Moreover, defects in the utopian moment were also there in
Michelet from the beginning: there was no perfect solidarity in Michelet's
circle dance as in the revolutionary women's salon. The weapons of the

armed men on the Champs de Mars foretell of violence and war. Michelet does not refer to the massacre that will occur a year later (1791) in the same spot, but the 'strong breeze' carries those remembrances too. Michelet does attend to the fundamental tragic irony of history – the Revolution he wants to portray does not exist in any of its events, or at least in very few, and those are quickly obscured by the political and historical appropriation of these events.

This utterly peaceful, benevolent, loving character of the Revolution seems today a paradox: so unknown is its origin, so misunderstood its nature, and so obscured its tradition, in so short a time! (1, p. 2).

Without an origin or a tradition, the Revolution Michelet would narrate shrinks to almost nothing. That is why his book is so important. The book stands for the Revolution, incarnates its living spirit. But the book is also obligated to tell the rest of the story, so finally the book itself threatens the fragility of the peaceful Revolution. Both Staël and Michelet, in spite of themselves, end up writing volumes that become monuments to silence and repression.

Michelet knew that the repression of enemies (the bourgeois monarch, the British) was not enough to complete the erasure of the benevolent revolution. An innocent forgetfulness did even more damage to the lost past. A 'forgetful generation' lost touch with the positive meaning of the Revolution and took the Revolution's destructive effects for its real identity. The young generation denied the existence of 'its own father, the great Eighteenth Century!' (I, p. 3). 'Her own tradition escaped from her, [France] forgot herself' (loc. cit.). Michelet had the eighteenth century living with him in his biographical father, so his father's death was a symbolic loss.

I have lost him who so often narrated the scenes of the Revolution to me, him whom I revered as the image and venerable witness of the great century, I mean the XVIIIth (1, p. 8).

Michelet went on to confess that he too was guilty of forgetfulness. But, like Staël who could not see her own subtle misogyny, Michelet never made the explicit connection between the 'forgetful generation' and his own lapsus.

When this [death of my father] happened to me, I was looking off, I was elsewhere, hastily finishing this work, so long the object of my dreams. I was at the foot of the Bastille, I was taking the fortress, I was planting on the towers the immortal flag . . . That blow came upon me, unforeseen, like a shot from the Bastille . . . (Michelet's ellipses, loc. cit.).

While Michelet was off constructing his own Bastille in his book (like Don Quixote's windmills), history was happening beside him, in his own house. History or the writing of history kept Michelet from seeing History. He got distracted by his own resurrections; he had his own race course. Neither Michelet nor Staël admitted their own complicity in the betrayal of the desired revolution.

In various passages of his preface of 1847, Michelet hints that the empty plain of the Champs de Mars will fill up again. The success of his whole history depends on his bringing back the life of that sterile place. 'And if this plain is arid, and if this grass is dry, it will grow green one day' (I, p. 2). Michelet does not specify what he means, but evokes, like Staël and Tocqueville, the principle of freedom. 'It is again through freedom that our time, awakened, recalled to its true tradition, will be able in its turn to begin its work' (I, p. 5). Michelet believed that education would act as the 'initiation' into a society of love and liberty, and this belief played up his own contribution as a professor. When Michelet wrote his preface, he was also preparing the lessons that would get his class suspended in 1848. He kept writing the lessons anyway, and they were eventually published in 1877 as *L'Etudiant*. In these lectures, Michelet designated university students as the new revolutionary class.[13]

The preface of 1847 may mark the end of the school year, but Michelet is already aroused by the reality of that new generation which will pour into his amphitheatre the next autumn. Murmuring, agitated, the students pressed together in anticipation of the luminous appearance of their evangelistic republican professor.[14] Did his lectures hasten the second coming of the Revolution, 1848? Michelet is like Whitman in *Crossing Brooklyn Ferry*, conjuring up before him the festive audiences of the future. The student throng unfolds itself, a palimpsest, over the race-track fans and over the revolutionary crowd: behind them or foregrounding them all, the ever-present, brooding professor, orchestrating past, present and future from his place on the empty Champs de Mars.

Tocqueville is not present in his narrative as an actor like Staël in her history of the Revolution, nor does he intrude himself passionately into the narrative like Michelet. Tocqueville's easy essayist first-person pronoun slips in and out of his analytical discourse with a tone of familiarity. That first person often promotes a self-image of the historian at work. The historian owes his authority as much to that mythico-professional image of himself as to his analysis and sources.

The 'I'-saturated preface of Tocqueville's text sets up the self-portrait:

> I have undertaken to penetrate up to the heart of this Old Regime, so close to us by the number of years, but that the Revolution hides from us. To succeed at this, I have not only reread the well-known books . . . I have wanted to study numerous works less known, less worthy of being so. (pp. 44–5).

So far the metaphor of penetrating the heart barely stands out, and Tocqueville merely portrays himself as a diligent researcher. He outlines his most important archival references: the debates of the state and provincial assemblies, the records of the public administration, and especially the *cahiers* of the three orders preceding the Estates General. The public administration is personified by an *elle* who knows and sees all 'interests' and 'passions' that strip themselves (*se montrer à nu*, p. 45) in *her* presence, revealing to her alone 'the most secret infirmities' (p. 46). Into such a charged, even sexual scene, the 'I' returns:

> There, as I expected, I found the Old Regime completely alive . . . because I had under my eyes what had never been released to [their contemporaries'] gaze. . . . I saw little by little uncover itself before my eyes all the physiognomy of this Revolution (p. 48).

If the reader can get beyond the echoes of Michelet,[15] a gesture that is totally Tocqueville's emerges. This repeats itself throughout the book in different pieces and forms and in at least one developed scene focuses on his reading of the prized *cahiers*.

The image of the historian doing research ('I found that', p. 220; 'When I researched . . . the archives of the intendance', p. 117; 'I read the letter', (p. 219) is supplemented by every other function of enunciation. The 'I' proliferates in Tocqueville's text, giving substantive commentary and taking a more formulaic stance, where 'I' does not seem to have a function other than calling attention to itself ('I do not think that', p. 267; 'I confess that', p. 270; 'I am not exaggerating', p. 261). The numerous examples of the 'I' as manipulator of the text (managerial functions) accentuate the continual relationship between writer and reader ('I said that elsewhere', p. 312; 'Now if you [*on*] would please consider', p. 304; 'I am getting to the facts', p. 229). It is as if Tocqueville were there all the time, yet not there. The most astounding instance of this reference to the self comes in the last paragraph of the book where the narrator says *Me voici* and then leaves the reader hanging: 'Here I am having arrived all the way up to the threshold of this memorable revolution; I will not enter here at this time' (p. 321). If the reader has not understood by now, Tocqueville must think there is no more that he can do.

Tocqueville's task as a historian, as he saw it, was hard, if not impossible. He had to penetrate through an even larger, immovable block of repression or silence than either Staël or Michelet, and the reference point of Tocqueville's history, its desired or utopian object which justified all the rest, was more illusive than Staël's 1791 salon or Michelet's *fête*.

A new, social form, 'simple, regular and grandiose' (p. 66), began to arise back in the Old Regime, becoming even stronger and widespread through the Revolution and post-revolutionary years until by the time of the Second Empire everyone took it for granted. The noise and self-propaganda of the Revolution hid this quieter, deeper change so that no one (but Tocqueville, eventually) saw it coming.

Out of the very entrails of a nation which had just thrown royalty over, all of a sudden one saw rise up a power more extended, detailed, absolute than those which any king had exercised (p. 319).

The new power derived from the centralized state and the institutions which extended its control. Tocqueville could recognize this power because he consciously located his historical point of view in the present of the Second Empire. But that situation in the present meant that he was a witness to the long advance of repression that composed modern history. 'The art of suffocating the noise of all resistance was then [eighteenth century] a lot less perfected than today' (pp. 199–200). This difficulty in breathing recalls the sensation Staël felt during the First Empire. For Tocqueville, as for Michelet on his Champs de Mars, history consisted of a blank space: 'It [central power in France] already managed to destroy all the intermediary powers, and . . . between it and particulars there no longer exists anything but an immense and empty space' (p. 141). The 'particulars' or whatever escaped the growing blank space were hard to see. We say today that Tocqueville refers back to the community and organic laws of feudal political culture, but the historian is reluctant in his text to fill in the effaced figure or 'last trace' (p. 148) of a lost era with categories of explanation. These mysterious traces hold the secret to renewing freedom.[16]

In order to overturn a monolith of historical blindness more extensive than anyone had ever imagined, Tocqueville needs the help of his image as a historian. Was that strategy conscious or not? As a result, Tocqueville's text does what would still be considered non-traditional in historical practice today – it integrates the historian's own process into the analytical narrative. In *The Secret Mirror*, L. E. Shiner emphasizes the ambition of Tocqueville's 'revisionism' that had to make a 'decisive break' with the prevalent interpretation of the Revolution. Shiner writes:

This discourse of "revision" or "disclosure" . . . is most often characterized by either a simple opposition to the received view or is marked by the use of a first-person voice to introduce the sources that have shown Tocqueville what is going on beneath the surface.[17]

The historian has set up the rhetoric of surface through which he can then penetrate to find the heart. The phrase 'before my eyes' ('I had before my eyes') sharpens the picture of the historian consulting his documents, or even better – the phrase, 'in my hands'. 'I am holding the facts in my hands' (p. 297; see also pp. 216 and 288). Touch makes the sources more real and his relation to them more solid. *L'Ancien régime et la Révolution* is not Arlette Farge's *Le goût de l'archive*, but the personal representation of the historical activity lends an authenticity to the argument that the sources could not alone elicit. This rhetorical strategy is as much another 'source of historical representation', to use Hans Kellner's words,[18] as the reality to which the documents refer.

In the case of the *cahiers* of the three orders, the experience of reading develops into its own little scene. The everyday details of sitting reading the archives take on a hallucinatory quality. 'I' appears seven times in the first lines of the paragraph:

I am attentively reading the *cahiers* that the three orders draw up before assembling in 1789; I say the three orders, those of the nobility and clergy, as well as that of the third estate. I see that they demand a change here in the law, there in practice, and I take note of this. I continue this tremendous work in such a way until the end, and when I come to pulling together all the separate declarations [*voeux*], I see with a kind of terror that what they ask for is the simultaneous and systematic abolition of all the laws and practices in use in the country; I see immediately that it is going to be a question of one of the most vast and dangerous revolutions that has ever appeared in the world. Those who will tomorrow be its victims know nothing about it. . . . The unfortunate ones! (p. 236).

More surprising than the narrator's present tense is the collapse of researching or writing present and revolutionary past. The time of the *énonciation* parallels the time of the *énoncé*.[19] Such a fantasy puts the historian in place, reading the right documents, before or as the events occur. He (alone) sees the monstrous concurrence that is preparing to take place and befall the unsuspecting population. This retrospective foresight or anachronism does not, unfortunately, change the historian's tragedy. There is still no power to warn the victims. This cursed visionary talent resonates throughout Tocqueville's text with the many repetitions of what seems to be simple variations of the phrase 'I see'. For instance: 'I suddenly see [*j'aperçois*] a glacial body, more compact and homogeneous than any that had perhaps ever been seen in the world before' (p. 153). The historian resembles the seer (echoes of Michelet or Hugo) as well as the dogged scholar.

The above passage has all the more chilling effect on the reader because it suggests that the general status of historical understanding is a constant 'Slouching towards Bethlehem to be Born'.[20] The twentieth-century reader is convinced that Tocqueville was right about the nineteenth-century state and society, and this modern reader knows how still more frightening terrors have yet to arise in apparently unprepared societies with more unsuspecting victims. The reader wonders what imperceptible change has already occurred in time which cannot be read and which will only become visible to the historian working through whatever evidence in horror and disbelief half a century later.

Shiner makes the association between Tocqueville's revisionary and visionary discourses: 'The discourse of commentary and wisdom . . . itself re-visions the Second Empire' (p. 187). Shiner wonders how liberty can possibly seem feasible in the face of these historical meditations on the long, invisible change. But Tocqueville implies (as Michelet did before him) that freedom is irreducible to easy causes; 'irregular' and 'deformed' (p. 204), it revives when least expected. Does Tocqueville's text let the reader off leaning into the abyss of the revolution that never comes because that is our symbolic relationship to history? A last irony has struck me about Tocqueville's strategy as a historian. Describing himself as a statesman, he reviled the man of letters (in the very chapter with the scene of reading the *cahiers*). He criticized the literary men for their superficial treatment of complex problems. But in *L'Ancien régime et la Révolution* the representation of the narrator doing literary activities is inseparable from the analysis put forth.

The reader of these three nineteenth-century histories has the personal, if not intimate, sense of a persona, a narrator involved in the process of coming to terms with a traumatic history. The historians appear as individuals in everyday situations, 'real people' (a rhetorical construction like any other): a woman giving dinner parties, a tired professor still affected by the death of his father, an independent researcher behind his stacks of folios. One of the most moving aspects of these three texts is their personal *longue durée*. The historians feel old. They are meditating on their own lives as they examine history. Their histories are attempts to 'work through', as Dominick LaCapra would call it,[21] nostalgia, frustrations and renewed desire for change. These nineteenth-century historians have not yet learnt to repress what later codes of objectivity say get in the way of an argument; they readily reveal a nervousness, a reliance on the reaction of the reader.

But subjectivity is not desirable in the historical text solely because it exposes the workings of historical reasoning. A radical, intimate impulse is what gave the historians their thesis in the first place. A trust in their subjectivity allowed them to strike through the overwhelming evidence of tradition that implied they must be crazy. Subjectivity provided these historians with their insight and gave them the ability to persist beyond the odds. They saw shocking revelations in the same document where others saw nothing of the kind. Who would believe Staël against Napoleon? After years of terror and backlash, who would believe the business in Michelet about a peaceful, loving Revolution? What was this idea in Tocqueville suggesting that the Revolution did not really exist?

Each historian spoke both as the lonely, beleaguered voice in the wilderness and sometimes – what also produced their conviction – as the mythic voice of a broad, almost timeless constituency. Staël was the voice of a liberalism that was older, she insisted, than despotism; Michelet appealed to his readers as if they were both one and the same, a part of the people, the true subject of history. Tocqueville spoke in the name of those ancient practices, almost beyond the tomb, which were silently being wiped out. These historians had both the greatest and slimmest authority; they stood on the most solid and slippery ground. Objectivity makes it appear that the reader is dispensable; subjectivity shows that the historian needs the reader's validation, now and hereafter.

In *Poetics of the New History: French Historical Discourse from Braudel to Chartier*, Philippe Carrard comes up with a paradoxical conclusion about twentieth-century history. The New Historians are beginning to slip and use more of those forbidden stylistic traits associated with Romanticism. But these same historians do not articulate the epistemological consequences of their new, almost furtive, practices. These modern French historians resort to broad narrative structures, *tableaux*, figurative language, varying points of view, and even the once-banished 'I'. Carrard calls this renewed reference to the enunciation 'the subjectivization of commentary'.[22] He notes a 'return to some of Michelet's textual machineries and to the attitudes which they inscribe' (p. 103). Instead of opening the way for a re-examination of positivist conventions, the more daring historians, like Le Roy Ladurie and Duby, are playfully asserting their independence that comes from succeeding in a field they do not want to challenge too much. Carrard is wittily sympathetic to what he calls the New Historian's timidity when confronted with the reality of the subject position:

The now commonplace argument that knowledge is always grounded in a subject keeps being made in the human sciences (and in this very sentence) through a rhetoric which signals the researcher's reluctance to leave marks of his involvement (p. 104).

Subjectivity is scary. More than timidity, it evokes anxiety. The 'Triangular Anxieties', that Hans Kellner saw threatening the historical profession (Marxism, psychoanalysis and structuralism)[23] shift and multiply. The consequences for the practice of history are often the same: epistemological challenges imply a loss of professional and personal value and identity. Is history more precautious when threatened by outside disciplines because history occupies a symbolic spot in our culture, maintaining our minimal, provisional truths? Writing this essay, I too experienced anxiety. I worried that I brought nothing to the subject but three charming images going nowhere. I was banking on that nagging feeling these images produced within me. Surely these images would tell me something I needed to know.

Among the human sciences, the fields of literary criticism and anthropology seem to have opened more readily to the challenge of subjectivity. (Natural science is also incorporating self-reflexivity into its methods, e.g. the work of Humberto Maturana or Stephen Jay Gould.) In literary criticism, feminism and later the politics of diversity have inspired what has become a critical movement. A kind of hybrid writing – autobiographical and analytical – has grown up (e.g. Nancy K. Miller, Marianne Hirsch, Alice Kaplan, Susan Suleiman) which attempts to renew agency and responsibility without losing the postmodern critique of the centred psychological subject. This hybrid writing, as expected or feared, has brought problems to our profession as an institution and as individuals. In literary criticism, for instance, we do not have predetermined criteria for judging 'personal criticism'. Such writing forces us to step back and examine our own presupposed standards and categories of evaluation. Upon what are they based?

The fear of blurred categories and unpredictable judgements affect a broader public beyond academic disciplines. The anxiety of a larger breakdown arises. Non-fiction and journalism use techniques from the novel (Joe McGinnis's *The Last Brother*), and the novel uses a current or historical event (Joyce Carol Oates's *Black Water*). Readers are confused and do not know what to think. For me, these writing strategies at the edges of different genres expose how we arrive at our personal, professional and national truths and give us a more complex appreciation of what is involved in the process. Such an appreciation can only enhance, not diminish, authority, even if each one of us is challenged to come to grips with her or his own ways of making ethical, political and epistemological decisions.

The work of French philosopher-historian, Jacques Rancière (*La Nuit des prolétaires*, 1981) suggests to me a constant self-searching investigation through historical writing. Rancière almost never uses the first person, but every moment of his study puts the historian as intellectual, i.e. Rancière himself, in question. Binaries fluctuate – thinker and worker, historical subject and historical objects (or rather subjects?[24]), language and silence – and in the 'difficult meeting'[25] that takes place, sometimes a 'voice' (p. 23), this other voice blended with one's own, is heard. 'The result is not scepticism but a certain kind of knowledge. It is empty knowledge, if you will, promising no mastery' (p. 18). Why not call a constantly renegotiated, painfully critical, passionate exchange between 'equal' subjects – knowledge, neither empty nor full?

Many forms of research and writing are waiting to be elaborated. The definition of narrative has expanded incredibly to become the structures in which we are obliged to think in general, and this narrative has rightly been criticized for its cultural totalizing power (Hayden White, Sande Cohen). But the other possibilities are not opportunities for playfulness within absolute limits. All kinds of possibility exist that are being initiated and will evolve – shifting an emphasis to process, looking back to one's own sequence of questions, not repressing where research has gone wrong, going into those impasses, writing about impasses, using fiction or scientific metaphor, folding in autobiography. This invitation to formal innovation interests me now as much as the questions of historical epistemology that used to preoccupy me. Unconventional forms of historical writing can work back and change someday the professional institution and its codes of authority.

Michelet felt strongly: 'The historian who . . . undertakes to erase himself while writing, to not be, . . . is not a historian at all'.[26] If Michelet is still too strident for us to hear in our states of anxiety, it is enough to remember whatever it was – a person, an event, 'chance', desire? – that made you a historian in the first place.[27]

5

Theory of a Practice:
Historical Enunciation and the Annales *School*

PHILIPPE CARRARD

French linguists, theorists and literary critics have often regarded historical discourse as constituting the objective pole of representation. They have described it as a discourse in which nobody speaks, or at least in which signs of enunciation have been carefully effaced. Emile Benveniste, for instance, draws on a piece of historiography (an excerpt from Glotz's *Histoire grecque*) to provide an example of *histoire* ('story'): the mode of communication in which events are reported 'as they occurred' and 'seem to be telling themselves outside the presence of a narrator'.[1] Roland Barthes makes similar assumptions when he identifies the basic features of what he takes to be 'the discourse of history'. In the area of enunciation, Barthes argues, such discourse functions without a speaker: promoting an 'objective subject', it seeks to cancel the 'emotional subject'.[2] Historians, therefore, cannot refer to themselves except in two types of utterance: the 'testimonials', where they may mention their authority for stating what they are stating, as in 'to my knowledge' or 'as I have heard'; and the 'discourse organizers', where they may point to other moments in the text, as in 'as I have said earlier' or 'I shall say no more on the subject'.[3] This erasure of enunciation, according to Barthes, contributes to the powerful reality-effect of historiography. Historical texts appear to be direct, unmediated representations of past events – representations that bypass the signified and provide direct access to the referent.

French textbooks present similar views when they take up the subject of historical enunciation. Whether they come in the form of introductions to the 'historical method' or of general guides to the proper way of writing up research in the human sciences, they generally instruct scholars to refrain from intervening personally in their texts. To begin with, according to these manuals, historians should avoid writing in the first-person singular. As French classicism has it, 'le moi est haïssable' ('"I" is despicable'), all the more so when this first person is a student's or a young scholar's whose personality is not 'entirely formed'. 'I', therefore, must give way to the more 'elegant' and (in French) more humble 'we', as well as to 'impersonal' ways of situating oneself.[4] More generally, historians should be careful not to exceed what Bernadette Plot calls the 'threshold of tolerance to subjectivity' in scholarly discourse.[5] Subjectivity, according to her, is acceptable in places where researchers describe their project or evaluate their data. But 'expressive traces' of the author's position must be eliminated when they take the form of 'polemical' and 'ironic' utterances. Indeed, such utterances are no longer situated on the true/false axis of 'scientific' search for knowledge; they are on the good/bad axis, and their authors commit the cardinal sin (for scholars) of 'investing themselves ideologically' in their research.[6]

Theorists and pedagogues, therefore, seem to bring the same assumptions when they consider history writing. Whether they look at such writing descriptively or prescriptively, they make it into a monolithic activity and one that exhibits essential features. Thus, as unlikely a foundationalist as Barthes seems to presume that there is such a thing as a 'discourse of history'. His title 'Le Discours de l'histoire' already implies the homogeneity of the object under consideration, as does the label 'historian' which he confers upon writers as disparate as Herodotus, Machiavelli, Bossuet and Michelet. Julia Kristeva proceeds similarly in her attempt to extend Bakhtin and map out a 'typology of discourses'. Indeed, she posits the existence of 'historical discourse', which she places with 'epic narrative' and 'scientific discourse' in the category 'monologic discourse': the texts that report everything from an impersonal viewpoint and do not enter into a dialogue with other texts.[7] As for authors of handbooks, they believe that there is a single, correct method of doing history. Using impersonal ways of writing is part of that method, and historians had better suppress all traces of enunciation if they want to turn out 'good' work.

I want to argue that the enunciator, however, is not necessarily erased in historical texts, and that his/her overtness is in fact a major trademark of present French historiography, especially of the *Annales* school. To be sure, the description of history writing as 'speakerless' is not ungrounded. But such a description does not originate in a review of current practices. Rather, it seems to be a legacy of positivism, more precisely of the conception of history which Charles-Victor Langlois and Charles Seignobos put forth in their influential *Introduction aux études historiques* (1898), and which Ernest Lavisse sought to implement in editing the monumental *Histoire de France* (1900–22). Langlois and

Seignobos, indeed, thought that one of the basic features of history writing was 'objectivity'.[8] They were thus scornful of Thierry, Michelet and other Romantic historians, whom they blamed for indulging in colourful, subjective evocations of the past at the expense of 'scholarly rigour'.[9] Along the same lines, they condemned German historians like Mommsen, Droysen, Curtius and Lamprecht for seeking to move their audience with 'personal, patriotic, moral, or metaphysical considerations'.[10] Such considerations, according to Langlois and Seignobos, were inappropriate in scholarly discourse, as was any sign of the researcher as artist or ideological subject. Historians had to report the facts only, and they were in violation of both the rhetoric and the deontology of their discipline if they left marks of their presence.

Whether the ideal which Langlois and Seignobos proposed in the *Introduction* was attained – and whether it is attainable at all – is of course open to question. Texts that claim to be objective and free from ideology are among the easiest to 'deconstruct', and critics like Guy Bourdé, Hervé Martin and Dominique Maingueneau have feasted on Lavisse's *Histoire de France* as well as on its public-school digest, the *Petit Lavisse*.[11] My point, however, is not that positivist historians have been unfaithful to their own programme. Rather, it is that 'history' is heterogeneous, both as a branch of knowledge and as a discursive practice. It has itself a history, as Pierre-Olivier Carbonell, Lionel Gossman and William R. Keylor have argued in recent studies of French historiography.[12] The rules which Langlois and Seignobos laid down in the late nineteenth century, therefore, should not be taken as eternal and universal: they are the signs of a dissatisfaction with what these historians perceived as the looser standards of their predecessors, and they point to the concerns of a discipline which was just establishing itself in the academic community at that time. The enunciative procedures advocated in the *Introduction*, in particular, do not denote some essential, atemporal feature of historiography. Langlois and Seignobos devised them to address what was in their eyes an urgent need of their discipline: the need to set boundaries, in this instance between history and literature on the one hand, 'scientific' history and slacker forms of research on the other. Historians of the eighteenth and nineteenth centuries, however, followed different conventions, and their writings would provide poor examples of 'historical discourse'. As for contemporary historians, if they still observe positivist regulations in such domains as the processing of documents, they no longer obey the positivist code in the area of enunciation. They have adopted different habits, and the works of the *Annales* school supply conspicuous examples of this discursive development.

'I' FOREGROUNDED

Annales historians, as critics often lament, have shown little interest in theoretical issues that concern the epistemology and poetics of their discipline. Thus, they have hardly participated in discussions about historical discourse, leaving to linguists and literary critics the responsibility for deciding – among other things – whether such a discourse can function without a speaker. When they have made statements on the topic of their presence in their research, these statements have tended to reinforce a certain non-critical view of 'objectivity'. Fernand Braudel, for example, writes in the introduction to *L'Identité de la France* that although he 'loves' his country, he will keep this feeling 'carefully out of the way'. Historians, according to him, must 'purge themselves' of the 'passions' originating in their 'social positions', 'experience', 'explosions of indignation', 'infatuations', and the 'multiple insinuations of their time', a feat which Braudel – with his usual optimism – thinks he is 'able to accomplish quite decently'.[13] Similarly, though in somewhat drier language, Marc Ferro insists in the preface to his *Pétain* (a biography of the marshal) that historians must 'preserve, clarify, analyse and diagnose', but 'never judge'.[14] As for François Furet, he proclaims from the first pages of *Penser la Révolution française* that the subject 'Revolution' can be studied anew only if 'disinvested', or in Levi-Straussian terms 'cooled down': the historian's motivation should be 'intellectual curiosity', as well as a desire to pursue 'the free activity of knowing the past'.[15]

These pronouncements clearly bear the trace of some of the polemics which have dominated the intellectual scene in France since the end of World War II, pointing in these instances to the controversies about nationalism and its potential dangers (Braudel), the assessment of the Vichy period (Ferro) and the value of Marxism as a political system and an interpretative tool (Furet). However, if these programmatic declarations make – given their context – legitimate cases for scholarly aloofness, they do not address in a theoretical manner the issue of writing from a neutral standpoint. For one thing, their authors take 'objectivity' to mean, as it did for Langlois and Seignobos, 'lack of partisanship', not 'independence from a cognitive subject'. They do not seem – with the possible exceptions of Furet and Paul Veyne – to be aware of Raymond Aron's work on the epistemology of the social sciences, nor of German and Anglo-Saxon research on the same topic. More precisely, *Annales* historians do not stop to consider how they can claim on the one hand – as Furet does in one of the school's best-known manifestos – to be moving from 'narrative history' to 'problem history',[16] that is to an admittedly more subjective communicative practice, while maintaining on the other hand that they can still absent themselves from their research. If, as Ferro puts it in a sentence which summarizes the two (conflicting) agendas, historians are now to 'analyse, clarify and diagnose', how can they perform these tasks without leaving traces of their presence as subjects? In other words, how can they abandon narrative and dissect problems (in Benveniste's terminology go from 'story' to 'discourse') while remaining absent from their texts as enunciators?

The answer is that they cannot. And readers who take up works of the *Annales* with an eye on these texts' rhetoric will immediately notice a recurrent feature: the overt presence of the enunciator, starting with numerous instances of the first-person singular. Indeed, such classics of the *Annales* as Braudel's *La Méditerranée*, Alain Corbin's *Le Miasme et la jonquille*, Georges Duby's *Le Dimanche de Bouvines*, Jean-Louis Flandrin's *Un Temps pour embrasser*, Emmanuel Le Roy Ladurie's *Montaillou* and Michel Vovelle's *La Mort et l'Occident* do what positivist historiography was not allowed to do and current handbooks still strongly denounce: they openly display the 'I' of the historian, together with the 'me', 'my' and 'mine'. Furthermore, they do not restrict these occurrences to sanctioned places like prefaces and footnotes. Pronouns and adjectives of the first person can be found throughout the text, and they refer to an enunciator who fulfils a whole range of functions.

This enunciator may initially perform the tasks of a commentator. Even hard-core positivist historiography shifts frequently from 'story' to 'discourse', as data do not speak for themselves, cannot produce meaning on the sole basis of their chronological arrangement, and must be interpreted to become intelligible. One of the major characteristrics of the *Annales* is the invasion of the text by commentary, and large sections of the works which Lawrence Stone takes to be examples of that school's 'return' to narrative (like Duby's *Le Dimanche de Bouvines* and Le Roy Ladurie's *Le Carnaval de Romans* are in fact devoted to extended discussions of the events.[17] Yet commentaries come in many guises, including the form of utterance that remains non-personalized and presents itself as shared knowledge of a specific subject matter. What is most interesting in the texts of the *Annales*, from this viewpoint, is the occurrence of many signs of the commentator where these signs could have been easily circumvented. Thus, when Furet states 'if Tocqueville never wrote a true history of the French Revolution, it seems to me [*il me semble*] that it is because he conceptualized only part of this history, that of continuity',[18] the 'to me' explicitly locates the explanation for the particularity of Tocqueville's endeavour in the historian as subject of the enunciation. But Furet could have written, as handbooks recommend,[19] 'it seems that', thus transferring the responsibility for the explanation to a community of observers of which he is only one. The observation would then have appeared more self-evident and more autonomous in relation to the historian.

This process of subjectivization of commentary is particularly noticeable in the large collective undertakings in which the *Annalistes* have been involved of late, that is in works whose authors could be expected to obliterate marks of their presence and play the part of self-effacing coauthors. *Le Moyen-Age*, Duby's contribution to the multi-volume *Histoire de France* published in 1987–8 by Hachette, is a case in point. Indeed, while describing the period, Duby makes himself directly accountable for many statements which he could have presented as originating in shared views about the matter he is discussing. He thus writes 'I am tempted to believe in the positive effects of a change in the relations of kinship'; 'But what interests me is the way that people in the past imagined things'; and – upon mentioning that for many specialists the modern state began between 1280 and 1360 – 'I claim that this beginning came earlier, at the threshold of the thirteenth century'.[20] Similarly, he on several occasions uses such phrases as 'in my eyes': 'I am not convinced'; 'I am inclined to think'; 'I deem it necessary'; and – like Furet – 'it seems to me'.[21] True, these utterances do not effect a high level of subjectivity. And yet *Le Moyen-Age* is offered as a reference work, that is as a text which is supposed to provide a synthetic overview of a period rather than an individual's interpretation of it. The enunciator's overtness tends to blur the distinction between the textbook and the essay, a confusion which would have been unthinkable in such collective endeavours of positivism as Lavisse's *Histoire de France*.

The presence of the enunciator in many texts of the *Annales* is also foregrounded in utterances that bear on the process of research. In his review of Veyne's *Comment on écrit l'histoire*, Michel de Certeau noted that one of the most promising characteristics of recent historiography was the 'resurrection' of the 'I' of the historian as researcher. He gave as examples 'extended prefaces' like Le Roy Ladurie's in *Paysans de Languedoc* and Pierre Vilar's in *La Catalogne dans l'Espagne moderne*, in which historians told both the story of the 'object' under investigation and that of the 'subject' who had undertaken the inquiry.[22] Yet prefaces (introductions, forewords, etc) are paratextual spaces where scholars have traditionally been allowed to express themselves in the first person. The pieces to which de Certeau refers thus make full use of an existing convention. But they do not really inaugurate a new one, as even positivist historians turned to the first person when introducing their project or commenting on their evidence in footnotes.

Applied to all four parts in *Paysans*, however, de Certeau's rhetorical mode of reading uncovers something more unusual. Indeed, Le Roy Ladurie sometimes displays himself as a researcher not in the paratext but in the text itself, where he plays the part of what Robert Scholes and Robert Kellog call a '*histor*': a narrator who is also an 'inquirer, constructing a narrative on the basis of such evidence as he has been able to accumulate'.[23] In *Paysans de Languedoc*, the enunciator as *histor* occasionally describes how he has been working in (and with) the archives, stating for example: 'From a list, I extract the most significant episodes'; 'I find again this demographic uprooting'; and 'in the sixteenth century, I note three main categories of signatures in notarial documents'.[24] Similarly, Le Roy Ladurie clarifies at times how he has generated the many numerical figures scattered throughout his study. Updating the role of the *histor*, he thus writes: 'I count 540 of them'; 'I therefore compiled'; and 'If I convert the price into gold'.[25] The historian even makes use of his occasional experience as an eye-witness, supplementing his depiction of southern France during the Old Regime with direct observation, for example: 'These wells can still be found and I have seen a few of them in the scrubland near Montpellier': and 'There are still fires in this area and on February 15th, 1958, I saw the Causses burn on all sides'.[26] True, these interventions of the *histor* are not systematic: it would be difficult to include with each piece of information a history of how this information was obtained – and to do so in the text itself. But such utterances as 'I note' and 'I count' still testify to the increasing presence of the first person in historical discourse, as well as to major changes in the rules which had previously determined the distribution of the data between the text and the paratext in that same discourse.

The *Annalistes*, finally, commit at times what positivist theory regarded as the ultimate sin and current writing guides still sternly condemn: they take sides, not only commenting upon their material in an academic manner (as Duby and Furet do with their polite 'I think' and 'it seems to me'), but actually expressing strong individual beliefs, feelings and opinions. These intrusions of the 'emotional subject', as Barthes calls it, take on different forms and vary widely in range. Women historians, for example, generally eschew the first person, and they tend to describe with great scholarly restraint customs which they find unjust, revolting or downright barbaric. Thus, Yvonne Knibielher and Catharine Fouquet intervene with discretion in their *Histoire des mères*, leaving to typographical devices like exclamation marks the task of indicating that there is something peculiar (usually something outrageous) in the situation which they describe. These exclamation marks often amount to a 'how + adjective' that comments on the utterance: in the nineteenth century, doctors (and Michelet) still claimed that because of their cycle women were 'destined to motherhood!' (i.e. how backward!); during the same period, a priest conducting an investigation in the country had obtained 'the confession of thirty-two infanticides!' (i.e. how bad was the condition of unwillingly pregnant women!); the mother was 'one of the pillars of rural society' during the Old Regime, 'but at the price of what fatigue, of what deprivation, of what anguish!' (i.e. how high was that price!).[27] Although these examples do not contain any 'I', they point to the existence of an enunciator. Indeed, the exclamation marks noticeably alter the nature of the utterances which they punctuate, transforming them from 'assertions of' to 'reactions to'. One can, as a test, substitute periods in the preceding quotations and measure the difference. If the change does not totally erase the trace of the emotional subject, it unquestionably tones it down and brings the utterances closer to assertions of what merely 'is'. Handbooks, for that matter, advise against exclamation marks, on the grounds that they inscribe too sharply the 'affectivity of the author'.[28]

Annales historians, however, may also express personal opinions with much more brutal directness, particularly when they comment on what they deem to be acts of violence or injustice against the oppressed. The *Annaliste* who most provocatively discards the conventions of scholarly reserve is probably Le Roy Ladurie, especially in *Montaillou* and *Le Carnaval de Romans*. Indeed, these books openly support the underprivileged, while they attack the establishment (the Clergue family in Montaillou, the ruling class in Romans) with utmost ferocity. The historian's interventions can be expressly grounded in an 'I', as when Le Roy Ladurie writes: 'The performance of the lower classes in Grenoble,

Vienne and Romans leaves me astounded. Admiring.'[29] But they can also come in the form of what some linguists call 'subjectivemes' (after 'phoneme', 'sememe', 'morpheme', etc), that is of words that contain one or several 'evaluative features'.[30] Le Roy Ladurie clearly draws on negative subjectivemes when he labels the upper class in Romans a 'clique' and a 'mafia', and when he describes its leader – Judge Guérin – as an 'evil genius', a 'character from a detective novel', a 'specialist in low blows', a 'Tartuffe' and finally a 'Machiavelli' who has plotted from the start to use the carnival for crushing the lower classes.[31]

Le Roy Ladurie draws on a similarly value-laden vocabulary to comment on Guérin's account of the events, that is one of the main sources for reconstructing what happened in the town during the carnival of 1590. For he speaks of 'malicious exaggeration', of 'laughable' and 'ridiculous' expressions, charges the judge with 'inventing' certain statements attributed to people and intersperses quotations from Guérin's report with parentheses containing derogatory remarks and the 'sic' of disapproval.[32] Le Roy Ladurie, therefore, goes much beyond the 'internal criticism' of the evidence which Langlois and Seignobos had made an obligatory step in historical research; he seeks to discredit Guérin's testimony, and he does so with a vehemence and a deliberateness which openly violate the ban on 'emotional' statements in scholarly discourse. *Le Carnaval de Romans* thus tends to blur the lines between the essay and academic writing just as Duby's *Le Moyen-Age* does. In this instance, the rhetorical usages of French journalism (which distinguishes less sharply between information and editorials than American journalism) creep into a scholarly endeavour, since Le Roy Ladurie uses the same tone and enunciative procedures in a text conceived for the very serious *Bibliothèque des histoires* as he does in one of his contributions to *L'Express* or *Le Nouvel Observateur*.

CIRCUMVENTING THE FIRST PERSON

If several important works of the *Annales* school are characterized by the overtness of their enunciator, this overtness does not always have the same form nor the same scope. As far as pronouns are concerned, for example, several *Annalistes* are reluctant to employ 'I' and prefer other, more discrete academic conventions. The most common consists of replacing the first-person singular with the first-person plural, of saying 'we' instead of 'I'. This practice is standard in French scholarly discourse, and official pronouncements periodically reaffirm its merits. The historian René Rémond, for instance, has defended the procedure, claiming that relying on 'we' is beneficial pedagogically (it associates readers with the research), psychologically (it protects the scholar's modesty), as well as epistemologically (it makes the endeavour into one which other members of the scientific community could have conducted). Turning to that form, according to Rémond, implies an 'act of faith in the universality of historical truth', as well as the 'conviction of being able to attain a certain objectivity'.[33] Similarly, though not as euphorically, de Certeau has pointed out that the use of 'we' fulfils an important ideological function: it makes it possible for historians to ground their discourse neither in an 'individual subject' (the 'author') nor in a 'global subject' ('time', 'society', etc), substituting instead an institutional 'site' [*lieu*] in which this discourse can originate without being reduced to it.[34]

The first-person plural is indeed frequent in current French historiography, and its use is not limited to 'traditional' historians who – like Rémond – specialize in politics: the *Annalistes* turn frequently to it when they treat such 'new' objects as books, cooking, festivals and mentalities.[35] The pronoun, however, is more polysemic than Rémond and even de Certeau think it is. Admittedly, 'we' often refers to both enunciator and reader. When Chartier, in *Lectures et lecteurs dans la France d'ancien régime*, writes 'We must now consider the apogee of the editorial formula', the shifter clearly includes a reader who is expected to follow the argument.[36] Similarly, when he states 'We do not have systematic investigations at our disposal', the pronoun and adjective of the first-person plural point to the community of historians which may be researching the same subject.[37] Other occurrences of 'we', however, do not fall as neatly into these obvious categories. When Chartier utilizes such formulations as 'It thus seemed to us','We have chosen to focus on the book's distribution', 'By "popular" classes, we mean' and 'We have tried to contribute', his 'we' admits neither the reader nor the peer group.[38] Verbs like 'seem', 'choose', 'mean' and 'try' refer to activities which in this instance can only be the individual researcher's. In other words, using 'we' does not serve here any pedagogical, psychological or epistemological purpose. The role of the pronoun is strictly rhetorical: it is to avoid the dreaded 'I' and make the text accord with academic standards.

Chartier is remarkably consistent in sidestepping the first-person singular. Indeed, I have not found a single occurrence of this form in his work, whether in *Lectures et lecteurs*, in his contribution to *Histoire de la France urbaine* (volume III) and *Histoire de la vie privée* (volume III) or in the French versions of the articles collected in *Cultural History*.

Tellingly, Lydia G. Cochrane, the American translator of this last volume, had to render 'nous' as 'I' in the cases where the first-person plural referred to the researcher exclusively. 'Le problème que nous proposons de traiter ici' thus became 'the problem that I intend to treat here', and 'il nous semble' turned into 'It seems to me'.[39] To be sure, the translator had few options: 'we' is now dated as a substitute for 'I' in scholarly American English, and this form would look inappropriate in the writing of a historian who is regarded as innovative and even trendy. The result is that the American edition of Chartier's essays misses an important rhetorical ingredient of the original, namely, the extreme purism of the historian's enunciative strategies. These essays, when read in translation, appear unremarkable in the domain of enunciation, whereas their French version provides some stunning examples of how the most progressive scholars can remain faithful to time-honoured standards, like those of academic 'modesty'.

The other main option available to historians wishing to eschew the first person is a pronoun of the third person, the 'indefinite "*on*"'. '*Nous*' and '*on*', however, do not share the same history, and they are not exact equivalents from a semantic standpoint. Whereas '*nous*' has a long tradition in French scholarship, '*on*' is of more recent usage in this kind of discourse, at least as a substitute for 'I'. Such usage probably started in the 1960s, as a part of what might be called 'structuralist enunciation': the attempt to import aspects of scientific discourse into the humanities, more precisely the effort to erase signs of the speaking subject by employing such devices as passive verbs ('L'analyse qui sera faite'), reflexive verbs ('le texte se lit', 'se donne') and impersonal expressions ('il convient', 'il suffit'). These strategies figured briefly in the works of literary theorists like Barthes and Tzvetan Todorov, who relied on them extensively when they sketched out their programme for a 'science of literature'.[40] For scientific discourse supposedly circulates without mediation, and for this reason it became the model to emulate when critics thought that their task – like the scientists' – was to describe regularities, in this instance the intrinsic features of literature, its 'literariness'.

Mona Ozouf's *La Fête révolutionnaire* could serve as a catalogue of the ways historians avoid 'I' and '*on*' figures prominently in that work in terms of frequency. Ozouf, in fact, is as consistent as Chartier in warding off forms of the first person. These forms, according to my computation at least, never appear in the text of *La Fête*, and can be found only once in the paratext: in a note where Ozouf mentions files 'which have been brought to my attention'.[41] '*On*', on the other hand, occurs repeatedly, functioning in a way comparable with 'we': referring to enunciator and reader ('Ce n'est pas, comme on va voir, si facile'), to enunciator and fellow researchers ('On a du mal à apercevoir la nouveauté de ces fêtes militaires'), and to the enunciator alone ('C'est cette polémique . . . qu'on voudrait d'abord écarter').[42] The last of these '*on*' is of course the most interesting, as its frequent occurrence links Ozouf's endeavour with the structuralist project I have just described – that of making the discourse of the human sciences more austere by purging it of signs denoting the individual subject.

If '*on*' certainly endows *La Fête révolutionnaire* with a supplement of impersonality, its consistent use cannot make the book pass for a scientific report in which the writer acts as a spokesperson for several researchers. Indeed, the '*on*' of those reports has the value of 'I + other scientists in the laboratory' 'or even of 'I + the scientists mentioned as co-authors': it refers to a group which has actual members.[43] The historian's '*on*', however, includes only virtual collaborators, and Ozouf never mentions what her study might owe to her colleagues at the Centre National de la Recherche Scientifique. The same remark applies to most literature criticism. Barthes, for example, celebrates the seminar format in his essay 'Au séminaire' and dedicates his book *S/Z* to the 'students, auditors and friends' who attended the classes during which it was developed at the Ecole Pratique des Hautes Etudes.[44] But he does not associate these participants with the presentation of the findings; in *S/Z* '*on*' remains the individual scholar effacing his involvement in the operations he is performing. *S/Z*, though a text which seeks to break the mould of structuralist criticism, conforms to the principles of structuralist enunciation in this respect. Utterances like 'On étoilera donc le texte', 'On n'exposera pas la critique d'un texte, ou une critique de ce texte' and 'Ce qu'on cherche, c'est à esquisser l'espace stéréographique d'une écriture' replicate in fact the model of impersonality which serious, 'scientific' critics had adopted in the 1960s.[45]

Several factors may account for a historian's preference for 'we' or '*on*' over 'I' as an enunciative device. The first consideration is probably gender. We have seen how Ozouf is highly consistent in averting the first person, and the same feature can be found in several other works by women historians, for example Odile Arnold's *Le Corps et l'âme*, Arlette Farge's *La Vie fragile*, Knibielher and Fouquet's *Histoire des mères*, Mireille Laget's *Naissances*, Anne Martin-Fugier's *La Place des bonnes*, Michelle Perrot's *Les Ouvriers en grève* and Anne Vincent-Buffault's

Histoire des larmes. One possible explanation for these historians' abandonment of 'I' is that they want to ward off the charge of 'subjectivity' often levelled against women's writing. Farge addresses this matter specifically in her contribution to the essays collected in *Une Histoire des femmes est-elle possible?* Asking whether women should aim at a 'distinctive practice of feminine history writing', she argues that the issue is raised regardless of what women historians purport to be doing: even when they 'do not claim for themselves a certain subjectivity in method and writing', their works are often read 'through that prism'.[46] This unindulgent look, according to Farge, determines distinct practices, and although Farge does not consider enunciative strategies *per se*, eschewing 'I' is certainly one way of steering clear of the label 'subjective'.

Besides (male) peer pressure, earlier and more generalized types of surveillance may account for the kind of self-censorship to which Farge is referring in this passage. Perrot, for example, traces what she takes to be her lack of assertiveness to her upbringing, more precisely to her having been taught in childhood to restrict her subjectivity. Considering the effects of this initial training on her enunicative habits, she writes 'Saying "I" has always been difficult for me' and goes as far as hypothesizing 'perhaps I have done history not to speak of myself, even not to think of myself'.[47] An examination of Perrot's *Les Ouvriers en grève* confirms the historian's own diagnosis. Indeed, there are very few instances of 'I'; they express a low level of subjectivity and they tend to occur in such authorized places as the preface or the beginning of a new section ('I shall only indicate . . .').[48] Ozouf's essays collected in *L'Ecole de la France* display similar characteristics: signs of the first person are many in the 'Presentation' but then appear in only five of the twenty texts which make up the book and are used in as restricted a manner as they are in Perrot's writings.

Gender, however, does not fully explain why some *Annalistes* exclude the first person from their enunciative practice. Indeed, as we have seen, male historians like Chartier also prefer using 'we' and '*on*' when they refer to themselves in their texts. The reluctance to employ 'I', and especially the 'I' of the 'emotional subject', thus has other causes, which are perhaps traceable to an (undeclared) generational conflict: to an impatience with what *Annalistes* of the third generation (like Ozouf, Perrot and Chartier) perceive as the one-man shows of their prestigious elders, more precisely with the polemical, essay-like aspects of works designated as scholarly. To be sure, the younger *Annalistes* do not endorse the idea of value-free research, and they would certainly disagree with Rémond's suggestion that 'we' inscribes a faith in the 'objectivity' of historical research and the 'universality' of historical truth. More likely, they consider that flaunting the signs of one's subjectivity to the degree that Duby and Le Roy Ladurie do in their works since the 1970s has no place in academic writings, and that editorials belong in newspapers and manifestos. Their enunciative habits, therefore, could be regarded as responses to what they perceive as the excesses of their predecessors, especially to the high interventionism displayed in such works as *Le Moyen-Age* and *Le Carnaval de Romans*.

One might conceive, finally, that historians who ward off the first person do so because of personal taste, and perhaps because they want to meet an aesthetic challenge. Although such serious scholars as Ozouf and Chartier are seemingly not given to finding their literary models among the writings of the experimental group Oulipo (a group that explores 'potential literature'), texts like *La Fête révolutionnaire* and *Lectures et lecteurs dans la France d'ancien régime* could be read as sorts of lipogram: as texts whose authors have striven not to use one sign in the language ('I' in this instance), as Georges Perec did in *La Disparition*, where what 'disappears' is both one of the characters and the letter 'e'. Similarly, Farge's fieldwork report in *Le Goût de l'archive* could be viewed as a rare instance of the genre which Philippe Lejeune calls 'autobiography in the third person'.[49] Farge, indeed, constantly discards 'I' and its byproducts in the account of her research in Parisian libraries, relying instead on a genderless 'le lecteur' and an anonymous 'elle' to designate the researcher.[50] Yet Farge is more clearly playing than Ozour or Chartier. Such sentences as 'She has just arrived; she is asked for an ID she does not have' and 'She does not know where the reference cards are and she sees nothing which signals them' can only incite readers to ask who that 'she' is and who is speaking about her.[51] Farge, in other words, is just pretending: pretending that she follows the conventions of history writing, and that she follows them with the zeal of a woman scholar who is wary of the charge of 'subjectivity' that male critics – as Farge argues in the essay I have quoted earlier – are prone to level at the writings of women historians. Such a selfconscious game, however, can only highlight the role of Farge as writer; and the absence of 'I' in a personal text where this pronoun could be expected makes *Le Goût de l'archive* closer to *Roland Barthes par Roland Barthes* than to a piece written to comfort the historical establishment.

ENUNCIATION AND EPISTEMOLOGY

While such historians as Chartier, Farge and Ozouf steer clear of the first-person singular, their doing so does not mean that they have become entirely invisible as subjects of enunciation. I have just mentioned how Farge's reliance on 'she' in *Le Goût de l'archive* foregrounds her role as an enunciator, and the same thing could be said of Ozouf's and Chartier's use of '*on*' and 'we' for the sole purpose of eschewing 'I'. The presence of an enunciator is especially obvious when the historian's scruples lead him/her to multiplying '*on*' and 'we' to the point of confusion, as in the following excerpt from *La Fête révolutionnaire*:

> Du dessein global que nous croyons pouvoir lire dans les fêtes de la Révolution française, il n'y a pourtant toujours pas d'expression organisée. Aucun système de fêtes. Non qu'on ait cessé de le souhaiter. On a, comme on l'a vu, sur la suggestion de Vergniaud et de Jean Debry, voulu fêter Jemmapes; le Comité d'instruction publique y a un peu songé.[52]
>
> There was still no organized expression of the overall purpose we have attributed to the festivals of the French Revolution. There was no system of festivals, though there were plenty of people calling for one. Vergniaud and Jean Debry proposed a festival to celebrate Jemmapes; the Committee of Public Instruction gave it some thought.[53]

It takes an alert reading here to determine that '*nous*' denotes the enunciator as an interpreter of the events, the first two instances of '*on*' the revolutionary leaders who wanted to 'organize' the festivals better, and the third one ('comme on l'a vu') both the enunciator and her addressees. In other words, Ozouf's choice of pronouns makes the situation of enunciation problematic, causing readers to ask: Who is speaking? To whom? About what and about whom? But such questions are not supposed to be raised about historical discourse, since this discourse, in theory at least, functions 'without a speaker'. Sidestepping the first person to the extent that Chartier and Ozouf do thus creates noise, calling attention to procedures which – to be fully operational – should have remained silent. '*On*' and especially 'we' are ultimately traces of the enunciator, and their frequent occurrence in works such as those of Chartier, Farge and Ozouf only points to the underlying presence of the 'I' which these works are trying to suppress.

The overtness of enunciative procedures in *Annales* historiography, whatever its exact nature and range, has epistemological underpinnings which critics' adverse comments have brought into sharper focus. Bernard Bailyn, at the publication of Braudel's *La Méditerranée*, took issue with the preface's opening sentence ('I have passionately loved the Mediterranean . . .'), arguing that if there is

nothing wrong with an historian's being emotionally involved with his subject . . . the formulation of a valid problem is as much the necessary ingredient for superior work in history as the sympathetic identification of scholar and subject.[54]

Thirty years later, reviewers of *Le Carnaval de Romans* similarly blamed Le Roy Ladurie for being 'excessively garrulous'),[55] for siding indiscriminately 'with the underdog'[56] and for developing the 'annoying mannerism' of attacking Guérin's testimony while quoting it.[57] These critiques, though unreasonably demanding at times (the preface may be regarded as the place where scholars are institutionally authorized to express their 'emotions'), have one significant merit: they show the endurance of the positivist model of 'objectivity'. Indeed, they assume the ideal neutrality of historical research and the possibility of reaching historical truth. Correspondingly, they posit that writing can mirror the disinterestedness of the researcher and become totally transparent to its object. History writing, in brief, must (and can) warrant the impartiality of the inquiry – an ideal which the reviews I have quoted propose with as much innocence as Langlois and Seignobos did about one hundred years ago.

Against this backdrop, the works of the *Annales* school seem to inscribe a new epistemology. More precisely, their reliance on visible signs of enunciation suggests that the *Annalistes* do not wish to go on pretending: pretending that historical research is conducted from some median spot, like Lord Acton's – who obviously did not suspect the Britishness of this definition of objectivity – 30 degrees longitude west; that historical texts write themselves from documents, of which they constitute the mere projection or continuation; and that those texts are therefore speakerless – the unmediated reflection of the events 'as they actually occurred'. Opposing this 'realist' epistemology, the *Annalistes* apparently endorse the position which critics of positivism have developed since the 1890s, and which 'pragmatist' linguists and philosophers reformulated in the 1970s and 1980s. According to that position, inquiries are always situated. Thus, even a so-called scientific utterance like 'water boils at 212 degrees' involves a context of enunciation: it can be made only by someone who is familiar with the Fahrenheit system, and it answers an explicit or implicit question asked by someone else who is, say, unfamiliar with this system or unaware of the temperature at which water boils.[58] In other words, utterances of the type 'A is B' are convenient short cuts which scientists use to summarize their findings; but scientific changes and debates show that these utterances should in fact be modalized, that is presented in the form 'X claims that A is B'.[59] Similarly, as Gérard Genette has argued, there is no such thing as a narrative told 'in the third person', thus there is no pure '*histoire*' in Benveniste's sense.[60] Every narrative has a narrator, the variable being the narrator's level of involvement: s/he may leave the text itself as the only sign of his/her presence, multiply the marks of subjectivity, use all kinds of intermediate modes, or even move from one mode to the other.

While the *Annalistes* rely on a highly involved enunciator, they do not seem, however, to have a clear awareness of the epistemology that underlies this textual usage. The 'theory' I am sketching here is thus the theory of a practice: one which is implicit in discursive habits, not explicit in self-reflexive comments. Such comments, for that matter, are very few in or about the texts we are considering. Indeed, the *Annalistes* seem to be more comfortable publicizing – as Furet has it – their 'colours' than their 'concepts'.[61] Thus, autobiographical sketches like Philippe Ariès' *Un Historien du dimanche* and Le Roy Ladurie *Paris–Montpellier* describe political trajectories rather than daily visits to the archives; tellingly, the subtitle of *Paris–Montpellier* reads *P.C.–P.S.U, 1945–1963*, emphasizing that one of the book's main themes is Le Roy Ladurie's shift of allegiance from the Communist Party to the Socialist Unified Party. Similarly, as I have mentioned earlier, the *Annalistes* occasionally report how they have used a specific document or reached a specific numerical figure. However, these interventions of the enunciator as researcher remain scarce and unsystematic. The *Annalistes*, to my knowledge, have to this day made no attempt to emulate what anthropologists have tried on occasion: to conduct in the first person a study that combines a story of the research with the presentation of the findings, as Jeanne Favret-Saada has done in *Les Mots, la mort, les sorts*, her investigation of sorcery in western France. Farge's *Le Goût de l'archive*, though unusually self-reflexive by *Annales* standards, thus grants little space to fieldwork: only 20 out of 156 pages describe visits to libraries, the rest of the book being devoted to discussions of Farge's favourite sources – judicial documents. It is not, moreover, a text which presents an investigation properly speaking, and there is little mention of the process of research in Farge's other works, for instances in *Délinquance et criminalité*, *La Vie fragile* and *Vivre dans la rue à Paris au 18e siècle*.

Let us stress, in conclusion, that if the overtness of the enunciative process in *Annales* historiography disproves the view of historical discourse as speakerless, an examination of other incarnations of that discourse would yield similar results. To put it differently, this overtness has intertextual aspects which critics could explore as they have explored intertextual relationships in literature. For one thing, the openness of the enunciator represents a return to earlier practices: to the habit of intervening in the story to comment upon the facts, make judgements, and draw conclusions, as historians did in the eighteenth century when they were confidently playing the role of what Gossman calls the text's 'unifying center',[62] and, perhaps more relevantly, to Michelet's textual machineries and the attitudes which they inscribe. For Michelet, too, relies heavily on forms of the first person: on the emotional 'I' of those citizens who despise the monarchy, support the Revolution and love their country, as well as on the 'I' of researchers who have done their homework, gathered the evidence and can proudly write such statements as 'I have before my eyes the minutes of the meetings of many rural federations'.[63] Braudel, for that matter, endorses Michelet's enunciative habits as well as his patriotism when he opens *L'Identité de la France* by proclaiming: 'I love France with the same demanding, complicated passion as Michelet did.'[64]

(Re)turning to the first person, moreover, constitutes a link between historiography and some of the other human sciences, where the overt enunciator has reappeared as well. Anthropology, as mentioned above, is a field where researchers have tried to stage themselves in their texts and present their investigation 'in progress' rather than 'as completed'.[65] But the same tendency can be observed in literary theory, where critics like Barthes, Genette and Todorov have moved away from the convoluted manoeuvres they used in the 1960s to confer 'scientific' impersonality upon their texts, opting in their later works (Barthes' *La Chambre claire*, Genette's *Seuils*, Todorov's *Critique de la critique*) for an open appropriation of the first person and its most visible signs. The changes I have described thus partake of a general relaxing of the rules which positivist theorists (and their unwitting disciples in the 1960s) had decreed in their attempt to control scholarly writing in general, scholarly enunciation in particular. They point to a questioning of the possibility of objective, non-situated knowledge, and – since this questioning started in the early twentieth century – to the lag between rhetoric and epistemology. For the now commonplace argument that research is always grounded in a subject keeps being made in the human sciences –

and in this very sentence – through a rhetoric which signals the researcher's reluctance to leave marks of his/her involvement, or even his/her hope of dispensing with them altogether.

6

Relevance, Revision
and the Fear of Long Books

ANN RIGNEY

Order is the most necessary of things in a piece of writing. . . . But I suspect that a historian has more trouble than any other writer in finding that order. He is overwhelmed by the sheer quantity of his materials; if he does not succeed in building these into a regular edifice, [the reader] will become lost in a labyrinth with no way out. Abbé de Mably, 1783[1]

Of the factors contributing to the success of a historical work, the most important perhaps is the historian's choice of a subject whose disposition will give rise . . . to a unified whole with a central point of interest. F.-J.-M. Raynouard, 1821[2]

I undertook to write a history which, in point of fact, lacked a body: my task involved making such a body by disengaging and abstracting it from all foreign substances, and by endowing a series of observations and general facts with the movement and the interest of a story. That was my ambition; did I succeed? Augustin Thierry, 1853[3]

'Especially when it comes to histories, we are all frightened by long books', wrote a certain Paul Lacroix ('bibliophile Jacob') in his preface of 1850 to Anquetil's popular *Histoire de France* (1805). Anquetil, the bibliophile argued, had basically rewritten in an abbreviated form the *grandes histoires* of Dupleix, Mézeray, Daniel and Velly and, in doing so, had done the public the favour of saving them a considerable amount of time. Whereas it would take more than two years, ten hours a day, to read all the original documents relating to the history of France, the whole History of France was now economically reduced, thanks to Anquetil, to a mere ten days' reading.[4]

Abridgements, *abrégés, précis, résumés, tableaux synoptiques*: the very existence of such genres suggests that historical works are constantly seen to be in need of abbreviation, re-editing.[5] Apparently, there is something

particular to history books that they so often go on too long, or threaten
to do so. Too long for the reader who has to follow them, but also too
long for the writer who becomes weary in producing them.[6] Indeed, some
books prove unfinishable according to the historian's original plan, while
others are simply not finished at all. Thus Macaulay's original intention
was to begin his history of England with 1688 and to continue it to 1830,
but after almost twenty-one years writing and several changes of plan, he
died having reached only 1702.[7] Thus Mézeray invoked the epic
dimensions of the task he had undertaken as writer (the work kept on
getting bigger and bigger) and the strategies he had adopted to help the
'tired reader' make it to the end. At the same time, however, he admitted
that, in spite of its monstrous length, his two-thousand-page history was
still incomplete. For to know the history of France truly, he wrote at the
end of his preface, by rights you must also know the history of all its
neighbouring countries, from the customs and deeds of the various
classes to the layout of all its rivers and mountains.[8]

    This paradoxical state of being 'over-extended' and yet 'incomplete'
would seem to be one of the historian's professional hazards. The
difficulties proclaimed by historians with respect to the question of length
reflect the difference, which in recent years has received so much
attention, between events and discourse. Or, as I would wish to formulate
the problem here, they reflect the differences between the nature of the
material the historian must deal with and the demands of discourse as a
communicative activity.

I

If history books threaten to go on too long, this is because there is
nothing in the nature of events which determines where they should stop,
or as importantly, where they should begin. For historical events, unlike
fictional plots with their tailor-made events, do not in themselves take the
form of an 'untold story' with a fixed beginning-middle-end structure
waiting to be transcribed.[9] It is up to the historians themselves, therefore,
to devise beginnings and ends and this being the case, inconsistencies and
changes of mind *en route* are always possible. Thus Macaulay presented
his work as a history of England 'since the accession of James the
Second', yet in fact first spent almost 300 pages sketching the 'prehistory'
of his subject, England since Roman times.[10] Thus Braudel, having
announced that the death of Philip II had no impact on the development
of the Mediterranean, nevertheless ended his history of the Mediterranean with the death of that king.[11] Where Macaulay spills out of or

modifies his self-imposed limits, Braudel ironically adopts a conventional sign of 'finality', the death of an individual, in order to justify calling a halt to the discourse.

In the evenemential continuum there are not only no fixed beginnings or ends, there are also no minimal event-units with permanently demarcated background and foreground features. As Paul Veyne has argued, the field of events is a continuous, ever-expanding network.[12] While the reality of certain phenomena can be established once and for all with the help of sources, their significance or importance cannot; for that is a function of their relationship with other phenomena as established by the point of view of an observer. In other words, the importance of particular historical phenomena is not absolute, fixed once and for all, but relative to the context in which they are considered. In the context of the history of textiles or the role of women, for example, the details of the making of the Bayeux tapestry are more important than the Battle of Hastings; in the context of the conquest of England, conversely, the making of the tapestry is incidental and the details of its making negligible.

If the objective field of events lacks an inherent hierarchical structure and fixed boundaries, the same cannot be said of discourse.[13] While everything which has ever been under the sun belongs to the objective field of events, and everything which is known to have occurred may potentially be included in historical discourse, not everything will or can be included in a single text. Not only because the making of the text would itself add to the sum total of things under the sun, and not only because of the physical restrictions of the medium (no matter how long or incomplete a work is, it must have a finite number of pages and volumes), but even more fundamentally, because the purpose of every text is to communicate.

When you use language you engage in an activity whose primary function is to transmit intelligible information to someone else. For discourse by definition involves trying to 'make sense'; that is, it involves making a point about the world and not reproducing the world itself in all its plenitude. For this reason, language is always a sort of shorthand, selection and categorization being a condition of meaningfulness.[14] Hierarchies are established among phenomena, the elastic nature of words allowing certain elements to be abbreviated and others to be expanded. And if it is to be followable by someone else, and 'come to' a point, an utterance cannot be endless.

To say that the use of language implies by definition the exchange of intelligible information is to suppose not only the currency of a linguistic code regulating the connections between sign and signifier, but also the currency of certain pragmatic principles regulating the expectations of the language users *vis-à-vis* communicative exchanges.[15] Among these principles, according to H. P. Grice, is the mutual understanding of sender and addressee that the information given is true to the best of the sender's knowledge, that the sender has tried to be as straightforward and as clear as possible, that the information is as complete and yet as concise as possible, and that the utterance is relevant, that is, it is designed to convey information to its receivers which is new and yet connected to their current preoccupations and representations of the world.[16] A reader always expects these maxims to have been respected except where generic conventions allow them to be flouted (truthfulness is not expected in a novel, for example, nor clarity and straightforwardness in a poem). As in other fields of activity, principles may be violated and transgressions censured, without the regulative function of such principles being undermined (indeed, as the phenomenon of irony illustrates, it seems that readers are prepared in the first instance to make considerable efforts to correct deviations or to rationalize them in terms of some ulterior purpose).

'Relevance' can be seen as the most important principle in communicative exchanges since it not only regulates the nature and quantity of information transmitted, but makes the information worth processing in the first place.[17] To use a term which recurs so often in pre-Romantic literary theory, relevance is what guarantees the 'interest' of the text for the public, in the root sense of 'that which makes a difference'. The principle of relevance is not only applicable to the relation between the utterance and its context, but also to the relations between the different propositions of which it is composed. In other words, where an utterance consists of different propositions, readers expect these to form not merely a finite sequence but also a coherent one.

Coherence is an effect, in the first place, of the local relations between particular propositions, each sentence being expected to 'make a difference' with respect to the previous one (and where the writer does not make connections explicit, the reader can be expected to supplement the text by filling in the gaps).[18] Coherence is, in the second place, a global effect of the utterance as a whole: with the exception of encyclopedias which are by definition piecemeal, the information supplied sentence by sentence in discourse is normally expected to add up to more than the sum of its parts.[19] In other words, information is expected to be articulated according to some unfolding global plan, designed on *narrative* principles (propositions are related on the grounds of their common reference to a particular sequence of events), *systematic* principles (propositions are related as expansions, explanations, specifications, generalizations with respect to one other) or *conceptual* principles (they deal with phenomena which are conceptually related), or on a mixture of the above.[20]

It is the nature of the implied subject – *what* it is you are on about – which in theory regulates what information is 'to-the-point', how much information needs to be included, and what details are more important than others. In other words, the subject establishes priorities and hierarchies with respect to the totality of things which *could* be said about the world, allowing some phenomena to be simply ignored, while others are presented in a more or less extensive fashion.[21] If the subject is 'the history of France', then what happened in neighbouring countries may legitimately recede to the background and be referred to only to the extent that it has a bearing on the central French issue; and other matters (for example, the development of literature in Brazil) may be ignored altogether without the charge of incompleteness being thrown at the writer.

The fact that a discourse is expected to be coherent does not mean that repetitions and irrelevancies may never occur without irrevocably impeding the communicative exchange. As readers are relatively tolerant of digression, some items of 'gratuitous' information may incidentally be included: pieces of *couleur locale*, for example, which although they do not contribute to the global design of the discourse, are interesting 'in their own right', that is to say, independently of the interest of the rest of the discourse. Every discursive representation of the world involves selection and schematization, as we have seen, but to the extent that historians claim to *represent* the world and not merely to impose an interpretative grid on it, over-schematization can be suspect. Following the same logic, the inclusion of apparently irrelevant details can also heighten the realism of an account.[22]

But the cost of thus avoiding over-schematization may be that of incoherence. For the more detail concerning events, persons and circumstances a writer includes, the more difficult it is to maintain the sense that the discourse as a whole is going somewhere in particular. The more one *fait divers* in Shandyan fashion leads to another, the more unclear it becomes that there is a *fil conducteur* leading out of the labyrinth, that there is a plan being followed. As late eighteenth-century literary theory stressed, foreshadowing modern discourse analysis, local points of interest in a discourse need to be subordinated to the ongoing thrust – the 'dramatic interest' – of the work as a whole if the reader is to be induced to continue reading.[23] As Blair put it, a writer 'will soon tire the Reader, if he goes on recording, in strict chronological order, a multitude of separate transactions, connected by nothing else, but their happening at the same time'.[24]

When discourse is thus viewed as a communicative activity, it follows that historical discourse in theory seeks to transmit to a reader interesting information which has been articulated into a coherent whole. Hayden White implies in his essay 'The Politics of Historical Interpretation: Discipline and De-sublimation' that historians have the choice whether or not to seek to render the 'manifest confusion' of events comprehensible.[25] The view of discourse presented here suggests, however, that once historians engage in communicative activity, they no longer have any choice in this matter. As Veyne argues, historical discourse as a cultural practice came into being with the recognition that the past was worth talking about, that is, that the narration of past events could 'give rise to a coherent, intelligible book'.[26] Further research is certainly needed into the specific expectations governing the production and reception of historical discourse – particularly as these are manifest in the critical reactions which, as Lionel Gossman has argued, are an integral part of historio-graphical practice.[27] But there are many indications to suggest that with respect to the transmission of relevant, coherent information, historical discourse conforms to the communicative norm. Blair, for example, asserted that the first duty of historians was to impart 'unity' to their material, so that their work 'should not consist of separate unconnected parts merely, but should be bound together by some connecting principle' and make the impression on the mind 'of something that is one, whole and entire'.[28] Mably wrote that 'unity of action and interest' was no less important for the historian than for the epic poet.[29] Augustin Thierry declared that he had done his best as a historian to 'multiply the number of details so as to exhaust the primary sources, but without breaking up the story and destroying the unity of the whole'.[30] Among the more recent (and for the present public, more directly relevant) indications of the 'coherence' norm is the review section of the *American Historical Review* of December 1991, in which one work is praised for its 'coherent structure' and the 'clarity, consistency, and absorbing quality of [its] argument',[31] while other works are criticized for the 'occasional fracturing of the story' and 'loss of overall forward movement';[32] for the lack of a 'firmer final outline';[33] and for an 'essay-like structure' which 'makes for repetition while obscuring links in the author's argument'.[34]

Such criticisms indicate that 'to-the-pointness' continues to be a regulative idea in historiographical practice: a historical work is expected to 'make sense' of – or, to use another term, to explain – something in the world. But such criticisms also point to the fact that the writers of history may fail in practice to realize these ideals or, more precisely, that they may fall short of them. If the function of the historical discourse is to communicate relevant, coherent (but not over-schematized) information about the past, numerous statements by historians attest to the fact that rendering the 'manifest confusion' of events comprehensible is easier said in normative statements than done in practice. How can a 'multitude of separate transactions', to recall Blair's words, all taking place at the same time in the open field of events, be reduced and articulated into an intelligible, readable whole? Where do you begin and where do you end? Given the limitless nature and the 'manifest confusion' of the field of events which the historian is claiming to represent with the help of disparate sources, the task may not be as straightforward as it is sometimes made out to be – by White, for example, who gives the impression that historians can freely impose any form they wish on their material, or by Veyne who suggests that historians are free to plot out *intrigues* across the field of events, which they subsequently and unproblematically represent in the 'accepted literary forms'.[35]

In what follows, I wish to consider some of the difficulties in finding a discursive form for events, the difficulty in articulating them.

II

While recognizing that difficulties exist, one should not exaggerate them. For in spite of romantic assertions to the contrary, historians do not operate alone.[36] Not only are they dependent on the sources in which events have been recorded (and initially interpreted), but they also have models of how to go about their business. To be sure, newcomers must always distinguish themselves from their predecessors, but 'what has already been said and done' within a particular cultural community functions as the background against which significant differences are measured.[37] The aspirations, methods, successes and failures of earlier historians provide both indications of things to be avoided and models to be followed. Thus the manner in which earlier historians (and, in some cases, writers in other genres) have organized their material may be emulated, adapted or criticized in later work.[38] The practice of devoting each chapter to a particular century or place, beginning a narrative with an orientational description of the setting, moving from a general overview of a situation to particulars, distinguishing main text from footnotes, adding detailed tables of contents, chapter titles and sub-headings: all of these can be seen as reflecting inherited solutions to the demands of clarity rather than any necessity linked to the 'nature of the material'. The influence of custom may be seen in the first instance, however, not in the manner in which historians write and the goals they set themselves, but in *what* they choose to write about, that is, in the range of topics they consider worth treating in discourse.

In keeping with the communicative function of discourse, historians do not write 'History' as such, but instead write 'histories of' X, Y, Z.[39] The evolution of history writing is characterized, on the one hand, by the fresh treatment of familiar topics like 'the history of France' or 'the history of the French Revolution' and, on the other, by the extension of the repertoire of topics available for treatment.[40] According to the 'system of relevance' of the particular period, certain subjects are considered more 'important', indeed more 'historical', and hence more worthy of being treated in historical discourse than others.[41] Those who treat these subjects consider themselves accordingly to be the 'real' historians (as LaCapra suggests in his critique of the current emphasis on cultural history).[42] The counterpart of this, of course, is that other areas of experience are effectively ignored as uninteresting, unintelligible, unworthy of historiographical attention. Thus, in an interesting projection of a cognitive dilemma onto the field of events, the Middle Ages were for long described as 'bizarre', 'chaotic', 'confusing', 'misty', 'obscure'.[43] In short, since they were incomprehensible for the latter-day historian and hence nothing interesting could be learnt from them, they did not constitute a 'subject' in the sense of a 'topic which could be elaborated in discourse'. They were not 'poetic' in the sense of having a shape which was recognizable in terms of existing discursive models.[44] As a result they were to be ignored, abbreviated, or relegated to a marginal, prefatory status. As Augustin Thierry complained:

It has almost become proverbial to say that no period of our history can measure up to the Merovingian period as regards confusion and barrenness. This period is the one which is most often abridged, which is most quickly passed over, which no one hesitates to ignore. Such disdain is more a reflection of indolence than of thought, and if the history of the Merovingians is a little difficult to disentangle, it is by no means barren. On the contrary, it is so full of unusual features, original characters, and varied incidents that the only problem for the historian is to impose order on such a wealth of detail.[45]

As Thierry's comments also suggest, however, periods, persons, domains which at one time seemed scarcely worth a passing comment in a discourse devoted to a different subject may be recognized at another period as potential subjects in their own right, as having discursive value. Thus, for reasons which often have to do with socio-cultural changes outside the sphere of history writing as such, phenomena which have hitherto seemed no more than 'irrelevant' details, good at most for a realistic effect, may move to the centre of attention and become the lodestone which attracts fresh items of relevant information and excludes others.[46] Particularly in recent years, there has been a rapid extension of the repertoire into all imaginable domains of daily existence, from leisure, tears and smells to childhood and old age, the discovery of new topics (frequently on the model of earlier topics) being one of the principal mechanisms behind historiographical evolution.[47] This emphasis on bringing marginalia to the centre of attention, in penetrating ever farther into the realm of the great unwritten, can be seen as a continuation of the Romantic project to 'make the silences of history speak',[48] to 'pass quickly over the points where history speaks, and to tarry over those where she is silent'.[49]

This Romantic project can be attributed in large part to the influence of the French Revolution which, in establishing the nation as the legitimate subject of political life, had also established 'the history of the nation' as the most relevant historical topic. Or at least, it had made the existing sovereign-centred histories à la Mézeray, those serial biographies of kings, irrevocably irrelevant. Reflecting the agonistic dimension of history writing, this *nouvelle histoire* was more often than not defined in oppositional terms as the contrary of that which had until then received attention. Thus historians now turned to the period before the monarchy and to the Middle Ages, for example, or to the life of the masses as opposed to that of their aristocratic and royal leaders, to manners and everyday customs as opposed to diplomatic, military and political events.[50] While all of this obviously opened up exciting new horizons for historians, it also brought its problems. To recall Thierry's words, hitherto neglected material was original and interesting, but could be 'difficult to disentangle' and hence difficult to arrange or order in discourse. Did 'everything unwritten' constitute one subject, or many? In what sort of discourse can silences be articulated?

As is well documented, one of the most important models for writing this *nouvelle histoire* was the novelistic work of Walter Scott – in particular, his treatment of manners.[51] The attention to detail characteristic of his novels was not merely seen as a way of making a narrative more vivid, that is, as a rhetorical device to interest the reader, but also as a substantial contribution to the non-evenemential history of culture or history of everyday life, as an addition to the repertoire of topics which were now open for historiographical (as distinct from merely antiquarian) treatment. As Macaulay put it, the novelist had brought to light those 'noiseless revolutions' which, although 'sanctioned by no treaties and recorded in no archives', are the locus *par excellence* in which the history of the nation, the history most calculated to interest the public, was manifest. Scott had taken up the fragments or gleanings of truth left over by eighteenth-century historians and fashioned them into a discourse, but it was now time that the historian did the same thing so as to 'reclaim those materials the novelist has appropriated'.[52] A discourse from gleanings?

For all their thematic innovation, Scott's narratives are traditional in the sense that they follow the familiar biographical model where the life of an individual provides the lodestone for discursive relevance. Using his novelistic freedom to invent, he integrated his diverse items of information regarding manners into his account of the experiences of a select number of fictional figures.[53] But how were historians to integrate such *faits divers* into discourse and yet abide by the truth-telling maxim to which their genre bound them? How were they to go about 'reclaiming' the revolutions of everyday life as a historiographical subject? I shall consider four attempts.

III: I

Augustin Thierry's *Récits des temps mérovingiens* (1840) opens, in traditional narrative fashion, with a description of a setting, Clother's royal residence in Braine. An initial generic description of this residence as an instance of a particular type ('It was . . . one of those immense farms in which the Franks used to hold court') is followed by an account of its particular layout. In a sequence which moves from centre to periphery in both social and spatial terms, mention is made first of the central building, then of the adjacent buildings occupied by important officials, the outhouses occupied by different artisans, and finally, the farm-labourers' cabins along the edges of the wood. The discourse then switches to Clother, the master of the whole complex, beginning with an account of the sort of activities he carried out in this place, and moving from there to an account of his activities in general and his dealings with women in particular; this topic then introduces the first narrative statement in the story: what his wife Indegonde said to him on a particular day.[54]

Thierry admitted in his preface that for the historian who wanted to treat not only political but also social matters, the history of the Merovingian period was simply a history which it was 'impossible to write in its entirety'.[55] If cultural phenomena are included in a large-scale political history of the period, they will 'impede at every step the progress of the discourse' and will make for a work 'of colossal dimensions'.[56] Rather than be colossal and still incomplete, Thierry chose to work on the basis of exemplification.[57] Instead of trying to weave together a continuous narrative involving all the different characters who played a role at this period, Thierry opted for a series of short narratives each of which has the actions of a limited number of characters as its *fil conducteur*.[58] In reducing the scale of his subject in this way, Thierry provided himself with a figurative focus in each narrative *and* allowed himself to enter into greater detail: as in Scott's novels, the focus on a select number of actors renders relevant the description of different aspects of their lives, from the disposition of their houses, to the manner of baptizing their children and marrying their wives. Such details are pertinent within the framework of the story of Galeswinthe and Fredegonde in a way which they would not be within the framework of a larger-scale narrative aiming to describe the political changes taking place within society at large over a whole period. As is illustrated by the description of Braine, the descriptions relating to the particular lives and actions of individual characters are used as a means to give information about phenomena which are characteristic for that social class or period.

If Thierry thus succeeds in integrating general information about Merovingian mores into his narratives of particular events, it cannot be said that this typification process always takes place without a hitch. In his account of the marriage between Chilperic and Galeswinthe, for example, Thierry explains the custom of the *morgane-ghiba*, the gift which the groom gives to the bride on the morning after the nuptial night, but he is unable to follow this up in the narrative with a quotation of the precise words which Chilperic spoke to Galeswinthe on the morning after. Although there are sources available relating to the customary words spoken on other such occasions, there are no sources relating to this particular *morgane-ghiba*. The focus on particular events which forms the organizing principle of the narrative is not abandoned, however, because of this informational gap. Neither is the reference to the speech. Instead, Thierry projects on the basis of his certain knowledge of other speeches a *hypothetical* speech – identified as such in advance – which is quoted verbatim as if it had actually taken place:

.I, Chilperic, king of the Franks, illustrious man, to you Galeswinthe, my beloved wife, to whom I am bound in wedlock according to the Salic law by the solidus and the denarius, I give today of the tenderness of my love, as a dowry and a morning gift, the cities of Bordeaux, Cahors.[59]

In order to maintain the focus on the particular marriage of Galeswinthe and Chilperic *and* impart the information he has from other sources regarding marriage customs in general, Thierry extrapolates from his material. In doing so, he also transgresses the truth-telling maxim so central to historiographical practice – but he flouts this maxim openly in the manner of fiction, not surreptitiously in the manner of lying.

III: 2

In the first chapter of his *History of England since the Accession of James the Second* (1848–61), Macaulay stated his intention to treat not only the history of government, but also the 'history of the people' – a topic which he presents as synonymous with the progress of useful and ornamental arts, the rise of religious sects, the changes of literary taste, the manners of successive generations, and 'even the revolutions which have taken place in dress, furniture, repasts, and public amusements'.[60] In contrast to Thierry, who reduced the scope of his history so as to 'make room' for information regarding manners, Macaulay presented the history of manners as complementing his narrative of political events. But where Thierry integrated information regarding cultural phenomena only intermittently into his various 'short stories', Macaulay devoted a separate chapter exclusively to the treatment of such phenomena.[61] In this 70-page survey of 'the state of a nation'[62] the giving of information regarding cultural phenomena is not subordinated to the narrative of political events, but is taken as a goal in its own right. Situated between the aforementioned account of English history since Roman times and the narrative of political events since James II, this chapter occupies a liminal position: like conventional descriptions of setting, it serves to mark the transition between the prehistory and the beginning of the history proper.[63]

As the table of contents and the topic-indicators in the margins make clear, this chapter treats one aspect of English culture after another, not a particular sequence of events, and refers mainly to generic phenomena, not to individual ones. After a general overview of the state of the country in 1685, the account moves to the population of England, north and south; thence to the state of the revenue; the army; the navy; the ordnance; the civil service; the state of agriculture; mineral wealth; country gentlemen; the clergy; the yeomanry; the growth of towns; Bristol; Norwich . . . London; the city; the fashionable parts of the capital; police; street-lighting . . . the difficulty of travelling; the badness of the roads; stage coaches . . . the post office; newspapers, newsletters . . . female education; the literary attainments of a gentleman; the influence of French literature . . . the state of the common people; agricultural wages; industrial wages . . . benefits derived by the common people from the progress of civilization. The treatment of each new subtopic generally begins with an explicit comparison between the state of affairs in England in 1685 and the situation at the time of writing/reading. In this way, Macaulay underlines the interest, the significant difference, which warrants the attention he pays to the phenomena in question.

As the abbreviated list above suggests, Macaulay treats an enormous range of phenomena in his survey. And as the list also suggests, the organization of his material is not random. There are local, non-narrative connections between the different chapter-sections, each one of which is almost invariably connected with the one preceding or following it. Some chapter-sections are related because one is a specification with respect to the other (thus 'Bristol' is a specification with respect to 'the growth of towns'). Others are connected because they relate to different aspects of the same phenomena (thus 'highwaymen' and the 'badness of the roads' are connected as part of the 'difficulties of travelling'). Yet others are connected as relating to members of a graded series (this is the case with 'country gentlemen', 'clergy', 'yeomanry').

Although the account is thus characterized by local coherence and by local points of interest, the global coherence of the chapter as a whole is much less evident. To be sure, the chapter opens and closes with general statements to the effect that English society tended to improve in all areas in the period under consideration; and this point is repeated with respect to many of the individual topics. But the information actually presented in the chapter is not organized to reflect this general development. At most, the global coherence of the chapter consists in a tendency to progress from the material to the cultural: from the general demographic

background to economic and political organizations, to the infrastructure, to the arts and sciences. This general tendency is disrupted, however,
by the abrupt move in the last seven pages to a new topic, the life of the
working population who have hitherto not been accommodated in
Macaulay's plan: 'It is time that this description of the England which
Charles the Second governed should draw to a close. Yet one subject of
the highest moment still remains untouched. Nothing has yet been said of
the great body of the people.'[64]

Already long enough and yet very much incomplete. Macaulay seeks
to excuse the *postscriptum* status of his treatment of the working classes
and the poor by his lack of sources: there is little which *can* be said about
the 'great body of the people' since their lives have largely gone
unrecorded. But this apologetic appendix can also be seen as symptomatic of the difficulties involved in taking 'the state of a nation' as a
discursive topic and the lack of models for doing so. Even more generally,
it can be seen as reflecting the problem of producing an extended
historical discourse on the basis of non-narrative principles and in the
absence of a figurative focus on a limited number of actors. Where should
one begin and where should one end? With the different participants in
the 'state of the nation' treated in a graded series from government to the
working classes (or vice versa, depending on your conceptualization of
politics), or with the different aspects of life, from the material to the
spiritual (or vice versa)? The difficulties posed by the lack of any single
structure for articulating information about social conditions perhaps
also explains why, despite the theoretical importance given to the 'history
of the people' in his statement of purpose, the attention paid to this
history in practice is so brief and marginal when compared with the
narrative of political events.

III: 3

The difficulties confronting Macaulay can be seen written large in
Amans-Alexis Monteil's *Histoire des Français des divers états aux cinq
derniers siècles* (1828–44). Rejecting history as it had hitherto been
written as mere *histoire-bataille*, as 'non-history', Monteil chose to
devote a work exclusively to the conditions of everyday life among the
great mass of people.[65] In his case, this history was not intended merely
to supplement political history, but to supplant it. Like more traditional
historians, however, he conceived his topic on a large scale. As the
complete history of all walks of life from the fourteenth century to the
time of writing, his work can indeed be seen as an alternative 'Histoire de

France'. Two volumes are devoted to each of the five centuries, and the sketch of each century is followed up by extensive, if impressionistic documentation. The general information Monteil has gleaned from his sources is imparted to the reader, as it is incidentally in Thierry, through the representation of particular fictional encounters or scenes. These scenes are not combined, however, to form a narrative.

How does one motivate talking at length about the conditions of everyday life? Macaulay, as we have seen, located his chapter on culture in the place traditionally reserved for 'the setting' of the political narrative. Monteil, in contrast, in rejecting customary historiographical subjects, also rejected the narrative model used to treat them. Instead, he opted for discursive models such as the letter, the travel description, the debate, and the diary apparently because these could provide pretexts for commenting on items of everyday life as points of interest in their own right.

Volumes I and II, devoted to the fourteenth century, take the form of a series of letters which a monk in Tours allegedly wrote to a friend in Toulouse. Each letter describes a different aspect of the society in which the monk is living, from lepers and the destitute to clocks, burials, schools, prisons and all the *arts et métiers*. The order in which the different topics are treated is apparently random and, in principle, the range of topics could have been extended at will. A very weak form of global, narrative coherence is provided by the fact that, in the final letter, the writer decides to contemplate his old age (he is nearly as old as the century) and look forward to death. Volumes III and IV (fifteenth century) take the form of a sort of 'parlement'; different groups have come together in the town hall of Troyes to debate the issue: which group has the most grounds for complaint? Representatives of thirty different groups, from the beggar to the astrologer, tell of their lot. Interspersed references to the situation in the town hall provide some sort of narrative continuity, but again the order in which the professions are treated is random and the ending a mere dropping of the curtain (the astrologer simply invites everyone to come outside and look at the stars). Volumes V and VI (sixteenth century) take the form of a journey made by a Spaniard around France: the beginning and end are motivated by his arrival and departure, and each of the sections, dealing with topics as diverse as rivers, canals, roads, printing-houses and architecture, corresponds to an overnight stay. Volumes VII and VIII (seventeenth century) are presented as an alternative to Voltaire's history of the same period, and take the form of a journal, written by a young man on the make. The topics treated in the different sections sometimes form coherent sequences (chapters 43–7, for example, deal with different aspects of the transport business; 73–4 deal with printers and booksellers), but there is no global coherence: after a series of sketches of life at the court, the view of the century closes with a chapter in which an encounter with a bellringer leads to a lengthy account of the different popular feasts celebrated every year in Paris. Finally, volumes IX and X take the form of no fewer than 125 'décades', which treat in apparently random fashion different aspects of life during the eighteenth century and the Revolution; closure is provided to the series simply by pronouncing a prolix 'adieu' to the eighteenth century.

Monteil's attempt to embody his limited amount of historical information in fictional scenes often leads to a lack of concision: the particular item of significant difference characterizing the age in question is often lost in the sketch given of the circumstances in which it was encountered. As the summary above suggests, moreover, the discursive models Monteil chose gave him the freedom to add as many subtopics as he wished and to treat them basically in any order he wished. But being above all models for short pieces, they provide no unifying principle for a more extended, composite discourse. The end result is that Monteil's reader is given no compelling reason to read the items in the order presented, or indeed to continue reading to the end. The fact that each century is treated according to a different plan and involves different topics makes it difficult, moreover, to conceive of the continuity and differences between the different centuries. In the words of one of Monteil's critics:

The variety of frameworks, into which so many different subjects are stuffed, destroys the unity of the composition. The detailed vision of things, seen from so close up, conceals from the reader's view the general appearance of the nation, its development as a whole and the connections between the different phases of its existence.[66]

Nevertheless, Monteil's experiment with different models enabled him to accommodate an extraordinarily wide range of cultural phenomena, from 'feast days', 'superstitions', and 'schooling' to 'printing', 'food', 'canals' and the different branches of the weaving trade – in many cases, topics whose historical interest has subsequently been recognized by historians. Even if his treatment of these topics was less than successful or definitive, he established them as potential topics for new treatment by others.[67] Thus Charles Louandre, in preparing the fifth edition of

Monteil's work in 1872, opted not to reproduce Monteil's ten-volume history as it had been conceived – 'this book, whose subject is even vaster than the number of volumes' – but to revise it on more methodical and orderly lines.[68] To this end, he compiled from the unsurveyable mass of Monteil's material a number of smaller-scale works based on much more narrowly defined topics, supplemented by tables of contents, indexes and general sketches of the changes taking place in the period under consideration: *Histoire de l'industrie française et des gens de métiers* (1872), *La Magistrature française* (1873), *Histoire agricole de la France* (1877), *Histoire financière de la France* (1881).[69]

III: 4

Michelet's *La Sorcière* (1862) is devoted exclusively to cultural phenomena over a long period of time. But where Monteil had tried to write a large-scale history of all aspects of culture, Michelet chose a much more narrowly defined topic which he treated in a mere 300 pages, made up of two books. Book 2 is largely a compilation of case studies extracted from his own history of France and forming a composite narrative structure reminiscent of Thierry's *Récits*: treated in chronological order, the cases together form a clearly defined narrative which traces the changes in witchcraft as a cultural phenomenon up to the eighteenth century.[70] Book 1 deals with the 'prehistory' of witchcraft as a juridico-cultural phenomenon and with popular beliefs in witchcraft.[71] Instead of relegating these topics to the marginal status of 'setting', however, Michelet treats them in the form of a continuous narrative on the biographical model. But since his material did not actually provide him with a historical figure who could exemplify the history he wanted to treat, he openly resorts to fiction (to avoid prolixity, as he puts it). In a manner which recalls 'Jacques Bonhomme', the allegorical figure used to give an abbreviated history of the French nation, Michelet invents 'the Witch':

To avoid getting bogged down in this lengthy historical and moral analysis of the creation of the Witch up to 1300, I have often followed a narrow biographical and dramatical strand, the life of the same woman across a period of three hundred years.[72]

The fragmentary and diverse material relating to popular culture which Michelet was dealing with here (in contrast to the relatively well-documented cases which are the subject of the second half) is integrated into the account of scenes typical for 'her' life. The discourse is organized both systematically and narratively: while each chapter deals with a different aspect of 'the witch' as an imagined figure, together they suggest a progression in her role from mediator between the living and the dead, and healer of woes, to satanic opponent of clerical repression. The recurrent reference to a nominally constant, grammatically singular figure called 'la femme' or 'elle' thus provides a fixed background against which varieties and changes in attitude and behaviour over hundreds of years are measured. Accordingly, it is with the account of her disappearance astride Satan's horse that the book ends.

If Michelet thus has openly recourse to a fictional figure in order to articulate his theme, to give it a beginning ('the woman was born') and an end ('On leaving, she laughed, with a terrifying cackle of laughter, and disappeared like an arrow') it is clear that there is no snug fit between the chosen biographical model and the material he is dealing with.[73] Where Thierry presented Chilperic's fictional speech as in all likelihood a good replica of a lost original, there is no possible – single – equivalent to Michelet's lady. Although 'she' is grammatically singular, it is understood, from the unabashed reference to her impossible longevity, that the name may correspond in different contexts to a number of different individuals; that she is the personification of an average. The life of the witch as a figure in popular culture thus approximates to a biography without literally being one. But this approximation can be seen as the price Michelet pays to overcome silence and make popular beliefs concerning witchcraft representable as the subject of a discourse. In the manner of a hypothesis or metaphor the figure of the witch is presented to the reader for the purposes of discussion *as if* it were an individual to whom others react, and of whom a biography can be written.[74]

IV

Although there has been much theoretical discussion in recent years about the role of 'narrative' and 'discourse', there has been a tendency to suppose the homogeneity of all history writing and to ignore the sheer variety of discursive forms adopted by historians (even within the same work). As my examples suggest, historical discourse may range from Macaulay's large-scale narrative of a country over a particular period (with its non-narrative account of culture), to Monteil's non-narrative history of culture over five centuries, to Thierry's 'short-story' collection, to Michelet's 'fictional biography' and series of case studies. But there is also the journal essay, the collection of essays by different historians, the single case study, the large-scale narrative account, the collection of case studies, the critical dictionary, and so on. Not only do these forms make different demands on their readers (a journal article or *récit* takes less time than a ten-volume monograph), they also allow readers to use them in different ways (a collection of essays, each of which is presumed to form a whole, for example, offers more possibilities for selective reading than does a monograph). As my examples also show, moreover, historical discourse does not always ask to be taken literally and sometimes has recourse to fiction.

All of this discursive variety is symptomatic of the lack of congruence between discourse and the world to which it refers. A lack of congruence does not mean, however, and I want to insist on this, that historical discourse is indifferent to events or that historians are free to compose their histories in any way they personally please. By virtue of their referential claim, historians are dependent on the information available in their sources and, by virtue of the same claim, their treatment of familar topics has to 'take into account' the work of predecessors and rivals.[75] As we have seen here, moreover, historians may also run into problems when trying to find appropriate models for dealing with the topic which interests them: representation supposes in the first case representability and, what is inseparable from this given the communicative function of discourse, intelligibility. At least one of the reasons for the persistence and popularity of the biographical model, even in situations where it is not directly applicable, may be the sheer difficulty in planning or imagining a large-scale discourse about particular historical phenomena *exclusively* on non-narrative principles. Or, to put this another way, the dramatic interest of a discourse – its 'overall forward movement' to recall the words of one of the reviewers quoted above[76] – may be one of the most efficient means of 'making sense' of a topic and ensuring the attention of the reader to the end of the text.

Transmitting coherent information sentence by sentence (and a necessary condition for this: ensuring the attention of the reader) can thus be seen as a regulative idea in the production of historical discourse. In order to realize this idea, however, the historian first has to find the 'connecting principle', to recall Blair's term, which makes intelligible as elements of a whole the different items of information at his or her disposal. This means that in actually carrying out their plan to treat a certain subject, historians may encounter difficulties: in reducing the quantity of information available and in organizing it, or conversely, in constructing a focussed account on the basis of disparate and fragmentary primary sources. Macaulay recognized the importance of the life of the common people as a topic, but gave this topic only a peripheral, *postscriptum* place in his discourse. Monteil attempted to include a maximum number of topics, but became prolix and incoherent. Monteil, Michelet and Thierry compromised the truth-claim of their discourse through the introduction of a fiction.

In other words, like every other human activity, the production of historical discourse involves failures, compromises, experiments.[77] What you may win on the swings of being interesting (e.g. by treating new subjects), you may lose on the roundabout of the quality of information.[78] What you win in the quality of the information, you may lose in terms of intelligibility and explanatory power. If a focussed point of view can be said to be the *desideratum*, many works are more or less off-focus – *flou*, blurred at the edges by an excess of information, an unsystematic organization of the material or an ill-defined subject. As is clear from the reviews of historical works, readers have a certain margin of tolerance. Just as Louandre reorganized Monteil's work on the grounds that the subject-matter was interesting, modern reviewers also show themselves ready to accept the interest of the subject, while criticizing, for example, the lack of straightforwardness and concision in the presentation, or the quality of the information. Indeed, one might argue that every historical work reflects its grounding in real events by the fact of always being at least slightly *flou*.

To be (partially) off-focus is to be open to revision in the form of a critical edition or abridgement, another version of the same topic involving a reorganization of the material, or, as my examples also show, a refinement of the topic. However flawed, a beginning has been made. Contrary to the received view that historians are uncreative from a literary point of view, history can be seen as proceeding by trial and error, sometimes even finding it necessary to suspend the truth-telling maxim by introducing fiction. What emerges in this process of trial and error, or more precisely, of trial and revisionism, is not only a store of information on the past and a store of interpretations, but also a store of topics, topic types and discursive models which can be used by other historians. The notion of experiment and 'imperfection' in history writing goes counter to the general tendency to consider historical writing only in those works considered masterpieces – ironically described by Lionel Gossman as the House of Lords of the historiographical institution.[79] In doing so, it gives theoretical recognition to the fact that many works are found wanting in some respect(s), and that many of them are explicitly and implicitly rewritten by others. By introducing the possibility of fuzziness and compromise into the theoretical consideration of historical writing, it becomes interesting to reconsider how historical writing evolves; how historians stimulate each other to follow up certain topics, how they may be influenced in their choice of subject by novelistic fictions, and how they learn from each other's mistakes. The works considered here suggest that this process involves the recycling and adaptation of discursive models, but also changes in the very conception of what is an appropriate and 'manageable' subject for historical discourse.

The fact that Michelet was my last example might seem to suggest that his fictional biography combined with case histories represented *the* solution to the problem of writing about cultural or 'mentality' history. This work, which has continued to be reprinted, might well be seen as one of the ancestors of contemporary micro-history and certainly as one of the ancestors of Le Roy Ladurie's *La Sorcière de Jasmin* (1983, a re-edition with commentary of a Provençal poem about a village-sorceress written down in 1842).[80] But it is by no means the only model in circulation. Thus, the *Histoire de la vie privée* (1985–7), written collectively under the direction of Philippe Ariès and Georges Duby, has much in common with Monteil's history, not only the fact of being divided into five parts, but also the fact that each part treats of a particular period in time and is organized according to different principles: where volume I, for example, is organized chronologically (each chapter deals with a different place at a different period), volume IV is arranged systematically following the metaphor of a theatre ('Lever de rideau', 'Les acteurs', 'Scènes et lieux', 'Coulisses'). Apparently, the project of writing a large-scale history of (an aspect of) culture is still alive, and historians are still experimenting with ways of writing coherently about it. The fact that at least one critic of the *Histoire de la vie privée* complained of 'its miscellaneousness and exasperating irrelevancies' suggests that the pattern of trial and revision is set to continue.[81]

ARGUMENTS

7
'Grand Narrative' and the Discipline of History

ALLAN MEGILL

ALLAN MEGILL

THE PRESUMED ABSORPTIVENESS OF PROFESSIONAL HISTORIOGRAPHY

Introducing a collection of essays on *New Perspectives on Historical Writing*, Peter Burke notes that 'in the last generation or so the universe of historians has been expanding at a dizzying rate.'[1] In this essay I wish to point out some limits to that expansion, even while applauding it. Long before the rise of the most recent 'new' histories; it was part of the mythology of the discipline that historiography is an absorptive enterprise, peculiarly open to whatever useful approaches, methods and the like it finds in other fields.[2] But for all its eclecticism, the discipline's absorptiveness, and its openness, are severely constrained. A particular assumption – at base, an ontological assumption – underlies and gives force to the belief in history's absorptiveness. In briefest terms, the assumption might be characterized as an assumption of ultimate world unity. Such an assumption lies behind the grand narratives that have prevailed in Western historiography.[3] In this essay, I survey the various modifications of the conception of grand narrative that have manifested themselves in the tradition of modern Western professional historiography. I do so with a view to casting some light on the current situation of historiography, a situation that has both a diachronic aspect, linked to this continuing tradition, and a synchronic aspect, linked to the particular conditions of present-day life and culture.

My aim is to offer an account of the deep intellectual bases for the disciplinization or departmentalization of historiography. Disciplines – history included – have boundaries. Scholars who are firmly within a discipline most often do not think about its boundaries. Instead, they feel its constraints as simply those of good scholarship generally. There are institutional reasons why this is so. It is a matter of community, and of modes of socialization into community. Except, sometimes, in a few multi-disciplinary fields – for example women's studies, cultural studies, science studies – participants in one discipline in the humanities and social sciences usually lack serious engagement with participants in other disciplines. Although they may on occasion borrow from other disciplines, they do not have the experience of entering into the modes of argument of those disciplines. Indeed, it seems often the case that the larger or more prestigious the academic institution, the higher the barriers. The institutions in question are most often set up in a heavily disciplinary way, and so is the larger scholarly world. The historian's departmental seminar operates in isolation from all the other humanities and social-sciences seminars, and each of these operates in isolation as well. (Indeed, the departmental seminar is often itself highly fragmented, drawing participation only from a particular field of specialists. This narrowness is often unfortunate, and could be corrected by greater attention to theory.) The awarding of tenure, too, is heavily departmentalized.

I deliberately operate in this essay at an extremely high level of generality, while acknowledging that accounts could be offered at other levels, yielding much more complex and historically specific views.[4] I do so because my aim is to engage in something of a *Grundlagenreflexion* on the assumptions and general character of the historical discipline. I apologise in advance for the abstraction that results, and urge careful attention to the definitions. Reflection of the sort that I attempt here – while obviously only a small part of what historians can and should do – is important because it brings to light what would otherwise remain unexamined prejudice. Such reflection, in short, has a theoretical significance. Moreover, I am persuaded that the argument also has a practical significance, for the researching and writing of history. For example, issues of synthesis have recently come up in historiographical discussion.[5] So, too, have issues of literary form, for example of fictiveness and of narrative coherence. Both sorts of issue might well be illuminated were one to bear in mind the schema that I shall present in this essay.

Obviously, an important issue here, perhaps the crucial one, is that of coherence. The subject is not capable of being exhausted in a single survey, but one can at least make some important distinctions. It seems useful to think of 'coherence' as occupying four distinct levels of conceptualization. These are: (1) *narrative proper*; (2) *master narrative* or synthesis, which claims to offer the authoritative account of some particular segment of history; (3) *grand narrative*, which claims to offer the authoritative account of history generally; and (4) *metanarrative* (most commonly, belief in God or in a rationality somehow immanent in the world), which serves to justify the grand narrative. In the present essay I focus specifically on the level of grand narrative. I do so because this will allow the development of a framework that I am inclined to think will help us to make sense both of the more specific issues, and of the fact that they have arisen *as* issues at that particular (postmodern?) moment that is ours. In essence, my concern is with the claim that 'professional' or 'disciplinary' historiography makes to a peculiarly authoritative role in the understanding of the past – that is, its claim to 'objectivity' in the broadest sense of that term.[6]

FOUR IDEAL-TYPICAL ATTITUDES TOWARDS THE OVERALL COHERENCE OF HISTORY

Observers of and participants in the tradition of modern Western professional historiography have generally held that every particular work of history ought to orient itself to history generally – that is, to a single history, which I shall here designate as History.[7] We can plausibly view the tradition as having related historiography to History in four ways, manifesting four 'attitudes' towards History. The attitudes can be ordered chronologically, although they can also be co-existent, and I would argue that in the best historiography they are so. They are conceptual types. Firstly, one finds belief in a particular 'grand narrative' claiming to make sense of history as a whole. The gist of 'attitude 1' is that there is a single coherent History and that it can be told (or retold) now. 'Attitude 2' holds that there is a single coherent History but defers its telling to a later date, after 'further research' has been done. 'Attitude 3' holds that there is a single coherent History, but that it can never be told. Obviously, if one thinks in narrativist terms one will find a paradox here, for a grand narrative that can never be told has nothing at all of the *form* of narrative. Instead, it manifests itself in the commitment of historians to the autonomy of their discipline, a commitment that serves to maintain the discipline's purity and coherence in the absence of any single story to which it converges. 'Attitude 4' calls even this form of coherence into question.

That professional historiography has presupposed the existence, although not necessarily the telling, of a vision of coherence has been largely invisible to historians themselves. Of course, historians are generally well aware of the problem of coherence at more specific levels, whether it is a matter of constructing a single (by definition coherent) narrative, or a matter of addressing the implicit or explicit 'master narrative' of some specific historical field (as Geyer and Jarausch do; see note 5). The issue here, however, is coherence at a 'world' level. Because the articulation of conceptual presumptions is a theoretical rather than a historiographical task, only rarely do historians articulate them. Moreover, there is a tendency for investigators, including historians of historiography, to miss precisely those features of a situation that are most 'natural' to them.

Still, *some* historians of historiography – invariably informed by extradisciplinary studies – have seen what is here pointed out. Reinhart Koselleck, a practitioner of *Begriffsgeschichte*, noted the emergence in late eighteenth-century Germany of the 'collective singular' use of the term 'Geschichte' and contended that, for writers within that frame, 'history in the collective singular establishe(d) the terms of all possible individual histories.'[8] A reading of literary theory led Robert F. Berkhofer, Jr., to find in professional historians' concern with context the assumption that the past is 'a complex but unified flow of events,' a 'Great Story.'[9] The philosopher Louis Mink found that the eighteenth-century notion of 'universal history' survives in twentieth-century historiography.[10] Finally, operating from a Kantian standpoint, Leonard Krieger emphasized professional historiography's persistent search for coherence.[11]

Krieger's account is especially telling. Krieger showed that when historians lack fundamental agreement concerning the character of human history, the coherence of the historiographical enterprise is threatened – and vice versa. Developing Krieger's point, from a present-day viewpoint we can see that professional historiography as it emerged in the nineteenth century was remarkably unified in its attitude to human history. Whatever their different national and ideological standpoints, almost all professional historians agreed that history was political, European and male. But in recent years professional historiography has found itself driven into a greater pluralism. The change strains the hope that a unified view of the past can be attained, even as it challenges the former homogeneity of the enterprise. It also strains the view that historiography can and ought to be autonomous in relation to other enterprises. Krieger was a professional historian's professional historian deeply committed to the autonomy of the discipline. He held that the historian, although learning from neighbouring disciplines, ought nonetheless to function as a 'pure historian' (that is, as a historian uncontaminated by other disciplines' modes of thinking), for the coherence of a 'distinctively historical knowledge' underwrites 'the coherence of the past.'[12] Yet Krieger's own emphasis on the relation between the subjective and the objective aspect calls into doubt the prospects for a coherent disciplinary vision in any time of social disjunction.

Attitude 1: There is a single History and we already know what it is.

Attitude 1 is embodied in the tradition of 'universal history.' Universal history is relevant to our problem of disciplinary boundaries, because in its secularized form it had an immense impact on professional historiography. Although its roots are to be found as early as the Patristic period, it first became a continuing tradition of scholarship and teaching in Protestant German universities after the Reformation humanist Philipp Melanchthon lectured on the subject at the University of Wittenberg in the mid-sixteenth century. In an age when a nation-state did not develop in Germany, as it did in France and Britain, universal history provided for Protestant Germans a vision of unity and glory that they otherwise lacked.[13]

Christian universal history emphasized the Hebrews and took its chronology and periodization from the Bible. In the course of the early modern period, the Biblical focus was challenged, and ultimately abandoned. But the undermining of Christian universal history did not destroy the idea of universal history itself, which continued in secularized (i.e. non-Biblical) form. In Germany, of course, the idea was supported by the existence of university chairs devoted to it.

The secularized tradition of universal history is the true beginning of the story that I tell here. Although the secularized tradition accorded no special privilege to the Bible, the basic idea of the earlier, Biblically-based conception remained in place – namely, the idea that there is finally a single history, whose unity is guaranteed by God. Conceptually, a new problem emerged in the move from universal history based on sacred scripture to one that, although presupposed by theism, granted no special privilege to scripture. In the first case, one can tell the grand narrative now because one's telling is actually *re*telling, whereas in the second case the telling has no pre-existing model. How is one to discover what the grand narrative is, since it is no longer prescribed by the Bible? Can one in fact *know* the grand narrative? To what degree, and by what means?

Immanuel Kant offered one answer. His essay 'Idea for a Universal History from a Cosmopolitan Point of View' (1784) explicitly contributed to the universal history tradition, and Kant returned to the matter in 'An Old Question Raised Again: is the Human Race Constantly

Progressing?' (1795).[14] In the former, Kant suggested that a 'philosophical history' of mankind could be written. The philosophical history would show how the apparently chaotic workings of individual freedom, when viewed 'from the standpoint of the human race as a whole,' may be seen as contributing to 'a steady and progressive though slow evolution' the end of which is 'the civic union of the human race.' Indeed, the writing of such a history would help to achieve the desired end.[15] But Kant knew that such a history could not be empirically justified, and disclaimed any wish to displace the world of 'practicing empirical historians.'[16]

In the essay of 1795 Kant again emphasized that 'the problem of progress is not to be resolved directly through experience'; yet he also contended that something in experience must at least *point* to 'the disposition and capacity of the human race to be the cause of its own advance toward the better.'[17] In considering his own time, Kant found just such an empirical indicator in 'the mode of thinking of the spectators' of the greatest event of his own time, the French Revolution. Observers who had nothing to gain from the Revolution greeted it with near enthusiasm, even in Prussia, where such enthusiasms were dangerous. Their sympathy for the Revolution, Kant held, could have been caused only by a 'moral predisposition' in the human race, the presence of which gives ground for believing that human history is progressive.[18] Hegel, too, claimed to be able to discern and to tell the essential shape of history, which he saw as a progressive realization of freedom: first one person is free, then some, then all.[19]

Yet the telling of the grand narrative carries risks, for future events may diverge from the suggested story-line. For example, in May 1789 Friedrich Schiller delivered his inaugural lecture as professor of history at the University of Jena. Inspired by Kant's 'Idea for a Universal History,' he spoke on the topic 'What is universal history and why do we study it ?' Schiller recounted a movement from barbarism, still visible in primitive races, to the civilization of eighteenth-century Europe, where truth, morality and freedom were growing ever more powerful. In his view, '(t)he European society of states seems transformed into a large family,' whose members could 'still show enmity to one another, but no longer tear each other to bits.'[20] Schiller apparently never commented on the discrepancy between his complacent account of European history in the inaugural lecture and the world-shattering events unleashed only two months later in France.[21]

A related problem concerns the level of detail to be included in the grand narrative. In a review of 1772 of August Wilhelm von Schlözer's *Universal-Historie*, Johann Gottfried Herder criticized Schlözer for not having implemented the plan of universal history that his book proposed. Responding, Schlözer agreed with Herder's observation that it is easier to propose something than to do it (*dass sich etwas leichter sagen als thun lasse*), but contended that 'where it is a matter of world history . . . it must be *proposed* (*gesagt*) before it is *done* . . . a *plan*, a *theory*, an *ideal* of this science must be drawn up.'[22] In other words, Schlözer held that the outline of the story can be told now, but he deferred its *complete* telling until later. Schlözer clearly must have thought of that later telling as a mere amplification of the outline. But what, one might ask, if the later telling were less amplification than correction? In such a case, we could not be said to know already what the single History is.

Attitude 2: There is a single History, but we can know what it is only after further research has been done.

Attitude 2 defers the telling of the story. Gaining prominence historically as a response to the upheavals of the Revolutionary and Napoleonic Wars, attitude 2 was intimately connected with the emergence of professional historiography. The canonical founder of the discipline, Leopold von Ranke, was critical of such universal historians as Gatterer, Johannes Müller and Friedrich Christoph Schlosser.[23] He was even more critical of such philosophers as Hegel, who attempted to posit *a priori* the course of human history. But he was not critical of universal history as such; on the contrary, it remained a continuing preoccupation for him.[24]

Consider the following passage, from a fragment that Ranke wrote in the 1860s:

[T]he investigation of the particular is always related to a larger context. Local history is related to that of a country; a biography is related to a larger event in state and church, to an epoch of national or general history. But all these epochs themselves are, as we have said, again part of the great whole (*Ganzen*) which we call universal history. The greater scope of its investigation has correspondingly greater value. The ultimate goal, not yet attained, will always remain the conception and composition of a history of mankind. . .Comprehending the whole and yet doing justice to the requirements of research will, of course, always remain an ideal. It would presuppose an understanding on a firm foundation of the totality of human history.[25]

Ranke here envisaged three distinct levels of historical concern. The first, 'the investigation of the particular, even of a single point,' evokes what historians today call micro-history. The second, which shows how the particular is part of a 'larger context,' is also visible in present-day historiography. The third level, concerned with 'the great totality' – with 'comprehending the whole' – is hidden, but the *idea* of it is familiar to us: it is the idea of grand narrative; of a unified history of humankind.

In his reference to 'the ultimate goal . . . not yet attained,' Ranke acknowledged a deferral of the telling of such a history. Similar statements are to be found elsewhere in his corpus; for example, in a lecture script of 1867 he wrote that '(T)he science of history is not yet mature enough to reconstruct universal history on new foundations.'[26] In fact, insistence on a deferral of the telling of grand narrative was necessary for history's emergence as a discipline. Kant, Schiller and Hegel believed that they already knew the basic outline of human history – or at any rate they believed that they knew which outline of human history it was best to posit as true. Their conviction deprived historical research of its rationale, for, persuaded by such accounts, one would 'seek only to know to what extent the philosophical principle can be demonstrated in history . . . (I)t would be of no interest at all to delve into the things that happened . . . or to want to know how men lived and thought at a certain time.' Furthermore, 'were this procedure [of constructing 'the whole of history' on an *a priori* basis] correct, history (*Historie*) would lose all autonomy (*Selbständigkeit*).[27] If through sacred scripture, or through knowledge of human nature, or in some other way we are able to tell the story now, what pressing need is there for the supposedly distinctive methods of professional historical research?[28]

Ranke's justification for continuing to believe in the reality of a single History, even in the absence of its present telling, was religious. God created the world and oversees everything in it, one God creating one History. Hints of this view are to be found in Ranke's 'Idea of Universal History,' where, in referring to the 'conception of totality' (*Auffassung der Totalität*) that is one of the features of universal history, he asserts that it is impossible for us to grasp universal history completely: 'Only God knows world history.'[29] But the connection between the idea of God and the idea of History's unity was perhaps stated most clearly in a letter that the young Ranke wrote to his brother in 1820:

God dwells, lives, and can be known in all of history. Every deed attests to Him, every moment preaches His name, but most of all, it seems to me, the connectedness of history in the large. It [the connectedness] stands there like a holy hieroglyph . . . May we, for our part, decipher this holy hieroglyph! Even so do we serve God. Even so are we priests. Even so are we teachers.[30]

There is thus a manifest continuity between Ranke and earlier, Christian conceptions of universal history.

Adherence to the notion of grand narrative by no means required religious faith, for forms of secular faith could also serve. Consider J. B. Bury's inaugural lecture of 1902 as Regius Professor of Modern History at Cambridge, entitled 'The Science of History.' Here Bury suggested that

the idea of the future development of man . . . furnishes . . . the justification of much of the laborious historical work that has been done and is being done to-day. The gathering of materials bearing upon minute local events, the collation of MSS. and the registry of their small variations, the patient drudgery in archives of states and municipalities, all the microscopic research that is carried on by armies of toiling students . . . This work, the hewing of wood and the drawing of water, has to be done in faith – in the faith that a complete assemblage of the smallest facts of human history will tell in the end. The labour is performed for posterity – for remote posterity.[31]

The justification for Bury's faith lay in the late nineteenth-century global expansion of Western civilization and in the ideals of science and cooperation that Bury thought had made the expansion possible. Bury's stance was structurally identical with Ranke's, despite its secular focus. Like Ranke, Bury adhered to attitude 2, deferring the telling of the grand narrative to the future. Bury's foil was an explicit adherent of attitude 1, Thomas Arnold, who in his inaugural lecture of 1841 as Regius Professor of Modern History at Oxford had suggested that the 'modern age' coincided with 'the last step' in the story of man – that it bore marks 'of the fulness of time, as if there would be no future history beyond it.'[32] Bury demurred, but not because he objected to the idea of a single History *per se*. He believed that it was too soon to know the shape of history, not that there is no single shape to be known.

One might be tempted to think that deferral of its telling would dramatically reduce the relevance of belief in a single History to the writing of history. But its relevance remains, for belief in universal history (albeit a universal history that is as yet untellable) has an important epistemological consequence. The belief allows historians to maintain that the historical account is an objective representation, connected to the standpoint of History itself. As Krieger noted, Ranke's 'assurance about the historian's objectivity' was predicated on belief in 'a single process' linking past and present.[33] In 'The Science of History,' Bury made precisely the same point. He began by insisting that history is a science – 'no less and no more.'[34] 'Science,' for Bury, implied purely objective representation: it 'cannot safely be controlled or guided by a subjective interest.'[35] Rejecting a relation to his own time and place, the historian claims to relate himself to the historical process as a whole. 'Principles of unity and continuity' exist within history, Bury believed.[36] These principles suggest the idea of man's future development, which serves as a 'limiting controlling conception' telling the historian what belongs in a historical account and what should be excluded.[37]

Attitude 3: There is a single History. However, it can never be told. It exists only ideally, as the unreachable end of an autonomous discipline. Coherence is now located not in the told or anticipated Story, but in the unified mode of thinking of the discipline.

Attitude 3 gives up the notion that the single History will ever be told, without giving up the notion that there is a 'single history'–that is, a single authorized mode of investigating the past. The historian and theorist of historiography Johann Gustav Droysen, who from 1857 to 1883 lectured on the theory and methodology of history, came close to articulating this attitude. Droysen maintained in his lectures that the grand narrative could never be told, at least not on the basis of historical investigation. '[T]he highest end' of history, he asserted, 'is not to be discovered by empirical investigation.'[38] As the mention of a 'highest end' suggests, Droysen believed that a coherent History exists. But whereas Ranke and Bury believed that the historian could discover coherence within the objective historical process, Droysen shifted attention to the subjective sphere. Without denying the existence of an objective coherence, he chose 'to establish, not the laws of objective History but the laws of historical investigation and knowledge.'[39] Further, 'historical investigation and knowledge' can embody laws guaranteeing coherence only if historiography is itself a coherent enterprise, clearly bounded off from competing enterprises and concerns. In consequence, Droysen insisted on the autonomy of historiography; indeed, Hayden White has suggested that he offered 'the most sustained and systematic defense of the autonomy of historical thought ever set forth'.[40]

While Ranke also emphasized the autonomy of history, defending the subject against those who would approach it with a ready-made grand narrative borrowed from philosophy, Droysen's insistence on autonomy had an additional role: it protected historiography not only from the first, pre-professional conviction that the story is already known but also from another threat, that of multiplicity and fragmentation. For a mid-nineteenth-century historian, Droysen (a Prussian nationalist of liberal bent) was remarkably sensitive to the possibility of past historical facts being recounted, explained and interpreted in vastly different ways. For whatever reasons, he seems to have been aware that adherents of competing identities would be inclined to claim legitimacy for their histories just as he claimed legitimacy for Prussia's.[41] Ranke, on the other hand, was protected from coming to grips with such threats by his conviction that Europe constituted a unified political system, and by his belief that the task of historiography is to write the history of that (European) system.[42] More sensitive, it appears, to the conflict of interests and identities, Droysen was correspondingly more able to see multiplicity as a *problem*; he recognized multiplicity as legitimate, but at the same time insisted on containing it.[43]

Attitude 3 abandons the hope of ever articulating an objective grand narrative (that is, an authoritative account of History as a whole), while retaining commitment to coherence at the level of the historical enterprise itself, which is seen as united by adherence to common methods and aims. Attitude 3 is an idealized version of what seems to have been the dominant stance of the historical profession in the twentieth century c.1914-91.[44] After the slaughter of World War I – carried out, it seemed, for naught – most professional historians no longer saw their task as the deciphering of a holy hieroglyph or as the telling of a great story of progress. Even if many continued to believe that history was fundamentally benevolent, they no longer saw it as the *historian*'s task to portray this benevolence.[45] Attitude 3 has the advantage of allowing adherence to a single ideal, without requiring that the ideal be embodied in a specific historical content.

Yet attitude 3 is deeply paradoxical and tension-laden, for behind commitment to historiography as a single, coherent enterprise there continues to reside the ghost of the hope for an objective grand narrative, yet the grand narrative cannot be told. Because Droysen, who studied under Hegel, was deeply influenced by German idealist philosophy and continued to believe in a 'moral world . . . moved by many ends, and finally . . . by the supreme end,' we cannot finally see him as embodying attitude 3 in a form that is clearly marked off from attitudes 1 and 2.[46] Among theorists of historiography, it is R. G. Collingwood who best exemplifies attitude 3, and thus best displays its inherent contradictions. (Admittedly, one might also look to Wilhelm Dilthey or Michael Oakeshott, who, like Droysen and Collingwood, focus attention on the subjective dimension, that is, on historians' *thinking*.[47] But Collingwood is the clearest thinker of the lot, and his clarity reveals what remains hidden elsewhere.[48])

Collingwood made two crucial 'third attitude' claims about historiography. Professional historians readily embraced the claims, for they conformed to how historians in the twentieth century 'always already' conceived of their enterprise.

Firstly Collingwood claimed that historiographical coherence has its roots in the mind of the historian. In a general sense, Collingwood's position on this issue was Kantian. Kant accepted David Hume's assertion that we cannot perceive causation (although we can perceive the spatial contiguity, temporal succession and constant conjunction that are normally associated with causation). Hume's view raised the threat of a totalized scepticism, to which Kant responded by asserting that causation is not something empirically discoverable but is an organizing principle in the mind. When, famously, Collingwood in *The Idea of History* attacked a passive 'scissors-and-paste' history and argued that the historian who depends on the documents to provide coherence will wait for ever, he was following out the implications for historiography of Kant's 'Copernican Revolution' in philosophy.[49]

Secondly, Collingwood repeatedly emphasized the 'autonomy' of history.[50] In invoking autonomy he actually referred to two different notions. In the first place, he was concerned to emphasize that the historian ought to have autonomy in relation to 'the sources,' making up his own mind about the past rather than relying on the supposed authority of the sources. This first emphasis is simply another way of saying that coherence is rooted in the mind of the historian. But 'autonomy' in Collingwood also refers to a different claim, namely, that historians ought to have autonomy in relation to other disciplines. Here Collingwood's argument is that historiography is an independent discipline, with its own rules (different from the rules of other disciplines) that have been worked out over time through a process of trial and error.[51] We can see why he would want to emphasize the autonomy of history in relation to other disciplines, for only if one holds that historiography is a clearly bounded field with its own distinctive set of rules can one expect historical thinking to provide coherence. In other words, the subjectivization of coherence – that is, its relocation into the mind of the historian – placed a premium on the claim that historiography is an autonomous enterprise.

Yet at various points Collingwood undermined, and even directly denied, the notion that historiography ought to be an autonomous enterprise in the sense just noted. For example, in his *Autobiography* he asserted this his life's work, as seen from his fiftieth year, 'has been in the main an attempt to bring about a *rapprochement* between philosophy and history.'[52] Collingwood's philosophical opponents of the time made a sharp distinction between historical questions (e.g. what was Aristotle's theory of duty?) and philosophical questions (e.g. was it true?), and saw only the philosophical questions as important.[53] Collingwood attacked the separation of the two enterprises. Further, he contended that '[t]he chief business of twentieth-century philosophy is to reckon with twentieth-century history,' a contention that connected with another *rapprochement* he wanted, namely, between theory and practice.[54] His position was not only that philosophy should become historical, but also that history should become philosophical, and that both should be written out of a profound concern with present problems – for events, he asserted, had broken up his 'pose of a detached professional thinker' and had moved him towards engagement.[55]

In *The Idea of History*, Collingwood's undercutting of the autonomy of historiography is less evident.[56] Yet the undercutting is clearly *there*. It is manifested, for example, in his otherwise quite puzzling contention that history is 're-enactment of past experience,'[57] a wording that seems intended to emphasize, to a greater degree than mere 're-thinking,' the activism of the historian. Similarly, his contention that '[e]very present has a past of its own, and any imaginative reconstruction of the past aims at reconstructing the past of *this* present,' has subversive implications that potentially demolish his more conservative assertion that 'all history must be consistent with itself.'[58]

Attitude 4: The assumption that there is a single History cannot be maintained, either subjectively as an enterprise or objectively as an actual grand narrative to be told now or in the future. Accordingly, a responsible historiography will call the assumption of a single History into question. Yet attitudes 1, 2 and 3, which assume a single History, can still be entertained: regulatively, in the case of attitude 1; heuristically or ironically, in the cases of attitudes 2 and 3. Attitude 4 both embraces these other attitudes and calls them into question.

Attitude 4 is perhaps best approached by reflection on table 1, which suggests the proximity of each attitude to the others. As ideal types, the four attitudes are distinct from each other. In reality, however, they shade off from one to the other; they can also coexist with each other, with the 'later' views taking account of the 'earlier' ones. Only a slight incredulity in the present tellability of History is needed for attitude 1 to shade off into attitude 2, as the exchange between Herder and Schlözer, noted

TABLE 1 *Four attitudes towards a single History*

Attitude 2: There is a single History, to be known only after 'further research' has been done.	*Attitude 3:* There is a single History, namely, the autonomous and coherent discipline of history.
Attitude 1: There is a single History, and we know it now.	*Attitude 4:* A single History is unjustified, but may be entertained. Border-crossing and methodological breaches *may* have justification.

above, shows.[59] Only a slight incredulity in the future tellability of History is needed for attitude 2 to shade off into attitude 3: recall Ranke, who in the same fragment wrote both that the telling of History was '[t]he ultimate goal, not yet attained,' and that '[c]omprehending the whole. . .will always remain an ideal.'[60] Similarly, in Collingwood, emphasis on the autonomy of historiography, which preserves subjective coherence even in the face of the permanent untellability of an objective grand narrative, tips over, when pushed hard enough, into the notion that the time within which historical thinking is being done is as important as the time of the past – to such a degree that past time gets reconfigured, at every moment, from the viewpoint of the present. In short, there is a conceptual instability pushing one type over into one or more of the other types.

More accurately, *beyond attitude 1* there is a conceptual instability. Attitude 1 is the only inherently stable position. Arising out of historically localized and scripturally authorized monotheism (Judaism, Christianity, Islam), it seems to have no reason to collapse as long as its religious justification is secure. But the other attitudes are different. Attitude 2 teeters between the possibility that 'further research' will *never* yield an objective universal history, and the heuristically or dogmatically maintained view that we already know, at least in outline, the objective universal history. Attitude 3 is caught between pride in the procedures of the historical discipline and unease that the procedures will never reveal an objective universal history. As for attitude 4, it occupies the difficult position of Pyrrhonian or Montaignean scepticism, which strives to be sceptical also of its own scepticism. From the point of view of attitude 3, attitude 4 is contradictory to the coherent way of thinking that is legitimate historiography. From the point of view of attitude 4, on the other hand, one ought not to exclude any mode of understanding the past on *a priori* grounds, whether methodological or ontological. Thus attitude 4 is not an argument against (for example) attitude 3, except insofar as attitude 3 seeks to dismiss attitude 4. Yet attitude 4 is constantly in danger of falling into one version or another of dogmatism – either through dogmatic adherence to the view that 'there is no single History' (which is itself a statement about the overall character of History), or through dogmatic rejection of disciplinary standards and convention.

My focus in this essay is of course on conceptual presumptions. Investigations of the institutional bases of the discipline would yield a more variegated picture. *Gross modo*, however, my central argument seems justified on an institutional level as well. The institutional structures of intellectual life include, among other things, professional organizations, disciplinary journals and the departmental organization of universities, all of which find intellectual justification in the presumption that historians are engaged in a single project. My argument here is that in the current situation both the institutional structures and the presumptions justifying them ought to be seen not just as supports for the production of knowledge, which they manifestly are, but as limits as well, and further that we ought to consider seriously the character of those limits.

The presumption that historiography is finally a single project has the effect of establishing a bias in favour of work written out of the conviction that there is a single, autonomous, historical mode of thinking – an approach, even a method, that aspires to 'unification' in 'history and the historical profession' in spite of a manifest disunity at the levels of subjects and subject matters. (I evoke here the theme of the American Historical Association annual meeting of December 1992[61]). The aim is to 'historicize' history's objects – that is, to subject them to the methods of a single historical thinking. The presumption of unity establishes a bias against work that reflects on the past in ways that involve commitments to other modes of understanding than the autonomously historical. Insofar as history so practised relates to other modes of understanding, it does so by way of 'appropriating' them for history. I do not reject such work, for that would be inconsistent with my rejection of *a priori* methodological criteria for judging scholarly work. Rather, my suggestion is that, because we have worked for so long from the standpoint of the 'autonomy' view – attitudes 2 and 3 – we have to reckon with diminishing marginal returns and to consider that it becomes difficult therein to produce new and surprising knowledge. This is a *suggestion*, not a solid assertion as to fact, for the future of any science is by its nature unpredictable.

There are other arguments as well that might be advanced for the partial de-disciplinization of history. The other arguments have for the most part already been developed, sometimes in considerable detail, although most often in contexts that historians do not attend to. Looking specifically at historiography, the historian and theorist of historiography F. R. Ankersmit points to what he calls 'the present-day overproduction in our discipline. . . We are all familiar with the fact that . . . an overwhelming number of books and articles is produced annually, making a comprehensive view of them all impossible'.[62] The result, Ankersmit argues, has been a move away from 'the essentialist tradition within Western historiography,' which focused attention on 'the trunk of the tree.' Instead, one can now see a 'pull' towards the margins, manifested in forms of historiography that no longer focus on 'meaning' (*sens*; that is, sense or direction) but instead address themselves to aspects of the past (such as mentalities, gender and the like) that were formerly seen as mere 'notations,' without significance for the general plot of history.[63]

Beyond historiography, there exists a philosophical line of argument, pre-eminently represented in certain aspects of the early writings of Jacques Derrida, which clearly has implications for the unity-claims of disciplines generally (I think especially of Derrida's notion of 'originary difference' or 'différance', which we can take as part of an argument against convergence).[64] The analytic philosopher Nicholas Rescher, arguing for the legitimacy of an 'orientational pluralism' in philosophy, advances a notion that seems as applicable to concerns with synthesis in historiography as it is to concerns with consensus in philosophy.[65] The political scientists Mattei Dogan and Robert Pahre argue, on the basis of empirical study, that 'hybridization' between disciplines, not specialization within them or unification between them, is currently the most reliable route to new knowledge. The Dogan and Pahre argument implies mixed or hybrid modes coexisting with continued disciplinarity.[66]

All the arguments point towards something much broader than historiography, or even than the human sciences generally. They point towards a cultural condition that has come to be identified as 'postmodern.' This is not the place to survey the immense literature that has emerged in an attempt to explicate just what the term and the reality of 'the postmodern' mean.[67] The term itself is both unsatisfactory and (at least for the moment) indispensable. A global definition does not seem possible (indeed, one suspects that a global definition would mean abandonment of the term). Still, one feature of the current social and cultural situation seems peculiarly salient to what is normally thought of as 'postmodern.' This feature is the juxtaposition of diversities. It is not that the social cultural situation is any more 'diverse' than it was before; rather, via contemporary modes of communication, the diversities are brought into closer proximity than before, so that the general feeling is of a quite amazing disjunctiveness.

It seems impossible and in any case undesirable to attempt to homogenize or synthesize the diversity. At most there is a syncretism, but even syncretism is no solution to the 'problem' of diversity in the (American) academy, in nation-states, or in the world generally. 'The postmodern condition' is manifest in a classroom inhabited by campus conservatives and liberals, by members of the bisexual, gay and lesbian alliance, by several varieties of Christian activism, by Asian-, European- and African-Americans and several varieties of admixture among them, by persons whose native languages are Spanish, Chinese, German and English, not forgetting people whose tastes in music and entertainment run a wide range from punk to soul to classical. In the teaching context, the challenge is somehow to hold the mixture together, without exclusion or explosion.

There is a close parallel between juxtaposed social diversities and juxtaposed disciplines. In both cases we are dealing with boundaries – boundaries, I contend, that should not be wished away. Incredulity towards the discipline's claim to autonomy (for that is what 'incredulity towards grand narrative' finally amounts to) means a questioning but not a denial of boundaries. In short, my argument is not an argument for interdisciplinary unification, not an argument for 'synthesis' at a broader level than that of historiography. For there are limits to 'openness.' The more that one learns about how practitioners of other disciplines argue, through the experience of having argued with them on their own grounds, the less likely one is to think that the modes of argument are compatible enough for any one person to practise them at the same time.[68] And yet these other modes of argument, when well done, also contribute to knowledge. My argument is rather for the *crossing* of boundaries, for temporary residence in other domains, for attempts to speak or at least to understand the foreign language (a different enterprise from translation), and for explicit recognition of the desirability of such projects *within* the historical discipline, to replace misguided views about the wonderful absorptiveness of professional historiography and about the unity of historical method.[69] It is also an argument for invention of hybrid states, possibly temporary Andorras, between the extant ones.

Since the story offered here ends not in the past, however recent, but in the present and future, it acquires inevitably a prescriptive dimension. To be sure, the only really satisfactory answer to the question 'How should science and scholarship be done now?' is to do it, for the answer is always a wager. But several prescriptive postulates do seem to follow clearly from the story. They also have, to a greater or lesser degree, an imbeddedness in the present situation (although it is not my aim here to articulate an authoritative description of the present situation, an impossible task in any case).

The Multiplicity Postulate: Never assume that there is a single authorized historical method or subject matter.

A phenomenon of third-attitude historiography in its most intellectually compelling form was the call for 'total history,' a call most closely associated with the name of Fernand Braudel. Braudel saw his *Mediterranean and the Mediterranean World* as 'an attempt to write' this 'new kind of history.'[70] But the aspiration towards 'total history' inevitably generates its opposite.[71] The greatest monument to this failure of unity is the journal *Annales: Economies, Sociétés, Civilisations.* One thinks also of *The Mediterranean and the Mediterranean World* itself, which is finally held together by a massive literary conceit.[72] One thinks too of Braudel's later *Civilization and Capitalism,* a vast collection of loosely-related disparates.[73] Not surprisingly, it is now commonplace for observers of the historiographical scene to point to the 'multiplication' or 'proliferation' of history, its conversion from 'history' into 'histories.'[74]

Multiplicity gained steam in part because of sociological changes bringing into the historical profession people who were inclined to see as interesting hitherto neglected subjects of investigation. For example, in the United States the emergence of social history was prompted in various important ways by the entry into the profession of people from non-WASP ethnic groups, people whose parents had been excluded from the exercise of political power and had devoted their energies to assimilation into and success within American society. The emergence of women's history had an obvious connection with the entry into the profession of more women (much could be said about the deep maleness of the professional tradition: at least in the United States, the increasing disciplinization of academic fields in the generation or two after 1920 correlated with a decline in the proportion of academics who were women). Previously excluded or discouraged groups were able to find new subjects of investigation interesting in part because personal and family experiences made them receptive to such subjects, just as, for similar reasons, earlier historians had focussed in their histories on a relatively small range of privileged political actors.

Investigators have several strategies available to them for coming to grips with the fact that they are engaged professionally with subject matters connected in a now 'obvious' way to their own social interests and experiences (earlier connections were generally not 'obvious' because of the lesser degree of social diversity). One strategy is assimilation. Hewing the 'third-attitude' standard of autonomy, historians may indeed acknowledge their social commitments, but claim that in their historiography 'objectivity' and professionalism hold sway. Here, nothing changes, at least not manifestly. A bolder variant continues to adhere to professionalism, but strives to change the 'grand' or at least the 'master' narrative, improving it by including what was previously excluded – for example, gender. The claim may even be made that an authoritative account of the past, 'the full story,' is finally being produced. Here, too, one is clearly within the bounds of attitude 3. Sticking with the example of gender, a further move is from 'women's history' to 'feminist history,' where the authority claimed is less a professional authority than a non-professional one. The move to feminist history can involve acceptance of received dogma, as in attitudes 1 and 2, or it can involve a dialectical relation to the past and to its own position. In the latter case, one would be tempted to see it as embodying attitude 4.

The Hybridization Postulate: Always establish residences outside the discipline.

By definition (and readers should recognise that much of my argument here is *per definitionem*), third-attitude history, committed to the autonomy of the discipline, does not *practically* recognise the existence of legitimate forms of argument about the human world other than its own. In attitude 3, other disciplines are seen as, at most, 'auxiliary' fields. Thus in the 1950s and 1960s connections developed between history and political science, leading to the importation into history of statistical methods for the study of human behaviour, and in the 1970s similar connections developed between history and anthropology, leading to the importation of new, culturally-oriented ways of looking at past societies.[75] In both instances the disciplinary boundaries guarding historiography remained unchallenged, whatever the insights that these cross-boundary raids brought.[76] In attitude 3, other disciplines are not seen as forms of argument in their own right, which in their very difference from historical thinking might reveal things that historical thinking cannot see, but as sources of methods and results to be imported into history without fundamental change of it.

By way of contrast, fourth-attitude history responds to the fragmentation of the discipline and its subject matters with partial or temporary residence in other intellectual communities. Cross-disciplinary hybrids, held together by some combination of theory and experience, emerge. Often these communities are *ad hoc* and local, dependent on accidents of character, geography and intellectual culture; they are hindered by walls and hierarchy and fostered by sociability and egalitarianism. But they share a concern for bridging the difference between different disciplines in temporary pursuit of some common approach or object of study. Within each such group, a new 'language game' emerges, a *lingua franca* different from the language games of the particular disciplines from which each participant comes (for participation *in* a discipline would still be a precondition for entry into a multi-disciplinary language game).[77] Work of a new type is produced in each 'hybrid' field, differing from that done in the contributing disciplines.

At present, multi-disciplinary interaction of a transformative sort is rare within the human sciences. It is perhaps more characteristic of the physical and biological sciences, where disciplinary boundaries are somewhat more fluid and are quite often altered in response to the emergence of new research problems.[78] It is no accident that the best-known instance of 'fourth-attitude' historiography comes from the history of science: Thomas S. Kuhn's *The Structure of Scientific Revolutions*.[79] Written by a physicist who turned himself into a historian of science, it was animated by important issues in the philosophy of science. In breaching disciplinary boundaries, it lost the benefit of disciplinary certitudes; its daring took it into problematic regions. But in part because of this, it also generated important insight; indeed, no other work by a historian writing in the twentieth century did so much to raise new problems and to suggest new approaches to old problems.[80]

The Fictionality Postulate: Always confront, in an explicit way, the fictionality implicit in all works of history.

Collingwood asserted in *The Idea of History* that whereas '[p]urely imaginary worlds cannot clash and need not agree' since 'each is a world to itself,' there 'is only one historical world.'[81] Taken generally, Collingwood's assertion about the historical world is incorrect (since the one historical world presupposes an infinity of counterfactual ones), but it is largely correct as an observation about third-attitude historiography, in which commitment to one way of thinking tends to generate one kind of historical object and to set limits on the kinds of explanation that will be entertained. Collingwood's assertion implies, further, that the more that historians find themselves at a distance from History, the more the 'fictional' aspects of their work come to the fore.

I touch here on issues that I do not think can be currently resolved, either in theory or in practice; but the issues need to be raised. The history/fiction dualism is one of many that is of limited analytical value: it is especially prone to polemical misuse, both by those who imagine that 'anything goes' and by those who would point with horror at precisely that view. Often, a useful method when one is confronted by such dualisms is to begin to complexify them. Even at first glance, it seems clear that within the general territory of 'fictionality,' one needs at the very least to distinguish between what I would call, respectively, the 'literary' and the 'fictive.' By the 'literary', I mean all those devices of literary craft that we commonly find leaping to our notice when we read works of fiction, but that we often see as abnormal and suspect in historiography, which in its professional mode has tended to cultivate a neutral voice. By the 'fictive,' I mean all those dimensions wherein works of history diverge from truth in its sense as correspondence to empirical reality. All causal analysis is fictive in this sense, because all causal analysis presupposes counterfactuals. All typologization is likewise fictive, because types are always idealizations of a messier reality. Indeed, given the complexity of reality, definition itself risks being fictive in this sense as well.

Much has been written on the literary dimension, by such theorists of historiography as Hayden White, Stephen Bann, Hans Kellner, Philippe Carrard and F. R. Ankersmit.[82] One also thinks of a small body of stylistically 'experimental' works of history written since the early 1970s that wittingly or unwittingly fall into a 'fourth-attitude' mould.[83] 'Voice' has been an important issue in many of the more experimental works;

other issues include a breaking away from the convention of the
smoothly-running narrative and a tendency for the historian to intrude
explicitly into the historical account being told. Such literary experiments
suggest a deeper, ontological point: that the historical object itself is a
'fictive' creation, something constituted *as object* by the mind of the
historian and his or her readers. This is not an assertion that 'there is no
there there'; it *is* an assertion that the historian makes (but not out of
nothing) the particular historical objects presented in his or her work.

The Theory Postulate: *Always theorize.*

In a world that no longer believes in a single History, historians can
awaken universal interest only insofar as their work addresses theoretical
issues. For example, in an America that no longer sees its history as
following directly from the political and constitutional history of Great
Britain, an account of say 'The Gunpowder Plot of 1605,' can have
interest only insofar as it raises issues of a theoretical sort, detached from
the specific events of 1605. Yet, at the same time, just as the conversion of
'history' into 'histories' problematizes boundaries between history and
fiction, so also it problematizes those between history and theory. Recall
Collingwood's hope that philosophy would become historical and that,
reciprocally, history would become philosophical. In the present
dispensation, which is one of multiplicity and disjunction, no happy
synthesis of this sort, no middle road, seems possible. Instead, one
envisages connections between history and theory that are more local
and limited.

Accordingly, one envisages (1) a historiography capable of bringing
(localized) aid to theory, contributing in serious ways to the discussion of
theoretical issues.[84] Clearly, *different* histories would be told, depending
on the different theoretical ends. One envisages (2) a greater attentiveness
of historians to theory; of course, there are different theories and different
ways of being attentive to them. One envisages (3) a more self-ironic
historiography than the current style, having a greater humility and
reflexiveness concerning its own assumptions and conclusions. It would
find its beginnings less in Thucydides than in Herodotus. In his
recounting of the advice of Solon to Croesus, Herodotus laid out a
principle – namely, that one cannot know history with certainty until
after the moment at which there is no more history to know – for the
writing of his own history, and perhaps for ours as well.[85] Finally, in view
of the vast, utterly unmanageable body of *primary* historiography that
has been produced, one envisages (4) a historiography more in the

manner of meditation or commentary, which, in a Montaignean spirit and in the essay form, would comment on the significance of that body for us, now. In its meditative mode, fourth-attitude historiography would engage not in the dredging up of new facts – would not, that is, engage in historical research as it is normally understood – but would instead engage in the philosophical task of reflecting on the significance of facts already in some sense 'known.'

Quoting, from memory it seems, an unnamed writer in an unnamed English periodical, Ranke once wrote: 'History begins with chronicle and ends with essay, that is, in reflection on the historical events that there find special resonance.'[86] As Ranke's observation begins to suggest, the four attitudes – which in the Western tradition range from pre-professional chronicle (relying on the coherence of a universal history assumed to be known already) to post-professional essay – are already present in the disciplinary tradition itself. Reading the tradition in a particular way, with a sensitivity to contradiction, we can begin to see its repressed self-questionings. In this sense, we merely develop something that is already there in the past. But the concrete social situation of our own time – in 'the West' and beyond – prompts, and lends authority to, such a reading.

8

A Point of View on Viewpoints in Historical Practice

ROBERT F. BERKHOFER, JR.

Much of what historians discuss under the rubrics of objectivity, perspective, partisanship and bias in historical productions resembles what literary theorists examine as point of view and voice. Historians confront obvious problems of voice and viewpoint each time they try to represent viewpoints and even voices of peoples of the past. What is the relationship between the historian in the present and the historical actors of the (postulated) past as mediated through the historian's text? Must a historian adopt the outlook as well as the words of the past actors in order to explain them and then present them fairly in their own terms? To what degree must historians be sympathetic to those they write about in their texts – no matter how repugnant their world views, behaviour or morals – in order to produce a valid history?[1]

These problems of voice and viewpoint in historians' works have particularly surfaced in recent times in the debates over who can understand whom in terms of gender, race, ethnicity, class and otherness in general. Who speaks for the so-called 'inarticulate,' or the undocumented, in history? To what extent do historians use traditional notions of otherness to promote dominant stereotypes of self and to conceal the past voices and therefore viewpoints of those others within a society? Does even the distinction between professional and folk history, documentary and oral histories, and learning over memory further this concealment? Can a history show various voices in its textual representation? Does attention to gender, ethnicity and class change the nature of story-telling in history or only the content of the story? Does a commitment to multiculturalism also require a commitment to multiple voices and viewpoints? Need multiculturalism therefore lead to the multiplication of Great Stories and therefore to plural pasts?[2]

Voice and viewpoint are united in a literary text, but what is joined by the author of the text can be separated by the reader of the text. Voice answers the question about who speaks in the text, while viewpoint answers from what perspective does a voice speak. Literary theorists discuss voice in texts in two complementary ways: (1) Who speaks for whom? (2) Who speaks to whom? Although the author speaks through the totality of the text (his or her creation), not all of the text need speak for the author. In what person(a) does the author insert him/her/self into the text? How blatant is the author's personal presence in the text as opposed to that of the subjects themselves? These questions about the relationship between the author and the text ask not so much what or who is an author in terms of professional and social context but where and in what ways does an author speak through the parts or layers of a text.[3]

When we turn to the historian's voice in the text or who is speaking, we can ask not only about the form of that voice, whether as author itself or as narrator, but also how obtrusive the author's voice or its surrogate is in the process. Narratologists discuss both these matters in terms of a scale ranging from explicit intrusive to implicit and unintrusive. Does the voice speaking in the text for the author designate itself as 'I' or 'we' and how often does the author in the text speak as and for him/herself? On the other side of the authorial voice spectrum lies the author who speaks in the third person only. Historians normally suppress or conceal the personal intrusive voice so that the facts seem to speak for themselves in a historical discourse. While not many historians today would assert, as did the nineteenth-century French historian Fustel de Coulanges, that it is 'not I who speak, but history which speaks through me,' they in effect follow this advice by presenting histories as if the past spoke for itself.[4] Hence the advice of Savoie Lottinville to the neophyte historian: 'he never – or almost never – intrudes the personal pronoun "I" into his account.'[5]

Historical actors can be given their own voices in historical discourses. By having (being given?) voice the historical actors move from being the subjects in and of the discourse to being subjects with their own views. As with the author, the actors' voices can range from explicit and personal to implicit and impersonal. The most explicit voice comes when past actors speak for themselves through quotation. The more removed method of giving past actors their voices is through historians' inclusion of their views through summary. A still more remote way comes from a generalization about a collective viewpoint.[6]

The relationships between the voices of authors and those of their postulated subjects point to the nature and problem of multiple voices; or polyvocality, in historical texts. Can historical actors ever speak for themselves in the end or must authors always speak for them ultimately in historical discourses? Can the reader discern the various voices and their associated viewpoints in a text through the tensions and contradictions embodied in the discourse itself? To ask who the Great Story Teller is, or who speaks for the Great Past raises the ultimate problem of voice in historical practice.

If we can ask who speaks for (or as) the Great Story-Teller, we can also inquire from what (or whose) viewpoint is the Great Story told? Historians like novelists must adopt a point of view along with its close ally, a voice, in their presentations. To the extent that novelists speak through their characters, they not only represent the novelists' views but limit their perspectives and knowledge in perceiving and understanding the imagined world they create. Though historians sometimes speak through the historical actors they (re)construct, more often they assume the more God-like view of omniscience and omnipresence in the world they supposedly (re)create from the past. Thus, according to Paul Ricoeur, historians rarely fuse (confuse?) who is speaking in their exposition with whence we perceive what is shown us.[7] In accord with such thinking, Savoie Lottinville divides viewpoint into two kinds in his primer for the fledgling narrative historian. 'Author viewpoint' is the predominant kind in historical practice and lies

somewhere between heaven and earth, high enough so that individual actions and the unified whole can be seen clearly ... we can call it 'omnipresent' viewpoint, principally because a historian is not permitted to do what a novelist is fully entitled to do, that is make himself, as narrator, part of the action.[8]

'Character viewpoint' sees matters from the perspective of those contemporary to the historical actors. According to Lottinville, such a viewpoint is particularly appropriate for biography but can be used in other kinds of histories.

These two kinds of viewpoints raise as many questions as they answer. Must, in short, our consciousness of the represented world come from either within or without that world in a historical text? Or, can we see from one or more consciousnesses both within and without it? If our consciousness comes from without, then does the reader see one or few or all consciousnesses and their viewpoints? Is the overall viewpoint God-like or limited? An omniscient view entails both omnipresence – perspectives from and in all places – and omniscience – knows all consciousnesses as well as what really happened and what caused everything.[9]

There is a difference between arguing for a point of view as opposed to arguing from a point of view. In the latter sense point of view refers to the prism, angle of vision, perspective, lens or focalization through which the narrative (and one might add argument in history) is presented. Although point of view is usually presented in ocular terms, it is a conceptual (point) as well as perceptual (view) position in terms of which the narrated situation and events are presented. At the literal level, point of view sees the represented world in the text through someone's eyes in terms of its physical aspects, as the quotation above from Lottinville on author viewpoint shows. This is the perceptual plane of viewpoint.[10] What spatial and temporal perspective does the historian need to adopt to produce the represented world presented in the discourse? In the end does the text offer a bird's-eye view of the represented world, a synoptic or a panoramic perspective?[11] At a more figurative or conceptual level, point of view understands a represented world from the perspective of a belief system, ideology or conceptual framework. Often the ideologies and belief systems from inside and outside the represented world are more fused than historians are aware as the arguments over liberal, conservative and radical history demonstrates in both issues and polemics. In the end, must not the very foundations of explanations in history and the social sciences be considered ideological from the plane of conceptual viewpoint?[12]

At an evaluative level, point of view assesses the represented world from the vantage-point of interest, well-being, profit or value system. On the evaluative plane of viewpoint, are interests in a situation, or profits from a system, or the well-being of humans in a society measured according to the standards and value systems of those from within or without the represented historical world? Seemingly neutral judgements are normally viewpoints favouring one or another of the participants. For this reason historians in favour of minority or radical representation in history see the viewpoint adopted in so many normal histories as hegemonic, for it supports the traditional or dominant power structure as the 'natural' way of viewing things social and political. Basic to the whole idea of hegemony is whose and what viewpoint defines reality.[13] At the psychological or emotive level, point of view feels the represented world according to someone's psyche: how does the implied author or narrator feel towards the actors; events and institutions in the discourse? How detached or involved is the historian with a past represented world? The big debate today revolves about who can share emotional and other viewpoints of and on race, gender, class and who can speak for the past and present experience of a group.[14]

Given the multiple kinds of viewpoint and the many places they enter a historical discourse, one might accede to F. R. Ankersmit's proposition that it is only by taking a point of view that historians create in the first place historical narrative or interpretation as such, for it provides *the* very way of 'seeing' the past as history.[15] It is this vital role of viewpoint in historical discourse, of course, that creates the biases that confound historical practice. No historian's supposed mediation between past and present on any level can occur without the aid of viewpoint in its many guises. The more the historian interprets in the text, the more aspects of viewpoint become incorporated into historical discourse. The more aspects of viewpoint embraced in discourse, the more biases create that history.

According to its advocates, a multicultural approach to scholarship and the educational curriculum challenges the traditional viewpoint that lies at the base of so many disciplines as hegemonic. No one has stated the multicultural implications of – and therefore, against – such a traditional viewpoint in the human sciences more succinctly or more baldly than Paula Rothenberg:

The traditional (educational) curriculum teaches all of us to see the world through the eyes of privileged, white, European males and to adopt their interests and perspectives as our own. It calls books by middle-class, white, male writers 'literature' and honours them as timeless and universal, while treating the literature produced by everyone else as idiosyncratic and transitory. The traditional curriculum introduces the (mythical) white middle-class, patriarchal, heterosexual family and its values and calls it 'Introduction to Psychology.' It teaches the values of white men of property and position and calls it 'Introduction to Ethics.' It reduces the true *majority* of people in this society to 'women and minorities,' and calls it 'political science.' It teaches the art produced by privileged white men in the West and calls it 'art history.'

The curriculum effectively defines this point of view as 'reality' rather than a point of view itself, and then assures us that it and it alone is 'neutral' and 'objective.' It teaches all of us to use white male values and culture as the standard by which everyone and everything else is to be measured and found wanting. It defines 'difference' as 'deficiency' (deviance; pathology). By building racism, sexism, heterosexism, and class privilege into its very definition of 'reality,' it implies the current distribution of wealth and power in society, as well as the current distribution of time and space in the traditional curriculum, reflects the natural order of things.

As a result of the hegemonic viewpoint grounding so many disciplines in the human sciences, she argues that 'women of all colors, men of color, and working people are rarely if ever subjects or agents. They appear throughout history at worse as objects, at best as victims.' Moreover, 'only people of color have race and only women have gender, only lesbians and gays have sexual orientation – everyone else is a human being.' Worse from her viewpoint, standard school curricula and scholarship embody traditional Western male hegemonic outlooks by valuing 'the work of killing and conquest over production and reproduction of life' and 'offers abstract, oppositional thinking as the paradigm for intellectual rigor.'[16]

These paragraphs suggest important and deeply disturbing implications for the traditional construction of history, but Rothenberg's own brief mention of her remedies for all these problems of misconception is to let students read the United States Constitution, Supreme Court decisions, and other public documents 'so that the 'founding fathers' and their descendants can *speak for themselves*'.[17] Such a solution does not say who provides the viewpoint(s) from which these voices from the past are contextualized and interpreted. Who becomes the Great Teacher, so to speak, in the multicultural classroom? Who gets to be the Great Contextualizer in the Great Story that interprets how these documents relate to each other, to their times, and to the present?

As with other disciplines multiculturalism challenges both the viewpoint basic to traditional history and in turn the authority of normal history. Multiculturalism highlights, first, the whole question of the relationship between the author's voice and viewpoint and those supposedly represented in any given text. For whom in the end does this text speak and from what viewpoint and by what authority? Second, multiculturalism challenges the whole idea of a single best or right Great Story in terms of its viewpoint for the practice of history. In questioning a single viewpoint as best for the Great Story and Great Past, multiculturalism also impugns the foundation of historical authority used traditionally to justify the discipline. As a result of this challenge to traditional authority, multiculturalism also raises fundamental issues about how politics are embodied in the paradigm of normal history practice itself through voice and viewpoint. Lastly, it poses the challenge of how to incorporate multiple viewpoints into historical texts, be they monographic histories, Great Stories or even the Great Past as history.

From the viewpoint of this essay, however, the question becomes rather what can be done about these matters from within the normal paradigm of historical discourse and what must be done outside that paradigm in order to convey the complexity of multiple viewpoints? What appears true of the difficulties of representing multiple viewpoints as well as voices in a single historical discourse applies to a Great Story and the Great Past when considered as a text. An extended example of old and new approaches to the history of the American West illustrates these limits of, as well as the potential in, the normal historical paradigm for realizing current multiculturalist ideals within the normal historical problematic. The comparison between the old and the new approaches to the American frontier highlight the relations among the various kinds of viewpoint: the understanding of space and time and the perspective from which to view them as perceptual viewpoint; the link between politics and objectivity in ideological viewpoint; the connection between past and present judgements of persons and actions as evaluative viewpoint; and feeling for and identity with the West as place and the empathy or repulsion for past (and present) persons who live(d) there.

One of the great narratives – if not the grandest – of the Great American Past has been (is?) the frontier interpretation of American history as expounded by Frederic Jackson Turner. From the vantage-point of our times and place, the viewpoint underlying Turner's history is painfully ethnocentric and chauvinistic because it represses the many voices and viewpoints of those peoples who lived in and fought over what Turner called the American West. As a consequence, the viewpoint of this history and his Great Story seem almost univocal and single viewpointed from a multiculturalist perspective, even though he made class conflict fundamental to his interpretation.[18]

When Turner did not silence the voices of many who had also participated in the adventure in the Great Story of the frontier, he denied or peripheralized their viewpoints. His Great Story of the American experience spoke for certain American males of Northern European descent and from the viewpoint of their dominant ideology and value system. Therefore, as Patricia Limerick observes in *The Legacy of Conquest: The Unbroken Past of the American West*, 'Turner's frontier rested on a single point of view.'[19] As she phrases the indictment on race, ethnicity and gender: 'English-speaking white men were the stars of his story; Indians, Hispanics, French Canadians, and Asians were at best supporting actors and at worst invisible. Nearly as invisible were women of all ethnicities.' (p. 21). Likewise, she accuses Turner of geographical provincialism and a preference for agrarianism over industrialism, because his (hi)story emphasized farming settlements and folk democracy in the humid Midwest and omitted deserts, mountains, mines and occupations of the far West. He neglected urbanization, railroads, territorial government, banking and commerce everywhere. In the end, she sees his division of a pre-1890s frontier from its post-1890s West as a nostalgia for small-town America, a nostalgia that repressed America's continuing industrial problems on the frontier as well as afterwards.

Almost a century after Turner first expounded 'The Significance of the Frontier in American History,' Limerick in her book attempts a synthesis incorporating those voices and viewpoints that Turner repressed or peripheralized. As her dual titles are meant to suggest, she seeks to represent (integrate) both the voices and viewpoints of the past and of her (our?) times. Her Great Story as opposed to Turner's shows the potential of multicultural viewpoints in historical practice as it also reveals the limits of normal history to achieve this goal.

In prose as vigorous in its own way as that of Turner, she denies the idea of the frontier as evolutionary process in favour of the West as a place 'undergoing conquest and never fully escaping its consequence.' Thus the American West becomes 'an important meeting ground' where Indian America, Latin America, Anglo-America and Asia 'intersected.'

The workings of conquest tied these diverse groups together into the same story. Happily or not, minorities and majorities occupied a common ground. Conquest basically involved the drawing of lines on a map, the definition and allocation of ownership (personal, tribal, corporate, state, federal and international), and the evolution of land from matter to property. The process had two stages: the initial drawing of lines (which we have usually called the frontier stage) and the subsequent giving of meaning and power to those lines, which is still under way. Race relations parallel the distribution of property, the application of labor and capital to make the property productive, and the allocation of profit. Western history has been an on-going competition for legitimacy – for the right to claim for oneself and sometimes for one's group the status of legitimate beneficiaries of Western resources. This intersection of ethnic diversity with property allocation unifies Western history (p. 27).

Although Limerick denies the social evolutionism and the racial hierarchy underlying Turner's conception of the frontier, she espouses both a recurring process and a social conflict model of society in the West as place. In accord with this model of social conflict and as part of the recurring process, she focuses on

The contest for property and profit . . . accompanied by a contest for cultural dominance. Conquest also involved a struggle over languages, cultures, and religions; the pursuit of legitimacy in way of life and *point of view*. In a variety of matters, but especially in the unsettled questions of Indian assimilation and in the disputes over bilingualism and immigration in the still Hispanic Southwest, this contest for cultural dominance remains a primary unresolved issue of conquest. Reconceived as a running story, a fragmented and discontinuous past becomes whole again (p. 25; my emphasis).

Even from these two paragraphs, it is clear that Limerick's stance towards the role of economic and political liberalism in America history is far more ambiguous than Turner's. The duties of American patriotism like the demands of American progress are far less certain in Limerick's West than in Turner's frontier, although there seems little doubt from the book that her attachment to her image of the West as a physical place is as great as Turner's was to the frontier as ideological geography. Surely she reflects the concerns of her times about race, class, gender and ethnicity as he did about class conflict, individualism and democracy. In fact, Limerick seems as dedicated to her version of what American democracy ought to be as Turner was to his version. For bringing the story up-to-date ideologically, Limerick's version was hailed as the New Western History.

Although Limerick accuses Turner of telling the Great Story of the American frontier from a single point of view, her own interpretation of the American West, as conveyed in these few quotations, does not seem to escape some of the same problems of viewpoint she set out to correct. Although she broadens the arena of competition, she too subscribes at bottom to the same basic materialist version of social conflict as Turner. She adds industrial class conflict and racial and other ethnic cleavages to Turner's agrarian conflicts. Although she disagrees with Turner's concentration on the white conquest of the West to the exclusion of other peoples, she too devotes the first half of her own book to those same 'conquerors.' These hegemons in many ways call the tune to which other peoples must dance – even though in the second half of the book she argues that 'The Conquerors Meet Their Match,' as the title phrases it. Though she denies the end of the West according to Turner's criteria by stressing the persistence of Western problems into the twentieth century, her text implicitly agrees with his starting-point of white settlements in the West. Although she gives ethnic priority of place to Native Americans in her (hi)story, her text starts off with a first part entitled 'The Conquerors' in its sequential arrangement of her discourse. Like Turner she too embodies the prevailing ideological currents of the contemporary academic and larger worlds in her interpretative focus. Both subscribe to their versions of the American Dream in their versions of the Great Story of the history of the American West. Both share an emotional bond with the Western part of the United States, although they may locate the West somewhat differently.[20]

Do both old and new historians in the end share so much because of the limits imposed upon any Great Story, and therefore the understanding of the Great Past, by the paradigmatic presuppositions of normal history? Although Limerick struggles mightily to escape Turner's ethnocentric and monologic voice and viewpoint, her book still surveys the Western landscape from her integrative viewpoint. Thus multiculturalism in the hands of many historians does not transform the presuppositions of the normal history paradigm so much as it expands their application to untraditional subject matter. Pluralism in, even of, interpretations need not result in plural pasts, because new like old historians insist upon their voices and viewpoints in the text as the single, ultimate mediator between the past and the present. In the end, the historian's authority depends upon such a practice.

That multicultural, polyvocal history is easier preached than achieved indicates that conceptual as well as ethical and political problems plague the enterprise. How much of this problem is due to the nature of the normal history paradigm as opposed to political partisanship or social inertia? Must the efforts of historians to reclaim the story of history in the name of gender, race, ethnicity, class or otherness also lead in essence to an attempt to pluralize viewpoints in history-telling? Or will such efforts merely (re)appropriate history as counter-hegemonic but still based at bottom on a single viewpoint? To what extent are the multiplication of voices and viewpoints in history limited to – as well as by – the traditional historical problematic and its paradigm of discourse?

An extended example of Limerick's very explicit attempt to represent multiple viewpoints within a single text offers lessons on both its potential and its problems for normal historical practice from a multiculturalist perspective. Since she defines the United States West as the meeting-ground for several societies and their contest for political, economic and cultural control of the land and each other, she tries to be particularly sensitive to the multiple viewpoints represented in the many conflicts. As she writes 'one skill essential to the writing of Western American history is a capacity to deal with multiple points of view,' (p. 39). 'The inclusion of these new angles of vision,' she concludes, gives 'added vitality and depth to Western American history'(p. 258).

One of her favourite methods of representing multiculturalist multiple viewpoints can be seen in her discussion of the Texas Rangers from the viewpoint of Anglo and Hispanic Americans. She writes:

In Hispanic history, as in every Western history, one never has the luxury of taking point of view for granted. Hispanics – like Indians, Anglos, and every other group – could be victims as well as victimizers, and the meanings of the past could seem, at times to be riding a seesaw. Consider, for instance, the dramatically different images of the Texas Rangers. Early in the Anglo colonization of Texas, the Rangers began 'as something of a paramilitary force' for fighting Indians. As the threat from the Indians diminished, the Rangers became a force for protecting the property of Anglo-Texans and for keeping Mexicans and Mexican-Americans subordinated. Surviving into the twentieth century as a kind of state police, the Texas Ranger had acquired a strong and positive standing in myth, 'eulogized, idolized, and evaluated to the status of one of the truly heroic figures in American history.' In 1935, the historian Walter Prescott Webb published an influential study that reinforced the image of the Texas Ranger as 'a man standing alone between society and its enemies,' a law officer who was also 'a very quiet, deliberate, gentle person who could gaze calmly into the eye of a murderer, divine his thoughts, and anticipate his actions, a man who could ride straight up to death' (p. 257).

After describing how President Nixon lauded the same virtues and praised the same public service tradition, she goes on:

Apparently, neither President Nixon nor his speech writers had consulted a study of borderlands folklore published by Américo Paredes in 1958. 'The word *rinche* from 'ranger' is an important one in Border folklore,' wrote Paredes. 'It has been extended to cover not only the Rangers, but any other Americans armed and mounted and looking for Mexicans to kill.' Adopting the Mexican point of view, scholars who came after Webb drew a different moral and political portrait of the Rangers. 'The Anglo community,' Julian Samore, Joe Bernal, and Albert Peña have written, 'took it for granted that the Rangers were there to protect Anglo interests; no one ever accused the Rangers operating in South Texas of either upholding or enforcing the law impartially.' The Rangers, moreover, kept up their traditional role in the twentieth century, lending a hand in strikebreaking and in cracking down on 'Mexican-American activism in politics and education. . .'

Through the use of quotations from those who hold opposing viewpoints in addition to summarizing such viewpoints, she tries to give the reader more than one side of the story. She achieves such a multicultural view, as the paragraphs make clear in this instance, through relegating the historically dominant white viewpoint to myth in light of the Mexican viewpoint as her ultimate reality.

Achieving a multiperspectival history poses its own kind of problems for the professional historian as Limerick's discussion of an 'Indian' point of view and voice illustrate. Should a new Indian history merely reverse the old stereotypes of who is savage and who is civilized? Limerick argues against such a flattened history because it still homogenizes the diversity of Native Americans as a 'unitary thing.' Native Americans were and are diverse in languages, customs, religions, tribal governments, economies and localities. They had and have varied histories as tribes and individuals as a result of differing times of contact with Euro-Americans and subsequent interaction plus the diplomatic and other relations with other tribes. Their concerns about intertribal rivalries and other native matters often loom larger in their own histories than the impact and implications of Euro-American contact. To speak of an 'Indian side' oversimplifies therefore not only the voices of Native Americans past and present but also their viewpoints (pp. 214-18).

She goes on to ask whether a changed perspective provides 'a sufficient corrective to the ethnocentric conventions of the past?' Is the traditional historian's 'leap to the high ground of objectivity and neutrality' enough? 'What if Indian people are now so certain of their injuries that they want condemnation and blame explicit in the writing of their history? How were white historians to respond when articulate and angry Indian people protested the fact that their history had been too long in the keeping of outsiders and invaders?' At first Limerick seems sympathetic to this point of view. After all, as she observes, 'much of what passed for objective frontier history was in fact nationalistic history, celebrating the winners and downgrading or ignoring the losers.' Thus 'defending the integrity of the profession, one can only hope that one's ethnocentric predecessors can be credibly and rapidly disowned. The nationalism of conventional frontier history carried an assumption that history was itself a kind of property in which Americans deserved to take pride.' But 'Indians have put forth a counterclaim: Indian history is not solely *about* Indians; it is history *belonging* to Indians, in which the owners should take pride and which should make them feel better about their inherited identity' (pp. 219-220; her italics). Such a claim, however, bothers her because corporations, governments, religions and even individuals in the dominant society have asserted the same claim to control and construct their own histories, and professional historians oppose such 'authorized histories' as blatantly partial and partisan.

Faced with the dilemma of whether each minority should write its own history its own way, Limerick voices sympathy for both sides of the proposition. On one hand, each partial perspective cannot be taken for the whole by the professional historian. In arguing that all the various versions of Western history ought to be read, she writes:

Of course, Indian people can and should write their own histories according to their traditions, just as pioneers and their descendants have every right to publish books enshrining their own version of the past. For the sake of national and regional self-understanding, however, there should be a group of people reading all these books and paying attention to all these points of view. In that process,

Western historians will always leave the serious individual emotionally and intellectually unsettled. In the nineteenth-century West, speaking out for the human dignity of all parties to the conflicts took considerable nerve. It still does (p. 221).

On the other hand, 'historians of the American mainstream' can learn much from such Indian histories. 'Take up this Indian perspective on the peculiar ways of white people, and you are set free of the intellectually crippling temptation to take white people's ways for granted' (pp. 220-21). Limerick proceeds to laud ethnohistory as a solution to the dilemma, because it 'places actions and events in a carefully explored context and culture and worldview.' Thus 'ethnohistory reaches its peak when its techniques are applied across the board, when white people as well as Indians are cast as actors in complex cultural worlds and when no point of view is taken for granted' (pp. 220-21).

As Limerick's discussion of the dilemmas of multiple viewpoints shows, she hopes to escape its relativistic implications for the Great Story as well as a single historical text by incorporating both the actors' viewpoints and their postulated context into the historian's own 'larger' multiculturalist viewpoint. Such a solution may be an improvement over texts denying actors' viewpoints but does not answer all the challenge of multiculturalism to viewpoint in historical practice. In the end, she solves the multicultural challenge to hegemonic viewpoint in history safely from within a single synoptic viewpoint customary to the normal paradigm of history even as she expands the number of viewpoints that normal history should embrace.

The paradigmatic limits as well as the moral implications of Limerick's approach are seen in her theoretical discussion of the problems of incorporating histories of minorities into the general history of the American West. Her ponderings illustrate the perplexities of combining multiple viewpoints with the historian's voice and viewpoint into a text and into history. First the problems as she sees them:

When the advance of white male pioneers across the continent was the principal concern of Western historians, the field had coherence to spare. But two or three decades of 'affirmative action history' have made a hash of that coherence. Ethnocentricity is out, but what alternative center is in? When it comes to centers, Western history now has an embarrassment of riches – Indian-centered history, Hispanic-centered history, Asian-centered history, black-centered history, Mormon-centered history, and (discredited as it may be) white-American-main-stream history.[21] If historians were forced to choose one of these centers, hold to it, and reject all others, we would be in deep professional trouble. But that is by no means the only choice available (pp. 291-2).

Her solution to the integration of multiple viewpoints into a history rests upon an analogy:

Take, for instance, a thoroughly un-Western metaphor for a complicated phenomenon – a subway system. Every station in the system is a center of sorts – trains and passengers converge on it; in both departure and arrival, the station is the pivot. But get on a train, and you are soon (with any luck) at another station, equally a center and a pivot. Every station is at the center of a particular world, yet that does not leave the observer of the system conceptually muddled, unable to decide which station represents the true point of view from which the entire system should be viewed. On the contrary, the idea of the system as a whole makes it possible to think of all the stations at once – to pay attention to the differences while still recognizing their relatedness, and to imagine how the system looks from its different points of view (p. 292).

In applying this subway metaphor, she argues:

What 'system' united Western history? Minorities and majority in the American West occupied common ground – literally. A contest for control of the land, for the labor applied to the land, and the resulting profit set the terms of their meeting. Sharing turf, contesting turf, surrendering turf, Western groups, for all their differences, took part in the same story. Each group may well have its own, self-defined story, but in the contest for property and profit, these stories met. Each group might have preferred to keep its story private and separate, but life on the common ground of the American West made such purity impossible (p. 292).

To explicate this analogy, she switches metaphors:

Everyone became an actor in everyone else's play; understanding any part of the play now requires us to take account of the whole. It is perfectly possible to watch a play and keep track of, even identify with, several characters at once, even when those characters are in direct conflict with each other and within themselves. The ethnic diversity of Western history asks only that: pay attention to the parts, and pay attention to the whole. It is a difficult task, but to bemoan and lament the necessity to include minorities is to engage, finally, in intellectual laziness. The American West was a complicated place for its historical participants; and it is no exercise in 'white guilt' to say that it is – and should be – just as complicated for us today (p. 292).

These are attractive metaphors but do they provide the solution multiculturalism seeks and needs to transform historical practice? Do they solve the problems of incorporating multiple viewpoints into a history text? How does Limerick know that the stations are all on the same subway system? Does someone still see the system as a whole? And if so, from what viewpoint is that system to be ultimately organized and described? Who, to use her metaphor, can view the subway system as a whole when one must travel from station to station? How can anyone know if it is a system, let alone speak for it? Who is the System-Maker, let alone its Great Story-Teller? In many ways her map analogy rests upon knowing the historical terrain in such a way that it can be mapped as it were from a spaceship. A better analogy from a multiculturalist perspective might be map-making before human flight in which the overview of the terrain is surveyed as much from guesstimation as observation, and no-one knows for certain the overview.[22]

In the end her advice on how to combine actors' and historians' viewpoints into a single text still privileges the historian's viewpoint over those of the actors. Her method, laudable as some of its results may be, frequently draws an overall conclusion above the relationship among the multiple viewpoints apart from any one of them. Such a solution offers the historian's stance ultimately as the integrative viewpoint regardless of the actor's viewpoints, even though such a solution may subvert the actors' viewpoints. Such a solution can be seen even in a single paragraph about the conflicts over managing the national forests for the public good.

The financial workings of the forests might engage the attention of few Americans, but when harvesting affected the appearance of the forest, public opinion became more audible. Clear-cutting (cutting all trees in a plot instead of cutting only mature, diseased, or dead trees) could trigger the greatest outrage. To timber companies and to Forest Service experts, a clear-cutting had undeniable charms; building one road to one site for one big haul certainly meant less expense and trouble. Moreover, clear-cutting left a plot of land in which trees could be scientifically replanted. To the commercial forester, old-growth virgin stands were troublesome, diverse in species and age, unmanageable. For management, progress meant getting rid of the old unplanned forest, planting intelligibly, and thus starting fresh with an orderly, sensible stand of trees. The hiker, the environmentalist, and the local tourist promoter, however, saw clear-cutting in different terms. It was an affront, a violation of the forest's integrity, an intrusion of ruthless industrialism into what should be a sanctuary, or a potential blow to local tourist income. Ugly and disruptive to its opponents, efficient and direct to its advocates, clear-cutting illustrates an axiom of Western history: one man's improvement is sure to be another man's defilement (pp. 302-3).

The 'axiom of Western history' presents many viewpoints in its argument but a single one in its stance towards the actors' viewpoints and therefore its conclusion. As Limerick admits elsewhere, 'My point is that the historian is obligated to understand how people saw their own times, but not obligated to adopt their terminology and point of view' (p. 25). In this she agrees with Wallace Stegner, the famous novelist and poet of the

American West, who opined: 'Unlike fiction, history can have only one voice, the historian's.'[23]

Plural viewpoints therefore do not lead to plural pasts in Limerick's theory or practice. In the end, as is typical of normal history, she too believes that multiculturalist blind men are still feeling different parts of the same elephant, or to use her own metaphor, travelling the same subway system. In this view a variety of multiculturalist viewpoints can – ought to – be combined by the historian because the very combination approaches ever more asymptotically to some (postulated) historical reality identified with a real past. Such an approach to historical reality, even if multiculturalist to some degree in practice, still conceives much of reality according to the conventions of objectivist historical realism, which pictures a represented world from a single synoptic viewpoint.

Is the lesson of Limerick's adherence to certain traditional tenets of normal history in spite of her multicultural ideals that the limits of multiculturalism in history are those of the normal paradigm of history itself? In the end by privileging the historian's version of multiculturalism in the text, she also insists that the historian be the single mediator ultimately between past and present in any given text. That the historian in the text acts as the single mediator in the end not only privileges that version's overall viewpoint above others but authorizes it as the best by doing so.

The challenge of dialogism in historical discourses lies less in introducing additional voices into a text or even a Great Story than in representing viewpoints in addition to that of the historian. That polyvocality need not produce a pluralistic let alone a multicultural history seems plain from actual practice. To introduce multiple viewpoints into historical discourse would appear to require both a revision of the normal history paradigm and a new vision of historical authority. A multicultural, dialogic ideal transforms not only the subject matter of histories but also the postulates of what a good history does and is. Ultimately, must multiple viewpoints issue forth in plural pasts and new approaches to the narrativization of histories?

Since any single viewpoint looks hopelessly partial by contemporary multicultural standards, the solution would seem to be the representation of the past and the present from multiple viewpoints in a single text as well as in the Great Story and Great Past. An ideal multicultural history should integrate multiple viewpoints as well as different voices from at least three sources: from within the represented world of the past; from without the represented world of the past in the light of subsequent events; and from the conflicting or at least diverse viewpoints existing in the present. Nothing less seems allowable in a multicultural history, if the author(s) seek(s) the fullest polyvocality and dialogue within the text. How does a historian or even a group of historians integrate into practice the tensions of past and present societies into a single text? To what extent must such a text also embody these tensions as well as represent them? Can a single text in the end be both multicultural and have multiple viewpoints, if the reader is to understand it?

Experiments of multivocality in history that attempt to embody multiple perspectives as the very framework of their discourse are few because they so challenge the normal historical paradigm on an ultimately single authorial viewpoint. If the text is not to be a collection of quotations or a book of documentary sources, what can it be? One of the most important attempts to embody multiple viewpoints as well as voices is by the historical anthropologist Richard Price in *Alabi's World*.[24] What Price started in *First-Time: The Historical Vision of an Afro-American People*[25] culminates so far at least in a text that reproduces various voices through quotations even using different typefaces and shades of print to emphasize the polyvocality. To convey the eighteenth-century history of the Saramaka maroons of Surinam, Price uses four voices, those of the German Moravians, the Dutch Planters, the Saramakas, and his own as historian and anthropologist. He translates the various languages into English and treats the Saramaka oral history on a par with those of his documentary sources; each group of people plus Price himself is distinguished by a different typeface throughout the book, including the notes. Although each voice and viewpoint is supposedly equal, his is dominant in the end, as one reviewer noted.[26] Even though Price argues that the Saramaka possess a strong sense of linear history, it is his views of history that ultimately organize the book, certify the validity of the various voices, and plot the dialogue of voices as diachronic and dialectic. Regardless of the problems of translation[27] or of authorial viewpoint, Price's book goes farther than almost any other towards achieving polyvocality and multiple viewpoints in a multiculturalist historical representation.

Must multiculturalist efforts to transform historical discourse eventuate in postmodern textualization(s) because they fragment the unified story-line in order to avoid the subjection of the other(s) through the imposition of an overall or totalized point of view? Must they embody the eclecticism of pastiche or collage as they blur genres by crossing the customary boundaries of the discipline between philosophy of history and historical sociology or anthropology, between oral and documentary history, between folk and professional history? Postmodern approaches point to a new way of narrativizing the past as histories and Great Stories. Should future historical discourses forgo customary closure through holism, continuity and consistency of authorship? Normal historicization constrains diversity of viewpoint and authority; so-called postmodern historicization surrenders an Archimedean overview for being just another participant in the dialogue(s) among the voices and viewpoints, just another text in time among other textualizations, another discourse among other discourses. It abandons its imperial, self-privileging position to become just one of the discursive bunch. By abandoning a totalized, holistic overview, postmodern historicization also surrenders its claim to a single right or best Great Story as the foundation of disciplinary and historical authority. Thus any attempt to practise such postmodern multiculturalist history demands not only recanting and renouncing traditional approaches to historicization but also reconceiving representation in and of history and the nature of historicization itself.[28]

IMAGES

9

History as Competence and Performance: Notes on the Ironic Museum

STEPHEN BANN

I

When Albertine de Broglie asserted in 1825 that 'we are . . . the first who have understood the past,'[1] she foreshadowed a further stage - let us say our own period – in which people would seek to understand that understanding. At the end of the twentieth century, the critical exploration of the diverse forms of historical consciousness that permeate our culture must surely be routed through that extraordinary half-century in which the mass public of the Western world learnt to assemble a comprehensive grammar of historical reference. They became competent to identify and assess the presence of the past, as representation, in the context of everyday appearances. Alois Riegl claimed at the beginning of the twentieth century: 'The most simple-minded farmhand is able to distinguish an old belfry from a new one.'[2] For all its empirical vagueness, this statement contains the essence of the matter. An eighteenth-century English gentleman would have been invited to view monastic ruins (as from the Terraces at Rievaulx Abbey) as the vestiges of an abhorred superstition. His successor, in the early nineteenth century, would have inserted them, free from religious ideology, within the viewing conventions of the picturesque. But Riegl's Austrian farmhand is an index of a more pervasive transformation: he implies that 'age-value' (to use Riegl's indispensable phrase) has become a culturally pervasive and ineradicable notion.

It is, of course, one thing to note these telling indexes of the process whereby the cult of the past spread from small, self-conscious groups of intellectuals to a much wider class of people. It is quite another thing to attempt to show what, precisely, was taking place in that process. If we take the obvious analogy between the dawning of historicalmindedness and the acquisition of a new language, then we are confronted immediately with the problem of what counts as a 'historically competent' statement of representation. And this means that what are usually taken to be the milestones in the progress of the new historiography may not repay scrutiny as much as the more popular manifestations, or indeed the random signs of a new mentality which can be gleaned from study of that period. For example, the fact that in 1824 both the German historian Leopold Von Ranke and the French historian Augustin Thierry published prefaces enjoining the new critical standards in historical scholarship does not, of itself, help us to understand by what stages the new understanding of the past was progressing.[3] In order to appreciate the force of Ranke's aspiration to show the past 'wie es eigentlich gewesen,' we must take a detour through the study of what counted, at that particular time, as the criteria for judging a life-like representation.

On the other hand, the examination of Alexandre du Sommerard's Musée de Cluny, which opened its doors to the Parisian public in the 1830s, enables us to understand how specific technical moves within the province of representation can be correlated with a particular acquisition of historical knowledge. When du Sommerard assembled the full range of contemporary furniture and domestic objects in what he termed his 'Salle de François Ier', he made concrete for an admiring audience the very specificity of a period, which we should now call the Renaissance. It seems probable that the use of that term, Renaissance, in a historically precise, rather than a general sense, is recorded for the first time in a story by Balzac, *Le Bal De Sceaux*. This is obviously not unconnected with the achievement of the Musée de Cluny. One might say that the perception of the Renaissance as a concrete, historical period was dependent on the prior acknowledgement of a similar status for the 'Middle Ages'. The eighteenth-century *philosophes* had elided the medieval period, and cherished an ideal notion of the antique world which corresponded with the utopian aspiration of their social and educational schemes. The engineers of the Revolution had been even more uncompromising in their unhistorical juxtaposition of the patterns of Roman heroism with the cruel obligations of the totalitarian state. Yet, as is all too well known, the Restoration brought back the study of the Middle Ages, operating almost as a metonymic displacement of the 'vieille France' that had been swept away by the tempest of revolutionary and imperial undertakings. If the Middle Ages became not a hollow notion, but a period replete with romance, then the emergence of the Renaissance as an independent temporal and cultural entity was bound to follow.

My argument so far has touched on very familiar themes, and proposed no radically new ideas. But I hope to have isolated a crucial point. If we argue that, even in the loosest sense, historical competence may be compared with the acquisition of a new language, then we have to posit as the next stage the recognition that language is before all else a system of differences. To perform, in the sense of reading and interpreting historical representations, implies a capacity for specific discriminations and distinctions. So the predecessor of du Sommerard, Alexandre Lenoir, arranges his Musée des Petits-Augustins in such a way that the distinct rooms coincide with the otherwise purely schematic notion of a 'century': he endows each century of French history with a material correlate, in the forms of monumental and decorative sculpture. Du Sommerard goes further than this. He has the pre-existent example of Lenoir to work against, first of all, and he decides not to confine his museum display to the venerable fragments of medieval and Renaissance buildings, but to engineer a representation of the 'lived life' of the period. Within the succession of rooms which he reclaimed from the former town house of the Abbots of Cluny, the appearance of the François Ier room must have seemed to embody both a culmination and a new start. Over the half-century which separated the opening of the Musée de Cluny from the publications of Pater, Burckhardt and a host of others, this initially tenuous concept of the Renaissance was, of course, to be pumped full of cultural content to the point of bursting.

My hypothesis is therefore a very simple one. In order to understand the growth of historicalmindedness from the nineteenth century to the present day, we have to look for the ways in which differences were introduced into the historical series. The mere achievement of Anno Domini dating was, one supposes, an immense cultural achievement which retrospectively endowed the whole Christian epoch with structure and significance. I would agree, moreover, with Hayden White that the conditions of narrativity are met by annals which refer, even in a lacunary way, to events collocated with a precise A D dating.[4] But in the nineteenth century, it would seem, it is the function of historical representation (novels, histories, paintings, museums, spectacles) to concretize past history as a repertoire of specific differences. The narrative of the past is punctuated with a plethora of images which have their own material form and their own location in space (in the room of a museum, or between the pages of an illustrated book); that they constitute not an exuberant disarray of discordant stimuli, but an orderly series, answerable to exact analysis, is the wager of the attentive student of historical representation.

I should add a connected point which is germane to the subject of this essay. Just as such analysis begins, in my view, with an awareness of specific differences with the 'language' of historical representation, so the critics and historians who have most notably contributed to the understanding of historicalmindedness have characteristically been those who posited differential systems of analysis in their turn. Nietzsche achieved a remarkable advance, in *Use and Abuse of History*, when he insisted that the past could be envisaged through three distinct, though not entirely exclusive attitudes: the monumental, the antiquarian and the critical.[5] It is not absurd to mention the contribution of St Augustine to politics and the theory of the state in this connection. For St Augustine argued that the difference between the *Civitas terrena* and the *Civitas Dei* was ultimately a difference between 'two loves': that is to say, the foundation of statecraft could be rooted only in man's disposition either to love God or to cleave to the things of this world. Nietzsche carried out a similar attack on the false reification of his object when he anchored historical consciousness in the psychological disposition to use the past in different ways: nonetheless, his analysis does not presuppose a wholly instrumental view of historicalmindedness, since his 'antiquarian' position (the one most redolent of early nineteenth-century concerns) implies a continuous dialectical interaction between the mind of the observer and the material vestiges of the past.[6]

In this respect, Nietzsche indeed shows the way for a succession of analysts which continues up to our own day. Alois Riegl, as already mentioned, pioneers the investigation of 'age-value' as a specific alternative to 'historical value' - which is the value objects have because of their particular causal function within the historical series - and 'art value' - which is their value estimated according to an ideal concept of worth. His essay was written for a government agency which was itself looking for guidelines in dealing with the upkeep of historical buildings, and one might say that Riegl anticipated the complexity of the issues that have dogged the practice of 'conservation' right up to the present. In a very different, but no less significant register, the writings of Hayden White from the 1970s onwards, have effectively entrenched the principle that, to understand how the historical message operates, we must approach the material to be analysed with a view to locating a series of specific differences. The differences which existed in the ambit of history of historiography before White's *Metahistory* appeared in 1973, were largely institutionalized differences: those between history, which was the province of historians; philosophy of history, which was the province of philosophers; and historical representation, which was the vast and incoherent territory of art historians, literary historians and specialists in theatre or spectacle. White showed that, for the first of these two domains, at any rate, it was possible to use the four-fold battery of rhetorical tropes, in order to discover a system of differences which cut across the institutionalized discrimination between historical and philosophical concerns.

Hayden White's strategy was therefore an exemplary one, within the brief sequence which I have been describing. It was, in these terms, an attempt to reconfigure an institutional difference, which served as an obstacle to the understanding of historicalmindedness, and afford expression to a new order of difference, which was to be revealed with the aid of the four tropes: metonymy, metaphor, synecdoche and irony. Although for White these tropes remained, in 1973, essentially tools of analysis, there is surely no inconsistency in going one stage further (or indeed returning to Nietzsche) and treating the various rhetorical strategies as differential dispositions of the human mind. I myself made this assumption in my introduction to *The Clothing of Clio* (1984), where I borrowed Dan Sperber's notion of a 'cognitive rhetoric'. According to Sperber, the question of whether the rhetorical mechanism is 'in the text' or 'in the mind' creates a false dualism. The point is that a 'figure' of rhetoric

is a function both of the text and of the shared knowledge. . . there are nothing but figures of thought, in relation to which phonological, syntactic or semantic properties could play the role of supplementary focalisers, without ever being either necessary or sufficient, to engage the mechanism of figural interpretation.[7]

This formulation appears to be just. But it also highlights the problem which is inherent in considering irony, as opposed to the other three tropes (a similar difficulty arises, let is be said, with Nietzsche's 'critical' attitude to the past). If we interpret historicalmindedness (or 'historical understanding') as the capability of projecting different modes of figural interpretation upon the objects and texts defined as 'historical' – if we agree that 'historical representation' is an effect of successful (or in Sperber's terms 'sufficient') focalisation of figures within a specific text or medium – then irony necessarily stands apart. It is, to use Vico's useful term, 'double vision'. It presupposes, not an effective focalization but (to continue the metaphor from optics) a condition in which two states of focus are achieved simultaneously. This looks like a recipe for not double, but blurred vision, if we translate the image from the well-tested domain of literature to the broader area of representation in general. And I must

confess to having implied, in *The Clothing of Clio*, that irony is not only
the stage which supervenes after the integrative procedures of metaphor
and synecdoche have done their work, but also the stage of figural
undoing.[8] In my account, it was easy to envisage the historical artists,
writers and impresarios of the advancing nineteenth century as being
engaged in a kind of figural dance of death, trying to repeat the
acknowledged successes of their predecessors by increasingly desperate
feats of ingenuity. To come late in the game of historical representation
was, I implied, to be dancing on hot coals.

I want, however, to use the rest of this essay, to test a new idea which is
not so much a revision as a reconfiguration of my original terms. One of
the reasons for doing so lies in the lessons of a remarkable study by
Jonathan Crary, *Techniques of the Observer*, which suggests that the
epistemic break in the history of Western representation since the
Renaissance comes precisely with the advent of 'double vision', or (to
give it its proper name) the development of the stereoscope. For Crary,
who revises Foucault without jettisoning his essential scheme of things,
the reign of monocular perception of space which begins with the
invention of perspective at the time of the Renaissance, comes to an end
in the second quarter of the nineteenth century, when a wholly new
bodily orientation to space is achieved:

The relation of observer to image is no longer to an object quantified in relation
to a position in space, but rather to two dissimilar images whose position
simulates the anatomical structure of the observer's mind.[9]

Is it worth considering (in line with the firmly epistemological
significance that Crary gives to this new development) that the 'irony' of
historical representation might entail not simply the disruption of
established patterns and the maintenance of separate levels of focus, but
the achievement of a higher level of figural synthesis, anchored within the
newly extended capacities of the mind? In that event, historical
competence would have marked an irreversible gain: the 'ironic'
viewpoint would, like the stereoscopic vista, imply an empathetic
projection into the reality of the other.

I began this essay by arguing that historicalmindedness developed
through the establishment of differences, and that the positing of
difference, on the level of analysis, is the best way in which we can come
to terms with the surprising phenomenon of historical competence. I do
not in any way retract this view. But the emergence of irony, within the
specific differential series of figural tropes, raises the question of whether

there is indeed a 'master trope' whose dominance might help to explain the continued evolution of historicalmindedness - at a stage when the simple figural strategies of the Romantic period no longer fully engage us. We might hesitate to use the term 'irony' in this connection, but we might still be unable to do without the notion of a figural effect which was both 'stereoscopic' and, on the level of perception, recomposed.

What follows is, I should add, a further stage in the exploration of a prospect originally suggested to me by Hayden White: the ironic museum.

II

They are talking to each other, the two gentlemen in top hats and frock-coats, who stand in the centre of the aisle of the ruined church. One of them, evidently the person who knows the site and its attractions, has his left arm outstretched in a generous gesture of reference: his companion, who is obviously a visitor being harangued, stands responsively with his face directed towards the objects indicated by his mentor. Close by, there is a third visitor, just as formally dressed but with the top hat, who balances a sketching block on his knees: he looks past his companions in the direction of the other side of the aisle, where a number of other sculptural objects are clearly on display.

I have been describing a wash drawing completed around 1850, which shows the thirteenth-century Eglise Toussaint, in Angers, a few years after the establishment by the town of a *Musée lapidaire* in its ruined buildings. The church had suffered the usual fate of abbeys of Augustinian Canons at the time of the Revolution, its clergy being dispossessed and its facilities being taken over by a series of *ad hoc* and destructive purposes. Around 1815, the vaults of the main nave had collapsed, and the epoch of the Restoration had witnessed no practical attempts to rebuild, or even shore up, the increasingly ruinous structure. The drawing of 1850 makes it very clear that the process of decay is quite far gone: a covering of plants, and even what appears to be a small tree, sprout from the heights of the walls while the amputated ribs appear to be bandaged with greenery. Yet the scene presents no threatening aspect. Quite the opposite, the visitors indicate an orderly discourse, a panorama of knowledge which is effectively mastered by the human mind.[10]

Two differential systems are put into play by this image: on the one hand, an antithesis between the medieval and the classical, and on the other, an antithesis (or shall we say a relation of complementarity) between the visual and the verbal. The Eglise Toussaint, however

1 Ernest Dainville, *Ancien Eglise Toussaint, c.* 1850, wash drawing.

2 Interior view of the Galerie David d'Angers (in the Old Church at Toussaint, restored
1977–83) from a contemporary postcard.

dilapidated, displays all the signs of its Gothic pedigree: quite a number (it is not clear exactly how many) of the standing figures obviously belong as adornments of the original church. But this is, after all, a *Musée lapidaire*, which had been urged upon the town by the local antiquarian and archaeologist V. Godard-Fautrier. A good proportion of the objects on view are of classical provenance, and at least one bears a partly legible Latin inscription. This brings into play, furthermore, the visual/verbal relation. The two standing visitors suggest that the museum is something to be spoken about: the funerary inscription visible to us (but not to them) insists on the high degree of legibility of the classical epigraphy (DIS - To the Gods - being the first word inscribed on two of the stones). The seated artist suggests that the museum is something to be figured: the statue which he orientates himself towards is probably a post-Renaissance one, and his relatively distant position from it implies that he is sketching a general, rather than a particularized view.

In the wash drawing which we see, there is therefore a recognition, one might almost say an assertion of differences. Unlike the Musée de Cluny, and unlike the Musée de Petits-Augustins, this *Musée lapidaire* of the town of Angers does not propose the perfection of a metonymic series, or the sedulous grouping of objects into a synecdochic integration. It states: this is, or was, a Gothic church. These objects placed on display are sometimes Gothic, but more usually Roman remains. The whole scene can be interpreted according the prescriptions of the Picturesque, no doubt – and that is what impelled the artist to linger upon the mouldering escarpment of flowering walls. But it is a scene for instruction, as well as for reverie. There is no attempt to soften the potentially jarring combination of the muteness of the ruin and the forensic eloquence of the contemporary mentor. This is a far cry from those beguiling lithographs of country churches, in Taylor's and Nodier's *Voyages pittoresques et romantiques* of the 1820s, where the human beings featured were allowed to appear largely as actors assimilated within the Picturesque convention.[11] No great claim is made for the wash drawing of the Eglise Toussaint described here, I should add, except that it indicates a certain sophistication in the expression and containment of differences.

Yet the very choice of this image depends on a further difference, which becomes evident if we juxtapose this scene from around 1850 with the view taken from roughly the same viewpoint over a century later, and perpetuated in the form of a colour postcard. The Gothic tracery of the rose window is recognizably the same, as is the arcading of the chancel. In place of the open sky, however, there is a severe modern structure of glass and steel which segments the blue sky necessary for a postcard image. In the wash drawing, soft light cuts obliquely across the walls of the church, casting some objects into a velvety gloom. In the postcard, light and shade intersect vividly across a mass of sculptured bodies and bas-reliefs subjected to a dizzying perspective. This is the Galerie David d'Angers.

It is worth taking a small detour back in time to understand the significance of this award-winning contemporary museum. The sculptor David d'Angers, solicitous from the start of his career for the aesthetic education of the townsfolk he had left behind in the provinces, had by the end of the 1830s constituted a substantial collection of works (and notably the original plasters of many celebrated statues) for the benefit of the town. As the rooms originally provided for the collection were progressively filled up, David began to think in terms of a museum, which would bring together casts relating to all periods, in addition to his own. In 1839, a solution was found with the enlargement and remodelling of the 'magasins de la bibliothèque', which became the repository of the ever-growing collection. But its inadequacy was soon revealed, piquantly enough, when the more than life-size statue of the seventeenth-century sailor Jean Bart (a model for the bronze erected in his home town of Dunkerque) had to have its base reduced in size, and its sabre clipped by several centimetres, before it could occupy the low-ceilinged space. Representations were made in the late nineteenth century about the need for a new home for the Galerie David d'Angers. But the citizens of Angers had to wait until 1977 for a decision to move the works into the former *Musée lapidaire*, the Eglise Toussaint. The reinstallation of the Galerie was finally completed in 1983.[12]

Jean Bart now has the ample space of a Gothic nave, covered in glass and steel, to rattle his sabre in. The educational project nurtured by France's greatest early nineteenth-century sculptor finds its fulfilment in an elegant postmodern environment. This is a pleasing thought. But is the ecclesiastical setting in fact appropriate for the stern non-classicist, with deeply held masonic convictions? Does the spectacular arrangement not sacrifice order and coherence to a homogenizing aestheticism, with each of the luminous plasters reduced to a common denominator of empty gesture and over-emphatic form? This building does not instil the cool radiance of Canova's Glyptothek at Posagno (doubtless David's model for a near-complete collection of original plasters). Its confrontation of codes cannot fail to be disruptive – does it then also disrupt the spectator's attention, and cancel out any possibility of historical understanding?

It would be possible to sustain an argument of this kind. But it would be more accurate, in my view, to examine the reasons why this museum, which I have deliberately called postmodern, succeeds in representing the life's work of David d'Angers quite remarkably well. For the assumption which I have been testing in my rhetorical questions is that a 'life's work' does indeed possess a coherence of its own, and that the museum should be, in a certain sense, the neutral receptacle for this coherent series. By contrast, the 'life's work' of David d'Angers must surely be seen as being fraught with ideological fissures, which were the absolutely faithful reflection of his bizarre historical role. Here was an artist sustained by the universalizing messages of heroic classicism, who was at the same time a faithful son of Anjou, impregnated with the memory of the counter-revolutionary Vendée wars. Faithful to the patrimony of his master, the painter David, he records the childish heroism of the little drummer-boy Barra, with no less pathos than we find in David's great, unfinished work. But he also records, in monumental form, the last words of the Vendée general, Charles de Bonchamps, whose decision to spare the republican prisoners saved the life of his own father.[13] Faced with the legacy of irreconcilable hatred, David d'Angers himself aspires to a reconciliation through art, in the interests of a 'humanity' which will transcend all historical antagonisms, taking 'great examples' from the historical repertoire without regard for divisions of ideology.

My point can thus be stated simply. Irony is integral to the vision of David d'Angers. The most distinctive quality of his work is, in fact, the excess of rhetoric with which he seeks to reconcile the tensions implicit in his style and subject matter. The postmodern museum espouses this irony, and enables the rhetoric to be grandiloquently expressed. More than that, it establishes a division within David's own work which is both intrinsically appropriate, and brilliantly reliant on the latent potentiality of the Christian church. Whereas the previous *Musée lapidaire* treated the Eglise Toussaint simply as an open shell, the new gallery establishes a barrier between the nave and the choir (artfully making use of a large frieze designed for the Pantheon). The nave is, to quote the curator, 'le lieu privilégié de présentation des grands modèles et le visiteur s'y promène à son gré, dans ces "Champs Elysées" de vertus, de gloire et de mérites'. By contrast, the space of the choir offers 'des espaces plus réduits, plus aptes à la présentation des esquisses, dessins, souvenirs personnels.'[14] One could go further in developing the striking opposition. The choir has as its focus the plaster of the little drummer-boy, with his tricolour cockade. David's own memories of a revolutionary childhood are mingled with acknowledgements to his master, and the Christian connotations of innocence and sacrifice. The nave presents us (as we see it on the postcard) with the grand image of Gutenberg, seen as the prophet of universal literacy and illumination. Where the *Musée lapidaire* invited us to linger over the dedications of the pagan altars, the Galerie David d'Angers confronts us with Gutenberg holding a sheet with the biblical inscription: *et la lumière fut* ('and there was light'). In its printed version (with the frame of type resting on the ground beside him), Gutenberg's text expresses precisely the message of *Genesis* subsumed into a universal religion of humanity and progress.

To recapitulate my argument, both the images of the Eglise Toussaint which have been discussed raise the issue of irony, or 'double vision', as a mode for the representation of the past. In the mid-nineteenth century wash drawing, the codes are deliberately mixed: classical and medieval, verbal and visual description, all are invoked simultaneously. In the contemporary photograph of the Galerie David d'Angers, this clash of codes takes place no longer in relation to ideal models of style, but through the medium of the life's work of an individual artist, who therefore becomes representative of a specific chapter of historical experience. But what is necessary, in the contemporary example, in order for the internal divisions and contradictions of that experience to be made manifest? The answer, obviously, lies in the way in which the museum space, itself possessed of a history, has been articulated in such a way as to express the discordant messages of the artist. Division of the space into nave and choir is the small, but necessary inflection which makes it possible for us to appreciate the two registers of David's work. The apparently wilful catachresis of glass roof and Gothic arcades prepares us to accept that David's own experience of the past was compounded of discordant impulses. His faith in universal enlightenment had to be reconciled with a local piety and a regard for the reactionary Pays de Bocage. To borrow Nietzsche's terms, his monumental preoccupation with the past as a repertoire of examples had to be reconciled with an antiquarian cult of locality, and a critical commitment to history as progress.

I began this essay by speculating on the preconditions of historical 'competence' in relation to a number of nineteenth century instances. My main point was that such competence develops as a direct result of the introduction of differences into the historical series. But I ended the first section with a query about the particular role which irony plays as the mode of rhetoric in which differences are openly and unapologetically declared. My question amounted to asking whether irony, as an analytic tool for looking at historical representation, was not implicitly the recognition that such representation had ended in failure. Crary's relevant illustration of the stereoscope as the mode of visuality which breaks with the perspectival order of post-renaissance space was a useful marker at this point, since it introduced the possibility that 'double vision' might imply a new sophistication in processing the messages of an apparently discordant visual field. And my discussion of the two successive incarnations of the Eglise Toussaint has been intended precisely to explore this possibility. In their structure, they are similar. But both can be interpreted as testifying to a strange kind of progress in historical competence, with the second example immeasurably more subtle in its representational strategy. Here is not simply the museum as a site of ironic juxtapositions, but the ironic museum.

I want, however, to extend the discussion a little further by looking at two more examples from the present day which may counteract the euphoric character of my previous argument. I have, undoubtedly, suggested that what passes for 'postmodern' architecture and museology can be seen not as a disavowal of historical representation, but as a mode of encapsulating its real discordances. But this does not mean that I recognize no need to discriminate between authentic and inauthentic cases of historical representation in the present period. It is a feature of the last two centuries that the mass public of the Western world has been called upon not only to be more and more historically competent, but also to 'perform' historically: by this, I am referring to the numerous special locations - from museums to country-houses and theme parks - where physical involvement in a space declared to be historical is proposed to them, and not rejected. What people experience as they journey through the signs and smells of Viking York, to take just one example, is an issue which can hardly be clarified by the usual indexes of consumer satisfaction, measured by sociological inquiry. It is an issue which is destined to remain opaque, unless we follow up Albertine de Broglie's invitation, to seek to understand historical understanding.

This is a very preliminary discussion of what might, and what might not, count as authentic in assessing such examples of historical 'performance'. Old Sturbridge Village, to begin with, is a splendid case of the maximal energy and commitment being devoted to historical education. Situated close to the border between Massachusetts and Connecticut, not far from the city of Springfield, it is, to quote the publicity material, 'a living history museum which presents the story of life in a rural New England town during the 1830s'. Restored buildings have been brought together from all parts of the area to compose a town which never existed, but now exists as a fully intelligible working model of a rural community. Yet this fact pales into insignificance beside the fact that the town is peopled, as well as being provided with all the tools and technologies of early nineteenth-century existence. If the 'Fenno House' is 'interpreted as the household of the elderly widow', then this means that a person resembling an elderly widow of the period will be in occupation. Volunteers from the entire region around Sturbridge spend occasional days as vicarious visitors to the past, appropriately clothed and obeying a complex choreography of movements which sometimes chimes in with, and sometimes departs from, the schedule of the ordinary public. A top-hatted figure, glimpsed from afar, begins his methodical walk from the Friends' Meeting House to the other side of the village green, furnished with a large covered basket which suggests that his destination is the rural store. How do we interpret the fact that his movements are 'other-directed' – that he will not stop and talk to us, even if we try to intervene in his time-travelling world ?

Other figures are not so pure in this historical vocation. The Manager of the Bank is irritated, not because of some putative financial worry of the 1830s, but because the confetti of American school children floats colourfully in and out of his sanctum without regard for sobriety and decorum. One comfortably dressed dame is willing to gossip out of character about her life in the 1990s, even though her companion, more sedulous, insists on displaying ignorance of what might be referred to as a tomato. Louis XVI, in Renoir's *La Marseillaise*, demonstrates his property of being 'a body too much'[15] in part by his enraptured consideration of the newly imported fruit (or vegetable), while the tides of revolution gather around him. Here the disavowed tomato serves as an index of one American lady's dedication to the past as otherness, and to her conviction that this little performance will be correctly interpreted by her motley contemporary audience.

All this reminds me of the plot of Jacques Rivette's film, *Céline and Julie go Boating*, where the two heroines visit a strange house which serves for the ceaseless re-enactment of some inscrutable intrigue. The characters in the past drama go about their doom-laden movements without seeing, or interacting with, the modern participants, and the outcome of the story obstinately resists their (and our) interpretation. In a similar way, the scene of Old Sturbridge Village presents the past as enacted fragments of a drama without conclusion. Yet, like Céline and

Julie, we cannot resist trying to naturalize the enigma within our modes of representation. The cottage interiors, with mob-capped women applying themselves to culinary tasks, resolve themselves into genre scenes, reminiscent of Dou or Chardin, while the kitchen gardens tended by their temporary proprietors offer spectacles of peasant life assimilable to Millet. A specific point can be made about the effect of distance in authenticating such a prospect. Hay-making in the far distance is all the more effective in that its participants are indistinct, and (as Marmontel recognized) the code of perspective comes to overdetermine the strategy of representing the past.[16] The problem is, however, that all these effects of representation and distancing offer no systematic ordering of differences. Old Sturbridge Village courts irony in the disruptive sense of the term, in that everything is mixed in with everything else. The issue is not, for our purposes, whether people enjoy themselves there. Clearly many of them do. Rather, the issue is whether their experience can become a vehicle for historical understanding – a focalization of historical competence. Here it must be acknowledged that the strategy of representation – Old Sturbridge Village as a re-created and re-composed totality which is at the same time infinitely permeable to the incursions of the contemporary world – is far too ambitious to succeed.

I cite this case not in a spirit of gratuitous criticism, but because it exemplifies the predicament of so much well-intentioned work of historical representation at the present day. The visitor, let us say the would-be historical performer, is precipitated into a contrast between past and present which is virtually without mediation. There can be little wonder that such a policy has produced its equally extreme reactions. Robert Hewison proclaims in the last sentence of his aptly named study, *The Heritage Industry* (1987): 'We must live in the future tense, and not the past pluperfect'.[17] Yet to live in the present, which is a certain precondition of the future, we have to be competent in using the imperfect, the perfect and – why not? – the pluperfect. In other words, we have to be competent in exploring the full range of tenses, or their temporal content will simply atrophy. Here again, Nietzsche is wise in suggesting that what is required is a balance of the 'monumental', the 'antiquarian' and the 'critical', rather than a striving for one particular type of relationship to history and temporality.

My conclusion therefore takes the form of a renewed plea for the representation of difference. Old Sturbridge Village is one model. But the scheme which seems to me much more rich in its implications - though it remains only at the stage of a proposal – is the one devised by the French landscape designer Bernard Lassus, for the recreational park of Duisburg-Nord, in the Ruhr district of Germany. In other pre-existing proposals, and notably the one for the restoration of the Jardin des Tuileries in central Paris,[18] Lassus has stressed that a historical location is a kind of palimpsest, and that the task of the landscape designer is to allow the different 'pasts' of each site to find expression, rather than fixing upon a single stratum of temporality to re-create. At Duisburg-Nord, he was confronted with a special challenge, since the vast, disused factories and blast-furnaces which survived from the industrial heyday of the Ruhr were an uncompromising presence on the site. He was determined that these monuments to a bygone industrial age should not simply be left like beached whales, but incorporated in an orderly vision of the past. Yet this raised a further question:

> how could we establish the difference between the Emscher (the river flowing through the site) of today and the Emscher of yesterday. . . if we did not also bring into play an Emscher of the day before yesterday, an Emscher from before the factory was built, an Emscher associated with the old countryside, with rippling clear water, fishes, birds and fields?

Lassus therefore correctly conceived the task of representing history as one of establishing perceptible differences. His scheme for Duisburg-Nord introduces the striking idea of the 'temporal pen' (sas temporel) which, in the same way as a pen on a canal marks the transition of water levels, is introduced to mark the transition from one historical level to another. Systematic planting of trees, in geometrical patterns which would instantly draw attention to their formal role, is used to demarcate the different time-zones. In this way, the area where the looming presence of the factories is felt becomes discontinuous with the area of the pre-industrial countryside. At one point the Emscher is strictly canalized, as in its industrial phase, and at another its sinuous course is re-established, through an 'idyllic garden' of old Westphalia, complete with grazing meadows and water mills. Establishing differences between yesterday and today, and between yesterday and the day before yesterday, permits not only a garden of the present – catering for all forms of contemporary recreation and sport – but also a garden of the future, where new, experimental facilities would be developed in laboratories of soil, sounds and smells . . . Lassus recalls that, in the past, the art of gardens has not been merely nostalgic, but a symbolic analogue to the explorations and discoveries of the time:

Surely the art of gardens has in the past opened up the horizons of the future, as, for example, in the 18th century, when monuments were raised, at the edge of parks, to the glory of Captain Cook?

Lassus's Park of Duisburg-Nord thus exemplifies a contemporary strategy of historical representation which would test, and arguably extend, historical competence. By insisting on the need for the 'temporal pen' – a materialization of historical difference which does not seek to efface itself – he courts the accusation of irony. How can we not note that this row of trees is a division of space, rather than time, just as we note that the 'idyllic garden' has had to be comprehensively 'reinvented'? The question would be grave in its implications, perhaps devastatingly so, if we had not become expert, over the past two centuries, at seeing double.

Statements, Texts and Pictures

F. R. ANKERSMIT

Il y a, dans toute réalité, dans tout fait qui s'accomplit, deux choses distinctes, deux choses, pour ainsi dire, concentriques: l'essence même du fait, et sa formule. On peut connaître le fait par l'une ou par l'autre. Connaître par la seconde, c'est *savoir*; connaître par la première, c'est *voir*. Savoir, cest connaître la formule, laquelle est toujours plus générale que le fait: savoir, c'est donc classer. Voir, c'est pénétrer, à travers l'enveloppe formulaire, dans l'intimité du fait, par conséquent dans son individualité: ce n'est pas classer, c'est nommer. L'un des actes appartient à l'intelligence, l'autre est exclusif à l'âme. L'intelligence ne connaît que des abstractions et des formes: l'âme voit des êtres et des substances: l'intelligence ne connaît que des genres et des espèces: l'âme voit des individualités: l'intelligence sait, l'âme voit. N'est-ce pas dire assez que c'est l'âme qui est poète? Et pour autant que l'historien complet est poète aussi, ne peut-on pas dire que pour lui, comme pour le poète, savoir c'est voir?
A. Vinet, *Mélanges littéraires*, 1955, p.158

INTRODUCTION

This essay stands at the crossroads of two controversies which at first sight seem independent of one another. The first is concerned with the relation between word and picture – so the question of whether there is a fundamental difference between the verbal and the pictural depiction of representation of reality. Are word and picture governed by two essentially different forms of representative logic or is Goodman right in holding that 'the boundary line between texts and images, pictures and paragraphs, is drawn by a history of practical differences in the use of different sorts of symbolic marks, not by a metaphysical divide'?[1] The second controversy under inquiry here requires a somewhat longer explanation. Its subject is the study of history. Both the way in which we intuitively talk about the study of history and our theoretical reflection on this subject show a strong inclination towards the use of visual metaphors: we like to speak of 'images of the past' of the 'point of view' from which the historian 'looks' at the past, of the 'distortions' of historical reality which an incorrect 'viewpoint' is liable to create. Over against these visual and optical metaphors, present-day philosophy of history is in the habit of linking the study of history to the novel and literature. Like the novel, the historical text is in the first place a text and so, it is argued, the metaphor of the 'picture' of historical reality presented by the historian is an incorrect characterization of the relation between representation and what is represented. Not the philosophy of the visual arts but literary theory is therefore the discipline to which the philosopher of history should turn. Thus in the introduction of his famous *Metahistory*, the manifesto of the literary approach to the historical representation of the past, Hayden White made the following programmatic statement: 'I will consider the historical work as what it most manifestly is – that is to say, a verbal structure in the form of narrative prose'.[2] In this book and in his later work White went on to develop a strong argument in favour of this literary conception of historical text. The success of White's conceptions means that the pictorial conception of the text must be pushed to the background as a naive and misleading metaphor.

For the following reason my aim in this essay is to create a short circuit between these two controversies. Whenever philosophy of history in the past appealed to visual and pictural metaphors, its concern was with the question of the truth, the reliability, or the adequacy of the historical text. The pictural interpretation of the historical text is thus closely connected with the cognitive claims of the study of history and the epistemological justification of those claims constantly stimulates the use of visual and pictural metaphors. On the other hand, the general objection to the literary, textual approach to the study of history is that it neglects the question of the truth and reliability of the study of history. In practice it seems that the historian and the philosopher of history cannot look to literature and literary theory for an answer to the question of what 'true' history is. It is significant that literary theorists rarely link the question of realism in the novel to the objectives of the historian, though one would expect this to be important common ground between literature and the study of history.[3] Here, then, lies the rationale for my wish to short-circuit the two controversies mentioned. For consider the study of history. It is true that it always manifests itself to us in the form of text – and because of this fact we are inclined to agree with White's literary approach to the study of history. On the other hand the historian wishes to tell us the truth about the past, and then the text assumes the form of a 'picture' of the past, just as the figurative painting aims to be a correct representation of a landscape or of a person sitting for a portrait. And from this we can conclude that it is the study of history where we can best examine the relation between picture and text, since the total historical text incorporates both pictural and textual elements. By concentrating on the historical text, we can study both controversies in the light of *one another*.

The conclusion of my argument will be the following. With regard to the historical text we have to distinguish between the level of the separate statements and the level of the text in its entirety. On the level of the text in its entirety one finds the existence of a surprising parallelism between text and picture. This is consequently a strong argument in favour of the pictural interpretation of the study of history. On the other hand, when the study of history and the novel, more specifically the historical novel, meet, this happens on the level of the separate statement. And since the problem of the true historical text obviously occurs on the level of the total historical text and not on that of the separate statement, we have to express our preference for the pictural over the literary approach to the study of history, even if this by no means involves a rejection of what theorists such as White have said about the historical text as such.

RESEMBLANCE

In the *Cratylus* Plato discusses the relation between representations of reality and the words or the names which represent objects in reality. He argues that there the words should resemble the things which they name just as pictures do. He introduces here the idea of 'the right name'. Whenever the name expresses the general character of a thing, even if it does not cover all the additional features of the thing in question, one is dealing with 'the correct name' of that thing.[4] He is particularly concerned here with phonetics. Thus Plato says that the letter 'r' in the verb 'rhein' (to flow) or in the noun 'rhoè' (current) correctly represents the phenomenon itself of flowing or the current. The name here is a *mimesis* of what it denotes, just as paintings are imitations of things, though in a different way.[5] Plato's considerations here – as we shall see, he expresses a different opinion elsewhere – thus seem to bring about a *rapprochement* between word and picture, since both words and paintings in this line of reasoning are imitations of the reality represented. Nevertheless, if we go along with Plato's line of reasoning, we come up against a difficulty here. For we should not lose sight of the role of the medium in which the resemblance is expressed. Thus it could be claimed that the medium of language and that of painting are so different that, despite the mimetic nature of both word and picture, we cannot really speak of a *rapprochement* between word and picture. Precisely the difference in medium creates an unbridgeable gap between word and picture.

We find this kind of argument in Lessing's *Laokoon*. For Lessing painting and poetry, picture and word, are irreconcilably different because each has an affinity with an entirely distinct part or aspect of reality:

it is true that paintings use different signs for mimesis than does poetry: painting uses figures and colours in space; poetry uses specific noises in time. And if it cannot be doubted that signs must have a satisfactory relationship to what they signify, it follows that signs that are placed next to each other can only stand for objects (or their parts) standing next to each other, whereas signs following each other can only stand for objects, or parts thereof, that follow each other.[6]

In other words, the painting offers a coordination of objects in its representation of the world and is therefore *sui generis* suitable for representing the spatial aspects of reality. By contrast, language, prose or poetry cannot be surveyed in a single glance; reading is a temporal process and language is therefore suitable for the representation of temporary processes. At the same time Lessing acknowledges that there is a certain continuity between word and picture. Historical paintings may suggest a certain drama and literature has the genre of so-called 'ecphrastic poetry', from which all temporality has been eliminated.[7] One also finds picturality in typographical experiments with poetic form. But these cases always involve hybrid forms which fail to detract from the 'satisfactory relationship' between word and time on the one hand and picture and space on the other. Such insights were defended in Kantian and neo-Kantian aesthetics in the twentieth century by, for instance, Ernst Cassirer and Susanne Langer. The 'Anschauungsformen' space and time each have their natural affinity with either the picture or the word. The paradox one constantly finds here is therefore the following: precisely the intuition that both picture and word are a mimesis of reality leads to an unbridgeable gap between word and picture.

Obviously, it is possible to imagine an empiricist variant of this Kantian, transcendentalist argument, a variant in which the distinction of word versus picture corresponds to that between auditory and visual perception. This empiricist variant seems unlikely to offer new angles, but it does present an interesting complication as soon as we realize that words can both be heard and seen. To put it differently, the word can present itself to us in a form which does not differ essentially from that of the painting. Of course, this is above all the case with pictographical, as opposed to phonetic, script. In the pictogram the word and picture approximate one another. Etymology confirms this. Thus in many languages the words for writing and painting are etymologically cognate. The Gothic word 'meljan' which means 'to write', is cognate with modern German 'malen'. Furthermore, German 'schreiben' ('to write') is probably an early derivation from Latin 'scribere', which in turn has the same root as English 'to carve' or German 'kerben', that is to say, with the word denoting the technique of scratching a picture in stone or wood.[8] Next, it is generally agreed that script developed out of the picture. The history of this development is instructive. The earliest script universally was ideography, that is to say, a system of more or less stylized pictures of certain states of affairs, or a pictography in the narrower sense, where the separate words are represented by separate pictures.[9] An interesting aspect here is that in both cases, ideography and pictography, the script is to a certain extent independent of language. It is possible to imagine an ingenious reader deciphering a message expressed in ideography or in a pictogram, even though he cannot speak the language of the person who formulated the message. In this sense the earliest script was more universalistic than its later, more practical descendants. But virtually everywhere pictography eventually had to give way to the phoneticization of script. Via an intermediate phase, in which the elements of the words are still represented by pictures, as in rebuses, a final stage is reached in which the script no longer represents the idea of a linguistic utterance, but merely its phonetic value. The intellectual daring of this oldest form of iconoclasm cannot be overemphasized: for how paradoxical it is that the script intended to convey ideas was stripped of every vestige of idea or conception and transposed into a system which merely reproduces sounds. A system was chosen in which the idea was represented by a medium which no longer 'resembled' the idea or conception in any way and which merely represents the completely arbitrary and external phonetic form of the idea. But precisely in this absurdity lies the secret of the power of phonetic script. 'The increasing use of simplified pictures had the further consequence,' writes Jensen, 'that out of the multitude of variants one commended itself as the most suitable, which then became generally used, *conventional* (Jensen's emphasis).[10] Not the *resemblance* between the picture and depicted,

between representation and represented, but *convention* governs phonetic script.

Of course, something similar can be said about the word itself. As
mentioned above, Plato claims in the *Cratylus* that the word is ideally a
picture of what it denotes. But in the same dialogue he also argues the
opposite thesis of the purely conventional character of the relationship
between the two theories. Thus towards the end of the dialogue Plato
writes:

both like and unlike letters, by the influence of custom and convention produce
indication. . . . We should henceforth be obliged to say that custom, not likeness,
is the principle of indication.[11]

Plato's second thesis sounds highly plausible and anyone who thinks
about the problem of the relation between word and picture for the first
time will be inclined to agree with it. Is it not true that the picture shows a
natural resemblance to what it is a picture of, whereas the word (and
phonetic script) are tied to the things in reality by essentially arbitrary
conventions? But the problem is more complicated. Plato himself puts us
on to a difficulty when he broaches the subject of numbers.

For, my friend, if you will just turn your attention to numbers, where do you
think you can possibly get names to apply to each individual number on the
principle of likeness, unless you allow agreement and convention on your part to
control the correctness of names?[12]

But are the names of numbers in fact merely conventional, as Plato
suggests here? Let us agree with, for instance, Frege and Russell that
numbers denote certain abstract entities. In that case it is clear that
precisely the *conventions* for counting in natural languages offer an
indication of the nature of what is denoted by the name of the number.
Dutch has a convention by which the name of the number twenty-five, in
contrast to fifty-two, is constructed as 'five-and-twenty' – a convention
which Dutch shares with German and in which it differs from English –
and in both cases the conventions determine the identity of the denoted
entity. It might be objected that these conventions do not offer us any
insight into the nature of the numbers, but that they merely help us to
identify numbers. And obviously this argument also requires the
acceptance of numbers as abstract entities – and this is a matter of
contention.

An example more suitable for undermining the value of the distinction
between resemblance and convention can be found in the system for
naming chemical substances. Thus industries use a solvent of which the

trivial name is xylene; this name offers no insight whatsoever into the name of the molecule. But such an insight is offered by the name 1,2-dimethyl benzene: the chemist who hears this name for the first time can directly reconstruct the nature of the molecule. Thanks to a series of semantic conventions which determine the reference of the elements of the chemical name and a number of syntactic conventions which determine the combination of these elements, this name is in effect a pictogram, a verbal model, indeed, a verbal *picture* of the molecule in question. Precisely owing to these conventions there is a resemblance between word and reality which we intuitively reserve for the relation between picture and reality. Convention and resemblance (as models for the relation between representation and what is represented) are parallel, not opposite, paradigms here. The system of names in chemistry puts one in mind of Faust, when he urges Mephistopheles to give him his name, for:

bei euch, ihr Herrn, kann man das Wesen/Gewöhnlich aus den Namen lesen.[13]

The verbal codes in chemistry run parallel to the properties of the entities which they name and they thus realize a transparency of language *vis-à-vis* reality which we would initially regard as the exclusive privilege of the picture. The distinction between the intensionality and the extensionality of linguistic utterances disappears, since the way in which reality is represented by the linguistic utterance is a copy of the relations existing in reality – just as the realistic picture tries to be a copy of real relations. One is reminded of Foucault's characterization of the Renaissance episteme:

Language partakes in the world-wide dissemination of similitudes and signatures. It must, therefore be studied itself as a thing in nature. Like animals, plants or stars, its elements have their laws of affinity and convenience, their necessary analogies. Ramus divided his grammar into two parts. The first was devoted to etymology, which means that one looked in it to discover not the original meaning of words but the intrinsic properties of letters, the syllables, and finally of whole words. The second part dealt with syntax: its purpose was to teach the building of words together by means of their properties; and it consisted almost entirely in the convenience and the mutual communion of properties, as of the noun with the noun or the verb, of the adverb with all the words to which it is adjoined, of the conjunction in the order of things conjoined.[14]

There is also a late reminiscence of the Renaissance episteme in Leibniz's speculations about a 'universal language' which would be capable of automatically generating true statements about the world.[15]

It is clear, however, that we find ourselves on a slippery slope if we accept the above argumentation against the intuitively albeit plausible distinction between resemblance and convention. For what was just said about the system of names in chemistry can ultimately, *mutatis mutandis*, be said about natural languages as well. After all, natural languages too, are governed by a series of semantic and syntactic conventions which enable us to represent the structure of reality in language. And, of course, this line of thought was in fact argued by the Wittgenstein of the *Tractatus*. For Wittgenstein the true sentence as a *picture* of reality was not merely a challenging metaphor, but the basis for a correct insight into the relation between language and reality. The distinction between word and picture would thus lose its meaning. Since we seem to have become gradually involved in a *reductio ad absurdum*, there is every reason to subject the distinction between (natural) resemblance and convention, in terms of which we have tried to define the difference between word and picture, to a more accurate inquiry.

GOODMAN ON WORD AND PICTURE

Anyone who studies the current literature on the relation between word and picture in the hope of finding an intuitive confidence in the differences between the two confirmed is in for a disappointment. The main explanation for this is that there has been a fairly general tendency to replace the neo-Kantianist view of the differences between word and picture with a semiotic or semiological approach to the picture. As a result of this development, the picture acquired a quasi-linguistic character. Pioneering work here was carried out by Ernst Gombrich. In his *Art and Illusion* and even more in his famous essay 'Meditations on a Hobby Horse', Gombrich severed the naturalistic ties which linked the picture to what it depicted. Gombrich arrived at his position because he was trying to find an explanation for the fact that the history of art shows an astounding number of styles, even though every one of these styles seems to aim at a realistic or naturalistic representation of reality. But it was above all Nelson Goodman who in many writings – in which he was not afraid of repeating himself – provided the semiotic approach with a number of arguments which were difficult to refute. Goodman's conceptions are therefore the obvious point of departure for a closer inquiry into the relation between word and picture.

Although Goodman does not radically reject the thesis of the resemblance between picture and what it depicts, he reduces this resemblance to a phenomenon of subsidiary importance. In any case resemblance cannot bear the load which the supporters of the resemblance thesis would have it bear. For this trivialization of the role of the resemblance he adduces a number of arguments which can all be traced back to the incongruence between the resemblance on the one hand and the relation between picture and depicted on the other. The idea is as follows. Resemblance is always a symmetrical relationship in the sense that if A resembles B, B also resembles A. By contrast, the relation between picture and pictured is asymmetrical: if A is a picture of B, B is not a picture of A. This insight could be applied as follows: nothing more resembles A than A itself and yet we do not say that A is a picture of itself. And, further, Constable's painting of Marlborough Castle more resembles any other painting than it resembles the castle itself – paintings and castles are, after all, totally different kinds of object – and yet Constable's painting is not a picture of another painting but of that castle.[16]

Of course, the edge of this argument cuts too keenly: to do away altogether with the criterion of resemblance would prevent us from properly explaining why Constable's painting is a picture of Marlborough Castle and not, for instance, of the Duke of Wellington. However, in general Goodman does not try to find the happy medium in a different definition of the notion of resemblance,[17] but in the answer which we should give to the question of what a 'realistic' representation of reality is. This seems a sound strategy. On the one hand the idea of the 'realistic representation' respects our intuitions with regard to the kind of requirements a true picture should meet; on the other hand this idea is less apt to prompt rash conclusions than the thesis of the resemblance between picture and depicted. The somewhat biased neutrality of the idea of the realistic representation makes it suitable for a further inquiry into the problem of the relation between picture and depicted. Goodman gives three definitions of realism – but only one of these is relevant here.[18] According to this definition, realism is 'a matter not of any constant or absolute relationship between a picture and its object but of a relationship between the system of representation employed in the picture and the standard system'.[19] That is to say, we characterize a painting as 'realistic': we believe that it offers a reliable and correct representation of reality if the painter represents reality in a way *that we are accustomed to* – whichever way that may be. To put it in terms of the word 'resemblance': we are dealing with a realistic representation if the work of art concerned represents reality in a way that *resembles* the way that the works of art familiar to us represent reality. The realistic representation is the representation which conforms to the existing pictural *conventions*. And this is the main point. For if the realism of the pictural representation of reality is, in fact, a matter of convention, we are not far from these semantic and syntactic conventions which relate the true statement to reality. Both in the case of the word and the picture, therefore, we can rely only on conventions; the picture is no less tied to conventions than the word – and now we understand why Goodman gave his *opus famosum* the title *Languages of Art* and why he supports a semiotic approach to the artistic representation of reality.

Nevertheless, Goodman draws attention to two differences between word and picture. First, he points out that, unlike the verbal representation, the pictural representation is such that for every distinction which is made in the notation system used by the artist, it is possible to make a distinction that is smaller and more subtle than that. In the painting there is, for instance, a perfect *continuity* of contours, colour and form: 'pictura non facit saltum', to paraphrase Leibniz. This continuity does not exist in the verbal representation, or at least we always find there a certain lower limit owing to which the verbal system of representation always meets the two 'syntactic requirements of disjointness and finite differentiation'.[20] This characteristic power of articulation in the verbal system is already seen at the level of words. Think, for instance, of the words 'mat', 'cat', 'rat' or 'bat': the syntactic conventions for the formation of words from letters leaves no room for a shadowy border area between 'cat' and 'mat' which one could subdivide: it is truly one or the other here. Something similar applies to the letters themselves: the letters 'a' and 'd' for instance, are such that there are no symbols which might be able to function as a kind of transition between them. There is a kind of notional space or void around these letters which makes a complete differentiation possible. Goodman characterizes the continuity which the pictural notation possesses, in contrast to this verbal notion, with the word 'density'.[21]

Goodman locates the second difference between word and picture in the so-called 'repleteness' of the pictural notation system. His point is the following. Compare the line on a cardiogram with the perhaps virtually identical line which the Japanese artist Hokusai (1760-1849) used to depict the contours of Mount Fuji. Of both notations one can indeed say that they are 'dense': there is a complete continuity between the elements of the representation. But the difference is that all kinds of detail of the line, such as colour, thickness, intensity or dimensions are irrelevant in the cardiogram's case, but form an essential part of the representation in

Hokusai's picture.[22] In the case of the verbal notation there is obviously even less 'repleteness' than in the cardiogram's case: one and the same letter can be written in entirely different ways. In short, not 'resemblance' but 'density' and 'repleteness' mark the (not very fundamental) difference between word and picture. Or, in Goodman's own words:

all this adds up to open heresy. Descriptions are distinguished from pictures not through being more arbitrary but through belonging to articulate rather than to dense schemes; and words are more conventional than pictures only if conventionality is construed in terms of differentiation rather than of artificiality. Nothing here depends on the internal structure of a symbol; for what describes in some systems may depict in others. Resemblance disappears as a criterion of representation, and structural similarity as a requirement upon notational or any other languages. The often stressed distinction between iconic and other signs becomes transient and trivial; thus does heresy breed iconoclasm.[23]

Indeed, heresy against the orthodoxy of the resemblance thesis leads to the iconoclasm which allows the picture no separate status over against the word.

Finally, if Goodman is still prepared to leave room for the difference between word and picture in terms of 'density' and 'repleteness', he is not very specific about the kind of linguistic utterances in which this difference manifests itself. In the last quotation above he talks about 'descriptions'; elsewhere he contrasts 'statements' and 'pictures' – and this suggests that he is mainly thinking of the true statement as the counterpart of the picture.[24] An interesting point here is the following. In *Of Mind and other Matters* Goodman expressly compares the picture with the narrative account of a development in time. But here, too, he has his back turned to the story, as it were: his concern is ultimately with the statement. For the question which Goodman asks himself is whether and how the narrative account of a temporal sequence can be split up into its independent components in such a way that when these independent components are arranged in a new order, in a 'twisted tale', the original sequence can nevertheless be reconstructed from them. The model of the text which he has in mind here is evidently the narrative account of a series of statements in which each of these statements describes the state of an object at a given point in time, without this series of statements coagulating into a whole that is more than the sum of the separate statements. Precisely this approach to the story or the text suggests how far the statement in Goodman's argument functions as the paradigm of the word, while the overall text is given no distinct status independent of the statement.[25]

STATEMENTS, TEXTS, PICTURES

And this brings me to the heart of my argument. For the interesting fact is that if, unlike Goodman, we award the text an autonomy with regard to the statement, the text, too, turns out to possess the 'density' and 'repleteness' which Goodman considered characteristic of the picture. That is to say, the differences which Goodman noted between the picture and the statement disappear when we contrast not the statement but the text or the story with the picture. And this, in turn, would mean that the visual and optical metaphors which we encounter so often in historical theory show a correct insight into the nature of the historical text after all. This radicalization of Goodman's semiological approach to the picture leads, in fact to a picturalization of the text.

Before the equivalence of picture and historical text from the viewpoint of the criteria of 'density' and 'repleteness' can be shown, it is necessary to devote a few remarks to the logical structure of the historical text. Elsewhere I have claimed that we can gain access to this logical structure only by postulating a new logical entity, which I called the 'narrative substance'. The narrative substance embodies the narrative – as distinct from the descriptive – meaning of the separate statements which make up a historical text. We gain access to the narrative substance by reading the statements p, q, r, etc, which comprise the historical text as 'N is p', 'N is q', 'N is r', etc, where N is the name of the narrative substance presented in the text in question and the statements 'N is p', 'N is q', 'N is r', etc express the narrative meaning of the descriptive statements p, q, r, etc. N, the narrative substance of the text, is individuated by the statements p, q, r, etc, which make up the text, and this means that the statements 'N is p', 'N is q', 'N is r', etc are analytical truths.

This process of the individuation of narrative substances can also be described as the process of the individuation of points in a narrative universe, a universe that is defined by all possible permutations of possible statements about historical reality. Furthermore, it can be shown that the conception of separate, individual points in this narrative universe can be satisfied only if we make the descriptive statements which comprise historical texts correspond with the dimensions of that universe. In other words, the point in the narrativistic universe that corresponds to the narrative substance N has the dimension p if and only if the narrative substance N contains the descriptive statement p.[26]

It is now possible to show that this narrative universe is 'dense' in the sense meant by Goodman. But first a preliminary remark. When

Goodman talks about the 'density' of the pictural denotation, he is thinking of the *components* of the painting as signs of the represented reality. The continuity of contours, colour and form referred to by him manifests itself in the presentation of the various components of one and the same painting. But since the narrative substance as a sign of (a part of) historical reality is expressed only in the total historical text, the question of the 'density' of the historical sign system is not a question of the relationship between the various elements of one and the same historical text, but a question of the nature of the narrative universe as defined above. The historiographical equivalent of the pictural signs which make up the picture is formed by *integral* historical texts.

Focusing our attention on the narrative universe, we can put forward the two following arguments for the 'density' of this universe. The first argument is as follows. We have to realize that although we can speak of distinct points in the narrative universe, we cannot give substance to the notion of *distance* in this universe. The explanation for this is that the space in which the distance between two (or more) narrative substances would have to be measured is co-dependent on other narrative substances. And the indeterminacy of the nature and the number of these other narrative substances results in the fundamental indeterminacy of all distances in the narrative universe. This combination of difference and nevertheless indeterminable distance corresponds to the lack of 'articulation' and 'disjointness' which Goodman attributes to the pictural representation of reality.[27] A second argument with the same result is the following. If we are to be able to compare narrative substances at all – and this is obviously the main issue of the historical debate – this comparison constantly requires an extensional typification of narrative substances. That is to say, comparison constantly requires us to be able to identify clusters of narrative substances and distinguish them from one another. Without this extensional typification, we are liable to compare, for instance, a narrative substance about the Industrial Revolution with one about the technological development at the end of the eighteenth and the beginning of the nineteenth century. For clearly the narrative substance about the Industrial Revolution will also make statements about this technological development. The problem which arises in connection with this extensional typification is that for every narrative substance N_1 and every narrative substance N_2 which belong to *different* clusters, we can think of a narrative substance N_3 which is closer both to N_1 and to N_2, a narrative substance which has more in common with N_1 and N_2 than N_1 and N_2 have in common with one another and on the cluster membership of which we can therefore only *decide* without having any objective criteria for *establishing* this cluster membership. And one should also realize that every statement contained by either N_1 or N_2 is a potential boundary between the two clusters to which N_1 and N_2 respectively belong. In the case of pictures the situation is less dramatic because there the components of the representation always come in more or less compact and coherent units: units such as figures, trees, ships, etc. Figures have no leaves and ships have no roots. But in the case of narrative substances *everything*, that is to say, each separate statement, may mark a boundary. And from this we can conclude that the syntactic 'density' which Goodman observes for the picture is even more present in the historical text than in the case of the picture.[28]

This brings us to the 'repleteness' criterion. A symbol is 'replete' in Goodman's sense when it has no properties of which we can say *a priori* that they offer no contribution to the representation – as is the case with, for instance, the thickness of the line of a cardiogram or the more or less arbitrary form of letters. And again the historical text satisfies this criterion even more than the picture. If we look at increasingly smaller surfaces of a painting, we will inevitably go beyond a limit below which the contribution of the element to the whole of the representation becomes indeterminate – below this limit the picture no longer satisfies the criterion of repleteness. But in the case of the historical text we have to read the statements of this text as statements which attribute these statements as predicates to the narrative substance in question. None of the statements which constitute the text is therefore irrelevant to the text's representation of the past as expressed in the narrative substance concerned. Finally, because the relationship between statements and narrative substance is not synthetic but analytical, one cannot think of a more complete satisfaction of the 'repleteness' criterion than by the historical text.

I will now leave Goodman for a moment and try to be more precise about the parallelism between pictures and texts. Let us imagine with Flint Schier in his excellent *Deeper into Pictures* that we are looking at a picture of Marlon Brando which depicts him as surly. There is a crucial difference here between the statement 'Brando is surly' and the picture in question. For we can divide the statement into a subject term which refers to Brando, and an element which Frege called 'an unsaturated expression' – 'is surly' – which predicates a quality. And this is not possible in the picture's case. As Schier writes:

obviously we cannot break down a depiction of Brando as surly into a part that barely denotes Brando (like 'Brando') and an expression which takes subjects into truth-values (like '-is surly'), which is a function taking objects as arguments and yielding the value true or false depending on whether the object is surly or not.[29]

But we can say the same for the historical text inasmuch as it presents a narrative substance; that is to say, for the historical text in its entirety. Suppose we are dealing with a historical text on the Cold War. We do not discover the narrative substance presented in this text by checking in which descriptive statements the term 'Cold War' occurs. Indeed, it is conceivable that we might be dealing with a narrative substance on the Cold War even if the term 'Cold War' does not occur as a subject term in any descriptive statement. Thus the work of Augustin Thierry could be seen as a contribution to the history of the class struggle, although this narrative substance is not mentioned *expressis verbis* in his work. The explanation for this is that the narrative substance is established only when we read the relevant statements p, q, r, etc as 'N is p', 'N is q', 'N is r', etc, where N is the name of the narrative substance on the Cold War. And for this very reason the narrative substance, like the picture of Brando, cannot be divided into a part that refers and a part that assigns a predicate. The narrative substance always comprehends *both*. For reference to a narrative substance is established only by attribution of predicates to a narrative substance and vice versa. The analyticity of statements of the type 'N is p', where N is the name of a narrative substance and not a narrative substance itself, confirms this: because of this analyticity we can say with Leibniz that the predicate is part of the notion of the subject.[30] And the conclusion of all this is that the logical structure of the historical text and that of the picture is therefore the same inasmuch as they differ in the *same* way from that of the statement. Both the historical text and the picture resist the differentiation between subject and predicate that is always achieved in every well-formed statement.

We can explore this similarity between text and picture even further. I return to one of Goodman's examples. Suppose, says Goodman, we look at the picture of a 'yellow, old, big, and ruined car' and we ask ourselves, still ignorant of the difference between pictures and statements, which true statement corresponds to this picture. According to Goodman, the picture is undetermined with regard to at least the following four statements: (1) 'the old, big, and ruined car is yellow'; (2) 'the yellow, big and ruined car is old'; (3) 'the yellow, old, ruined car is big'; (4) 'the yellow, old, big car is ruined'. And, as before, Goodman's conclusion here too is 'that a picture is no statement'.[31] In view of the fact that the narrative substance also admits of the (analytical) derivation of every statement of which it is comprised, we find exactly the same situation there.

However, an interesting problem arises here. Goodman's example illustrates more dramatically the coalescence of subject and predicate which we observed in the cases of both the picture and the text. For everything that is a part of the subject term can also be part of the predicate term and vice versa; and any fixation one might wish to seek here remains completely arbitrary. Certainly this is the rule for pictures, and here, in fact, lies the logical equivalence of pictures and historical texts which we just noted. Nevertheless, a problems crops up here. For, unlike the picture in Goodman's example, the picture of Brando does justify one particular statement – the statement 'Brando is surly'. In certain circumstances the picture can apparently deviate from the general rule of the asymmetry of picture and statement. And we can say the same for the verbal equivalent of the picture – the integral historical text. The narrative substance expressed by the integral historical text also compels a preference for a certain category of statement about the part of the past with which the text in question is concerned. A text on, for instance, the Cold War, also effects a polarization between the meaningful and non-meaningful statements which we might be able to make about the relations between East and West after World War II. All this seems to be at odds with the above thesis of the incompatibility of the statement on the one hand and the text and the pictures on the other. How is this deviation to be explained?

An initial explanation is suggested in J. G. Bennett's essay 'Depiction and Convention'.[32] The example this time is a very attractive postcard of what the postcard itself indicates to be Diddle Beach. But having decided to spend our summer holidays in Diddle Beach, we find on arrival that the postcard offers a completely unreliable impression of the seaside resort. According to Bennett, this proves the importance of the *name* or *title* of a picture or painting. And he continues:

I believe that we have found something which can be true or false: the combination of a picture and label. Our example suggests that in this case the picture is analogous to a *predicate* and the label analogous to a *name*. Combining the predicate and the label gives something which can be true or false like a sentence.[33]

It is now possible to explain the difference between Goodman's picture of the yellow car and Schier's picture of Brando. For the picture of the yellow car in Goodman's example is not accompanied by a 'label' and this causes the indeterminacy of the picture with regard to various descriptive statements. This would have been different if it had said under the picture: the ruined car. In that case the picture would have had the following statement as equivalent: 'the ruined car is yellow, old and big'. True enough, the picture in Schier's example is not accompanied by a label either, but we can plausibly assume that this label is supplied by the person who looks at the picture. We see the picture, immediately recognize Brando, and give the picture the 'label' 'Brando'. We do not recognize the old car and as a result the reference – and so the required 'label' – is not forthcoming. Two objections can be urged to this explanation. First, suppose that Schier's picture does not show Brando but a person with whom we are as unfamiliar as with Goodman's old car. In that case there is no reason to assume that Schier's picture predisposes more strongly to the statement 'Brando is surly' than this picture to the statement 'the person depicted here is surly'. Wolterstorff sees another problem in Bennett's suggestion. Bennett's proposal requires the acceptance of a conception of language which allows labels to function as subject terms in statements and pictures as predicates. Bennett in fact tries to develop a linguistic theory which leaves room for such unusual linguistic utterances. But the result is a language which no longer has much in common with what we usually take a language to be. Thus one cannot conceive of false statements in Bennett's 'language'. Suppose for instance, that we attach the 'label' Brando to the postcard of Diddle Beach. This does not produce a false statement, that is to say, a statement of which the negation would be true, but something which at most we could characterize as 'nonsense' or 'non-applicable'. Hence Bennett's proposal to conceive of the picture as a series of predicates which can be attributed to a label cannot help us further.[34]

For a different explanation I propose to distinguish between the representation of qualities and the representation of aspects by the picture. Goodman's picture can be said to represent a number of qualities of the depicted car: oldness, yellowness and ruinousness. But Schier's picture shows us Brando under a certain aspect: the picture shows us Brando *as* surly. The crucial difference between the two kinds of pictures is that aspects always relate to qualities of the picture *itself* and *not* of what is depicted. For it is a quality of the Brando picture that it represents Brando *as* surly to us; indeed, it is quite possible that Brando was not at all surly when the picture was made: he is, after all, a great actor. The qualities which are at stake in Goodman's picture are *not* qualities of the picture but of what is depicted. Certainly it is true that in the case of Goodman's old car, too, we can decide on qualities of the depicted only via qualities of the picture, But the qualities of the picture efface themselves with regard to the depicted. The picture is transparent with regard to the depicted. But in the case of the representation of an aspect, the picture insinuates itself between us and the depicted. The picture displays its opacity.

And here we find the reason why Schier's picture predisposes to one particular statement ('Brando is surly'), whereas Goodman's picture is indifferent with regard to various statements. The components of Goodman's picture retain a relative independence from one another because these components are not represented from an aspect which integrates the components. The picture therefore does not compel a preference for certain statements. But in the case of the Brando picture such an integration does take place. For although some elements of the picture will contribute more than others, the heart of the matter is still that it is a quality of the picture as a *whole* to represent Brando *as* surly. And it is this highly specific quality of the picture which predisposes us to make a particular statement: 'Brando is surly'. We therefore ought to distinguish between 'representing that -' and 'representing as -'. In the first case the accent lies on qualities of the depicted and in the second case on those of the picture. And this difference clearly has nothing to do with some or other categorical difference between the qualities 'yellowness' on the one hand and 'surliness' on the other. We do not have to conceive of the yellowness of Goodman's car as a 'primary quality' and Brando's surliness as a 'secondary quality' in roughly the Lockean sense.[35] Not differences in objects and their potential qualities but the difference between the transparency and the opacity of the picture explains the different ways in which these qualities function in pictures. It does seem likely, however, that some qualities of depicted objects are more suitable for 'representing that –' than for 'representing as –'. It is as if the representation of certain qualities (like surliness) require an effort of the *entire* picture, whereas other qualities (like yellowness) modestly content themselves with only a *part* of the picture. But there are no hard and fast rules here. Thus in 'The Vision after the Sermon' Gauguin represents the grass *as* red and here, too, it is the totality of the work of art in which such inversions become possible and acquire their aesthetic plausibility. The fact that, since the end of the nineteenth century inversions like the one in Gauguin's painting have been the rule rather than an exception may justify the conclusion that 'representing as -' and the totality of the work of art have triumphed over 'representing that -' and its components. But perhaps in our postmodern era, with its preference for an 'aesthetics of the fragment' – the term derives from Friedrich von Schlegel – the pendulum is swinging in the opposite direction again.

And all this has its counterpart in the historical text. Like 'representing as -' the historical text also gives rise to an interaction between the descriptive elements (here: the true statements which are made about the past) and this interaction also makes for a dimension in the historical work which cannot be merely reduced to these descriptive parts and their truth-claims. The narrative substance in which this interaction takes place is a 'representation as -', a representation of the past under a particular aspect which is established by the narrative substance. And as in the case of 'representing as -' in the picture, this showing under a particular aspect is far from being exclusively a question of viewpoint, of seeing the past from an angle that as such is independent of past reality itself. For just as a certain quality of the represented reality actually corresponds to the 'representing as -' in the picture – think of Brando's surliness –, so this is also true of the 'representing as -' in the writing of history. The interesting thing about the 'representing as -' in the integral historical text is that a nominalistic and a realistic interpretation of the text are complementary here. For in the first place the quality suggested by the 'representing as -' is, in fact, only a quality of the text, as the nominalistic interpretation prescribes. But in the second place the text clearly also predicates a quality of the historical reality itself. It is true that the quality in question is defined only by the integral historical text, that is to say, by the narrative substance which it presents, but this is by no means merely a matter of a 'projection' onto the historical reality, for there is most certainly an agreement between text and reality here. And here we have the realism of the historical text.

FORM AND CONTENT

'I began by dropping the picture theory of language and ended by adopting the language theory of pictures' – thus Goodman describes his intellectual development.[36] Indeed, insofar as word and picture are comparable, Goodman is less in favour of the pictural approach to the word than of a linguistic or semiotic approach to the picture. The explanation for this preference is mainly that Goodman associates the word above all with the statement or with texts or textual components

which are best regarded as conjunctions of statements. The convention-
alism of Goodman's attack on the resemblance thesis and of his views on
the meaning of the realistic work of art indeed require the sentence and
not the text as the verbal counterpart of the work of art. And the result is
a 'language theory of pictures'. But when we realize that not the
statement but the text is the most obvious equivalent of the picture, the
question of the 'picture theory of language' comes to be seen in an
entirely different light. I would therefore like to return to some questions
which we discussed earlier about the relation between the depicted and
its pictorial or verbal depiction.

In the discussion of this relation the point of departure was the
commonsense intuition that, unlike statements, pictures resemble what
they depict. Goodman's criticism of the resemblance thesis is that
resemblance is not an independent but a derived phenomenon –
resemblance occurs in the case of adaptation to the pictorial codes, the
systems of representation which we *habitually* employ in the representation of reality. In the literature there is general agreement on the
effectiveness of Goodman's attack on the naive resemblance thesis. But
there is also a general belief that precisely the success of this attack should
stimulate us to inquire more closely into what we (may legitimately)
mean when we speak about the resemblance between picture and
depicted rather than to concur with Goodman's more extremist remarks
to the effect that resemblance plays no role *whatsoever* in pictural
representation. The following statement by Schier is representative:

the primitive resemblance theory of iconic reference is doomed, since on that
theory it would follow, given Goodman's premises, that all icons are icons of
each other.. . . While it is all very hard-nosed and literal minded of Goodman to
point this out, it can't be denied that he is right. Goodman uses the point to get *us*
thinking seriously about resemblance so that we appreciate what is involved in
claiming that a picture resembles what is depicts.[37]

This is indeed the challenge to which most present-day theorists are
trying to find an answer. Thus Schier's own explanation of 'resemblance'
is that the same 'recognitional abilities' are activated by both the picture
and the depicted – an unsatisfactory explanation which reminds one of
the 'virtus dormitiva' by means of which Molière explains the soporific
effect of opium.[38] Richard Wollheim argues in this connection that we see
the picture 'as' the depicted or that we see the depicted 'in' the picture.[39]
Following Gombrich's suggestions in 'Meditations on a Hobby Horse',
Walton views the picture as a 'prop', that is to say, as 'generative of

fictional truths, things which by virtue of their nature or existence make propositions fictional'.[40] All these proposals can be seen as emendations of the naive resemblance theory which avoid the shortcomings of this theory noted by Goodman.

This is not the place to pass judgement on such theories. The question which demands our attention in the context of this argument is how the idea of resemblance can be explained more precisely for the study of history (as Schier, Wollheim and Walton did for the visual arts), in such a way as to produce a theory which is relevant to both the study and the theory of history. Like the above authors I will take my starting-point in Goodman's criticism of the naive resemblance theory. I should add, however, that in a certain sense my route will be opposite to the one followed in art theory; it has rarely been held in philosophy of history that the historical text resembles or should resemble the past, as might be claimed to some extent for the work of art. I shall therefore try to defend a counter-intuitive rather than an intuitive position. Nevertheless, it will turn out that a certain variant of the resemblance thesis can be argued for the study of history too.

For Goodman' 'resemblance' is the compliment we pay to the realistic representation. And we are dealing with a realistic representation if the conventional codes and a conventional system of representation are used. Now here arises a problem for the study of history. In the previous section we considered the historical text (and the picture) by focussing on the text as a whole rather than on its constituent parts. However, it is difficult to devise representative schemes and codes for the *whole* historical text. It is true that certain historiographical styles were developed through the ages, and by analogy with the styles from the history of the visual arts one might exspect to find the desired representative schemes and codes here. But the difficulty is that the historical debate always focuses on individual historical studies – is Le Goff's study of the Middle Ages better than Genicot's, and if so, why? There are no representative codes and schemes here, and if there are, they will probably be included in the debate over which of the two historical studies is the most 'realistic' account of the Middle Ages, or over the question, in our new terminology, of which of the two studies most 'resembles' the Middle Ages. The inevitable conclusion seems to be that in the study of history and the theory of history there can be no room for Goodman's representative codes and schemes; thus the comparison between the realism of the visual arts on the one hand and the study of history on the other seems to lead to a dead end.

But there is a surprisingly simple solution to this problem if we ask what such a representative code or representative scheme really is. A code enables us to give the correct form to a content. The codes of writing teach us what the correct orthographical form of the word of the sentence is; the codes of speech what the semantic and syntactic forms are which we should give to the content of our thoughts when we wish to express them – and so art from a certain period has its own representative codes for how the portrait-sitter or the landscape should be depicted in order to obtain a maximum 'reality effect'. In short, the represented code establishes which form matches which content.

We can do two things with this simple fact. First, if the representative code is in fact a question of the right form for the right content, for the relation between form and content, we are viewing the code in a way that can also certainly be applied to the individual historical work. For with the eighteenth-century rhetoricians we can require of the individual historical work that its form and content agree, since in itself agreement of form and content is not an appeal to a universalistic code. A second step is to interpret the agreement of form and content of the 'realistic' historical work as a *resemblance* of form and content. Obviously this second step is legitimate only if there are considerations independent of this argument which lend plausibility to the notion that in the realistic historical work the form *resembles* the content. And that is what I wish to show in the concluding part of my argument. Below I will give three examples of historiography which demonstrate that it is by no means problematical or hazardous to speak of resemblance of form and content in the historical text. And to avoid the impression that I am manipulating the reader, I will choose these examples from three totally different periods in the history of historiography.

My first example is Leonardo Bruni's *Historiarum Florentinarum Libri XII* from 1416. Bruni (1369-1444) centres his history on the intimate relationship between political freedom and the public, rhetorical debate. 'For Bruni', writes Struever:

the central motif of Florentine history is the formation of a public space; the purpose of the changes in government was "to establish and keep in existence a space where freedom as virtuosity can appear", the creation of a sphere of good faith, where we can debate without fear of intimidation or restraint, in which men talk and act in real "libertas".[41]

Two formal aspects of Bruni's historiography correspond to this definition of the content of the Florence of history. The first formal aspect is found in the speeches which Bruni puts in the mouths of the main actors in his history. But this is a stylistic characteristic of much humanistic historiography from the fifteenth and sixteenth centuries. The following aspect is therefore more important. The presence or absence of the public, rhetorical debate also enables Bruni to divide the history of Florence into periods of political freedom and lack of political freedom. In a surprising manner Bruni thus succeeds in harmonizing the form and the content of his historiography. For certainly the periodization he uses is one of the main formal features of the historical text – hence we see here that the chosen form (periodization) suggests a content which agrees with the content actually presented in the historical work.

My second illustration is Tocqueville's analysis of democracy in his *De la démocratie en Amérique* (1835 and 1839). Elsewhere I have argued that the form of this work is determined by Tocqueville's acceptance of the paradox as a trope and his rejection of the metaphor. Now the metaphor in the metaphorical text always supposes or generates a certain point of view from which part of historical reality is considered. By contrast, the paradox necessitates the destruction of such centres of meaning. I also showed that for Tocqueville democracy – unlike the benevolent despotism into which democracy constantly threatens to devaluate – is characterized by the absence of a clear political centre. We should realize here that Tocqueville would never have been able to formulate this insight into the nature of democracy if he had privileged the metaphor over the paradox. Whatever Tocqueville might have wanted to say about democracy, any attempt to express this centrelessness of democracy would have been effectively frustrated by the centripetality of the metaphor. The form of Tocqueville's analysis as expressed in his choice of the paradox as trope agrees with the *content* of his views on democracy.[42]

My last example is Braudel's *Méditerranée*, the book which many regard as the historical masterpiece of this century. In his 'anatomy' of this book Hans Kellner asked the question:

what is the genre of this text? Why is it cast in its present form? What does the form itself say? This, I believe, is the precise issue on which attempts to grasp the book have foundered, and the area that best reveals the nature of the work.[43]

Kellner's answer to this question is that Braudel's book is a Menippean satire, that is to say, the book displays enormous erudition in a quasi-encyclopedic way and with a riotous profusion of fact and details. A further characteristic of this genre is a preference for catachresis and oxymoron.[44] The effect of the Menippean satire is that it shows us reality as a mosaic of autonomous, self-contained units. And this stylistic effect also agrees here with what the content of Braudel's text says about the economic reality of the sixteenth-century Mediterranean world. As was the case in the historiography of Bruni and Tocqueville, so here too the style, the Menippean satire, suggests a content which agrees with the actual content of the text.

Two matters deserve our attention in these three cases of resemblance of form and content. First, the relevant formal aspects cannot be systematized within a certain fixed and well-defined repertoire of historical forms. In Bruni's case the form is the way in which the past described is divided into periods; in Tocqueville's case we are dealing with one of the tropes which Hayden White sees as the vehicles of the historical form *par excellence*; and in Braudel's case the encyclopedic character of the historical text embodies the *mimesis* of the historical reality described. As this variety shows, the historical form is not a selection from a fixed and predetermined catalogue of historical forms. In each historical masterwork the form may have a different character and the form manifests itself in different features of the text. Certainly it is true that a historical form once discovered may lead to imitation and thus to the development of a historical style. But it is important to realize that the relation between form and content as defined in this section is such that we can speak of an agreement of form and content in the *individual* historical work, that is to say, without there being any question of a *style* belonging to *several* historical works. The resemblance of form and content concerned here by no means requires adaptation to a particular 'code' or to a particular 'scheme of representation'.

In the second place we have to realize that a resemblance of form and content is conditional on a relative independence of form and content from one another. In other words, the historical text should be constructed in such a way that a certain polarization occurs between form and content. For instance, in Tocqueville's analysis of democracy the formal characteristic of the text – the text's affinity with paradox – is clearly distinct and independent from what the content of the text says about the origin and nature of democracy. If we endorse the common insight into the continuity between form and content,[45] this means that the distinctive feature of the historical masterwork (and clearly we can regard the works of Bruni, Tocqueville and Braudel as such) is that is avoids the transitional area between form and content as much as possible. But if there is such independence of form and content, while at

the same time we can discern a resemblance of form and content, as in the
work of Bruni, Tocqueville and Braudel, then we can rightly say that the
historian has found the *correct* form for the content presented. If, on the
other hand, the historian gets stuck in the transitional area between form
and content, we cannot characterize his work in this way. In the latter
case we are dealing with what I would like to call the 'ideological'
historical text: the form of the text predominates here over the content
and the required independence of form and content has not been
achieved, so that historical reality and the content of the text have
succumbed to the pressure of a preconceived idea. As White has noted,
the narrative form is often responsible for such a subordination of the
content to the form:

historiography is by its very nature, the representational practice best suited to
the production of "law-abiding" citizens. This is not because it may deal in
patriotism, nationalism, or explicit moralizing but because in its featuring of
narrativity as a favoured representational practice, it is especially well suited to
the production of notions of continuity, wholeness, closure and individuality that
every "civilized" society wishes to see itself as incarnating, against the chaos of a
merely "natural" way of life.[46]

In other words, if historiography uses the form of narrativity, it readily
suggests an ideological content as indicated by White. But his 'ideologiza-
tion' of historical reality may also have an entirely different character, as is
shown by Fogel's study of the influence of railway construction in
nineteenth-century America on the economic growth of the country in
that period. The form of Fogel's counterfactual analysis transforms here
the content of historical reality into a reality of which it is already assumed
ex hypothesi that it never really existed. It is hard to think of a more
striking example of the predominance of form over content.

   If the historian does respect the mutual independence of form and
content and the form moreover resembles the content, we could see in
this a criterion for the *truth* or possibly the *objectivity* of the historical
study in question. And here we have a criterion for the truth of the
historical text as a whole which cannot be reduced to the truth of the
separate descriptive statements which make up the historical text. For
this kind of historical truth Buffon used the term 'the tone of the text',
which he described as follows:

the tone of the text is nothing but the agreement between style and nature of the
topic dealt with in the text; it should never be forced; it should be developed quite
naturally from the nature of the topic and depends on the level of generality from
which the topic is considered.[47]

The difference between the true and ideological historical text can be also specified in another way. And this brings us back to Goodman's theory of the pictorial representation of reality. According to Goodman, the work of art stands at a crossroads. On the one hand the work of art refers to the reality depicted; but on the other hand the work of art is capable of expressing a certain emotion, mood, atmosphere, etc and Goodman believes that what the work of art expresses lies, as it were, 'on the other side' of what the work of art denotes or refers to. What the work of art expresses is 'exemplified', as Goodman says, by the work of art.[48] A name refers to or denotes that to which the name belongs; by contrast, 'exemplification is reference running from denotation back to label'.[49] Thus the tailor's sample exemplifies the fabric of which it is a sample; in doing so the sample does not refer to the fabric, but the fabric refers to the sample, since the sample is an example of it. The denoted generates its denotation here and not vice versa. And the difference between the true and the ideological historical text can be characterized in the same terms. The form of Tocqueville's text about democracy is an exemplification of the content of this text; just as the sample is exemplification of the fabric. For the *form* of Tocqueville's text is an example of the centrelessness which Tocqueville attributes to democracy in the *content* of his text. The autonomy of historical reality, the content of the text, is not affected here by the form of the text; in the ideological text the form always re-creates the content in a reproduction of itself. In short, a mutual independence of form and content and a resemblance of form and content are possible only if the form does not *determine* the content but *exemplifies* it. Goodman's notion of 'exemplification' enables us, therefore, to specify the nature of the resemblance of form and content in the true historical text.

CONCLUSION

In the foregoing we ascertained the equivalence of text and picture and the difference between these two and the statement. We can draw the following conclusions from this. First, we have a new argument in support of the distinction between the study of history and historiography; the former corresponds to what we can say about the past in terms of separate statements and the latter to the historical text in its entirety. On account of the formal distinction between the statement and the text and the distinction between descriptive and narrative meaning based on it, the formal distinction between historical inquiry and historiography is unassailable.

But what follows is more important. Ever since the criticism of the scientific model of historical investigation, philosophers of history have become interested in the common ground between historical investigation and the arts. In particular they have focused on literature. In view of the common textual character of literature and history, this is an obvious step. And if the inquiry is into the textual and rhetorical forms of the historical argument – compare what was just said about the work of Tocqueville and Braudel – this literary approach to the historical text is certainly valuable and has enriched our understanding of the nature of historical research.

But the ascertained equivalence of text and picture suggests a 'renversement des alliances', in which not literature but the visual arts function as a model or metaphor of the study of history. Admittedly such a reorientation may seem premature at first sight, for is it not true that both historical inquiry and the novel have a textual character and that therefore the equivalence of text and picture applies just as much to the novel as to historical inquiry? But we should reflect that, from the standpoint of what one might call 'a genealogy of genres', it seems arguable that the historical text is the protoform of the novel and not the other way round. I would be the first to admit that a literary genre like epic is already older than the study of history and that, from at least as far back as Aristotle's *Poetics*, theory presents literature as being more original than historical inquiry. However, it is only after a conception has been created of the (proto)historical description of an event that actually occurred – no matter how simple this event and how primitive this conception of the (proto)historical account may be – that it becomes possible to vary this conception of a (proto)historical account in the *literary* representation of a *fictional* reality. Logically, therefore not a literary genre but the historical text offers the 'Urphänomen' of the text (and it is surprising that the interaction between historical and literary theory has always been so one-sided). And if this genre genealogy is essentially correct, it seems advisable to play down the relevance of literary theory for a better understanding of historical inquiry. After all, from this viewpoint literary theory is a reflection on an evolution which started only *after* historical research and literature in its many forms went their separate ways and little is to be expected from this reflection for the understanding of the historical representation of reality. Thus the proliferation of subspecies within the species of anthropoids does not increase our insight into hominids and vice versa, once the branching off between anthropoids and hominids has taken place in evolution.

Nonetheless, it might now be objected on the basis of the textual nature of both historical inquiry and literature and the novel that the analogies between historical inquiry and literature are more obvious than those between historical inquiry and the visual arts. To answer this objection I will briefly pursue my evolutionist metaphor. Within my genre genealogy the historical novel could be regarded as the 'missing link' between historical investigation and literature, and any meaningful comparison between historical investigation and literature will therefore have to concentre on the relationship between historical inquiry and the historical novel. And, in fact, if the relationship is reorganized in this way, it will transpire that historical inquiry is closer to the visual arts than to literature – in this case the historical novel.

It can be argued that the historical novel is an *application* of the historical insight gained by the historian to a particular, concrete historical context.[50] For example, in the ingenious historical novel *The Ninth Thermidor* by Aldanov – pseudonym of Max Landau[51] – the protagonist Julius Stahl travels from St Petersburg via London to Paris, where he witnesses the fall of Robespierre's Reign of Terror. A particular historical evaluation of the French Revolution and a thorough knowledge of the Revolution are applied here by the author in or to the protagonist. The result of this process of application is found in Stahl's experiences as related by the novel. The difference between the study of history and the historical novel can therefore be expressed as follows. The study of history integrates the historical knowledge expressed in descriptive historical statements within a certain *picture* of the past; the historical novel applies this historical insight gained in the study of history, in order to generate fictional statements about the past. Historical inquiry is 'inductive' and therefore works from statement to picture; the historical novel is 'deductive' and works from picture to statement. Bearing in mind the equivalence of picture and text (the latter viewed as an integrated totality of statements), we thus find that the visual arts and the study of history have more in common than the study of history and the (historical) novel. The study of history is more a 'depiction' than a 'verbalization' of the past.

I admit at once that this genre genealogy, resulting in the logical priority of historical inquiry over literature, seems far from modern and recalls the aprioristic way that people in the eighteenth century were accustomed to theorize on various aspects of culture and society. But even if we defer our judgement on the genre genealogy, I hope that this essay may justify a greater interest in an approach to historical inquiry that includes the visual arts than has been the case in the theory of history so far. The countless visual and optical metaphors in the study and theory of history contain a lesson which we should take to heart.

References

Hans Kellner: Introduction: Describing Redescriptions

1 Richard Lanham, *Literacy and the Survival of Humanism* (New Haven and London, 1983), pp. 45–6.

2 The phrase 'linguistic turn' was originally coined to describe Wittgenstein's reflection on ordinary language, as opposed to ideal philosophic language; this distinction foreshadows the division in the 1960s of narrativist from covering-law models of historical inquiry. The first use known to me of this phrase is in Gustav Bergmann's essay of 1953, 'Logical Positivism, Language, and the Reconstruction of Metaphysics', reprinted in Richard Rorty, ed., *The Linguistic Turn: Recent Essays in Philosophical Method*, (Chicago and London, 1967), pp. 63–71. Neither Bergmann nor other users of the phrase seem to have noted that a 'linguistic turn' is 'literally' a trope, or figure of speech.

3 Precisely such a venture was attempted in *The Historians' History of the World*, published by the *Encyclopaedia Britannica* in five editions between 1904 and 1926. In twenty-odd volumes, classic and authoritative histories were spliced together with so little indication of boundaries that the editors could write that 'the casual reader might scan chapter after chapter without suspecting that the whole is not the work of a single writer'. On this work, see my 'Beautifying the Nightmare: The Aesthetics of Postmodern History', in *Strategies: A Journal of Theory, Culture, and Politics*, V/4–5 (1991), pp. 300–303.

4 Carrard's *Poetics of the New History: French Historical Discourse from Braudel to Chartier* (Baltimore and London, 1992) describes in a thoroughly original way the uses of historical language in recent French practice. Few works demonstrate more dramatically the change in the grounds of historiographical discussion.

5 Barthes' *Michelet par lui-même* (Paris, 1954) inaugurated the reawakened interest in the representational revolution of romantic historiography. Hayden White's *Metahistory* (Baltimore, 1973), with its discussions of Michelet, Tocqueville, Marx and Burckhardt, carried forward the literary interest in the Golden Age. More recently, Bann's *The Clothing of Clio: A Study of the Representation of History in Nineteenth-Century Britain and France* (Cambridge, 1984) and *Inventions of History: Essays on the Representation of the Past* (Manchester, 1990), Linda Orr's *Jules Michelet: Nature, History, Language* (Ithaca, 1976) and *Headless History: Nineteenth-Century French Historiography of the Revolution* (Ithaca, 1990), Lionel Gossman's *Between History and Literature* (Cambridge, MA, 1990), Hans Kellner's *Language and Historical Representation: Getting the Story Crooked* (Madison, 1989), Ann Rigney's *The Rhetoric of Historical Representation: Three Narrative Histories of the French Revolution* (Cambridge, 1990) and Jörn Rüsen's 'Rhetoric and Aesthetics of History: Leopold von Ranke' in *History and Theory*, XXIX/2 (1990), all extend the list of topics to be explored in this area.

6 Ankersmit develops the consequences of this distinction in *Narrative Logic: A Semantic Analysis of the Historian's Language* (The Hague, 1983).

7 Rorty has noted the association of pictures and metaphor: 'It is pictures rather than propositions, metaphors rather than statements, which determine most of our philosophical convictions.' See his *Philosophy and the Mirror of Nature* (Princeton, 1979), p. 12.

8 Rorty, *Contingency, Irony, and Solidarity* (Cambridge, 1989), p. 89.

9 Russell Jacoby, 'A New Intellectual History?', *American Historical Review*, XCVII/2 (1992), p. 424.

10 Perez Zagorin, 'Historiography and Postmodernism: Reconsiderations', *History and Theory*, XXIX/3 (1990), 271.

11 See Gossman, op. cit., p. 303.

12 Friedrich von Schiller, *Naive and Sentimental Poetry* and *On the Sublime*, trans. Julius A. Ellis (New York, 1966), pp. 84–5.

13 Ibid., p. 92.

14 Ibid., p. 116.

15 Hayden White, *The Content of the Form: Narrative Discourse and Historical Representation* (Baltimore and London, 1987), p. 45.

16 Schiller, op. cit., pp. 111–2.

17 White, *Tropics of Discourse* (Baltimore, 1978), p. 118.

18 Friedrich Nietzsche, *The Will to Power*, ed. Walter Kaufmann (New York, 1967), section 428. The revival of interest in the Sophists marks the recent work of Susan Jarratt, John Poulakos, Takis Poulakos and Edward Schiappa. Roger Moss's essay 'The Case for Sophistry' (in *Rhetoric Revealed*, ed. B. Vickers, Binghamton, NY, 1982) presents a good account of the reasons for reconsidering their status, as do several of the essays in *Rethinking the History of Rhetoric: Multidisciplinary Essays on the Rhetorical Tradition*, ed. T. Poulakos, Boulder, 1993).

19 Susan Jarratt, *Rereading the Sophists: Classical Rhetoric Refigured* (Carbondale, 1991).

20 R. G. Collingwood, *An Autobiography* (Oxford, 1939), pp. 78–9.

21 The telescope metaphor is detailed in Timothy Reiss, *The Discourse of Modernism* (Ithaca, 1982).

22 The phrase seems to originate in Nietzsche's 'On the Uses and Disadvantages of History for Life', in *Untimely Meditations* [1874], trans. R. J. Hollingdale (Cambridge, 1983). Sande Cohen has critically examined the modern implications in *Historical Culture* (1986).

23 Georg Iggers, *The German Conception of History: The National Tradition of Historical Thought from Herder to the Present* (Middletown, CT, 1983).

24 Johann Gottfried Herder, *Reflections on the Philosophy of the History of Mankind* [1791], abr. F. Manuel (Chicago, 1968), pp. 57–8.

25 Leopold von Ranke's famous comment that 'every epoch is immediate to God' was made in 1854; see Ranke, *The Theory and Practice of History*, ed. G. Iggers and K. v. Moltke (Indianapolis, 1973), p. 53.

26 White, op. cit. (n. 5), p. 276.

27 Wilhelm von Humboldt [1821], in Ranke, op. cit., pp. 22–3.

28 Jean-François Lyotard, *The Postmodern Condition: A Report on Knowledge* (1979), trans. Geoff Bennington and Brian Massumi (Minneapolis, 1984), p. 79.

29 Rorty writes that the culture critic 'is the person who tells you how all the ways of making things hang together hang together'; see 'Pragmatism and Philosophy', in *After Philosophy: End or Transformation?*, ed. K. Baynes, J. Bohman and T. McCarthy (Cambridge, MA, 1987), p. 58.

30 Peter Novick, *That Noble Dream: The 'Objectivity Question' and the American*

Historical Profession (Cambridge, 1988), pp. 599–607.

31 *After Philosophy* (see n. 29), includes essays by a number of postmodern philosophers, including Alasdair MacIntyre, whose publications include *After Virtue* (South Bend, IN, 1984). The 'End of History' debate was sparked by an article by Francis Fukuyama in *The National Interest* (1989); the book in which Fukuyama develops his ideas is called, typically, *The End of History and the Last Man* (New York, 1992).

32 On existentialism and *Metahistory*, see Kellner, op. cit. (n. 5), p. 212.

33 Jean-Paul Sartre, cited in Novick, op. cit., p. 629.

34 Nietzsche, op. cit. (n. 18), section 312.

35 The essay of 1931 is included in Carl Becker's collection *Everyman his Own Historian: Essays on History and Politics* (Chicago, 1966).

36 See, for instance, Carol Berkin's article '"Dangerous Courtesies" Assault Women's History', *Chronicle of Higher Education* (11 December 1991), p. A44. Of feminist, Marxist and minority historians, Berkin notes, '[t]heir attempts to redefine and reinterpret what should be taught and studied now has been met with a counter-attack from supporters of the established canon'. Her essay, however, stresses the enormous amount of discourse and professional advancement of these groups. How could opposing points of view possibly remain unexpressed? What she seems to be lamenting, in fact, is the absence of an established canon which the 'new perspectives' can change or dominate.

1 *Nancy F. Partner: Historicity in an Age of Reality–Fictions*

1 For the discipline of history, awareness of the full claims of language and literary form to a major, intrinsic role in historical writing was prompted mainly by Hayden White's *Metahistory: The Historical Imagination in Nineteenth-century Europe* (Baltimore, 1973). This presented ideas and modes of analysis which White expanded and refined in many subsequent essays, for example *Tropics of Discourse: Essays in Cultural Criticism* (Baltimore, 1978) and *The Content of the Form: Narrative Discourse And Historical Representation* (Baltimore, 1987), which contains an especially cogent and useful introduction to the topic of narrative, 'The Question of Narrative in Contemporary Historical Theory', pp. 26–57. A survey of the incursion of language theory among other anti-empiricist contenders into history can be found in Peter Novick's *That Noble Dream: The 'Objectivity Question' and the American Historical Profession* (Cambridge, 1988), section IV: 'Objectivity in Crisis'. An early and still important collection of essays is *The Writing of History: Literary Form and Historical Understanding*, ed. Robert H. Canary and Henry Kozicki (Madison, 1978). The sensitivity of quite specialized fields to these questions is shown by the special issue of *Speculum*, journal of the Medieval Academy of America, called 'The New Philology', LXV (1990), especially Gabrielle M. Spiegel's article, 'History, Historicism, and the Social Logic of the Text', pp. 59–86.

2 The general tone and intensity of the debate can be sampled in 'AHR Forum: Peter Novick's *That Noble Dream*: The Objectivity Question and the Future of the Historical Profession', *American Historical Review*, XCVI (1991), pp. 675–708; and the exchanges between F. R. Ankersmit and Perez Zagorin in *History and Theory*: Ankersmit, 'Historiography and Postmodernism', *History and Theory* XXVIII (1989), pp. 137–53; Zagorin, 'History and Postmodernism: Reconsiderations', *History and Theory*, XXIX (1990), pp. 263–74; Ankersmit, 'Reply to Professor Zagorin', *History and Theory*, XXIX (1990), pp. 275–96. A non-polemical, sophisticated meditation on language and history is Hans Kellner's *Language and Historical Representation: Getting the Story Crooked* (Madison, 1989); I attempt some reflections on the debate in 'History without Empiricism/Truth without Facts', in *Transformations: The*

Languages of Culture and Personhood after Theory, ed. Christie McDonald and Gary Wihl (State College, PA, 1994), pp. 1–10. A useful survey of the 'where we are now' sort is *New Perspectives on Historical Writing*, ed. Peter Burke (Cambridge, 1992).

3 In the United States, the most controversial case in the 1980s about, or ostensibly about, scholarly ethics as a function of scholarly method concerned David Abraham's book *The Collapse of the Weimar Republic: Political Economy and Crisis* (Princeton, 1981); the controversy, touching on archival accuracy, accusations of fraud and counter-accusations of tendentious zealotry, is surveyed by Novick, op. cit., pp. 612–21.

4 It should be noted that the kinds of criticism and controversy that appear most commonly in the book reviews of learned journals and written debates (articles followed by commentary and author's reply as in the AHR forum cited above) in the same journals are not about what sort of discourse *is* history, but which particular discourse offers the most adequate, accurate and perceptive account of some topic.

5 A rigorous yet generous-minded and entirely non-polemical approach to the descriptive analysis of prose is Richard Lanham, *Analyzing Prose* (New York, 1983), especially chap. 9, 'Opaque Styles and Transparent Styles', pp. 199–225, which offers a lucid mode of analysis addressed to the psychological, social and intellectual purposes attempted and achieved by style. An earlier work by the same author is *Style: An Antitextbook* (University Park, PA, 1992).

6 The essential premises and strategies of this argument are those laid out by Lionel Gossman, 'History and Literature: Reproduction or Signification', in Canary and Kosicki, op. cit. (n. 1), pp. 3–39. Also see the same author's *Between History and Literature* (Cambridge, MA, 1990).

7 My own interest began with medieval historical writing, *Serious Entertainments: The Writing of History in Twelfth-Century England* (Chicago, 1977), and extended chronologically in both directions and more abstractly into narrative theory and epistemology, as in 'Making Up Lost Time: Writing on the Writing of History', *Speculum*, LXI (1986), pp. 90–117; and currently the problem of insufficient attention to basic genre definitions, 'Notes on the Margins: Editors, Editions, and Sliding Definitions', in *The Politics of Editing Medieval Texts*, ed. Roberta Frank (New York, 1993), pp. 1–18, and the article in *Transformations* (see n. 2).

8 I complain, perhaps wistfully, in my article 'Notes On The Margins' (see n. 7) that the editors of medieval histories systematically slight and even draw attention away from the wealth of fictional inventions (anecdotes, speeches, conversations, etc) incorporated and developed within medieval historical writing, thus making the task of analysing these developments much harder than it should be; modern scholars betray a deep embarrassment with the practices of their favourite medieval historians in their editorial decisions.

9 It should be noted that this distinction between constructed vs. copy is merely a convenience for the sake of emphasis; even the remaining positivists do not claim that it is possible for anyone to make a neutral 'likeness' of virtually anything in language, much less a complex historical event.

10 Jeffrey M. Masson brought a libel suit against Janet Malcolm which reached court in 1993, charging that he had been libelled in a two-part profile of him published in the *New Yorker* magazine several years earlier (later published as a book); the articles were based on a long series of interviews conducted in various places over several months. Although the suit focusses on several specific passages, the real interest of this case lies in the fact that Ms Malcolm is a journalist with a high reputation for her knowledge of difficult subjects (here psychoanalysis), her intelligent and painstaking research, and the excellence of her writing; her confidence that her certain grasp of 'the meaning' allows her the fullest possible freedom to use her evidence for maximum

dramatic and literary effect (here piecing together scraps of interviews to make one long coherent speech presented as a whole and in quotation marks) is what has held my attention. The case was followed by the *New York Times*; articles specifically on these issues appeared on 14 and 18 May 1993.

11 In this case a civil suit was being conducted (and won in 1993) against General Motors, claiming that negligence in automotive design was the ultimate cause of a specific fatal explosion. The televised *Dateline* programme was attempting to replicate the circumstances in which a statistically probable explosion would occur; the problem was that although too many of these badly designed trucks exploded during side impacts, not *all* of them did every time and the show's producers could not make their truck explode for the camera, so they faked it. Experts examining the footage were able to point out crude errors and contrivances.

12 This simplest taken-for-granted fact of all truth-claim texts – that the narrator in the text is established as identical with the known author – is perhaps the most stable and indispensable of all the formal conditions for establishing 'history' as the primary status or genre of a text. That is, having a narrative voice identical with that of the known author is not itself sufficient to assert 'non-fiction', but is a necessary *condition* of historicity; if the author chooses to narrate in an impersonated voice, then the entire text, whatever is thus narrated, becomes fiction (regardless of the truth status of any or all statements offered in the impersonated voice). A fictional voice utters fiction because the privilege of fiction has been invoked, even if that privilege is not used for any further act of invention (this sort of case is true if unlikely). Homer invokes the muse and immediately speaks with omniscient knowledge, that is, in an impersonated voice since his own voice, limited to human sources of knowledge, could not be omniscient unless invoking the privilege of fictional invention. Herodotus specifically offers the reader/listener his own voice *without* the announced privileges of fictional licence.

13 I am using the translation by David Grene, Herodotus, *The History* (Chicago, 1987), p. 33; Grene's introductory essay is acute and sensitive, as well as learned, especially on the endlessly complex relations between the reality of event and the reality of mind-mediated experience in Herodotus: 'His is a kind of universal history; that is, it is the record of all the logical possibilities, political and human, that coexist in the human world. The *kleos* is the tale that makes one understand and admire this; that obtrudes itself between one's bewilderment at the diversity of experience and one's inner single moral certainty of man's nature' (p. 21).

14 Herodotus, I.5, in Grene, p. 35.

15 Most famous among these fictional episodes which establish the meaning-bearing themes which hold together this expansive and leisurely yet coherent narrative are the meeting of Solon and Croesus (I.29–33) and many others; an intermediary kind of narrative, with a strong evidentiary base of information that is then dramatized to bring out its moral and political significance is the stand of the Spartans at Thermopylae (7.207–228).

16 The entire book is adjudicated in a balanced yet hesitating way which usually refrains from awarding single-version status to any one story, as, from among endless examples: 'Concerning the oracles, the one that is among the Greeks and the other in Libya, this is the story that the Egyptians tell' (2.54); and 'That is what I heard from the priests in Thebes, but the following is what the priestesses of Dodona had to say' (2.55).

17 Aristotle, *Poetics*, trans. Ingram Bywater (Oxford, 1920 and many reprints), chap. 9, p. 43. In other passages he insists that history, by definition (his), is trapped at the level of the contingent, the local, the specific; see esp. chap. 23, pp. 79–80. The things that have been, the fragments and accidents of past actuality, have no necessary

participation in the logical relations that establish probability; the fiction writer has the positive obligation to sort out and select those aspects of human choices and their consequences which illuminate permanent qualities of life, while, in Aristotle's view, the historian is prevented from this crucial philosophic manipulation by his very commitment to actual events.

18 Probably the strongest statements about the deep interrelations between rhetorical practice and ancient history are by T. P. Wiseman, *Clio's Cosmetics: Three Studies in Greco-Roman Literature* (Leicester, 1979), and the exhilaratingly fearless study by A. J. Woodman, *Rhetoric in Classical Historiography* (London, 1988) with its detailed demonstrations of textual analogues and tropes. The importance of their work, especially that of Woodman, is very great; its limitation is that both scholars work with a rather stiff and positivist definition of history as 'scientific', objective and the like, and so the import of exposing the rhetorical armature tends to sound merely debunking. This encourages classical scholars to fall into a debunk or defence mode; for the defence which argues that ancient historians were honestly trying to be accurate and critical, see among endless examples, Charles Fornara, *The Nature of History in Ancient Greece and Rome* (Berkeley, 1983); these excellent studies tend to talk past rather than to one another. Some very sophisticated literary-critical essays are in *Lies and Fiction in the Ancient World*, ed. Christopher Gill and T. P. Wiseman (Austin, TX, 1993), especially Wiseman's 'Lying Historians: Seven Types of Mendacity'. For a non-polemical approach to rhetoric, George Kennedy has several lucid books on the uses and significance of rhetoric for all intellectual and literary life in antiquity, and the discussion of the rhetors by Bernard Knox in *The Oldest Dead White European Males* (Cambridge, 1992) is refreshingly sympathetic.

19 E. M. Forster, *Aspects of the Novel* (Harmondsworth, 1927), pp. 69–70.

20 Woodman, op. cit., chap. 2, 'Theory: Cicero', is indispensable here, and it should be more widely noted that most of Cicero's less celebrated passages on history writing in the *De Oratore* are not about truth, and certainly not about accuracy, but entirely about attractiveness and fullness of presentation.

21 Sallust, *Conspiracy of Cataline*, trans. S. A. Handford (Harmondsworth, 1963), pp. 188–9; this passage is a *tour de force* of the historian's moral confidence and near-omniscient knowledge.

22 Tacitus, *The Histories*, trans. Kenneth Wellesley (Harmondsworth, 1964), p. 21; for a brilliant passage of dramatic expansion, see the last hours of Vitellius, pp. 198–9; and a discussion of Tacitus' self-plagiarism of the battle scenes, see Woodman, op. cit., chap. 4.

23 Tacitus' *Dialogue on Oratory*, trans. W. Peterson (London, 1970). This comparatively seldom cited work is very revealing in that it offers a purely upper-class description of livelihoods, ambitions and literary achievements entirely in aesthetic terms, as rhetorical competitions which are closely related versions of one another.

24 By far the most lucid and thorough analysis of the meaning of basic genre categories in terms of the entire range of signals and understandings obtaining between writers and readers is that offered by Meir Sternberg in the first chapter of his book *The Poetics of Biblical Narrative* (Bloomington, IN, 1985), 'Literary Text, Literary Approach: Getting the Questions Straight'; this densely but lucidly written book deals with every essential literary critical question of textual intention and interpretation in terms which are directly applicable to all literature, fiction and non-fiction alike.

25 Arnaldo Momigliano's essays remain the classic statements on these topics: 'Greek Historiography, *History and Theory*, (1978), pp. 1–28; 'The Place of Herodotus in the History of Historiography', *Studies in Historiography* (London, 1966), pp. 127–42.

26 Sternberg offers the right questions about genre, intention, and the implicit rules for reading: 'Both historiography and fiction are genres of writing, not bundles of fact or

nonfact in verbal shape. In either case, then, it all boils down to the rules of the writing game, namely, to the premises, conventions, and undertakings that attach to the discourse as an affair between writer and audience. What kind of contract binds them together? What does the writer stand committed to?'; Sternberg, op. cit., p. 26.

27 The philosopher of history Louis Mink offers the most useful approach to understanding the irresolvable competition between different modes of comprehension and why there cannot be one incorporating all others; see 'Modes of Comprehension and the Unity of Knowledge', in *Historical Understanding*, ed. Brian Fay, Eugene O. Golob and Richard T. Vann (Ithaca, 1987), pp. 35–41.

28 The question of terminology is admittedly troublesome since there is generally accepted philosophic language one can appeal to; after a good deal of fumbling and deliberation, I have decided that *protocol* is reasonably useful because: (1) it does not invoke the inappropriate model of the physical sciences as does 'method'; (2) it suggests a system or set of rules for engaging in a complex activity as the rules of baseball might accurately, if funnily, be termed a protocol; and (3) the word is common enough to be intuitively accessible.

29 Natalie Davis is an exception here in her deeply informed concern with visual literacy; see, for example, '"Any Resemblance to Persons Living or Dead": Film and the Challenge of Authenticity', *Yale Review* (1987): 457–82.

30 I think that historians might read over, say three or four times a year, that passage from Kingsley Amis's novel *Lucky Jim* (1954), in which Jim contemplates the opening of his hapless article on medieval shipbuilding: 'In considering this strangely neglected topic, it began. This *what* neglected topic? This strangely *what* topic? This strangely neglected *what?*'

31 An exceptionally careful and detailed treatment of the process by which a dramatized non-fiction becomes fiction is the long article by Betsy Sharkey in the *New York Times* (5 September 1993), describing the pressures and hesitations surrounding the making of the film *And the Band Played On*. Based on the book of the same title by the journalist Randy Shilts, it is about the early years of the AIDS epidemic. The project went through three directors including Joel Schumacher who found the fictional freedoms of the script disturbing: 'I don't understand where the line is. This work was going to be a strong indictment of many people. How would I explain what parts to believe and what not to?' He offered to do extensive research, was turned down by the US HBO cable TV channel, and left the project.

32 Thucydides points in his introduction to the credulity surrounding traditional stories and uses the case of Harmodius and Aristogiton as his example, then expands the episode in detail in Book VI; *History of the Peloponnesian War*, trans. Rex Warner (Harmondsworth, 1954), pp. 46–7, 442–6.

33 Notable works on medieval historiography include: Gabrielle Spiegel, *Romancing the Past: the Rise of Vernacular Prose Historiography in Thirteenth-Century France* (Berkeley, 1993); Walter Goffart, *The Narrators of Barbarian History* (Princeton, 1988); Karl Morrison, *History as a Visual Art in the Twelfth-Century Renaissance* (Princeton, 1990); and Ruth Morse, *Truth and Convention in the Middle Ages: Rhetoric, Representation, and Reality* (Cambridge, 1991).

34 The question of genre and the ambiguities of presentation, or textual intention, surrounding several of Defoe's works have not attracted much scholarly attention. Defoe himself attempted to deal with questions of literary verisimilitude and morality in several chapters of his *Serious Reflections during the Life and Surprising Adventures of Robinson Crusoe, with his Vision of the Angelic World*, ed. George Aitken (London, 1895) where his thoughts are painfully involved and tortuous. One modern critic has attempted to sort out Defoe's religious and literary intentions in his use of supernatural stories: Rodney Baine, *Defoe and the Supernatural* (Athens, GA, 1968).

2 *Richard T. Vann: Turning Linguistic: History and Theory and* History and Theory,
1960–1975

1 Frank Kermode, 'Novel, History and Type', *Novel* I (1968), p. 236.
2 This helps explain why the density of subscribers to the journal *History and Theory* is greater in the Netherlands than anywhere else.
3 Jurgen Herbst, 'Theoretical Work in History in American University Curricula', *History and Theory*, VII (1968), pp. 336–54.
4 See William H. Dray, 'Toynbee's Search for Historical Laws', *History and Theory*, I (1961), 32–54 and the review essay on *A Study of History* by Kenneth Bock, ibid. II (1962), 301–7.
5 *The History of Childhood*, ed. Lloyd DeMause (New York, 1974), chap. 1; Shulamith Firestone, *The Dialectic of Sex* (New York, 1970).
6 *Journal of Philosophy*, XXXIX (1942), pp. 35–48; frequently anthologized. It is symptomatic of the marginality of history as an object of philosophical reflection that Hempel wrote to show that even this apparently intractable subject (about which he exhibited no real knowledge) could be brought within the same framework of explanation used in physics.
7 This phrase was used by William H. Dray in his *Laws and Explanation in History* (London, 1957). Denying that subsumption under some general law was necessary or characteristic of historical explanation, Dray emphasized the historian's search for the motives for action of the people written about. This brought him close to R. G. Collingwood's position in the posthumously published *The Idea of History*, ed. and compiled T. M. Knox (Oxford, 1946) and even, curiously, to Karl Popper's notion of 'the logic of the situation'; see *The Poverty of Historicism* (Boston, 1957), pp. 149–52.
8 'The Science of History', in J. B. Bury, *Selected Essays*, ed. H. W. V. Temperley (Cambridge, 1930), p. 4.
9 G. M. Trevelyan, *Clio, A Muse and Other Essays* (London, 1913), pp. 9, 14.
10 Emery Neff, *The Poetry of History* (New York, 1947), p. 193.
11 Hayden White, 'The Burden of History', *History and Theory*, V (1966), p. 111; reprinted in *Tropics of Discourse* (Baltimore, 1978), pp. 27–50.
12 Isaiah Berlin, *Historical Inevitability* (London, 1954).
13 Patrick Gardiner, *The Nature of Historical Explanation* (London, 1952). The direct influence here was undoubtedly J. L. Austin, and behind him the later philosophy of Wittgenstein (see for example the Wittgensteinian argument deployed by Michael Scriven in 'Truisms as a Ground of Historical Explanation', in *Theories of History*, ed. Patrick Gardiner (Glencoe, IL, 1959), 443–75. The theory of speech acts developed by Austin and John Searle became important for literary criticism in the 1960s and has had some influence on criticism of historical writing as well.
14 'On Explanations in History', *Philosophy of Science*, XXIII (1956), p. 22. See the comments by Leon J. Goldstein, 'A Note on the Status of Historical Reconstructions', *Journal of Philosophy*, XLV (1958), pp. 475–9.
15 See the exchange between Danto and Walsh in *Journal of Philosophy*, L (1953), pp. 173–82 and LV (1958), pp. 479–84.
16 'Explanatory Narrative in History', *Philosophical Quarterly*, IV (1954), p. 24.
17 Presidents of the American Historical Association, as the prestige of scientific models of historiography receded in the profession, have been particularly lavish with this recommendation; see Russel B. Nye, 'History and Literature: Branches of the Same Tree', in *Essays on History and Literature*. ed. Robert H. Bremner (Columbus, OH, 1966), p. 136.
18 A volume would consist of three numbers and a possible supplement or *Beiheft,*

appearing on no fixed publication schedule. Commitment to appear regularly in February, May, October and December (not always kept) was made only in 1974, when the new publishers, Wesleyan University Press, had to meet the requirements for second-class mailing privileges.

19 It is instructive to compare this article with the summary of it by Louis Loeb (in *History and Theory*, VI (1967), p. 133. Raymond Aron's 'Thucydide et le récit des événements' could have been included in volume I, but (much to its author's annoyance) was saved for the lead article in volume II.

20 *History and Theory*, I (1961), pp. 32–85, 163–85.

21 I refer to Mazlish's review essay; see *History and Theory*, I (1961), pp. 219–227. Mazlish was associated with *History and Theory* from its inception, and for the first four years was an associate editor.

22 White, 'Introduction', *From History to Sociology* (Detroit, 1959), pp. xviii, xxiii–xxiv.

23 Mazlish, op. cit., p. 225. Note that Mazlish equates response to plays and paintings, despite the fact that plays unfold in time to a much greater extent than paintings do.

24 White, op. cit. (n. 22), p. xxi.

25 Ibid., p. xxii.

26 Morton White, *Foundations of Historical Knowledge* (New York, 1965), pp. 221–2.

27 Thus the 49-page review essay – in small print – by John Murrin (*History and Theory*, XI, 1972, pp. 226–75) and the instruction invariably given to contributors not to excuse themselves from discussing certain topics on grounds that there was no space to do so.

28 Arthur Danto, 'Narrative Sentences', *History and Theory*, II (1962), 146–79 and *Analytical Philosophy of History* (Cambridge, 1965), pp. 143–81.

29 W. B. Gallie, 'The Historical Understanding', *History and Theory*, III (1964), pp. 149–202. Some idea of George Nadel's editorial skill can be gained by comparing this article with Gallie's *Philosophy and the Historical Understanding* (London, 1964).

30 Ibid., p. 149.

31 The same point was made even more forcefully by Danto: 'The difference between history and science is not that history does and science does not employ organizing schemes which go beyond what is given. Both do. The difference has to do with the kind of organizing schemes employed by each. *History* tells stories.' (*Analytical Philosophy of History*, p. 111.)

32 An editorial effort to change the example from cricket to baseball proved abortive; but baseball was to enter the literature as a multi-page example in J. H. Hexter's *Doing History* (Bloomington, 1971), pp. 30–43 and *The History Primer* (New York, 1971), pp. 149–97. It is noteworthy how many critics of Gallie proceeded to talk mainly about watching cricket, rather than understanding historical accounts.

33 A point made by Louis Mink, 'Philosophical Analysis and Historical Understanding', in *Historical Understanding*, ed. Brian Fay, Eugene O. Golob and Richard T. Vann (Ithaca, 1987), p. 135. This review essay on Morton White, Gallie and Danto originally appeared in the *Review of Metaphysics* XI (1968), pp. 667–98.

34 Mink, op. cit., p. 136.

35 Mink, 'Modes of Comprehension and the Unity of Knowledge', in *Historical Understanding*, pp. 36–8; see also the editors' introduction, pp. 13–14. Mink appears to have used 'comprehension' and 'understanding' interchangeably.

36 Mink, 'The Autonomy of Historical Understanding', *History and Theory*, V (1966), p. 33. This article is reprinted in *Historical Understanding*, pp. 61–88.

37 Ibid., p. 37.

38 White in fact resigned from the editorial committee of *History and Theory* in 1965, the only person to do so. Mink and Danto of course had more to say; the latter

published 'Historical Language and Historical Reality' in *Review of Metaphysics*, XXVII (1973), pp. 219–68 and added this and two new chapters to a reprint of *Analytical Philosophy of History* entitled *Narration and Knowledge* (New York, 1985). Mink's later articles in this field are all reprinted in *Historical Understanding*.

39 Maurice Mandelbaum, 'A Note on History as Narrative', *History and Theory*, VI (1967), p. 419. Despite his long-standing hostility to historical relativism, it does not appear that Mandelbaum was always so sceptical about narration. The 'historian's whole purpose as historian is to describe, to narrate', he wrote in *The Problem of Historical Knowledge* (New York, 1938), p. 3.

40 Morton White, op. cit. (n. 26), p. 223. An almost identical formulation, differing only in that overtly causal language is used instead of 'led to', can be found in White's essay 'The Logic of Historical Narration', in *Philosophy and History*, ed. Sidney Hook (New York, 1963), p. 3. The example originally comes from Forster's chapter on plot in *Aspects of the Novel* (London, 1927); Forster distinguished between story and plot in roughly the same way that White contrasted chronicle with history.

41 Mandelbaum, op. cit., p. 417.

42 C. J. Arthur, 'On the Historical Understanding', *History and Theory*, VII (1968), pp. 203–16.

43 'Mandelbaum on Historical Narrative: A Discussion', *History and Theory*, VIII (1969), pp. 275–83.

44 Ibid., p. 284.

45 Ibid., p. 289.

46 Ibid., pp. 292–303.

47 A. R. Louch, 'History and Narrative', *History and Theory*, VIII (1969), pp. 54–70.

48 Frederick A. Olafson, 'Narrative and the Concept of Action', *History and Theory*, IX (1970), pp. 265–89.

49 Forster, op. cit. (n. 40); W. H. Walsh, '"Plain" and "Significant" Narrative in History', *Journal of Philosophy*, XLV (1958), pp. 479–84.

50 This is the argument of Danto, *Analytical Philosophy of History*, pp. 116–42; but see Dray, 'On the Nature and Role of Narrative in Historiography', *History and Theory*, X (1971), pp. 157–61.

51 McCullagh, 'Narrative and Explanation in History', *Mind*, LXXVIII (1969), pp. 256–61, with a rejoinder by Richard G. Ely, *Mind*, LXXXII (1973), pp. 89–94. The state of play at the end of the 1960s was well analysed by W. H. Dray, op. cit. (n. 50), pp. 153–4.

52 H. Stuart Hughes, *History as Art and as Science: Twin Vistas on the Past* (New York, 1964), p. 72. Hughes however was making a different point: that the nature of the historical material and the inherent limitations of the historian obliged him to 'proceed like a dramatist'. Unfortunately Hughes did not follow up this point.

53 J. G. A. Pocock, review essay on J. H. Hexter, *Reappraisals in History*, in *History and Theory*, III (1964), p. 121.

54 Ibid., 122.

55 Mink, op. cit. (n. 36), p. 25. He goes on to point out that although philosophers cite pertinent works by historians in their bibliographies, and vice versa, they do not cite them in their footnotes, strongly suggesting that in fact neither paid any real attention to what the others were writing.

56 Review essay on *Philosophy and History: A Symposium*, ed. Sidney Hook (New York, 1963), in *History and Theory*, IV (1965), p. 329.

57 Ibid., p. 330.

58 *History and Theory*, VI (1967), pp. 3–13. Hexter has set a pretty puzzle for his future bibliographers by incorporating this article into another much longer article, also called 'The Rhetoric of History' (*International Encyclopedia of the Social Sciences*,

VI, pp. 368–94). It was then reprinted as chapter 2 of *Doing History*. Much of this article also appears in *The History Primer*. Since my principal interest is in how the issues were reflected in *History and Theory*, and since Hexter's main ideas are represented *in nuce* in this article, I shall largely confine my discussion to it.

59 Ibid., p. 3.

60 At least as practised in 1967; a growing number of historical works are now issued without any footnotes.

61 'Rhetoric of History', p. 4.

62 Ibid., p. 5.

63 Ibid., p. 6.

64 Ibid., p. 8.

65 Ibid., p. 6.

66 Ibid., p. 11.

67 Quoted in Mink, 'The Theory of Practice: Hexter's Historiography', in *After the Reformation: Essays in Honor of J. H. Hexter*, ed. Barbara Malament (Philadelphia, 1980), p. 15. The quotation from Hexter is from his article in the *International Encyclopedia of the Social Sciences*, p. 389, with italics added by Mink.

68 Idem.

69 On this see his 'Personal Retrospect and Postscript' in *Reappraisals in History* (London, 1961), pp. 188–91.

70 Mink, op. cit. (n. 67), p. 19.

71 E.g., alas, Richard T. Vann, *The Social Development of English Quakerism, 1655–1755* (Cambridge, MA, 1969), p. x. I owe this reference to Philip Pomper.

72 To take a recent example of the former, see Raymond Martin, *The Past within Us: An Empirical Approach to Philosophy of History* (Princeton, 1989).

73 Such essays were generally rejected by *History and Theory* on grounds of want of rigour. An exception is Igor Sevcenko, 'Two Kinds of Historical Writing', *History and Theory*, VIII (1969), pp. 332–45, which however is not primarily about writing.

74 Sevcenko makes this point – obvious to any historian – forcefully. Marvin Levich is one of the very few philosophers to pay attention to the enormous variety of histories; see his review essay on *History and Philosophy* in *History and Theory*, IV (1965), p. 337.

75 Another exception must be made for Peter Munz; see his 'The Skeleton and the Mollusc: Reflections on the Nature of Historical Narrative', *New Zealand Journal of History*, I (1967), pp. 107–24 and *The Shapes of Time: A New Look at Philosophy of History* (Middletown, CT, 1979). Munz believed that he had reconciled narrativism and positivism by calling every generalization a historian might use or presuppose – such as 'If a person has a pain, he will see a doctor' – a 'covering law'.

76 From a memorandum to the Director of the Center for the Humanities at Wesleyan University, quoted in Richard T. Vann, 'Louis Mink's Linguistic Turn', *History and Theory*, XXVI (1987), p. 4.

77 Published in the bilingual *Social Sciences Information*, VI (1967), pp. 65–75. An English translation by Peter Wexler was published in *Structuralism: A Reader*, ed. Michael Lane (London, 1970), pp. 145–55 and another by Stephen Bann in *Comparative Criticism*, III (1981), pp. 3–20. Barthes' other two articles were 'Introduction à l'analyse structurale des récits', *Communications*, VIII (1966), pp. 1–27, translated in *New Literary History*, VI (1975), pp. 237–72 and 'L'Effet du réel', *Communications*, XI (1968), pp. 84–9, translated by R. Carter as 'The Reality Effect' in *French Literary Theory Today*, ed. Tzvetan Todorov (Cambridge, 1982), pp. 11–17. As Bann notes in the introduction to his translation, Barthes had a long-standing interest in historical representation; his second book, *Michelet par lui-même* (Paris, 1954), was published in the Ecrivains de Toujours series.

78 Barthes, trans. Bann, 'The Discourse of History', p. 7.

79 Ibid., p. 7.
80 Ibid., pp. 9–10.
81 Ibid., p. 14. Schizophrenics are alleged to be 'incapable of submitting an utterance to a negative transformation', on the basis of an article by Luce Irigaray, 'Négations et transformation négative dans le langage des schizophrènes', *Langages*, v (March 1967), pp. 84–98.
82 Barthes, trans. Bann, p. 15; Hegel, *The Philosophy of History* (Ger. orig. 1837), trans. J. Sibree (New York, 1956), pp. 5–7.
83 Barthes, trans. Bann, p. 16.
84 Ibid., pp. 16–17.
85 Bann translates this as 'realistic effect'; Wexler renders it 'reality effect'.
86 Michelet, *Histoire de la France, La Révolution*, v (Lausanne, 1967), p. 292, quoted in Barthes, 'The Reality Effect', pp. 11–17.
87 Barthes, trans. Carter, 'The Reality Effect', p. 14.
88 Ibid., p. 17.
89 Barthes, trans. Bann, p. 18.
90 Idem.
91 Hayden White is a possible exception. Bann ('Discourse of History', p. 5) says that White's *Metahistory* (Baltimore, 1973) testifies 'both implicitly and explicitly' to the influence of Barthes. Parallels are certainly there, and White had read Barthes' edition of Michelet, but explicit reference to Barthes (unlike, say, Northrop Frye) is undetectable in *Metahistory*.
92 Kermode, op. cit. (n. 1), p. 232.
93 Ibid., pp. 236–7.
94 Fredric Jameson, 'T. W. Adorno, or Historical Tropes', *Salmagundi* III (1967), p. 5.
95 No exact breakdown of subscribers by disciplinary affiliation can be made; but a telling statistic is that in 1991 only about one per cent of members of the American Historical Association listed 'philosophy of history and historiography' as either a primary or secondary field of scholarly interest. Although there are many fewer American philosophers than historians, about seven times as many philosophers identified themselves as interested in the philosophy of history.
96 Haskell Fain, *Between Philosophy and History* (Princeton, 1970), pp. 42–3, 209.
97 Danto, *Analytical Philosophy of History*, p. 117.
98 Ibid., pp. 216–17.
99 Ibid., p. 228. Substitute 'ideology' for 'speculative philosophy of history' and this statement could have been made by Barthes.
100 White, 'The Abiding Relevance of Croce's Idea of History', *Journal of Modern History*, xxxv (1963), p. 109.
101 White, op. cit. (n. 11), pp. 130, 124, 127.
102 Ibid., p. 126. White insisted that this article have no footnotes; the reference is to *History as Art and as Science*, p. 70.
103 Ibid., p. 130.
104 Ibid., pp. 130–31.
105 Ibid., p. 131.
106 Quoted in Vann, op. cit. (n. 76), p. 12.
107 White did brilliantly run Foucault's *Les Mots et les choses* through his tropological machine in 'Foucault Decoded: Notes from Underground', *History and Theory* xII (1973), pp. 23–54. This and 'The Burden of History' were both solicited articles; if the editors had solicited more vigorously, some of the pieces which appeared in *Clio* and *New Literary History* might have been published in *History and Theory*.
108 *New Literary History*, Iv (1973), pp. 281–314; reprinted in *Tropics of Discourse*, pp. 51–80.

109 Ibid., fn. 42, p. 310.
110 Ibid., p. 313.
111 White, 'The Structure of Historical Narrative', *Clio*, 1 (1972), p. 13
112 Ibid., pp. 15–19.
113 It is in fact the theme of John S. Nelson's review essay of *Metahistory* in *History and Theory*, XIV (1975), pp. 74–91.
114 Printed in *Clio*, III (1973), pp. 35–53, together with a critique by W. H. Dray, pp. 55–76.
115 Ibid., p. 53.
116 Comments on a paper by Arno Mayer, 'Domestic Causes and Purposes of War', delivered in November 1972; quoted in Vann, op. cit. (n. 76), p. 9.
117 'Narrative as a Cognitive Instrument', manuscript of a paper Mink delivered at the Midwest MLA in Chicago in 1974; quoted in Vann, ibid., pp. 9–10.
118 Quoted in Vann, ibid., p. 10, fn. 24.
119 Ranke, quoted in *Varieties of History*, ed. Fritz Stern (New York, 1956), pp. 59–62.
120 'History and Narrative', paper delivered at Toronto in March 1974; quoted in Vann, op. cit. (n. 76), p. 10. This paper was published, in revised form, in *The Writing of History: Literary Form and Historical Understanding*, ed. Robert H. Canary and Henry Kozicki (Madison, 1978), pp. 129–49.
121 Canary and Kozicki, op. cit., p. 140.
122 Ibid., p. 143.
123 Quoted in Vann, op. cit. (n. 76), p. 12.
124 Ibid., p. 16.
125 Ibid., pp. 12–13.
126 Ibid., p. 13.
127 '[H]istorical events differ from *fictional events* in the ways that it has been conventional to characterize their differences since Aristotle.' See White, 'The Fictions of Factual Representation', in *The Literature of Fact*, ed. Angus Fletcher (New York, 1976), p. 21; reprinted in *Tropics of Discourse*.
128 He was not elevated to *History and Theory*'s editorial committee until 1991.
129 Arnaldo Momigliano, 'The Rhetoric of History and the History of Rhetoric: On Hayden White's Tropes', *Comparative Criticism*, III (1981), 259–68.
130 Three out of the four editors considered Sande Cohen's 'Structuralism and the Writing of Intellectual History', to be unintelligible, but were persuaded by Louis Mink that it should be published; see *History and Theory*, XVII (1978), pp. 175–206.

4 *Linda Orr: Intimate Images: Subjectivity and History – Staël, Michelet and Tocqueville*

1 See Roland Barthes, 'Historical Discourse', *Structuralism: A Reader*, ed. Michael Lane (London, 1970), pp. 145–55; 'Le discours de l'histoire', *Poétique*, 49 (February 1982); pp. 13–21.
2 François Furet, *Penser la Révolution française* (Paris, 1978), pp. 33. See his comparison of Tocqueville and Michelet, pp. 30–31.
3 Jules Michelet, *Histoire de la Révolution française*, 7 vols (1847–53), ed. Gérard Walter (Paris, 1952), 1984.
4 Alexis de Tocqueville, *L'Ancien regime et la Révolution*, ed. J.-P. Mayer (Paris, 1967), p. 61.
5 Germaine de Staël, *Considérations sur la Révolution française*, 2 vols (1818), ed. Jacques Godechot (Paris, 1983), pp. 228–29. All translations from the three French histories are mine; after initial citations, subsequent references will be in the text.
6 See chapter 3 of Madelyn Gutwirth's *Madame de Staël, Novelist: The Emergence of the Artist as Woman* (Urbana, 1978) for details about slander against Staël.

7 See Joan De Jean, 'Staël's *Corinne*: The Novel's other Dilemma', *Stanford French Review*, XI/1 (1987), pp. 77–87. 'The only creative avenue seemingly still open to them (literary women) would require them to take possession of their production in the male script, thereby silencing the conversational voice, a lesson borne out by the future of women's writing in nineteenth-century France' (p. 87). Among interesting studies of the eighteenth-century and revolutionary salon, see Dena Goodman, 'Enlightenment Salons: The Convergence of Female and Philosophic Ambitions', *Eighteenth-Century Studies*, XXII/3 (1989), pp. 329–50, and Joan B. Landes' *Women and the Public Sphere in the Age of the French Revolution* (Ithaca, 1988).

8 For a more elaborate discussion of this thesis, see my 'Outspoken Women and the Rightful Daughter of the Revolution: Madame de Staël's *Considérations sur la Révolution française*', in *Rebel Daughters: Women and the French Revolution*, ed. Sara E. Melzer and Leslie W. Rabine (Oxford, 1992), pp. 121–36. For another view of sibling rivalry, see Lynn Hunt's *The Family Romance of the French Revolution* (Berkeley, 1992).

9 See Godechot's Introduction to Staël, op. cit. (n. 5), p. 24.

10 Constant and Staël were involved (sometimes lovers) off and on from 1795 to 1806 and continued a relationship up to the end of Staël's life. Staël reacted angrily to *Adolphe*, which Constant read to her in 1806 (because she saw herself or because she saw another woman?). She also did not appreciate his rallying to Napoleon in 1815.

11 Marilyn Yalom, *Blood Sisters: The French Revolution in Women's Memory* (New York, 1993), p. 161.

12 Marie-Hélène Huet, 'La Signature de l'histoire', *Modern Language Notes*, C (1985), pp. 715–27.

13 See *L'Etudiant* (1877), ed. Gaëten Picon (Paris, 1970). A quote from the dust jacket: 'Read in light of the events of May 1968, these pages written in anticipation of the events of '48 seem to have a surprising actuality.'

14 See the painting by Brouilhet, 'Michelet and Quinet retaking possession of their course at the College de France in 1848', reproduced in Roland Barthes' *Michelet par lui-même* (Paris, 1954), pp. 46–7. The white-haired Michelet is standing beside the taller Quinet in the rays of sunshine beaming through the window behind them. They face a dense crowd of men of all ages leaning towards them with hands and hats outstretched.

15 Cf. Michelet: 'I came upon all of that, whole, burning hot, as if from yesterday, after sixty years, when I recently opened these papers, that few people had read' and 'Me too, I will penetrate inside there'; op. cit. (n. 3), I, pp. 405, 650.

16 See the chapter, 'The Freedom and Terror of Unknowable History: A Reading of Tocqueville' in my *Headless History: Nineteenth-Century French Historiography of the Revolution* (Ithaca, 1990) for a discussion of historical periods in Tocqueville, their shadowy relationship one inside another, and the status of freedom in such a history.

17 L. E. Shiner, *The Secret Mirror: Literary Form and History in Tocqueville's 'Recollections'* (Ithaca, 1988), p. 186. All subsequent references are in the text.

18 Hans Kellner, *Language and Historical Representation: Getting the Story Crooked* (Madison, 1989), p. 2. Kellner also states that Michelet uses the strategy of self-representation very specifically to establish his authority as a historian: 'To establish his own authority requires a narrative subject; and for Michelet, a personal identification with that subject is the only acceptable form of narrative authority' (p. 115).

19 In *Narrative Discourse: An Essay in Method* (1972), trans. Jane E. Lewin (Ithaca, 1980), Gérard Genette speaks of a 'double narrative' resulting from analepsis or retrospection. 'This return retroactively confers on the past episode a meaning that in its own time it did not yet have' (p. 56). The example from Tocqueville is still different since the past event and retrospection supposedly happen in the same moment.

20 The title of Joan Didion's novel *Slouching towards Bethlehem* (1968) is derived from the last line of W. B. Yeats's poem *The Second Coming*.

21 In the chapter 'History and Psychoanalysis' of *Soundings in Critical Theory* (Ithaca, 1989), Dominick LaCapra's continued elaboration of the concepts 'working through' and 'transference' provide an important reflection on subjectivity in history.

22 Philippe Carrard, *Poetics of the New History* (Baltimore, 1992), p. 88. Subsequent references are in the text.

23 'Triangular Anxieties: The Present State of European Intellectual History' is a chapter in Kellner, op. cit. (n. 18). Behind the epistemological and personal fears, Kellner saw a 'primal anxiety fear of *the domination of the past by the present*' (p. 279). Or, to paraphrase: fear of the domination of the enunciation, of reading and writing processes over the *énoncé* or events of the past.

24 The ambiguity of the word 'subject' is useful. The old binary – the historian and (his) subject – sounded like the relationship of a king to his underlings. The more structuralist binary – historical subject and object – brought back the Cartesian cliché. Now subject refers to both the investigators and the investigatees.

25 Jacques Rancière, *La Nuit des prolétaires* (Paris, 1981), p. 21. Subsequent references are in the text.

26 Jules Michelet, preface of 1869, *Histoire de France* (Paris, 1876), I, p. ix.

27 Thanks to my writing group and to the Triangle French Studies Seminar whose discussions echo in this essay. William M. Reddy's 'Denial and Historical Research: Honor in Nineteenth-Century France' is an example of work in this group, blending private, critical and scholarly modes of discourse. A particular thanks to Philip Stewart.

5 Philippe Carrard: Theory of a Practice: Historical Enunciation and the Annales *School*

1 Emile Benveniste, *Problèmes de linguistique générale* (Paris, 1966), p. 241. Benveniste's choice of the term *histoire* is certainly infelicitous given its polysemy in French.

2 Roland Barthes, 'Le Discours de l'histoire', *Informations sur les sciences sociales*, VI/4 (1967), p. 69.

3 Barthes, op. cit., p. 66.

4 Denis Huisman, 'A. B. C. de la dissertation', in Roland Mousnier and Denis Huisman, *L'Art de la dissertation historique* (Paris, 1965), pp. 80–81.

5 Bernadette Plot, *Ecrire une thèse ou un mémoire en sciences humaines* (Paris, 1986), p. 252.

6 Plot, op. cit., p. 257.

7 Julia Kristeva, *Semiotike: Recherches pour une sémanalyse* (Paris, 1969), pp. 158–9.

8 Charles-Victor Langlois and Charles Seignobos, *Introduction aux études historiques* (Paris, 1898), p. 260.

9 Ibid., p. 261.

10 Ibid., p. 273.

11 Guy Bourdé and Hervé Martin, *Les Ecoles historiques* (Paris, 1983), pp. 137–70; Dominique Maingueneau, *Les Livres d'école de la République 1870–1914 (discours et idéologie)* (Paris, 1979).

12 Pierre-Olivier Carbonell, *Histoire et historiens: Une Mutation idéologique des historiens français, 1865–1885* (Toulouse, 1976); Lionel Gossman, *Between History and Literature* (Cambridge, MA, 1990); William R. Keylor, *Academy and Community: The Foundation of the French Historical Profession* (Cambridge, MA, 1975).

13 Fernand Braudel, *L'Identité de la France*, I (Paris, 1986), pp. 9–10.

14 Marc Ferro, *Pétain* (Paris, 1987), p. iii.

15 François Furet, *Penser la Révolution française* (Paris, 1978), pp. 26–7.

16 Furet, 'De l'histoire-récit à l'histoire-problème', in *L'Atelier de l'histoire* (Paris, 1982), pp. 73–90.
17 Lawrence Stone, 'The Revival of Narrative: Reflections on a New Old History', *Past and Present*, LXXXV (1979), pp. 3–24. For a different view, see my 'To Tell or Not to Tell: The New History and the Rebirth of Narrative', *French Forum*, XIV (1989), pp. 219–28.
18 Furet, op. cit. (n. 15), p. 34.
19 See for instance Mousnier and Huisman, op. cit. (n. 4), p. 81.
20 Georges Duby, *Le Moyen-Age: de Hughes Capet à Jeanne d'Arc, 987–1460* (Paris, 1987), pp. 67, 103, 345.
21 Duby, op. cit., pp. 164, 78, 82, 102, 263.
22 Michel de Certeau, 'Une Epistémologie de transition: Paul Veyne', *Annales ESC*, XXVII (1972), p. 1325.
23 Robert Scholes and Robert Kellog, *The Nature of Narrative* (New York, 1966), p. 265.
24 Emmanuel Le Roy Ladurie, *Paysans de Languedoc* (The Hague, 1966), pp. 48, 93, 345.
25 Ibid., pp. 276, 282, 514.
26 Ibid., pp. 86, 88.
27 Yvonne Knibielher and Catherine Fouquet, *Histoire des mères du Moyen Age à nos jours* (Paris, 1982), pp. 150, 226, 349.
28 Plot, op. cit. (n. 5), p. 258.
29 Le Roy Ladurie, *Le Carnaval de Romans: De la Chandeleur au mercredi des Centres, 1579–1580* (Paris, 1979), p. 367.
30 Catherine Kerbrat-Orecchioni, *L'Enonciatio: De la subjectivité dans le langage* (Paris, 1980), pp. 70, 74.
31 Le Roy Ladurie, op. cit. (n. 29), pp. 135, 297, 129, 129, 274, 153, 277.
32 Ibid., pp. 126, 248, 251, 247.
33 René Rémond, 'La Thèse', *Sources*, VI (1986), p. 294.
34 Certeau, *L'Ecriture de l'histoire* (Paris, 1975), p. 72.
35 For a more complete list of these objects, see *Faire de l'histoire III: Nouveaux objets*, ed. Jacque Le Goff and Pierre Nora (Paris, 1974).
36 Roger Chartier, *Lectures et lecteurs dans la France d'ancien régime* (Paris, 1987), p. 247.
37 Ibid., p. 97.
38 Ibid., pp. 10, 87, 88, 156.
39 Chartier, *Cultural History: Between Practices and Representations*, trans. Lydia G. Cochrane (Ithaca, 1988), pp. 127, 146.
40 See for instance Barthes, *Critique et vérité* (Paris, 1966), p. 56, and Tzvetan Todorov, *Qu'est-ce que le structuralisme? 2. Poétique* (Paris, 1968), p. 18.
41 Ozouf, *La Fête révolutionnaire* (Paris, 1976), p. 281, n. 1.
42 Ibid., pp. 150, 53, 46.
43 For an analysis of enunciative procedures in French scientific discourse, see Anne-Marie Loffler-Laurian, 'L'Expression du locuteur dans le discours scientifique: "Je," "Nous," "On" dans quelques textes de chimie et de physique', *Revue de linguistique romane*, XLIV (1980), pp. 135–57.
44 Barthes, 'Au séminaire', in *Le Bruissement de la langue* (Paris, 1984), pp. 369–80. This text was written in 1974.
45 Barthes, *S/Z* (Paris, 1970), pp. 20–21.
46 Arlette Farge, 'Pratique et effets de l'histoire des femmes', in *Une Histoire des femmes est-elle possible?*, ed. Michelle Perrot (Paris, 1984), p. 22.
47 Michelle Perrot, 'L'Air du temps', in *Essais d'ego-histoire*, ed. Pierre Nora (Paris, 1987), p. 291.

48 Perrot, *Les Ouvriers en grève: France, 1871–1890*, I (The Hague, 1974), p. 101.
49 Philippe Lejeune, 'L'Autobiographie à la troisième personne', in *Je est un autre: L'Autobiographie de la littérature aux médias* (Paris, 1980), pp. 32–59.
50 Farge, *Le Goût de l'archive* (Paris, 1989), pp. 61, 62, 63, 139.
51 Ibid., pp. 61, 62.
52 Ozouf, op. cit. (n. 41), p. 98.
53 Ozouf, trans. Alan Sheridan as *Festivals and the French Revolution* (Cambridge, MA, 1988), p. 83. The English version is clearer than the French original. As an expert in this kind of prose – he has also translated Foucault – Sheridan knows how to cut through pronominal ambiguities.
54 Bernard Bailyn, 'Braudel's Geohistory: A Reconsideration', *Journal of Economic History*, XI (1951), p. 280.
55 R. J. Knecht, Review of Le Roy Ladurie's *Carnival in Romans*, *History*, CCXVII (1981), p. 298.
56 Lawrence Stone, 'In the Alleys of Mentalité', *New York Review of Books* (8 November 1979), p. 23.
57 Edward Benson, Review of Le Roy Ladurie's *Carnival in Romans*, *Sixteenth-Century Journal*, XI/4 (1980), p. 128.
58 I am borrowing this example from Gérard Genette, who says that he is 'not sure whether the present tense in "Water boils at 212 degrees" (iterative narrative) is as intemporal as it seems'. See *Figures III* (Paris, 1972), p. 225.
59 For a more thorough demonstration, see for instance Bruno Latour and Paolo Fabbri, 'La Rhétorique de la science: Pouvoir et devoir dans un article de science exacte' *Actes de la recherche en sciences sociales*, XIII (1977), pp. 81–95.
60 Gérard Genette, 'Frontières du récit', *Poétique*, VIII (1966), pp. 152–63.
61 Furet, op. cit. (n. 15), p. 29.
62 Gossman, op. cit. (n. 12), p. 243.
63 Jules Michelet, *Histoire de la Révolution française*, 7 vols (1847–53), ed. (Paris, 1939), I, p. 305.
64 Braudel, op. cit. (n. 13), p. 9. This sentence, of course, echoes the opening sentence in *La Méditerranée* – the one which so much outraged critics.
65 For an account of these attempts, see for instance James Clifford, 'On Ethnographic Authority', in *The Predicament of Culture: Twentieth-Century Ethnography, Literature and Art* (Cambridge, MA, 1988), pp. 21–54.

6 Ann Rigney: Relevance, Revision and the Fear of Long Books

1 Gabriel Bonnot, Abbé de Mably, 'De la manière d'écrire l'histoire' (1783), in *Oeuvres complètes* (London, 1789), XII, p. 455. All translations in this essay are mine.
2 François-Juste-Marie Raynouard, review of A.-J.-S. Nougarède de Fayet, *Histoire de la Révolution qui renversa la République romaine et qui amena l'établissement de l'Empire* (1820), *Journal des savants* (March 1821), pp. 142–9 (p. 142).
3 Augustin Thierry, *Essai sur l'histoire de la formation et des progrès du tiers état; suivi de deux fragments du receuil des monuments inédits de cette histoire* (1853) (Paris, 1867), p. 7.
4 Louis-Pierre Anquetil, *Histoire de France: Depuis les temps les plus reculés jusqu'à la Révolution de 1789* (1805), 6 vols (Paris, 1850), I, pp. 7, 13. On the popularity of Anquetil's history, see Martyn Lyons, 'Les best-sellers', in *Histoire de l'édition française*, III (*Le Temps des éditeurs: du Romantisme à la Belle Époque*), ed. Henri-Jean Martin and Roger Chartier (n.p., 1985), pp. 369–97.
5 For a brief recognition of the importance of abbreviations and summaries ('organized on new principles') as an element in historiographical production, see Charles

Louandre, 'Statistique littéraire de la production intellectuelle en France depuis quinze ans', *Revue des deux mondes*, 20 (1847), pp. 192–219, 318–45, 512–41 (p. 332).

6 See also Linda Orr's vivid evocation of the sheer physical effort and the amount of time involved (months, not days) in reading the monumental histories of the French Revolution which are the subject of her *Headless History: Nineteenth-Century French Historiography of the Revolution* (Ithaca, 1990), pp. 2f.

7 See Thomas Babington Macaulay, *The History of England*, (1848–61), ed. and abridged, Hugh Trevor-Roper (Harmondsworth, 1979), pp. 20–25.

8 François Eudes de Mézeray, *Histoire de France, depuis Faramond jusqu'a maintenant: Oeuvre enrichie de plusieurs belles et rares antiquitez; et d'un abrégé de la vie de châque Reyne, dont il ne s'étoit presque point parlé cy-devant*, 3 vols (Paris, 1643–51), 1, p. [vi].

9 Louis O. Mink, 'Narrative Form as a Cognitive Instrument', in *The Writing of History: Literary Form and Historical Understanding*, ed. Robert H. Canary and Henry Kozicki (Madison, 1978), pp. 129–49 (p. 134).

10 The supplementary status of this lengthy preamble is reflected in the fact that it was scrapped in Trevor-Roper's abridgement; see Macaulay, op. cit. (n. 7).

11 Fernand Braudel, *La Méditerranée et le monde méditerranéen à l'époque de Philippe II* (1949), 2 vols (Paris, 1966), 11, pp. 512–4.

12 Paul Veyne, *Comment on écrit l'histoire: Essai d'épistémologie* (Paris, 1971), p. 51.

13 In making this theoretical distinction between the objective field of events (the totality of what happens) and the discursive representation of what happened, I am not denying the connection in practice between discourse and events. As Lynn Hunt in particular has shown with respect to the French Revolution, 'making sense' of past events through discursively representing them can also play a role in directing the course of what happens next; see Lynn Hunt, *Politics, Culture and Class in the French Revolution* (Berkeley, 1984), pp. 19–51.

14 In comparing film and natural language as media, Seymour Chatman argues that whereas filmic shots are characterized by a plenitude of details, making it difficult for the viewer to know *which* details are the significant ones, a verbal description involves selecting those features of a phenomenon which are of significance; the basis of language is thus *assertion* and not mere presentation; Seymour Chatman, 'What Novels Can Do That Films Can't (and Vice Versa)', in *On Narrative*, ed. W. J. T. Mitchell (Chicago, 1981), pp. 117–36.

15 On the distinction between 'correlative' codes, bearing on semantics, and 'institutional' codes, bearing on pragmatics, see Umberto Eco, *Semiotics and the Philosophy of Language* (Bloomington, 1984), pp. 164–88.

16 H. P. Grice, 'Logic and Conversation', in *Syntax and Semantics*, 111 (*Speech Acts*), ed. P. Cole and L. Morgan (New York, 1975), pp. 41–58.

17 See Dan Sperber and Deirdre Wilson, *Relevance: Communication and Cognition* (Oxford, 1986).

18 See Sperber and Wilson, op. cit., pp. 65–117; Wolfgang Iser, 'Die Appellstruktur der Texte', in *Rezeptionsästhetik: Theorie und Praxis*, ed. Rainer Warning (Munich, 1979), pp. 228–52; Teun van Dijk and Walter Kintsch, *Strategies of Discourse Comprehension* (Hillsdale, 1983).

19 The individual propositions making up a sequence may be *locally* coherent without the sequence as a whole being *globally* coherent. Consider, for example: 'This morning I had a toothache. I went to the dentist. The dentist has a big car. The car was bought in New York'; see Teun van Dijk, 'Semantic Discourse Analysis', in *Handbook of Discourse Analysis*, 11 (*Dimensions of Discourse*), ed. Teun A. van Dijk (London, 1985), pp. 103–35.

20 This triadic division follows Van Dijk (see n. 19) who distinguishes between

conditional, functional, conceptual coherence. Although Van Dijk reserves the notion of conceptual coherence for texts which have no recognizable propositional structure (e.g. poems) and so do not fit into the other categories, it is clear that the specifications, generalizations and expansions upon which functional coherence are based are also dependent on the associations pertaining between concepts. For a more detailed account of the 'sense relations' between concepts, see John Lyons, *Semantics*, 2 vols (Cambridge, 1977), 1, pp. 270–335. Particularly in the light of current debates within historiography on narrative form and the alternatives to it, further research is undoubtedly needed into the varieties of 'non-narrative' coherence. Such research should start, however, from the premise that a text may be designed according to different principles, and that non-narrative elements may be combined in different ways with narrative ones. As I have argued elsewhere, there are degrees of narrativity; see Ann Rigney, 'Narrativity and Historical Representation', *Poetics Today*, XII/3 (1991), pp. 591–605. Carrard's discussion of the narrative dimensions of the history writing of the *Annales* school offers support for this view; Philippe Carrard, *Poetics of the New History: French Historical Discourse from Braudel to Chartier* (Baltimore, 1992), esp. pp. 47–54.

21 On the elasticity of language and the shifting scale characteristic of verbal representations, see Ann Rigney, *The Rhetoric of Historical Representation: Three Narrative Histories of the French Revolution* (Cambridge, 1990), pp. 63–90.

22 See Roland Barthes, 'L'effet de réel', *Communications*, XI (1968), pp. 84–9.

23 On the term 'dramatic interest', see for example Prosper de Barante, *Etudes littéraires et historiques*, 2 vols (Paris, 1858), II, p. 238; Augustin Thierry, *Dix ans d'études historiques* (1835), *Oeuvres d'Augustin Thierry* (Brussels, 1839), X, p. 116; Ségur in n. 43 below.

24 Hugh Blair, *Lectures on Rhetoric and Belles Lettres* (1785), 3 vols (New York, 1970), III, pp. 26–7.

25 Hayden White, *The Content of the Form: Narrative Discourse and Historical Representation* (Baltimore, 1987), p. 72.

26 Veyne, op. cit. (n. 12), p. 102.

27 Lionel Gossman, *Between History and Literature* (Cambridge, MA, 1990), pp. 307–8.

28 Blair, op. cit. (n. 24), III, p. 21.

29 Mably, op. cit. (n. 1), p. 363.

30 Thierry, *Dix ans*, (n. 23), p. 19.

31 Albion Urdank, review of Robert Hole, *Pulpits, Politics, and Public Order in England, 1760–1832* (1989), *American Historical Review*, XCVI/5 (1991), p. 1539.

32 Arden Bucholz, review of Dennis E. Showalter, *Tannenberg: Clash of Empires* (1991), *American Historical Review*, XCVI/5 (1991), p. 1526.

33 Robert Zaller, review of Thomas Cogswell, *The Blessed Revolution: English Politics and the Coming of War, 1621–1624* (1989), *American Historical Review*, XCVI/5 (1991), p. 1535.

34 Sarah Maza, review of Dorinda Outram, *The Body and the French Revolution: Sex, Class, and Political Culture* (1989), *American Historical Review*, XCVI/5 (1991), pp. 1553–4 (p. 1554).

35 Veyne, op. cit. (n. 12), pp. 51, 103.

36 'I am alone', wrote Thomas Carlyle of his work on the French Revolution, 'without models, without *limits*' (letter written 21 September 1834; quoted in Fred Kaplan, *Thomas Carlyle: a Biography*, Cambridge, 1983, p. 216). In practice, of course, Carlyle repeatedly used the model of epic, if only to show how the French Revolution did not fit into it. See also Jules Michelet's self-portrayal as Prometheus, Orpheus, and as a 'poor solitary dreamer'; Jules Michelet, *Journal: texte intégral*, ed. Paul Viallaneix and Claude Digeon, 4 vols (Paris, 1959–76), 1, p. 378; Idem, *Oeuvres complètes*, ed.

Paul Viallaneix (Paris, 1971–), v, p. 27; Idem, *Le Peuple* (1846), ed. Paul Viallaneix (Paris, 1974), p. 195.

37 For a more detailed account of the intertextual and agonistic basis of historical representation, see Rigney, op. cit. (n. 21), pp. 47–61.

38 See in this context the discussion of the Braudellian model in Carrard, op. cit. (n. 20), pp. 54–62.

39 Veyne, op. cit. (n. 12), pp. 37–8.

40 On the 'dynamics of historiographical topology', see also F. R. Ankersmit, *The Reality Effect in the Writing of History: The Dynamics of Historiographical Topology* (Amsterdam, 1989).

41 For the term 'system of relevance', see Irmline Veit-Brause, 'Paradigms, Schools, Traditions: Conceptualizing Shifts and Changes in the History of Historiography', *Storia della storiografia*, XVII (1990), pp. 50–65 (p. 63).

42 Dominick LaCapra, *History and Criticism* (Ithaca, 1985), p. 69.

43 See, for example, Mézeray (op. cit., n. 8): 'the obscurity is so great as regards our first and second race of monarchs that one can compare those periods to the Polar regions, where even daytime is never more than a faint twilight' 1, p. [v]). Also the Comte de Ségur's criticism in 1823 of Sismondi's treatment of the Middle Ages in his *Histoire des Français* (1821–44): 'The lack of historical interest exists . . . obviously in the subject itself and in the savage barbarity of our ancient institutions. This chaos also destroys any dramatic interest. Only with difficulty can one distinguish the foreground from the background, the king from his subjects, the suzerain from his vassals. There is no unity for the mind to grasp, it being impossible to make a whole from such anarchic elements' (quoted in Boris Reizov, *L'Historiographie romantique française 1815–1830*, authorized trans., Moscow, n.d., p. 77). Also Hallam's comment that: 'Many considerable portions of time, especially before the twelfth century, may justly be deemed so barren of events worthy of remembrance, that a single sentence or paragraph is often sufficient to give the character of entire generations, and of long dynasties of obscure kings'; Henry Hallam, *View of the State of Europe during the Middle Ages*, 3 vols (London, 1819), 1, p. v.

44 It is in the light of this problem that one can explain such a phenomenon as Marchangy's study of ancient Gaul which, through multiple parallels with classical figures and a highly florid, conventionalized use of language, attempts to show that ancient Gaul is after all worth writing about; Louis-Antoine-François de Marchangy, *La Gaule poétique, ou l'Histoire de France considérée dans ses rapports avec la poésie, l'éloquence et les beaux-arts*, 8 vols (Paris, 1813–19).

45 Augustin Thierry, *Récits des temps mérovingiens; précédes de Considérations sur l'histoire de France* (1840), 2 vols (Paris, 1887), 1, p. 3.

46 According to the 'canonization of the junior branch' principle of the Russian Formalists, literary evolution is also characterized by shifts from periphery to centre: in the process of literary innovation, previously marginalized genres and neglected writers are retroactively canonized as models; see Victor Erlich, *Russian Formalism: History-Doctrine* (1955) (New Haven, 1981), p. 260.

47 See, for example, Witold Rybczynski, *Waiting for the Weekend* (New York, 1991); Alain Corbin, *Le Miasme et la jonquille: l'odorat et l'imaginaire social, XVIIIe–XIXe siècles* (Paris, 1982); Anne Vincent-Bouffault, *Histoire des larmes, XXIIIe–XIXe siècles* (Paris, 1986); Shulamith Shahar, *Childhood in the Middle Ages* (London, 1990); Georges Minois, *History of Old Age: From Antiquity to the Renaissance*, trans. S. H. Tenison (Cambridge, 1989). It would be interesting to study in detail how the *inventio* or discovery of one topic leads to another on the basis of some conceptual link (see n. 20 above); thus, 'smell' may suggest 'touch' or 'sight' while 'childhood' and 'old age' may suggest 'middle age' and 'adolescence'.

48 Michelet, *Journal*, (n. 36) 1, p. 378.

49 Thierry, *Essai*, (n. 31) p. 200.

50 Surveying developments in 1835, Sarazin characterized the aim of the new historiography as the inclusion of every imaginable aspect of national life: 'It is not enough, therefore, for the historian to relate in an interesting fashion the course of wars and diplomatic missions, the deaths and coronations of kings . . . what is called for is an account of society as a whole, of everything which makes it what it is.' See J. Sarazin, *Du progrès des études historiques en France au dix-neuvième siècle* (Strasburg, 1835), pp. 19–20. Such statements have recently been echoed by Carlo Ginzburg in the preface to his study of the cosmos of a sixteenth-century miller: 'In the past historians could be accused of wanting to know only about 'the great deeds of kings,' but today this is certainly no longer true. More and more they are turning toward what their predecessors passed over in silence'; Carlo Ginzburg, *The Cheese and the Worms: The Cosmos of a Sixteenth-Century Miller* (1976), trans. John and Anne Tedeschi (Baltimore, 1980), p. viii.

51 See Klaus Massmann, *Die Rezeption der historischen Romane Sir Walter Scotts in Frankreich (1816–1832)* (Heidelberg, 1972). As one commentator wrote in 1828: 'Until now . . . the only history written was the history of kings; we are going to trace that of the people; we shall above all endeavour to make known the history of manners' (quoted in Massmann, p. 88). Scott's influence on topology was not restricted, however, to the history of manners. According to Augustin Thierry, for example, Scott's focus on intercultural conflict had enabled him to bring out the poetic, dramatic qualities of the history of Scotland, i.e. to show its suitability as a discursive topic (Thierry, *Dix ans*, (n. 23) pp. 113–17). Thierry himself used the same model of intercultural conflict in writing the history of the Norman conquest of England; see Augustin Thierry, *Histoire de la conquête de l'Angleterre par les Normands, de ses causes et de ses suites jusqu'à nos jours, en Angleterre, en Ecosse, en Irlande et sur le continent* (1825), 4 vols (Paris and Brussels, 1835), I, p. xvi.

52 Macaulay, 'History' (1828), in *Complete Works*, 12 vols (London, 1906), I, pp. 304, 307. See also Barante's comments in the preface to his history of the Dukes of Burgundy: 'Since [as readers] we wanted not only to learn but to watch and to listen, the novel form offered more truth than history'; 'I have attempted to restore to history proper the attractions which the historical novel had borrowed from it'; *Histoire des Ducs de Bourgogne de la maison de Valois 1364–1477* (1824), 2 vols (Brussels, 1838), pp. 13, 16. In this poetics, 'vividness', 'truth' and 'relevance for the public' were closely linked (see Rigney, *The Rhetoric*, (n. 21), pp. 1–6).

53 As I have shown elsewhere with respect to *Old Mortality* (1816), both Scott's inventions and his deviations from facts can be seen as serving, on the one hand, to reduce the diversity of the historical record and, on the other, to increase the connectedness between events as elements of a single plot; see Rigney, 'Adapting History to the Novel', *New Comparison*, VIII (1989), pp. 127–43 (pp. 134–9).

54 Thierry, *Récits* (n. 45) 1, pp. 291–4.

55 Ibid., p. 6.

56 Ibid., p. 5.

57 On the importance of exemplification in Thierry's work, see also Marcel Gauchet, '*Les Lettres sur l'histoire de France* d'Augustin Thierry', in *Les Lieux de mémoire*, II (*La Nation* 1), ed. Pierre Nora (Paris, 1986), pp. 247–316 (pp. 275–8).

58 As he explains in the preface, Thierry looked for 'central facts' around which a complete discourse could be organized (*Récits*, (n. 45), I, p. 7). In response to similar compositional problems, Capefigue opted to organize his account of the Middle Ages around the famous name of Philippe Auguste 'in order to reduce to a unified whole all the large-scale changes underway at that time'; J.-B.-H.-R. de Capefigue, *Histoire de*

Philippe-Auguste, 5 vols (Brussels, 1830), 1, p. v). Barante opted to organize his history around the different reigns of the Dukes of Burgundy, a strategy which allowed him to 'attach the narrative of each period to a great individual' and provided 'a thematic line guiding the reader across the confused mass of facts' (*Histoire des Ducs* (n. 52), 1, p. 16). Whereas the form chosen by Barante resembles the serial biographies of traditional sovereign-based histories, the form chosen by Thierry is novel in the sense that the short stories he treats consecutively in fact ran partly concurrently (as do the different lives treated by Balzac in *La Comédie humaine*, 1842–8).

59 Thierry, *Récits*, (n. 54) 1, p. 326.

60 Macaulay, *The History of England from the Accession of James the Second* (1848–61), 2 vols (London, 1883), 1, p. 2.

61 Ibid., 1, pp. 136–209.

62 Ibid., 1, p. 138.

63 As Kellner notes, Michelet's *Tableau de France* is situated in similar fashion between the antecedents of his history of France and the main body of his narrative; Hans Kellner, *Language and Historical Representation: Getting the Story Crooked* (Madison, 1989), pp. 108–9.

64 Macaulay, *History* (1883) (n. 60), 1, p. 202.

65 The history which has been written until now is 'the history of kings, of clerics, of military men . . . it is not the history of the different estates, it is not history'; Amans-Alexis Monteil, *Histoire des Français des divers états aux cinq derniers siècles*, 10 vols (Paris, 1828–44), 1, p. v. For the term *histoire-bataille*, see Monteil, *Les Français pour la première fois dans l'histoire de France; ou Poétique de l'histoire des divers états* (Paris, 1841), p. 73.

66 Pierre Larousse, *Grand dictionnaire universel*, 17 vols (Paris, 1865–90), VIII, p. 716.

67 Reflecting the ongoing exchanges between historians and novelists at this period, Monteil's work also provided a model for Balzac. When in the preface of 1842 to *La Comédie humaine*, the novelist announced his intention to write a history of nineteenth-century manners (on the grounds that it was 'the history which had been forgotten by historians'), he invoked the 'patient and courageous' Monteil as one of his predecessors; Honoré de Balzac, *La Comédie humaine*, ed. Pierre-Georges Castex and Pierre Citron, 7 vols (Paris, 1965–6), 1, p. 52.

68 Charles Louandre in Monteil, *Histoire de l'industrie française et des gens de métiers*, with introduction, supplement and notes by Louandre, 2 vols (Paris, 1872), 1, p. 3.

69 To this list may be added *La Médecine en France*, ed. A. Le Pileur (1874). Having been 'extracted' from Monteil's original history, these works are fragmentary and follow different discursive models. But they are much shorter and, thanks to editorial additions, they are more surveyable: from the index to the *Histoire de l'industrie française*, for example, we can learn that 'Tuiliers' are discussed in three different places in the first volume (pp. 160, 227, 297).

Through indexes, textual subdivisions, detailed tables of contents, and summaries, writers may thus enable their readers to take short cuts through the work (with this idea in mind, it would be interesting to take a closer look at the paratext of historical works: the tables of contents, the guides in the margins, the arguments at the beginning of chapters, the use of titles to indicate the topics of chapters, and so on). On the concept of 'paratext' see Gérard Genette, *Seuils* (Paris, 1987).

The alphabetical classification which takes place in an index might be seen as the ultimate achievement in the imposition of order on diverse material, but also as the ultimate in entropy: the reduction of a discourse to single items or micro-sequences of information in which every combination of items is possible – if the reader is willing and able to do the work. That readers in practice may read even monographs selectively through the back door of the index is illustrated by a recent review of a biography of Lord Kelvin: the work is praised for its scholarship, detailed table of contents and index, and recommended as being potentially of interest for historians working in a number of different areas, and 'so well written and presented that the reader runs the risk of reading the whole biography'; Henry Steffens, review of Crosbie Smith and W. Norton Wise, *Energy and Empire: A Biographical Study of Lord Kelvin* (1989), *American Historical Review* XCVI/5 (1991), pp. 1522–3 (p. 1523).

70 Book 2, chapter 2 and chapters 4–12 were taken almost literally from Michelet's *Histoire de France*, VII (1855), XI (1862) and XIII (1860).

71 According to Wouter Kusters, among Michelet's most important models in the first part of *La Sorcière* was Louandre's *La Sorcellerie* (1853) and Charles Nodier's *Trilby: ou le Lutin d'Argail* (1822): see Jules Michelet, *La Sorcière* (1862), ed. Wouter Kusters (Nijmegen, 1989), pp. 44, 51–4.

72 Jules Michelet, *La Sorcière* (1862), ed. Paul Viallaneix (Paris, 1966) p. 296. For other uses of an allegorical figure, see Augustin Thierry's 'Histoire véritable de Jacques Bonhomme' (1821) in *Dix ans*, (n. 23) pp. 201–7; also Prosper de Barante's 'Jacques Bonhomme' (1832), in *Mélanges historiques et littéraires*, 3 vols (Brussels, 1835), II, pp. 298–326.

73 *La Sorcière*, ed. Viallaneix (1966), pp. 62, 139.

74 This hypothetical mode can also be found in Amédée Thierry's *Histoire des Gaulois, depuis les temps les plus reculés jusqu'à l'entière soumission de la Gaule à la domination romaine*, 3 vols (Paris, 1828). This work is presented as a 'biography which has as its hero one of those collective characters known as *peoples*' and as being based on the 'hypothesis of the existence of a Gaulish family different from other human families' (I, pp. i, xi). On Thierry's mixing of metaphors here (is the nation an individual or a family?), see my 'Mixed Metaphors and the Writing of History', *Storia della storiografia*, XXIV (1993), pp. 149–59. As this recourse to metaphor and approximation indicates, representing groups was one of the principal challenges facing these post-Revolutionary historians (see also Rigney, *The Rhetoric* (n. 21), pp. 103–36).

75 On this point, see also Rigney, *The Rhetoric* (n. 21) pp. 47–62.

76 Bucholz op. cit. (n. 32).

77 On the 'experimental' character of historical writing, see also Daniel S. Milo, *Trahir le temps (histoire)* (Paris, 1991).

78 For a brief discussion of the devices which contemporary cultural historians have incidentally adopted in order to make up for the deficiencies of their sources, see Carlo Ginzburg, 'Checking the Evidence: the Judge and the Historian', *Critical Inquiry*, XVIII (1991), pp. 79–92.

79 Gossman, op. cit., (n. 24) p. 307.

80 Emmanuel Le Roy Ladurie, *La Sorcière de Jasmin: avec la reproduction en fac-similé de l'édition orginale bilingue (1842) de la Françouneto de Jasmin* (Paris, 1983).

81 Peter Laslett, 'Elusive Intimacy', review of *A History of Private Life*, V (*Riddles of Identity in Modern Times*), ed. A. Prost and G. Vincent, trans. A. Goldhammer (1991), *Times Literary Supplement* (28 February 1992), p. 15.

7 Allan Megill: 'Grand Narrative' and the Discipline of History

The argument of this paper owes much to my experience as a member of the University of Iowa Project on Rhetoric of Inquiry (POROI) in the period 1980–90; I owe a special debt to Donald N. McCloskey and John S. Nelson. Over a period of several years, the following research assistants contributed to the paper: Lori Brandt, Kevin Burnett, Ann Gallagher, Carey Goodman, Addison Howe, Susan Peabody, Trent Watts and Harwell Wells; I am also indebted to several groups of graduate students in my historiography courses at the universities of Iowa and of Virginia. Successive versions of the argument were presented in the Faculty Rhetoric Seminar, University of Iowa; the Center for the Humanities, Memphis State University; the Center for Cultural Studies, Rice University; the History Department seminar, Johns Hopkins University; Georg Iggers's graduate seminar, State University of New York at Buffalo; the History Department, University of Vermont; and a POROI- and N.E.H.-sponsored workshop on the rhetoric of social history, University of Iowa. For the invitations, I am indebted to David Hiley, Thomas Haskell, Dorothy Ross, Georg Iggers, Patrick Hutton, Jeffrey Cox and Shelton Stromquist. I am indebted to many other persons for their useful comments.

1 Peter Burke, 'Overture: The New History, its Past and its Future', in *New Perspectives on Historical Writing*, ed. Peter Burke (Cambridge, University Park, 1991), p. 1.

2 See, for example, the discussion of 'History the Great Catch-All', in Jacques Barzun and Henry F. Graff, *The Modern Researcher* (San Diego, 4/1985), pp. 8–13.

3 With reservations and modifications, I borrow the term 'grand narrative' from Jean-François Lyotard, *The Postmodern Condition: A Report on Knowledge* (1979), trans. Geoff Bennington and Brian Massumi (Minneapolis, 1984), p. xxiii. The term might well be taken as designating an all-embracing story, arranged in beginning-middle-end order – the most obvious meaning, given Aristotle's influence on our view of narrative. Without necessarily rejecting the Aristotelian view (for it does fit part of the history recounted here), I intend the term more broadly, to designate a vision of coherence – in particular, a vision of coherence broad enough to support objectivity claims.

4 See, for example, Horst Walter Blanke, *Historiographiegeschichte als Historik* (Stuttgart-Bad Cannstatt, 1991), an 809-page account of the German tradition of historiography since 1750.

5 See especially Thomas Bender's widely noticed article, 'Wholes and Parts: The Need for Synthesis in American History', *Journal of American History*, LXXIII (1986), pp. 120–36; responses by Nell Irvin Painter, Richard Wightman Fox and Roy Rosenzweig and a response to the responses by Bender were published as 'A Round Table: Synthesis in American History', *Journal of American History*, LXXIV (1987), pp. 107–30. See also, on the question of a 'master narrative' for German history, Michael Geyer and Konrad H. Jarausch, 'The Future of the German Past: Transatlantic Reflections for the 1990s', *Central European History*, XXII (1989), pp. 229–59 (esp. pp. 234–47).

6 For an account operating on a more specific level, that of American historiography, see Peter Novick's important and provocative book, *That Noble Dream: The 'Objectivity Question' and the American Historical Profession* (Cambridge, 1988). The present paper might be read as an attempt to get at a deep background to Novick. For a multi-disciplinary take on objectivity, see Allan Megill, ed., *Rethinking Objectivity* (Durham, NC, 1994), esp. Megill, 'Introduction: Four Senses of Objectivity', pp. 1–20.

7 The striking exception, among historians whom one would otherwise be tempted to designate 'professional', is Jacob Burckhardt. When, at the beginning of his *Civilization of the Renaissance in Italy* (Ger. orig., 1860), Burckhardt wrote that 'the same studies which have served for this work might easily, in other hands, not only receive a wholly different treatment and application, but lead also to essentially different conclusions', he denied the notion of History (see Burckhardt, *The Civilization of the Renaissance in Italy*, trans. S. G. C. Middlemore, Harmondsworth, 1990, Part I, Introduction, p. 19).

8 See Reinhart Koselleck, 'Die Entstehung des Kollektivsingulars', in Otto Brunner, Werner Conze and Reinhart Koselleck, eds, *Geschichtliche Grundbegriffe: Historisches Lexikon zur politisch-sozialen Sprache in Deutschland* (Stuttgart, 1972–), II, p. 652. For a brief account in English, see Koselleck, 'On the Disposability of History', in Koselleck, *Futures Past: On the Semantics of Historical Time*, trans. Keith Tribe (Cambridge, MA, 1985), pp. 200–202 (cf. n. 28 below). Koselleck develops a point

made by his teacher Karl Löwith, who contrasted the 'substantive singular' character of the German *die Geschichte* with the lack of any equivalent term in Greek; see Löwith, 'Mensch und Geschichte' (1960), in *Der Mensch inmitten der Geschichte: Philosophische Bilanz des 20. Jahrhunderts*, ed. Bernd Lutz (Stuttgart, 1990), p. 228.

9 Robert F. Berkhofer, Jr., 'The Challenge of Poetics to (Normal) Historical Practice', in Paul Hernadi, ed., *The Rhetoric of Interpretation and the Interpretation of Rhetoric* (Durham, NC, 1989), pp. 188–9. How does one get from a concern with context to the notion that there is finally only a *single* context? In practice, it is an easy passage from the observation that a work of history is 'contextually rich' to the conclusion that 'every meaningful precinct, person, or decision has been accounted for and integrated' by the story that it tells; see Michael Kammen, 'Historical Knowledge and Understanding', in *Selvages and Biases: The Fabric of History in American Culture* (Ithaca, 1987), p. 37.

10 Louis O. Mink, 'Narrative Form as a Cognitive Instrument', in *Historical Understanding*, ed. Brian Fay, Eugene O. Golob and Richard T. Vann (Ithaca, 1987), pp. 194–5.

11 Leonard Krieger, *Time's Reasons: Philosophies of History Old and New* (Chicago, 1989), p. xi and *passim*. Krieger's commitment to 'the traditional discipline of history' led him into some polemical misreading when he turned to the historiography of the 1960s and 1970s (see esp. pp. ix–xii, 1–6), but this is no denial of the larger merits of the book. See also Krieger, *Ranke: The Meaning of History* (Chicago, 1977), where a similar argument is advanced, although in less general a form.

12 Krieger, *Time's Reasons*, p. 170.

13 The standard account of universal history in the early modern period is Adalbert Klempt, *Die Säkularisierung der universalhistorischen Auffassung im 16. und 17. Jahrhundert: Zum Wandel des Geschichtsdenkens im 16. und 17. Jahrhundert* (Göttingen, 1960). See also the discussion of 'Universal History: A Troubled Tradition' in Ernst Breisach, *Historiography: Ancient, Medieval, and Modern* (Chicago, 1983), pp. 177–85. Universal history has recently been revived in a very different, but still quasi-theological context: see Francis Fukuyama, *The End of History and the Last Man* (New York, 1992), esp. chap. 5, 'An Idea for a Universal History', pp. 55–70.

14 Immanuel Kant, 'Idea for a Universal History from a Cosmopolitan Point of View' (1784), trans. Lewis White Beck, in Kant, *On History*, ed. Lewis White Beck (Indianapolis, 1963), pp. 11–26; Kant, 'An Old Question Raised Again: Is the Human Race Constantly Progressing' (1795), trans. Robert E. Anchor, in Kant, *On History*, pp. 137–54. For a meticulous, deconstructive investigation of Kant's writings on universal history, see Peter D. Fenves, *A Peculiar Fate: Metaphysics and World-History in Kant* (Ithaca, 1991).

15 Kant, 'Idea for a Universal History', pp. 11, 23–36.

16 Kant, op. cit., p. 25.

17 Kant, 'An Old Question Raised Again', pp. 141–2.

18 Kant, op. cit., pp. 143–5. On Kant's attitude toward the French Revolution, see Krieger, *The German Idea of Freedom* (Boston, 1957), pp. 104–5.

19 For the most detailed statement of this view, see G. W. F. Hegel, *The Philosophy of History*, trans. J. Sibree (New York, 1956). For an abbreviated presentation, see Hegel, *Philosophy of Right*, trans. T. M. Knox (Oxford, 1952), pp. 216–23. In Hegel, the theological underpinnings of grand narrative are particularly evident; note his famous assertion that 'the History of the World . . . is the true *Theodicaea*, the justification of God in History' (*Philosophy of History*, p. 457). On the role of 'Christian theology of history' in Hegel, see Laurence Dickey, *Hegel: Religion, Economics, and the Politics of Spirit, 1770–1807* (Cambridge, 1987), p. 149.

20 Friedrich von Schiller, 'Was heisst und zu welchem Ende studiert man Universal-

geschichte?', in Wolfgang Hardtwig, ed., *Über das Studium der Geschichte* (Munich, 1990), pp. 18–36 (27).

21 As Mink observes; op. cit. (n. 10), p. 189.

22 See Johann Gottfried Herder, 'A. L. Schlözers Vorstellung seiner Universal-Historie', in Herder, *Sämmtliche Werke*, ed. Bernhard Suphan, 33 vols (Berlin, 1877–1913), v, pp. 436, 438. See also August Wilhelm von Schlözer, *Vorstellung seiner Universal-Historie*, 2 vols (Göttingen, 1772–3), ii, 'Vorbericht'. For the Schlözer quotation, I depend on Peter Hanns Reill, *The German Enlightenment and the Rise of Historicism* (Berkeley, 1975), pp. 47, 232–33 n. 59.

23 See Ranke's excursus, entitled by his editors 'Die Universalgeschichtsschreibung seit dem 16. Jahrhundert', appended to the introduction to his course of Summer Semester 1848 ['Erster Teil der Weltgeschichte oder Geschichte der alten Welt'], in Leopold von Ranke, *Aus Werk und Nachlass*, ed. Walther Peter Fuchs and Theodor Schieder, 4 vols (Vienna, 1964–75), IV: *Vorlesungseinleitungen*, ed. Volker Dotterweich and Walther Peter Fuchs, pp. 208–10.

24 As Krieger established in great detail: see his *Ranke* (cited in n. 11), pp. 103, 107, 112–15, 124, 151–2 and *passim*. For documentation of Ranke's concern with universal history, see the entries for 'Universalgeschichte, -Historie', in the *Sachregister* of Ranke, op. cit. (n. 23), IV.

25 Ranke, [Die Notwendigkeit universalgeschichtlicher Betrachtung], ibid., IV, pp. 297–8; trans. Wilma A. Iggers as 'The Role of the Particular and the General in the Study of Universal History (A Manuscript of the 1860s)', in Ranke, *The Theory and Practice of History*, ed. Georg G. Iggers and Konrad von Moltke (New York, 1983), pp. 58–9.

26 Ranke, 'Neuere Geschichte seit dem Anfang des 17. Jahrhunderts (28. Oktober 1867–10. März 1868)', in op. cit. (n. 23), IV, p. 411. As Krieger rightly noted, '[r]epeatedly, [Ranke] insisted that the historian's success in perceiving the objective coherence of universal history was only a matter of time' (op. cit., n. 11, p. 103).

27 Ranke, 'Idee der Universalhistorie' [lecture script of 1831–2], in op. cit. (n. 23), pp. 74–5; abridged trans. Wilma A. Iggers as 'On the Character of Historical Science (A Manuscript of the 1830s)', in Ranke, op. cit. (n. 25), p. 36.

28 Koselleck has argued that the emergence of the term 'history' (*die Geschichte*) as an objectless 'collective singular' dates from the late eighteenth century: 'Only from around 1780 can one talk of "history in general", "history in and for itself" and "history pure and simple"', as distinguished from talking about 'the history of X' and 'the history of Y'; see Koselleck, trans. Tribe, op. cit. (n. 8), p. 200. One might speculate that the growing dominance, in the nineteenth century, of the 'collective singular' notion of history compensated for the deferral to the future of the telling of the grand narrative. When the grand narrative is seen as (re)tellable now, there is no need to insist semantically on History's unity. The situation changed, however, when the telling of the grand narrative was deferred.

29 Ranke, op. cit. (n. 27), pp. 82–3; trans. Iggers, p. 44.

30 Leopold Ranke to Heinrich Ranke, letter of March 1820, in Leopold von Ranke, *Das Briefwerk*, ed. Walther Peter Fuchs (Hamburg, 1949), p. 18; trans. from Krieger, op. cit. (n. 11), p. 361 n. 13.

31 J. B. Bury, 'The Science of History', in Fritz Stern, ed., *The Varieties of History from Voltaire to the Present* (New York, 2/1972), p. 219.

32 Ibid., p. 217, quoting Thomas Arnold, *Lectures on Modern History* (New York, 1874), p. 46.

33 Krieger, op. cit. (n. 11), p. 242.

34 Bury, op. cit. (n. 31), p. 210.

35 Compare Ranke's famous statement: 'I wished to extinguish, as it were, my self, and only to recount those things that powerful forces allowed to appear, that over the

course of centuries emerged and became strong with and through one another.' Ranke, *Englische Geschichte, vornehmlich im Siebzehnten Jahrhundert*, Fünftes Buch, 'Einleitung', in *Sämtliche Werke*, 2. Gesammtausgabe, 54 vols (Leipzig, 1867–1890), XV, p. 103.

36 Bury, op. cit. (n. 31), pp. 213, 216.

37 Ibid., p. 219.

38 Johann Gustav Droysen, *Outline of the Principles of History*, trans. E. Benjamin Andrews (translation of Droysen, *Grundriss der Historik*, rev. 3/1882) (Boston, 1893), sect. 81, p. 47. The *Outline* offers an encapsulated version of reflections that are presented at greater length in the posthumously published manuscript of his lectures: Johann Gustav Droysen, *Historik*, ed. Peter Leyh, 3 vols (Stuttgart, 1977 [vols II and III forthcoming]). The Leyh edition includes, pp. 413–88, a transcription of the 1882 edition of the *Grundriss*.

39 Droysen, trans. Andrews, Appendix II, 'Art and Method', p. 118. Cf. Droysen, *Historik*, p. 69: 'the activities that our science concerns itself with . . . are only historical because we conceive of them as historical, not in themselves and objectively, but rather in and through our examination [*Betrachtung*]' [the passage comes from the manuscript of Droysen's lectures of 1857].

40 Hayden White, 'Droysen's *Historik*: Historical Writing as a Bourgeois Science', *The Content of the Form* (Baltimore and London, 1987), p. 99. See also Jörn Rüsen, *Begriffene Geschichte: Genesis und Begründung der Geschichtstheorie J. G. Droysens* (Paderborn, 1969), 119.

41 Note Droysen's statement (trans. Andrews, part 1, p. 6): 'Observation of the present teaches us how, from different points of view, every matter of fact is differently apprehended, described and connected with others; how every transaction in private as well as in public life receives explanations of the most various kinds. A man who judges carefully will find it difficult to gather out of the plenitude of utterances so different, even a moderately safe and permanent picture of what has been done and of what has been purposed.' See also, on this theme, the manuscript of his 1857 lectures, *Historik*, pp. 113–14, 236–8.

42 Ranke, 'The Great Powers' (1833), trans. Hildegarde Hunt Von Laue, in Ranke, op. cit. (n. 25), pp. 65–101, esp. 99–101. Here Ranke contended that '[w]orld history does not present such a chaotic tumult, warring, and planless succession of states and peoples as appear at first sight' (p. 100). Ranke's discovery of a basic unity was aided by his insistence, endemic among nineteenth-century European intellectuals, on seeing *European* history as *world* history. On Ranke's universalism generally, see Krieger, 'Elements of Early Historicism: Experience, Theory, and History in Ranke', *History and Theory*, XIV (1975), pp. 1–14, esp. 9–14. On Droysen's rejection of the concept of a European system of the great powers, see Georg G. Iggers, *The German Conception of History: The National Tradition of Historical Thought from Herder to the Present*, rev. ed. (Middletown, CT, 1983), pp. 106–7. On Droysen's 'maverick' status in the German historical tradition, see Michael J. MacLean, 'Johann Gustav Droysen and the Development of Historical Hermeneutics', *History and Theory*, XXI (1982), pp. 364–5.

43 See Droysen, trans. Andrews, op. cit. (n. 38), sect. 73, p. 44: 'Even the narrow, the very narrowest of human relations, strivings, activities, etc., have a process, a history, and are for the persons involved, historical. So family histories, local histories, special histories. But over all these and such histories is *History*.'

44 Novick, op. cit. (n. 6), generally supports my claim that twentieth-century professional historians (at least, *American* professional historians) largely conformed to the third attitude. A substantial essay could be written on how this is so, but note the following points: (1) Novick established that insistence on autonomy was widespread in the

historical profession (pp. 361–411). Insistence on autonomy is perhaps the most characteristic 'third attitude' position, since it implies that historians are in principle capable of arriving at a view of history untainted by irrelevant external influences, without requiring that they actually do so. (2) He established that historians had a widespread, but consistently thwarted, concern with 'convergence' in historical interpretation (pp. 206–7, 320–21, 438, 457–8, 465 and *passim*). Desire for a single authoritative narrative, combined with its perpetual failure to appear, is definitive of the third attitude. (3) He established that the fragmentation was widely seen as a bad thing (pp. 577–92 and *passim*). This suggests the view that a single authoritative narrative is a good thing, even if it can never be told. (4) He established the long-standing persistence of 'the idea and ideal of "objectivity"' (p. 1), a notion that historians were perfectly willing to concede could never actually be realized. Again, grand narrative is relegated to an ideal level.

45 Consider H. G. Wells, *The Outline of History, Being a Plain History of Life and Mankind*, 2 vols (London, 1920; New York, 1921), which emphatically does not conform to the view just noted (see esp. chap. 41, 'The Possible Unification of the World into One Community of Knowledge and Will', 11, pp. 579–89). In their embarrassed reaction to Wells, professional historians ever since the 1920s have demonstrated their conviction that this sort of thing is just not done in historiography.

46 Droysen, trans. Andrews, op. cit. (n. 38), sect. 15, p. 15. See also Droysen, *Vorlesung über das Zeitalter der Freiheitskriege*, 1/2 (Gotha, 1886), p. 4: 'Our faith gives us the consolation that a divine hand bears us up, that it directs the fates of great and small. And the science of history has no higher task than to justify this faith: thereby is it science. It seeks and finds in that chaotic ocean [*wüsten Wellengang*] a direction, a goal, a plan'. Rüsen, op. cit. (n. 40), particularly stresses Droysen's commitment to a Hegelian grand narrative of freedom (see esp. pp. 126–30).

47 See Wilhelm Dilthey, *Introduction to the Human Sciences* (Ger. orig., 1883), ed. Rudolf A. Makkreel and Frithjof Rodi, trans. Michael Neville (Princeton, 1989), p. 50; Michael Oakeshott, *Experience and its Modes* (Cambridge, 1933), esp. pp. 92–6; and Oakeshott, 'The Activity of Being an Historian', *Rationalism in Politics and other Essays* (New York, 1962), pp. 137–67.

48 Collingwood's philosophy generally, and his theory of historiography in particular, raise many interesting theoretical and exegetical puzzles that cannot be considered here. Among discussions of Collingwood's work, see especially Louis O. Mink, *Mind, History, and Dialectic: The Philosophy of R. G. Collingwood* (Bloomington, 1969); W. Jan Van Der Dussen, *History as a Science: The Philosophy of R. G. Collingwood* (The Hague, 1981); and 'Reassessing Collingwood', *History and Theory*, XXIX (1990) [essays by James Patrick, James Connelly, W. Jan Van Der Dussen, Leon J. Goldstein, Michael A. Kissell and G. S. Couse].

49 Much of the 'Epilegomena' to *The Idea of History* is aimed at arguing out this point: R. G. Collingwood, *The Idea of History* (Oxford, 1946), pp. 205–334, esp. 266–302; in this book he noted the Kantian roots of his theory several times (pp. 60, 236, 240).

50 For some relevant passages, see Collingwood, op. cit., pp. 209, 236, 256.

51 Ibid, pp. 210, 231.

52 Collingwood, *An Autobiography* (Oxford, 1939), p. 77.

53 Ibid., p. 59.

54 Ibid., pp. 79, 147–67.

55 Ibid., p. 167. In this chapter Collingwood identified three R. G. Collingwoods, one of whom lived 'as a professional thinker' (p. 151), while the other two respectively believed in and agitated for the unity of theory and practice.

56 Historians who read Collingwood generally fail to attend to *An Autobiography*; combined with their 'third attitude' prejudice for well-defined disciplinary boundaries,

this may explain why Collingwood's denials of historiographical autonomy have so often been overlooked. For example, the methodology for the history of political thought associated with Quentin Skinner, J. G. A. Pocock and several other historians was partly inspired by an 'autonomist' reading of Collingwood; see Skinner, 'Meaning and Understanding in the History of Ideas', *History and Theory*, VIII (1969), pp. 3–53. But when Pocock, for instance, wrote that intercourse between history and theory begets pseudo-history, so that, like owl and eagle, the two ought to 'stay out of each other's flight-paths', or, in another striking simile, that history and theory are like ships passing in the night between which information might be exchanged, but which are bound on radically different courses, he articulated a position in sharp opposition to Collingwood's; see Pocock, 'Political Theory, History, and Myth: A Salute to John Gunnell', *Annals of Scholarship*, I (1980), pp. 23, 24. It is a standard hermeneutic observation that interpreters find, in what they interpret, only those things that they are ready to see. In the present paper a Collingwood is shown for whom historians were not ready until now.

57 Collingwood, op. cit. (n. 49), pp. 282–302.
58 Ibid., p. 247 [my italics], 246.
59 Schlözer, op. cit. (n. 22), II, 'Vorbericht'.
60 Ranke, op. cit. (n. 25), p. 297.
61 American Historical Association, *Program of the One Hundred Seventh Annual Meeting, December 27–30, 1992, Washington, D.C.* (Washington, DC, 1992), p. 40.
62 F. R. Ankersmit, 'Historiography and Postmodernism', *History and Theory*, XXVIII (1989), p. 137.
63 Ibid., p. 149; for Ankersmit's reflections on 'the pull of the frame', and on 'notation', see his *The Reality Effect in the Writing of History: the Dynamics of Historiographical Topology* (Amsterdam, 1989), esp. pp. 27–30, 32. On the concept of notation, see Roland Barthes, 'The Reality Effect' (Fr. orig. 1974), *The Rustle of Language*, trans. Richard Howard (New York, 1984), pp. 141–2.
64 See especially Jacques Derrida, 'Différance', *Margins of Philosophy* (Fr. orig. 1972), trans. Alan Bass (Chicago, 1982), pp. 1–27. The notion of originary difference is distinct from the radical textualism that is sometimes – but I think mostly mistakenly – inferred from Derrida's writings.
65 See Nicholas Rescher, *The Strife of Systems: An Essay on the Grounds and Implications of Philosophical Diversity* (Pittsburgh, 1985), pp. xi, 276–7 and *passim*.
66 Mattei Dogan and Robert Pahre, *Creative Marginality: Innovation at the Intersections of Social Sciences* (Boulder, CO, 1990). See also Clifford Geertz, 'Blurred Genres: The Refiguration of Social Thought' (first pubd 1980), *Local Knowledge: Further Essays in Interpretive Anthropology* (New York, 1983), pp. 19–35. The term 'blurred genres' is potentially misleading, however, since 'blurring' might suggest lack of clarity and 'genre' that the change is simply a matter of *literary* mode.
67 Perhaps the central text – if 'central' is the appropriate term here – is Lyotard, op. cit. (n. 3). See also Allan Megill, 'What Does the Term "Postmodern" Mean?', *Annals of Scholarship*, VI (1989), pp. 129–51.
68 See, for example, the comments of a university administrator concerned with matters of tenure, promotion and review: 'We rarely recognize that "multicultural" tensions can be found not only in matters of ethnicity and race, but also between and among our disciplines. . . . I have been struck by how utterly distinct the world views of faculty members from different disciplines can be.' Raymond J. Rodrigues, 'Rethinking the Cultures of Disciplines', *Chronicle of Higher Education* (29 April 1992), pp. B1–2.
69 See, *inter alia*, Sharon Traweek, 'Border Crossings: Narrative Strategies in Science Studies and among Physicists in Tsukuba Science City, Japan', in Andrew Pickering,

ed., *Science as Practice and Culture* (Chicago, 1992), pp. 429–65. Traweek's theme of marginality, or the condition of being *bachigai* (out of place), is much larger than the title suggests; she offers an entire intellectual itinerary. On the epistemological benefits of concern with marginality, see Sandra Harding, 'After the Neutrality Ideal: Science, Politics, and "Strong Objectivity"', *Social Research* LIX (1992), pp. 567–87, esp. pp. 577–85.

70 Fernand Braudel, *The Mediterranean and the Mediterranean World in the Age of Philip II* (2/1966), trans. Siân Reynolds, 2 vols (New York, 1973), II, p. 1238.

71 So too does the vaunted third-attitude standard of autonomy. For if the autonomy of history is a value, why not 'the autonomy of intellectual history'?; see Krieger, 'The Autonomy of Intellectual History', *Journal of the History of Ideas*, XXXIV (1973), pp. 499–516. And if the autonomy of intellectual history is a value, why not the autonomy of all other histories, such as early modern French or late modern American?

72 As demonstrated by Hans Kellner, 'Disorderly Conduct: Braudel's Mediterranean Satire', *Language and Historical Representation: Getting the Story Crooked* (Madison, 1989), pp. 153–87.

73 Braudel, *Civilization and Capitalism: 15th–18th Century* (Fr. orig. 1979), trans. Siân Reynolds, 3 vols (New York, 1981–4).

74 Paul Veyne, *Writing History: Essay on Epistemology* (Fr. orig. 1971), trans. Mina Moore-Rinvolucri (Middletown, CT, 1984), p. 26: 'History with a capital H . . . does not exist. There only exist "histories of . . ."' (this is, of course, a reversal of what Koselleck, op. cit., n. 8, observed as happening in the late eighteenth century). See also Furet, whose move from 'narrative history' to 'problem-oriented history' was aimed at overcoming the present 'proliferation of histories'; see his *In the Workshop of History* (Fr. orig. 1982), trans. Jonathan Mandelbaum (Chicago, 1982), p. 16.

75 For the former, see William O. Aydelotte, Allan G. Bogue and Robert William Fogel, eds, *The Dimensions of Quantitative Research in History* (Princeton, 1972), esp. pp. 3–14; for the latter, Lynn Hunt, ed., *The New Cultural History* (Berkeley, 1989), esp. pp. 1–12.

76 See Novick, op. cit. (n. 6), p. 591 n. 20, discussing the University of Chicago History Department: 'At the University of Chicago . . . as of 1987 fully half of the members . . . also held appointments in other units of the university, and others were heavily involved in area studies programs without appointive powers. Yet for all this, the overwhelming majority would unhesitatingly and unequivocally identify themselves as historians, with other commitments relegated to a subordinate position.'

77 Here the work of Lyotard is suggestive: see op. cit. (n. 3), esp. sect. 13, 'Postmodern Science as the Search for Instabilities', pp. 53–60.

78 Consider the following announcement, from the University of Chicago: 'As of July 1 [1984], the departments of biochemistry and molecular biology and the department of molecular genetics and cell biology replaced the departments of microbiology, biochemistry, and biophysics and theoretical biology.' *University of Chicago Magazine*, VII (1984), pp. 3–4; quoted in Novick, op. cit. (n. 6), p. 585 n. 13). Common commitment to 'scientific method' makes it easier to move the locations of what are thus perceived as mere *internal* boundaries. See also Gérard Noiriel, 'Foucault and History: The Lessons of a Disillusion', *Journal of Modern History* LXVI (1994), p. 567.

79 T. S. Kuhn, *The Structure of Scientific Revolutions* (orig. edn, 1962; rev., enlarged, Chicago 2/1970). For another, more accessible hybrid work, see Geoffrey Hawthorn, *Plausible Worlds: Possibility and Understanding in History and the Social Sciences* (Cambridge, 1991).

80 Since the popularity of history has been raised as an issue, it is perhaps worth pointing out that *The Structure of Scientific Revolutions* has sold far more copies than any other

academic work by a historian in living memory, and more copies than all but a few 'popular' works of history. From its original publication on 5 March 1962 through January 1991 it sold 768,774 copies (I owe these data to Douglas Mitchell, sociology and history editor at the University of Chicago Press). Moreover, citation data give clear evidence that many scholars have actually *read* the book, at least in part.

81 Collingwood, op. cit. (n. 49), p. 246. He of course omits to note (see Hawthorn, op. cit., n. 79) that the historical world is accompanied by an infinite number of counterfactual – that is, fictional – ones.

82 See Hayden White, *Metahistory: The Historical Imagination in Nineteenth-Century Europe* (Baltimore, 1973); Stephen Bann, *The Clothing of Clio: A Study of the Representation of History in Nineteenth-Century Britain and France* (Cambridge, 1984); Hayden White, op. cit. (n.40); Kellner, op. cit. (n. 72); Philippe Carrard, *Poetics of the New History: French Historical Discourse from Braudel to Chartier* (Baltimore, 1992) and the essays of F. R. Ankersmit, especially 'The Dilemma of Contemporary Anglo-Saxon Philosophy of History', *History and Theory*, XXV (1986), pp. 1–27; 'The Use of Language in the Writing of History', in Hywell Coleman, ed., *Working with Language: A Multidisciplinary Consideration of Language Use in Work Contexts* (Berlin, 1989), pp. 57–81; and op. cit. (n. 62, n. 63).

83 See, for example, Jonathan D. Spence, *The Death of Woman Wang* (New York, 1978); Natalie Zemon Davis, *The Return of Martin Guerre* (Cambridge, MA, 1983); Davis, *Fiction in the Archives: Pardon Tales and their Tellers in Sixteenth-Century France* (Stanford, 1987); Robert A. Rosenstone, *Mirror in the Shrine: American Encounters with Meiji Japan* (Cambridge, MA, 1988); and David Farber, *Chicago '68* (Chicago, 1988).

84 The obvious example is Kuhn, op. cit. (n. 79). Bringing aid to theory was a conscious intent on Kuhn's part: 'History, if viewed as a repository for more than anecdote or chronology, could produce a decisive transformation in the image of science by which we are now possessed' (p. 1).

85 Herodotus, *The History*, trans. David Grene (Chicago, 1987), 1.32, pp. 47–8; 1.91, pp. 76–7; and 1.5, p. 35.

86 Ranke, op. cit. (n. 26), IV, p. 412: 'Geschichte beginnt mit Chronik und endigt mit Essay, das ist, in der Reflexion über die historischen Ereignisse, die dort besonders Anklang findet.' (Ranke appears to have used this passage as early as the Summer Semester 1853 offering of the course; I have not found the source.)

8 Robert F. Berkhofer, Jr.: A Point of View on Viewpoint in Historical Practice

1 I leave aside the presumptions in these questions about the mimetic reconstruction of the postulated past, since I am trying to represent what I think is a normal viewpoint of normal historians through what I believe is a typical voice. For an earlier version of my views, see 'The Challenge of Poetics to (Normal) Historical Practice', *Poetics Today*, IX/2 (1988), pp. 435–52.

2 'Great Story' is my coinage to designate the larger context of monographic histories or the overall interpretative context of general histories. Although metanarratives are always Great Stories, a Great Story need not be one of the classic metanarratives as defined by Jean-François Lyotard in his *The Postmodern Condition: A Report on Knowledge* (Fr. orig. 1979), trans. Geoff Bennington and Brian Massumi (Minneapolis, 1984). The supposed mimetic foundation postulated by most historians for the Great Story is what I term the Great Past. These terms are developed and applied in my book *Beyond the Great Story: History as Text and Discourse* (Cambridge, MA, 1995). This essay derives from sections of two chapters in that manuscript.

3 Voice and viewpoint apply to historical practice in two different ways: in reading a

272 *References*

historian's text; and in reading the historical sources themselves. I treat only the former here. The whole topic of voice and viewpoint in historical practice deserves its own book. The best we have about contemporary historical practice is Phillipe Carrard, *Poetics of the New History: French Historical Discourse from Braudel to Chartier* (Baltimore, 1992), parts 2–3. Good starting surveys of the subject in literary theory in English are Wallace Martin, *Recent Theories of Narrative* (Ithaca, 1986), chap. 6; Shlomith Rimmon-Kenan, *Narrative Fiction: Contemporary Poetics* (London, 1983), chaps 6–8; Mieke Bal, *Narratology: Introduction to the Theory of the Narrative* (Toronto, 1985), pp. 100–49; Paul Ricoeur, *Time and Narrative* (Fr. orig. 1984), vol. 2, trans. Kathleen McLaughlin and David Pellauer (Chicago, 1985), pp. 88–99. The following are more detailed studies: Seymour Chatman, *Coming to Terms: The Rhetoric of Narrative in Fiction and Film* (Ithaca, 1990) and *Story and Discourse: Narrative Structure in Fiction and Film* (Ithaca, 1978); Boris Uspensky, *A Poetics of Composition: The Structure of the Artistic Text and Typology of a Compositional Form* (Russ. orig. 1970), trans. Valentina Zavarin and Susan Wittig (Berkeley, 1973); and Susan Sniader Lanser, *The Narrative Act: Point of View in Prose Fiction* (Princeton, 1981).

4 Quoted in *The Varieties of History: From Voltaire to the Present*, ed. Fritz Stern (New York, 1956), p. 25.

5 Savoie Lottinville, *The Rhetoric of History* (Norman, OK, 1976), p. 104. See Carrard, op. cit. (n. 3), p. 23, for earlier French advice to the same effect.

6 Carlo Ginzburg, *The Cheese and the Worms: The Cosmos of a Sixteenth-Century Miller* (orig. 1976), trans. John and Anne Tedeschi (Baltimore, 1980), offers an interesting example of various approaches to actors' voices as well as his own, but see Renato Rosaldo, 'From the Door of his Tent: The Fieldworker and the Inquisition', in *Writing Culture: The Poetics and Politics of Ethnography*, ed. James Clifford and George E. Marcus (Berkeley, 1986), pp. 77–97, for a critique of the inquisitorial source of those voices. Ginzburg replies to this criticism in 'The Inquisitor as Anthropologist', in his *Clues, Myths, and Historical Method* (orig. 1986), trans. John and Anne Tedeschi (Baltimore, 1989).

7 Ricoeur, op. cit. (n. 3), 11, p. 99.

8 Lottinville, op. cit., p. 104.

9 See Norman Friedman, *Form and Meaning in Fiction* (Athens, GA, 1975), pp. 145–50, 153–6, on types of omniscience in novels. Narrative theorists dispute whether to call perspective 'viewpoint', 'focalization' or another term. See 'Point of View' and 'Focalization' in Gerard Prince, *A Dictionary of Narratology* (Lincoln, NE), pp. 31–2, 73–6. See Chatman (n. 3) for new terms to distinguish between narrator and character perspectives (*Coming to Terms*, chap. 9). Carrard, op. cit. (n. 3), uses the term 'focalization' but entitles the relevant section 'Perspective', pp. 104–21. What those advocating viewpoint call 'omniscience' becomes 'zero focalization' under the other terminology. Elizabeth Deeds Ermarth, *Realism and Consensus in the English Novel* (Princeton, 1983), chap. 3, eschews 'point of view' as too bound to a notion of individual consciousness; she prefers 'perspective' to designate the supposedly faceless, omniscient narrator conventional to realism in literature.

10 This plane or level and the following three are derived from combining Chatman, *Story and Discourse*, pp. 151–2; Uspensky, op. cit. (n. 3); Roger Fowler, *Linguistic Criticism* (Oxford, 1986), chap. 9. I leave out the phraseological plane of Uspensky and Fowler. Other systems are proposed by Prince, op. cit. (n. 9), pp. 31–2, 73–6; Rimmon-Kennon, op. cit (n. 3), chaps 6–8; and Lanser, op. cit. (n. 3). Friedman, op. cit. (n. 9), pp. 134–42, offers a brief history of the idea of point of view as an explicit concept.

11 Uspensky, op. cit. (n. 3), uses the term 'birds-eye view' but 'panoramic' and 'synoptic' are my terms and not those of literary theorists. For a repudiation of the whole

'visualist ideology' associated with traditional approaches to point of view, see Stephen A. Tyler, 'Post-Modern Ethnography: From Document of the Occult to Occult Document', in *Writing Culture: The Poetics and Politics of Ethnography*, ed. James Clifford and George E. Marcus (Berkeley, 1986), esp. pp. 130–1.

12 Such would seem a major contention of the 'rhetoric of inquiry' movement, for which see *The Rhetoric of the Human Sciences: Language and Argument in Scholarship and Public Affairs*, ed. John S. Nelson, Allan Megill and Donald S. McCloskey (Madison, 1987). Compare Christopher Lloyd, *Explanation in Social History* (Oxford, 1986).

13 The defining of ideology and hegemony is its own intellectual industry today, an industry that illustrates all too well the relationship between viewpoints and political interests and how they issue forth in conflicting theories and competing languages and definitions. One guide to recent theorists of ideology is offered by John B. Thompson, *Studies in the Theory of Ideology* (Berkeley, 1984), but see his own attempt to theorize the field: *Ideology and Modern Culture: Critical Social Theory in the Era of Mass Communication* (Cambridge, 1990). Ernesto Laclau and Chantal Mouffe, *Hegemony and Socialist Strategy: Towards a Democratic Politics* (London, 1985), chap. 1, provide what they term a 'genealogy' of the concept. See also Michèle Barrett, *The Politics of Truth: From Marx to Foucault* (Cambridge, 1991).

14 For two important statements on both the advantages and limits of self-referential experience as the basis for multicultural history, see Ruth Roach Pierson, 'Experience, Difference, Dominance and Voice in the Writing of Canadian Women's History' in *Writing Women's History: International Perspectives*, ed. Karen Offen, Ruth Roach Pierson and Jane Randall (Bloomington, 1991), pp. 79–106; and Joan W. Scott, 'The Evidence of Experience', *Critical Inquiry*, xvii (1991), pp. 773–97.

15 F. R. Ankersmit, *Narrative Logic: A Semantic Analysis of the Historian's Language* (The Hague, 1983), pp. 216–24, argues the crucial importance of point of view to constructing what he calls the 'narratio', but he does not distinguish its many aspects. See also his concept of the 'frame' in his *The Reality Effect in the Writing of History: The Dynamics of Historiographical Topology* (Amsterdam, 1989), p. 24.

16 Paula Rothenberg under the headline 'Critics of Attempts to Democratize the Curriculum are Waging a Campaign to Misrepresent the Work of Responsible Professors', *Chronicle of Higher Education*, xxxvii/30 (10 April 1991), p. B3.

17 My emphasis. That such documents are not self-interpreting lies at the centre of the original intent argument about what the founding fathers meant in the Constitution, for which see Jack N. Rakove, ed., *Interpreting the Constitution: The Debate over Original Intent* (Boston, 1990).

18 Grand Narratives, or what I call Great Stories, matter greatly, because they establish the larger context of monographic histories and historical context of interpretations of the past itself. Thus they become the explicit battleground for multiculturalist claims for the revision of history in the classroom and in professional discourse. Who gets to be the Great Story-teller and from whose viewpoint is the Great Story told are the questions around which multiculturalist debates over Afro-centrism or whether to frame the 500th anniversary of Columbus' navigational feat as discovery, invasion, encounter, genocide, collision or other general noun.

Of the multitudinous studies of Turner's ideas, see the rhetorical analysis of Ronald H. Carpenter, *The Eloquence of Frederick Jackson Turner* (San Marino, CA, 1983); and William Cronon, 'Revisiting the Vanishing Frontier: The Legacy of Frederick Jackson Turner', *Western Historical Quarterly*, xviii (1987), 157–76, and 'Turner's First Stand: The Significance of Significance in American History', in *Writing Western History: Essays on Major Western Historians*, ed. Richard Etalain (Albuquerque, 1991), pp. 73–101.

19 (New York, 1987), p. 25. Further references to this book are parenthesized in the text.

20 Will some historian in the future write a book about Limerick's version of the West as a summation of the mythology of her time, as Henry Nash Smith did about Turner's West? See *Virgin Land: The American West as Symbol and Myth* (Cambridge, MA, 1950, 2/1970). That the new Western history presumes the Great Story of the expansion of European economies and nation-states on the 'American frontier' is even more explicit in William Cronon, George Miles and Jay Gitlin, eds, *Under an Open Sky: Rethinking America's Western Past* (New York, 1992), for example, pp. 8–10.

21 Should she have put these histories in the plural to show conflicts and different viewpoints within each group?

22 Compare the analogy of James Clifford, *The Predicament of Culture: Twentieth-Century Ethnography, Literature, and Art* (Cambridge, MA, 1988), p. 22: Observers should 'dislodge the ground from which persons and groups securely represent others. A conceptual shift, "tectonic" in its implications, has taken place. We ground things, now, on a moving earth. There is no longer any place of overview (mountaintop) from which to map human ways of life, no Archimedean point from which to represent the world. Mountains are in constant motion. So are islands: for one cannot occupy, unambiguously, a bounded cultural world from which to journey out and analyze other cultures.'

23 Wallace Stegner, 'On the Writing of History', in *Sound of Mountain Water* (Garden City, NY, 1969), p. 20.

24 Baltimore, 1990.

25 Baltimore, 1983.

26 Michael Craton in *William and Mary Quarterly*, n.s. 3 XLIX (1992), pp. 697–703, offers a critical but sympathetic review from this standpoint.

27 Talal Assad, 'The Concept of Cultural Translation in British Social Anthropology', in Clifford and Marcus, op. cit. (n. 11), esp. pp. 156–63, argues that translation imposes the viewpoint as well as the voice of the self on the other as a part of the power of imperialist language, because a language is both an orientation to the world and a mode of thought.

28 Of the many books on postmodern narrative, particularly pertinent for the historian is Linda Hutcheon, *A Poetics of Postmodernism: History, Theory, and Fiction* (New York and London, 1988). Comments germane to a postmodernist approach to voice and viewpoint are scattered throughout Elizabeth Deeds Ermarth, *Sequel to History: Postmodernism and the Crisis of Time* (Princeton, 1992).

9 *Stephen Bann: History as Competence and Performance: Notes on the Ironic Museum*

1 Quoted in P. de Barante, *Souvenirs* (Paris, 1890–97), III, p. 248.

2 A. Riegl, 'The Modern Cult of Monuments: Its Character and its Origin', trans. K. W. Forster and D. Ghirardo, *Oppositions* XXV (1982), p. 33.

3 For Ranke's Preface, see Fritz Stern (ed.), *The Varieties of History: From Voltaire to the Present* (London, 1970), pp. 55–8; for Thierry's, see A. Thierry, *History of the Conquest of England by the Normans*, trans. W. Hazlitt (London, 1856), pp. xvxx. These statements are discussed further, in the context of other contemporary examples, in S. Bann, *Romanticism and the Rise of History* (New York, 1995), pp. 3–29. A number of other themes implicit in this essay are also developed there.

4 See H. White, 'The Value of Narrativity in the Representation of Reality', in *The Content of the Form: Narrative Discourse and Historical Representation* (Baltimore, 1987), pp. 1–25. See also H. White, *Metahistory: The Historical Imagination in Nineteenth-Century Europe* (Baltimore, 1973).

5 Nietzsche, *Use and Abuse of History*, trans. A. Collins (Indianapolis, 1978). The essay was originally published in 1873.

6 See S. Bann, *The Inventions of History: Essays on the Representation of the Past* (Manchester, 1990), pp. 100–21.

7 D. Sperber, 'Rudiments of rhétorique cognitive', *Poétique*, XXIII (1975), p. 415 (my translation).

8 See S. Bann, *The Clothing of Clio: A Study of the Representation of History in Nineteenth-Century Britain and France* (Cambridge, 1984), pp. 112–37.

9 J. Crary, *Techniques of the Observer: On Vision and Modernity in the Nineteenth Century* (Cambridge, MA, 1990), p. 128.

10 For the history of the Galerie David d'Angers, and the visual representations referred to here, see the excellent catalogue of the Musées d'Angers, *Galerie David d'Angers*, with texts by Viviane Huchard and Pierre David (Angers, 1989). For a timely reconsideration of David d'Angers' achievement, see Jacques de Caso, *David d'Angers: Sculptural Communication in the Age of Romanticism*, trans. Dorothy Johnson and Jacques de Caso (Princeton, 1992).

11 The 26-volume *Voyages pittoresques et romantiques dans l'Ancienne France*, begun by Isadore Taylor, Charles Nodier and Alexandre de Cailleux, were published in Paris from April 1820 onwards. They have been called 'arguably the most influential illustrated publication of the nineteenth century' in Patrick Noon, *Richard Parkes Bonnington: On the Pleasure of Painting* (New Haven and London, 1991), p. 22.

12 *Galerie David d'Angers*, (n. 10) p. 12.

13 Ibid., p. 34.

14 Ibid., p. 14.

15 See Bann, op. cit. (n. 6), p. 193.

16 See Bann, op. cit. (n. 8), p. 28.

17 Robert Hewison, *The Heritage Industry: Britain in a Climate of Decline* (London, 1987), p. 160.

18 See Bernard Lassus, *Le Jardin des Tuileries* (London, 1991). Lassus's text on Duisburg-Nord, from which the quotes in this essay are drawn, is published in my translation in 'The Landscape Approach of Bernard Lassus II', *Journal of Garden History*, XV, 2 (1995), pp. 67–106.

10 F. R. Ankersmit: Statements, Texts and Pictures

1 Thus Mitchell sums up Goodman's findings. See W. J. T. Mitchell, *Iconology: Image, Text, Ideology* (Chicago, 1986), p. 69.

2 H. V. White, *Metahistory: The Historical Imagination in Nineteenth-Century Europe* (Baltimore, 1973), p. 2.

3 Thus S. Kohl's authoritative *Realismus: Theorie und Geschichte* (Munich, 1977) fails to mention a single prominent philosopher of history. An exception to this rule – the lack of interest in the study of history among literary critics – is Roland Barthes' essay on the reality effect in the historical text. Also there is Auerbach's brief note on historism in his *Mimesis: The Representation of Reality in Western Literature* (Princeton, 1974), pp. 443–8. But both authors are concerned with the literariness of the study of history rather than with the historicity of the literary representation of reality.

4 Plato, *Cratylus*, trans. H. N. Fowler (Cambridge, MA, 1970), p. 137.

5 Ibid., p. 139.

6 *Lessings Laokoon* (orig. 1766), ed. R. Gosche (Berlin, 1876), p. 141.

7 Mitchell, op. cit., p. 99.

8 H. Jensen, *Sign, Symbol and Script: An Account of Man's Efforts to Write* (London, 1970), p. 32.

9 Ibid., pp. 40, 41.

10 Ibid., p. 51.

11 Plato, op. cit., p. 173.

12 Ibid., pp. 173–4.

13 'The nature of gentlemen like you/Can often be guessed from your names'. W. Goethe, *Goethes sämtliche Werke: Jubiläum-Ausgabe*, XIII (Stuttgart and Berlin, n.d.), p. 54.

14 M. Foucault, *Les Mots et les choses* (Paris, 1966), p. 50; trans. as *the Order of Things* (New York, 1970), p. 35.

15 H. Ishiguro, *Leibniz's Philosophy of Logic and Language* (London, 1972), p. 12.

16 N. Goodman, *Languages of Art* (Indiana, 1985), p. 5. See also his *Ways of Worldmaking* (Hassocks, 1978), pp. 130, 131.

17 Goodman defines his tolerance threshold with regard to resemblance as follows: 'to Beardsley's proposal to distinguish depiction – or what we usually consider to be "naturalistic" or "realistic" representation – in terms of resemblance between picture and depicted, I have little objection as long as we bear in mind that resemblance is a variable and relative matter that as much follows as guides customs of reprsentation.' See N. Goodman, *Of Mind and other Matters* (Cambridge, MA, 1984), pp. 80, 81.

18 See Goodman, *Mind*, pp. 126–30; Goodman also relates realism to the depiction of non-fictional objects and, next, to the originality of the representation, which makes for a 'new' insight.

19 Goodman, *Languages*, p. 38.

20 Ibid., p. 137.

21 Ibid., pp. 130ff.

22 Ibid., p. 229.

23 Ibid., pp. 230, 231.

24 See, for instance, Goodman's reaction to the objections of R. Rudner in *Mind*, pp. 94ff.

25 Goodman, *Mind*, pp. 109–22.

26 See F. R. Ankersmit, *Narrative Logic* (The Hague; 1983), pp. 134–50; see 'Reply to Professor Zagorin', *History and Theory*, XXIX (1990), pp. 279, 280.

27 Ankersmit, *Narrative Logic*, p. 146.

28 Ibid., p. 159.

29 F. Schier, *Deeper into Pictures* (Cambridge, 1986), p. 118.

30 Ankersmit, *Narrative Logic*, pp. 140–55.

31 Goodman, *Ways of Worldmaking*, p. 131.

32 J. G. Bennett, 'Depiction and Convention', *The Monist*, LVIII (1974), pp. 259–69.

33 Cited in N. Wolterstorff, *Works and Worlds of Art* (Oxford, 1980), p. 271.

34 Ibid., pp. 276, 277.

35 J. Locke, *An Essay Concerning Human Understanding* (London, 1690), ed. J. W. Yolton (London, 1972), I, p. 109.

36 Cited in Mitchell, op. cit. (n. 1), p. 66.

37 Schier, op. cit. (n. 29), p. 183.

38 Ibid., pp. 186ff.

39 Compare the first and second editions of R. Wollheim, *Art and its Objects* (New York, 1968 and 1980).

40 K. L. Walton, *Mimesis as Make-Believe: On the Foundation of the Representational Arts* (Cambridge, MA, 1990), p. 37.

41 N. Struever, *The Language of History in the Renaissance* (Princeton, 1971), pp. 118.

42 See F. R. Ankersmit, 'Tocqueville and the Sublimity of Democracy', *Tocqueville Review*, XIV (1993), pp. 173–201; XV (1994), pp. 193–218.

43 H. Kellner, 'Disorderly Conduct: Braudel's Mediterranean Satire', *Language and Historical Representation* (Madison, 1989), p. 161.

44 Ibid., pp. 166ff.

45 See, for instance, Goodman, *Ways of Worldmaking*, pp. 24–7.

46 H. V. White, *The Content of the Form* (Baltimore, 1987), p. 87.
47 G. L., Comte de Buffon, 'Discours sur le style', in A. Vinet, *Chrestomathie* (Lausanne, 1978), III, p.157.
48 Goodman, *Languages*, p. 85.
49 Ibid., p. 63.
50 Ankersmit, *Narrative Logic*, pp. 19–27.
51 M. Aldanov, *De negende Thermidor* (Zutphen, 1930).

Bibliographical Essay

As a reorientation of historical theory, 'the new philosophy of history' has several roots. Reorientation in a discipline normally requires in the first place a restructuring of its affiliations with other related disciplines. Part of this bibliographical essay consists, therefore, of an enumeration of works from related disciplines that have proven to be of significance for historical theory. Second, a reorientation in a discipline always entails a different assessment of its past and of the theorists who ought to be seen as determining the discipline's history. Hence, this bibliographical essay also mentions several books of less recent date that have obtained a new and different influence with the coming into being of 'the new philosophy of history'.

The first book that must be mentioned as exemplifying such a different view of the history of historical theory is J. G. Droysen's *Historik* (Munich, 1971). Two aspects of this book, the first sketch of which dates back to 1870, require mention here. First, in what he referred to as 'der erste grosse Fundamentalsatz', Droysen argues that the historical text could never be seen as a simple mimesis or reflection of the past 'as it has actually been' since we can never compare the text to the past itself. The historical text is a 'construction' of the past, based on the evidence that we presently possess and not a 'reconstruction' of the past. A similar observation can be found in Friedrich Nietzsche's *Vom Nutzen und Nachtheil der Historie für das Leben* (Stuttgart, 1970) – though Nietzsche, in contrast to Droysen, does not present this insight as propaedeutic for a proper attitude towards historical writing, but rather as an irremediable defect that can be overcome only by focusing on 'das Ueberzeitliche' as we mainly find it in the beauty of the work of art. Here Nietzsche was undoubtedly inspired by Jakob Burckhardt, at the time his colleague in Basle. But, though Droysen openly embraced what Nietzsche saw as the fundamental flaw of all historical writing, both men recognized the autonomy of historical writing with regard to the past itself. And this recognition is certainly of fundamental importance for 'the new philosophy of history'. Droysen elaborated the consequences of this insight for historical writing in the section on 'Topik' in his *Historik*. He argued that there are constraints upon the presentation of the past that do not have their origin in the past itself but in the nature and the aims of the historical text as such.

Droysen's *Historik* has been most fully analysed in Jörn Rüsen's *Begriffene Geschichte: Genesis und Begründung der Geschichtstheorie J. G. Droysens* (Paderborn, 1969). Rüsen presents us here with a Droysen whose theoretical position is in many ways remarkably similar to the one that was defended in H. G. Gadamer's *Wahrheit und Methode* (Tübingen, 1960). Moreover, the aestheticist propensities of Droysen's 'Topik' have their counterpart in the way Gadamer investigates the hermeneutic experience of the past within the context of aesthetic experience as such. Both Droysen and Gadamer develop their positions against the background of German historism (not to be confused with its near opposite: Popperian historicism). The historist antecedents of the aestheticism of 'the new philosophy of history' can therefore best be traced in their work and the discussions provoked by it. The aestheticist dimensions of Ranke, who is customarily seen as the founder of German historism, was expounded in Rüsen's 'Rhetorics and Aesthetics of History: Leopold von Ranke', *History and Theory*, XXIX (1990), pp. 190–204. For an account of the historist tradition and for the relevant bibliographical information, see F. Jaeger and J. Rüsen, *Geschichte des Historismus* (Munich, 1992). Rüsen's own position with regard to 'the new philosophy of history' can best be understood from his *Studies in Metahistory* (Pretoria, 1993) and from Allan Megill's 'Jörn Rüsen's Theory of Historiography between Modernism and Rhetoric of Inquiry', *History and Theory*, XXX (1994), pp. 39–61.

Droysen's 'erster Fundamentalsatz' was echoed in Michael Oakeshott's *Experience and its Modes* (Cambridge, 1933) and in L. J. Goldstein's *Historical Knowing* (London, 1976). Both argued, like Droysen, that the past itself is no ingredient in the process of obtaining historical knowledge. We have only the evidence that the past has left us and it is the historian's duty to develop the most plausible hypothesis about the nature of the past on the basis of this evidence. And both agreed with Droysen that this implied the autonomy of the historical text with regard to the past. It is striking that Goldstein recoiled from the unexpected importance that was thus granted to the text: Goldstein attempted to evade the revolutionary implications of his constructivism by focussing exclusively on what he referred to as the 'infrastructure' of historical writing. This 'infrastructure' corresponds, mainly, to the phase in historical research in which the historian acquires the kind of knowledge of the past that can be expressed by separate statements about the past (either constative or causal). He dismissed the 'superstructure', on the text itself, as mere icing of the cake of 'infrastructure'. For a discussion of Goldstein's views, see *History and Theory* (*Beiheft*, 1978).

This attitude changed with Peter Munz's *The Shape of the Past* (Middletown, CT, 1978); Munz rephrased the constructivist argument with the help of the following memorable metaphor about the nature of historical narrative: 'but the ineluctable truth is that there is no face behind the mask [i.e. historical narrative (F.A.)] and that the belief that there is one is an unsupportable allegation. For any record that we could have of the face would be, precisely, another mask.' And, though by a different route, namely a criticism of the Humean notion of causality, Haskell Fain reached roughly the same conclusion in his *Between Philosophy and History* (Princeton, 1970). Both Munz and Fain developed the constructivist thesis into a cautious rehabilitation of speculative philosophy that was almost universally condemned as a metaphysical delusion in the heyday of critical philosophy of history of the 1950s and 1960s. Their argument was that the 'super-structure' of historical writing, to use Goldstein's terminology, since it could not be determined by the past 'an sich', necessarily had to rely upon the models that had been proposed by the constructors of the great speculative systems. It is these models that guide historians in their efforts to arrange the results of historical research into a meaningful, narrative whole. And, indeed, there has been since then a modest increase in the interest for speculative systems.

The disadvantage of their position was, needless to say, that these speculative systems tended to operate like a Procrustean bed and could not account for the variety of historical narrative. The first study in which these disadvantages were spelt out was A. C. Danto's *Analytical Philosophy of History* (Cambridge, 1965). An enlarged and revised version of this most influential book appeared under the title *Narration and Knowledge* (New York, 1985) and has been translated into several languages. Danto offered here, among other things, an analysis of what he referred to as the 'narrative sentence' and that would be the point of departure for many later discussions. Danto argued that the historical text typically consists of 'narrative sentences' and that this type of sentence always describes the past while implying, at the same time, a reference to the point of view of the historian. This going together of description and implicit reference to point of view amounted to a rejection of traditional critical philosophy of history that was exclusively interested in description. Danto's book can therefore well be seen as the watershed between the traditional and 'the new philosophy of history'. It should be added, by the way, that Danto's no less influential *The Transfiguration of the Commonplace* (Cambridge, MA, 1983) developed an analysis of the nature of the work of art that is also quite interesting from the point of view of an aestheticist historical theory.

A further development in the analysis of the nature of historical narrative can be found in the essays written by Louis O. Mink (collected in *Historical Understanding*, ed. B. Fay, E. Golob and R. Vann, Ithaca, 1987); these may still be considered among the best philosophical frameworks for the theoretical implications of 'the new philosophy of history'. Like the constructivists, Mink argued that there is no 'untold story' in the past itself, but, unlike Munz and Fain, he did not rely upon speculative systems for an explication of the nature of historical narrative. Instead Mink investigated 'the modes of comprehension' that make historical narratives into what they are. He thus tried to define the logical properties of historical narrative. One of Mink's best essays (together with, among others, one by L. Gossman) was originally published in *The Writing of History: Literary Theory and Historical Understanding*, ed. R. Canary and H. Kozicki (Madison, 1978). For an exposition of Mink's historical theory, see R. T. Vann, 'Louis Mink's Linguistic Turn', *History and Theory*, XXVI (1987), pp. 1–14. This effort to identify the logical structure of narrative was continued in F. R. Ankersmit's *Narrative Logic* (The Hague, 1983). The notion of 'narrative substance' was introduced here as a logical entity beside the subject and the predicate terms of statements in order to develop a philosophical logic (in the sense meant by Strawson) for historical narrative. Though Leibniz's monadology was Ankersmit's main source of inspiration, his argument about the 'narrative substance' came close to views that had been proposed by Walsh and Gallie. Ankersmit elaborated these views and placed them within the wider context of twentieth-century historical theory in *Denken over geschiedenis* (Groningen, 1986) and *De navel van de geschiedenis* (Groningen, 1990).

In his influential (and still surprisingly fresh) *Introduction to Philosophy of History* (London, 1965), W. Walsh introduced the notion of the 'colligatory concept' (the term was derived from the work of the nineteenth-century logician W. Whewell) to suggest that historians propose concepts like 'the Renaissance' or 'the Cold War' in order to 'colligate' a maximum variety of historical phenomena within one (explanatory) notion. A first step in elucidating the behaviour of such concepts – baptized 'essentially contested concepts' – was made by W. B. Gallie in his *Philosophy and the Historical Understanding* (New York, 1964). A further elaboration of the consequences of constructivism along the lines suggested above can be found in the writings of Allan Megill. Megill wrote a brilliant book on the origins of contemporary deconstructivism – *Prophets of Extremity* (Berkeley, 1985) – but then turned to an analysis of historical writing taking the self-interpretation of historians more seriously than the high-handed approach of the deconstructivists would ever be prepared to do. His essays 'Recounting the Past: Description, Explanation and Narrative in Historiography', *American Historical Review*, XCIV/3 (1989), and 'Four Senses of Objectivity', *Annals of Scholarship*, 8 (1991), have been most successful in reinvigorating the debate between historians and historical theorists.

But far more influential and successful than any of these has been the work of Hayden White, whom one might well see as the progenitor of 'the new philosophy of history'. The classic text is his *Metahistory: The Historical Imagination in Nineteenth-Century Europe* (Baltimore, 1973). White detailed his views in two collections of essays, namely *Tropics of Discourse* (Baltimore, 1978) and *The Content of the Form* (Baltimore, 1987). He requires us to consider the historical text as what it most manifestly is, that is, as 'a verbal artefact'. When characterizing historical writing in this way, White accepts constructivism more consistently than was ever done before him: he emphasizes that historical insight as expressed in historical narrative is not so much 'found' (as the objectivist historian believes) as 'made' (in the way the artist produces his work of art). But of even greater importance is that White went far beyond efforts to model historical narrative on speculative philosophies or to define the logical properties of narrative; he succeeded in giving to 'the new philosophy of history' a research programme that would inspire a great number of historical theorists after him. For *Metahistory* – and especially its introduction – not only assumed a different position on the kind of topics that used to be discussed in (critical) philosophy; it also provided a discourse for framing and considering these topics. White's appeal, in the main part of the book, was to literary theory in order to come to a better understanding and a more fruitful analysis of the historian's text. Though White's literary apparatus was initially strongly based on Vico's theory of the tropes, his approach invited the use of other instruments borrowed from literary theory. And White has been the first to exploit systematically these possibilities.

A combination of a careful analysis of White's historical theory, a further development of White's conceptions and an application of tropology to new subjects can be found in Hans Kellner's *Language and Historical Representation: Getting the Story Crooked* (Madison, 1989). Only if 'we get the story crooked' can we become aware of the thing-like nature, or the 'substantiality' of the historical text and only then can the secrets of the text be revealed to us. Kellner has extended White's insights to contemporary historical writing as in the case of Braudel. The whole issue of *Storia della storiografia*, 24 (1993) is devoted to a discussion of White's views and their impact on contemporary historical theory. White has often been associated with postmodernism (for example, by Christopher Norris); in opposition to this (profoundly mistaken) view Kellner emphasizes the modernist and structuralist character of White's tropology in his essay 'Hayden White and the Kantian Discourse', in *The Philosophy of Discourse*, ed. C. Sills and C. Jensen (Portsmouth, 1992). For a postmodernist interpretation of 'the new philosophy of history', see L. Hutcheon, *A Poetics of Postmodernism: History, Theory, Fiction* (London, 1988); truth, reference, mimesis – all that historical writing used to strive for since the days of Thucydides – succumb here ingloriously to the pressure and presuppositions of literary theory.

The main consequence of White's redefinition of the nature and the tasks of historical theory has been that it now has all but lost the abstract, apriorist character that it used to share with philosophy (of science); historical theory gradually became a new and highly sophisticated form of historiography (i.e. the history of historical writing). Formerly historiographers concentrated on questions of influence and political bias; with and after White interest focussed on the peculiarities of their texts and this resulted in a hitherto unparalleled deepening of our understanding of the great historical texts, past and present. It must be emphasized, however, that White has not been the only one to promote this reorientation of historical theory.

A first specimen of this new kind of historical theory could be found in Roland Barthes' *Michelet par lui-même* (Paris, 1954). Mention should also be made here of his no less perceptive essays, written in 1974 and collected in *Le Bruissement de la langue* (Paris, 1984; trans. R. Howard as *The Rustle of Language*, New York, 1986). Barthes' oeuvre has been more influential in historical theory than that of other French theorists, such as Paul Veyne's *Comment on écrit l'histoire: Essai d'épistémologie* (Paris, 1971; trans. Middletown, CT, 1984) – where the story-telling character of historical narrative is presented as a matter of course – or M. de Certeau's *The Writing of History* (New York, 1988). Barthes has deeply influenced Lionel Gossman, as in *Between History and Literature* (Cambridge, MA, 1990); Gossman's readings of Michelet and Augustin Thierry must be reckoned among the finest and most convincing examples of the approach to historical theory advocated within 'the new philosophy of history'. Part of the subtlety of Gossman's reading originates in his extreme tact and prudence when making use of the instruments of literary theory (see for this, especially, the final chapter of the book).

Derrida is very much present in the work of Dominick LaCapra, notably in his *History and Criticism* (Ithaca, 1985), *Rethinking Intellectual History: Texts, Contexts, Language* (Ithaca, 1983) and in the volume that he edited with S. Kaplan, *Modern European Intellectual History: Reappraisals and New Perspectives* (Ithaca, 1983). It should be added, though, that LaCapra has always remained as much a literary as a historical theorist.

Among French theorists, the significance of Foucault for 'the new philosophy of history' is certainly not negligible – one need only think of White's fascination with his writings. Nevertheless, his impact on historians has probably been greater than on historical theory. Theoretical debate, however, has been much stimulated by Ricoeur's most influential *Time and Narrative*, trans. Kathleen McLaughlin and David Pellauer (Chicago, 1984–8); in this trilogy historical writing, the novel, literary theory and the relevant philosophical traditions since Aristotle are discussed from a predominantly phenomenological point of view. Conclusions quite similar to those reached by Ricoeur can be found in D. Carr, *Time, Narrative and History* (Bloomington, 1986) that was likewise informed by phenomenology. Both Ricoeur and Carr argue for a continuity of the life-world and historical interpretation. Both studies embody, therefore, a challenge to the thesis of the autonomy of historical narrative that has been, since the constructivist argument, one of the pillars of 'the new philosophy of history'. Few theorists, if any, are more agile and surprising in their approach to historical texts, have a better command of literary and aesthetic theories and apply them in a more restrained and careful manner to such an amazing variety of subject matters than Stephen Bann. Here historical theory shades off into what one might call historiographical connoisseurship; each of Bann's analyses are as surprising as their subjects, as is especially evident in his *The Clothing of Clio* (Cambridge, 1984) and *The Inventions of History: Essays on the Representation of the Past* (Manchester, 1990).

The reorientation of historical theory towards historiography has resulted in a new reading of Romantic historical writing. Illustrative are Linda Orr's *Jules Michelet: Nature, History and Language* (Ithaca, 1976) and *Headless History: Nineteenth-Century French Historiography of the Revolution* (Ithaca, 1990), in which the writings of Michelet, Blanc, Quinet and Tocqueville are investigated with the help of a wide variety of instruments borrowed from literary theory. Another study devoted to early nineteenth-century histories of the French Revolution is Ann Rigney's *The Rhetoric of Historical Representation* (Cambridge, 1990). Both the title and the method adopted in this book testify to the rehabilitation of rhetoric within 'the new philosophy of history' that N. Struever had already argued for in *The Language of History in the Renaissance* (Princeton, 1970). In this study, which one may well see as one of the first examples of 'the new philosophy of history', Struever analysed the work of three humanist Florentine historians and defended the view that history and politics share with rhetoric a concentration not on the realm of absolute truth (the world of philosophy and science) but on the sphere of 'the intermediate and the relative'. Rhetoric is thus presented as the natural vehicle for all historical insight and the rhetorics of the text ought, therefore, to be the main focus of historiography. Tocqueville's 'rhetoric' and tropology was analysed by L. Shiner in *The Secret Mirror: Literary Form and History in Tocqueville's Recollections* (Ithaca, 1988) and by Ankersmit in 'Tocqueville and the Sublimity of Democracy', *Tocqueville Review*, XIV (1993), pp. 173–201 and XV (1994), pp. 193–218. Important contributions to the revival of rhetoric in the study of historical texts have been made by Nancy Partner in her 'Making up Lost Time: Writing on the Writing of History', *Speculum*, 61 (1986), pp. 90–117 and 'The New Cornificius: Mediaeval History and the Artifice of Words', in *Classical Rhetoric and Mediaeval Historiography*, ed. E. Breisach (Kalamazoo, 1985), and by Linda Orr in 'The Revenge of Literature: A History of History', *New Literary History* (1986), pp. 1–22.

The fascination of the historiography inspired by 'the new philosophy of history' for

Romantic historiography is, in fact, surprising. For if we recall the origins that 'the new philosophy of history' has in structuralism and closely related theories of the text, one would have expected it to have much more affinity with the kind of well-structured and disciplined historical writing that came into being in most European countries in the course of the last quarter of the last century. Further, it might seem that Romantic historical writing, with its outright acceptance of the presence of the historian's self in his writing, would necessarily escape structuralist analysis. The paradox is reinforced by the fact that the recent interest for these later, 'structuralist' phases in the history of historical writing comes into being when few theorists would still be prepared to describe themselves without qualification as being a structuralist. Especially illustrative in this context is Philippe Carrard's *Poetics of the New History: French Historical Discourse from Braudel to Chartier* (Baltimore, 1992), where the 'poetic' dimensions of (and especially the presence of the subject) in one of the most scientistically minded variants of twentieth-century historical writing are demonstrated. As was the case twenty years ago, Hayden White best exemplifies this new development in 'the new philosophy of history'. In his essay 'Historical Emplotment and the Problem of Truth', in S. Friedlander, *Probing the Limits of Representation* (Cambridge, MA, 1992), White elaborated suggestions by Barthes and Berel Lang (to be found in Lang, *Act and Idea in the Nazi-genocide*, Chicago, 1990), about so-called 'intransitive writing'. This is a form of literary or historical writing in which the author 'writes himself', just as the neurotic 'speaks himself' in psychoanalysis and where, therefore, the self of the historian obtains a hitherto unparalleled predominance. Categories like '(collective) memory' (cf. the writings of M. Halbwachs), experience, consciousness, trauma, testimony and the 'privatization' of the past in commemoration and 'lieu de memoire' (Pierre Nora) thus acquire a significance that they could never have had in the structuralist phase of 'the new philosophy of history'. The ingredients in this new development are summed up in P. Hutton's *History as an Art of Memory* (Hanover, 1994); the theoretical implications of this shift in emphasis are explored in Ankersmit's *History and Tropology: the Rise and Fall of Metaphor* (Berkeley, 1994) and *De historische ervaring* (Groningen, 1993). Problems of the representation of the Holocaust and of the relationship between the film and the historical text as representations of the past have triggered this 'personalization' or 'privatization' of our attitude towards the past. See for these recent developments the contributions by H. Kellner, W. Kansteiner and R. Braun in *History and Theory*, XXXIII (1994), pp. 127–98; S. Felman and D. M. D. Laub, *Testimony: Crises of Witnessing in Literature, Psychoanalysis and History* (New York, 1992); V. Sobschack, *The Address of the Eye: A Phenomenology of Film Experience* (Princeton, 1992); and R. A. Rosenstone, 'The Future of the Past? Film and the Beginnings of Postmodern History', in *Cinema, Modernism and the Representation of History*, ed. V. Sobschack (London, 1994).

Index